How to Do *Everything* with

Dreamweaver 4

D1494615

About the Author

Michael Meadhra is an author, consultant, and web designer. After working as a photographer, graphic designer, media producer, and manager for a number of years, he discovered that his best efforts were directed toward writing and teaching others how to use the computer technology that figured so prominently in all those occupations. So, he turned to writing as a full-time career, first as a writer/editor of technical journals, then as a freelance book author. To date, Michael has written or contributed to more than 30 computer books and countless articles on topics such as graphics, presentation, and publishing software.

Michael is also a consultant who provides advice, training, system administration, web design, and web-hosting services to small and mid-size business clients. And, of course, he uses Dreamweaver and Fireworks in his web design work.

How to Do *Everything* with

Dreamweaver 4

Michael Meadhra

Osborne/**McGraw-Hill**

New York   Chicago   San Francisco
Lisbon   London   Madrid   Mexico City
Milan   New Delhi   San Juan
Seoul   Singapore   Sydney   Toronto

Osborne/McGraw-Hill
2600 Tenth Street
Berkeley, California 94710
U.S.A.

To arrange bulk purchase discounts for sales promotions, premiums, or fund-raisers, please contact Osborne/**McGraw-Hill** at the above address. For information on translations or book distributors outside the U.S.A., please see the International Contact Information page immediately following the index of this book.

How to Do Everything with Dreamweaver 4

1234567890 FGR FGR 01987654321

ISBN 0-07-213369-4

Publisher:	Brandon A. Nordin
Vice President &	
Associate Publisher:	Scott Rogers
Editorial Director:	Roger Stewart
Project Editor:	Patty Mon
Acquisitions Coordinator:	Alissa Larson
Technical Editor:	Michael Raucci
Copy Editor:	Stacey Sawyer
Proofreader:	Paul Tyler
Indexer:	David Heiret
Computer Designers:	Melinda Moore Lytle
	Kelly Stanton-Scott
Illustrators:	Michael Mueller
	Alex Putney
	Lyssa Sieben-Wald
	Beth Young
Series Design:	Mickey Galicia
Cover Series Design:	Dodie Shoemaker
Cover Design:	Greg Scott
Cover Illustration:	Victor Stabin

This book was composed with Corel VENTURA™ Publisher.

Contents at a Glance

Contents

Acknowledgments

This book would not exist without the contributions of a lot of different people. I'm glad that tradition allows me this opportunity to acknowledge some of those people for their efforts.

Thanks to Roger Stewart for the vision that resulted in this book and for giving me the opportunity to write it. Alissa Larson, acquisitions coordinator, and Patty Mon, project editor, were my regular contacts and have been a pleasure to work with. Michael Raucci, technical editor, helped ensure the accuracy of the text and offered many good suggestions. Stacey Sawyer, the copy editor saw to it that my prose was readable. I didn't have much direct contact with the rest of the Osborne/McGraw-Hill staff working on this book, but their contributions are appreciated nonetheless. My thanks to all of you!

When time ran short, some fellow authors stepped up to contribute chapters to the book—among them, Norbert Herber and Richard Schrand. Thanks to all of you guys! I also want to thank my friend and colleague, Michael Boatman, for his invaluable insights. His comments made this a better book. And finally, I wish to thank my agent, David Fugate, Waterside Productions, for getting me this gig and for his continued support and help to make it a reality.

Introduction

This book is for anyone wanting to learn how to use Macromedia Dreamweaver 4, the leading web site development tool on the market today. It targets beginning to intermediate Dreamweaver users and assumes no previous experience with the software. It does presume, however, that the reader is an intelligent and interested person with basic computer skills and at least a beginner's understanding of the Web and web page design.

Dreamweaver is a versatile and powerful tool for developing web pages and web sites. But Dreamweaver is just a tool. It can't supply the vision of what your web site should be or what features will make your pages attractive and effective. Dreamweaver can, however, enable you to transform your vision for a web site into reality.

In some ways, Dreamweaver is like a car. A car gives you the means to make short trips quickly and easily and makes practical journeys too long to undertake on foot. Of course, you must learn to drive the car if you expect to use it as your primary means of transportation; but there wouldn't be much point in learning to drive if you didn't have somewhere to go. The destination is an essential element of the driving experience, and yet selecting a destination and planning the trip have very little to do with the mechanics of steering, breaking, and acceleration that are necessary to control the car.

This book is about learning to drive the car (using Dreamweaver); it's not about planning a road trip (designing a web site). Web site design is a huge topic, the exclusive subject of many books, and the art of design is beyond the scope of this book. Also, this book's focus is Dreamweaver 4, not Dreamweaver UltraDev 4's advanced features for producing database-driven web sites. But all the coverage of the common Dreamweaver feature set applies to UltraDev as well.

The book starts with an introduction to the Dreamweaver user interface: Part I, "Get to Know Dreamweaver." This part covers how to work with the various windows and panels that make up the Dreamweaver working environment. You also learn how to define a site in Dreamweaver, which is the first step in developing a web site.

Part II, "Create Basic Web Pages," covers the basics of how to create a web page, add and edit text, build hyperlinks among pages, and add images to your pages. This is also where you discover how to access the HTML source code for your pages.

In Part III, "Go Beyond the Basics," you learn how to work with tables in Dreamweaver, including Dreamweaver's new Layout Table feature. You also discover how to use frames and framesets, how to build interactive forms, and how to use Dreamweaver templates to make creating and updating web pages fast and easy.

Part IV, "Add Graphics and Media," starts with an introduction to Fireworks 4, the popular image editor that is the other half of the Dreamweaver 4/Fireworks 4 Studio bundle. The two programs are engineered to work closely together, with Fireworks being the tool you use to create the web graphics and optimize the images that figure so prominently on most web pages. But it's not all Fireworks in Part IV. You also learn how to use other external editors and how to add sounds, Flash animations, movies, and other media to your web pages.

In Part V, "Expand Your Horizons," you learn how to use CSS style sheets and how to create layers and animate them with timelines. This part also covers Dreamweaver behaviors, which enable you to create rollovers and other JavaScript effects without programming.

Part VI, "Manage Your Site in Dreamweaver," covers how to publish your site using Dreamweaver's built-in file transfer features. You also learn how to use Dreamweaver's testing and reports features to detect and correct problems on your web pages and how to use Design Notes and File Check In/Out to work in a collaborative environment.

In Part VII, "Customize Dreamweaver," you discover how to adjust Dreamweaver's many preference settings to adapt the program to your preferred working style. This is also where you find out how to use the History panel and Assets panel to make your work faster and easier.

Finally, in the Appendixes you find instructions to get you started installing the Dreamweaver program and all the other programs that Macromedia ships on the Dreamweaver CD. There are also instructions on how to find and install Dreamweaver Extensions—objects, commands, and behaviors that you can download and install to add features or productivity enhancements to Dreamweaver.

All the books in this series include special features that call out certain bits of information to make them easily accessible. Among them are the following:

- **How to...**   A boxed section giving instructions on how to perform a specific task
- **Did you know...**   A boxed section that provides background information or explores a topic related to the main text
- **Note**   Supplemental information
- **Caution**   Something to watch out for
- **Tip**   A time-saving alternative
- **Shortcut**   A keyboard shortcut for a command

Here are a few resources you might want to refer to as you read this book and go on to develop web pages and sites of your own. For web site design issues, check out *Web Design: The Complete Reference*, by Thomas A. Powell. You'll also need a good reference for HTML codes, such as *HTML: The Complete Reference*, by Thomas A. Powell; or *HTML: A Beginner's Guide*, by Wendy Willard. For information on the critical issue of browser compatibility, refer to **http://www.webreview.com/browsers/browsers.shtml** or **http://hotwired.lycos.com/ webmonkey/reference/browser_chart/**.

Part I

Get to Know Dreamweaver

Chapter 1

Get Started with Dreamweaver

How to...

- ■ Get to know Dreamweaver
- ■ Work with the Document window
- ■ Work with panels
- ■ Work with the Site window
- ■ Get help

What is Dreamweaver anyway?

The name may sound like the title of a sci-fi novel or a term for a spiritualist or shaman that engages in guided imagery. But web developers instantly recognize Dreamweaver as the leading program for web page design and editing. Dreamweaver wasn't the first program in this class of software, but it's grown to become the premier web development tool on the market today. Dreamweaver 4, the subject of this book, is the fourth release of the Dreamweaver program, and it continues to get more powerful and sophisticated with each new version.

First and foremost, Dreamweaver is a graphical web page editing program that enables a web author to work with text, images, and other web page elements in a WYSIWYG (What You See Is What You Get) editing environment. Dreamweaver enables web authors to create and edit web pages in much the same way that desktop publishing programs enable layout artists to create page designs for print publication.

Using Dreamweaver, you can design web pages without directly manipulating the HTML code that defines the web page. However, Dreamweaver also provides easy access to the HTML code, so you can work with it when you need to.

Dreamweaver is more than just a web page layout tool—it's also a complete web site development environment. Besides making it easy to create and edit multiple web pages, Dreamweaver includes powerful features to help web developers build links between pages, map their relationships, manage all the related files, post those files to a remote web server, and keep the local files and the files on the remote server synchronized.

You don't need to use one program for creating web pages and then a host of separate utilities for diagramming the site, managing files, and transferring files to the web server— Dreamweaver does it all! Dreamweaver even includes features, such as Design Notes and file Check Out, that facilitate collaboration by teams and workgroups developing a web site. Dreamweaver is a complete solution for the web developer needing to build and maintain web sites ranging from simple home pages to sophisticated web sites that include dozens of pages with text, graphics, and rich media.

Dreamweaver is a product of Macromedia, Inc., which also develops and markets a full range of other web and multimedia development tools. The Macromedia programs are designed to compliment one another and work together to provide a comprehensive set of media development tools. The following list shows where Dreamweaver fits in the Macromedia product line.

- **Dreamweaver 4**   The leading graphical web site development tool on the market today
- **Dreamweaver UltraDev 4**   All the features of Dreamweaver, plus tools to develop database-driven web applications using ASP, Java, and ColdFusion
- **Fireworks 4**   The tool for creating and optimizing web graphics
- **Flash 5**   Animation tool for creating vector-based web content
- **Freehand 9**   Artist's tool for creating vector-based illustrations for use in Flash animations and in print
- **Director 8 Shockwave Studio**   Multimedia authoring tool for creating interactive rich-media content for the web and for distribution on CD-ROM
- **Flash and Shockwave players**   Browser add-ons to enable viewing of Flash animations and Shockwave movies
- **Generator**   Dynamic graphics server
- **Aria**   Customer-behavior analysis system
- **LikeMinds**   Personalization server

In addition, as of this writing, Macromedia is in the process of merging with Allaire, the developers of ColdFusion application server technology, the JRun Java server, and the HomeSite HTML text editor. Even before the merger, Allaire and Macromedia were cooperating in several significant ways. Dreamweaver UltraDev supports both Java and ColdFusion application development, and a copy of HomeSite, an external HTML editor, ships with every copy of Dreamweaver. It's safe to assume that the merger will lead to even tighter integration of Allaire technologies with future versions of Macromedia products such as Dreamweaver.

This book, of course, is about Dreamweaver 4. And, since Fireworks 4 comes bundled with Dreamweaver 4 in the Dreamweaver Studio package, I've also included a couple of chapters on Fireworks. The advanced database connectivity and server-side programming capabilities of Dreamweaver UltraDev are beyond the scope of this book, but all the basic Dreamweaver features covered in this book apply to Dreamweaver UltraDev as well.

Dreamweaver and Fireworks are both cross-platform products that are available in both Windows and Macintosh versions (as are the other Macromedia products). All the figures, examples, and instructions in this book show the Windows versions of the software. However, with few exceptions, the programs look and act the same on both Windows and Macintosh computers. Sure, there are minor cosmetic differences imposed by the different operating systems and some differences in terminology (COMMAND key on the Macintosh versus CTRL key on a Windows machine), but other than that, the Windows and Macintosh versions are essentially the same.

Now it's time to start learning about the key components of Dreamweaver and how to get around in the Dreamweaver working environment.

Get to Know Dreamweaver

At times, Dreamweaver seems to have a split personality. One moment it's a web page creation program, and the next moment it's a web site management program. Creating individual web pages and managing all the files that make up an entire web site are obviously related activities, but they are very different tasks. Given the different natures of those tasks, it's not surprising that Dreamweaver presents you with different tools for handling them.

You can find a detailed exploration of how to perform all those tasks in other chapters of this book. This section gives you an introduction and overview of the various windows and menus that make up the Dreamweaver user interface, so you'll know where to find things.

Get Acquainted with the Dreamweaver Work Area

When you're working on an individual web page, you're in a Dreamweaver *Document window* displaying the web page document you're editing. The Document window is surrounded by an assortment of smaller windows, called *panels*, which contain the various tools and resources for creating and manipulating objects on the web page.

The combination of a Document window and multiple panels, all open at once, means that the Dreamweaver work area can spread out across your entire screen, as shown in Figure 1-1, even when the main Document window isn't maximized to full-screen size. You can open, close, and move the panels independent of the main Document window.

This arrangement of a main Document window and separate panels for the various tools you need for editing the document is common to all Macromedia design products (and to many other graphics programs as well). However, it's a stark contrast to the all-in-one-window approach of common word processor and spreadsheet software. The following sections of this chapter explore Dreamweaver's Document window and panels in more detail.

NOTE   *One of the notable new features of Dreamweaver 4 is improved consistency of the Macromedia user interface as implemented in different programs. Details such as the naming and arrangement of menu commands are now standardized across all the Macromedia products. Attention to such details makes it much easier for users to switch from one product to another. That's an important consideration because many projects require the capabilities of more than one program. For example, it's common to use Fireworks to create a graphic that you then insert into a web page that you are editing in Dreamweaver.*

When it comes time to deal with site management chores, Dreamweaver presents a somewhat different face. Instead of an individual web page, the key feature of the *Site window* (see Figure 1-2) is a list of local files in the current web site, which is usually defined as a folder on your computer's hard drive.

Alongside the list of local files you can view either a Site Map diagram or a list of files on the remote web server that is linked to the local site. From the Site window, you can perform all sorts of site management tasks, including posting newly created or edited files to the remote

1

Objects panel   Document window   Toolbar   CSS Styles panel

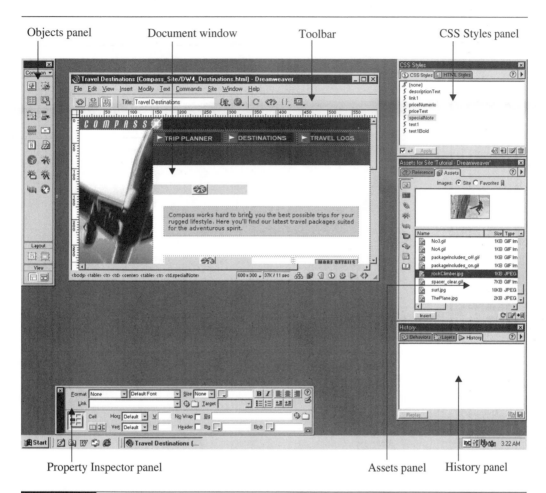

Property Inspector panel   Assets panel   History panel

FIGURE 1-1   The Dreamweaver work area is composed of several individual windows.

server. You can learn about defining a site in Dreamweaver in Chapter 2, and Chapters 17 and 18 explore Dreamweaver's site management capabilities in more detail.

As you might expect, the Dreamweaver Document window and Site window exhibit the common characteristics found in the windows of just about every program you've ever used.

The title bar at the top of the window identifies the contents of the window and includes the standard set of buttons in the right corner to minimize, maximize, and close the window. Below the title bar is the menu bar and, below that, a toolbar with buttons that give you quick access to commonly used commands. The status bar across the bottom of the window displays some status information about the contents of the window but is more notable for the assortment of buttons and special features tucked away in there (more on that later in this chapter).

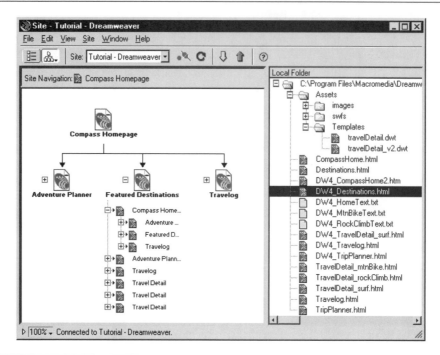

FIGURE 1-2 The Site window is where you tackle file management tasks for your web site.

Most of the window is used to display the web page you're editing or, in the Site window, the file list and Site Map. If necessary, scroll bars appear along the edge of the window to accommodate lists and pages that are too big to fit completely within the window.

Of course, you can move a window around on the screen by dragging its title bar and resize a window by dragging the window border. You can have multiple Document windows open simultaneously displaying different web pages. However, you can have only one Site window open at a time.

The panels—the smaller windows surrounding the main Document window—are hybrids of a window and a dialog box. The panels display detailed information and options such as you might find presented in a dialog box in some other programs, but, unlike dialog boxes, panels are designed to stay open on your computer desktop while you work on a web page document in Dreamweaver. Some panels contain resources that you can use to develop your web page, while other panels display the properties of selected objects on the page. Panels enable you to do things like drag-and-drop resources from a panel onto the page you are editing and edit the properties of an object in a panel and see the changes reflected immediately in the Document window.

You can move, resize, and close panels just as you can Document windows. However, unlike Document windows, the Dreamweaver panels will disappear from your computer desktop when you open or switch to another program, and you can't minimize panel windows. You'll find a list of available panels and more information about working with panels later in this chapter. The details of how to use the individual panels are covered elsewhere in the book, in context with the tasks for which you use the panels.

Use Dreamweaver Menus and Toolbar

Working with the menu bar in Dreamweaver is essentially the same as using the corresponding component of any other Windows (or Macintosh) program, so I won't rehash the general procedures here. The individual menu commands and what they do are covered in context throughout this book.

In addition to making commands available from the drop-down menus on the menu bar, Dreamweaver makes extensive use of *context menus* to present menu commands that are applicable to a selected object. To access a context menu, simply right-click on an object in most any Dreamweaver window. A context menu, such as the one shown below, will pop open showing a list of commands that are available for use with that object.

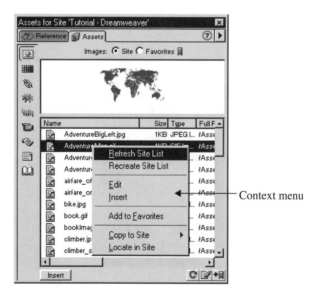

Selecting a command from the context menu has exactly the same effect as selecting the same command from the menu bar—it's just faster and more convenient. You'll find context menus available almost everywhere in Dreamweaver. There are context menus available for text, graphics, and other objects on a web page in the Document window, for files and folders in the Site window, and for many of the resources shown in the various floating panels.

The Dreamweaver toolbar is relatively straightforward. The buttons on the toolbar provide shortcuts to several frequently used commands and options. The standard Dreamweaver toolbar, shown below, includes the following buttons (from left to right):

- **Show Code View**   Switches the Document window into HTML code view
- **Show Code and Design View**   Switches the Document window into the split-screen code view and design view
- **Show Design View**   Switches the Document window into the WYSIWYG design view, which approximates the way the page will appear in a browser
- **Page Title**   A convenient editable display of the current document title
- **File Management**   A drop-down list of file management commands
- **Preview/Debug in Browser**   A drop-down list of available browsers for previewing and debugging pages
- **Refresh**   Refreshes the design view display after you make changes to the HTML code in one of Dreamweaver's code windows
- **Reference**   Displays context-sensitive reference information about the currently selected object in the Reference panel
- **Code Navigation**   A drop-down list of code navigation commands
- **View Options**   A drop-down list of view option commands

Work with the Document Window

The Dreamweaver Document window is where you design and edit web page documents. As such, the Document window is your main base of operations in Dreamweaver—it's where you'll spend most of your time as you interact with the program to perform most web page development tasks.

It's usually easy to identify the Document window as the big window that appears in the middle of your screen when you work with Dreamweaver, but that's not always so. (Dreamweaver is highly adaptable to individual working styles, so you can configure the program to show the Site window first instead of the Document window.) You can have multiple Document windows open in Dreamweaver, each showing a different web page—even pages from different sites. You can also resize, move, and minimize each Document window independent of the others.

The Dreamweaver Document window can display a web page using one of three different views:

- **Design View**   Approximates the way a page will display in a browser
- **Code View**   Displays the HTML code for the page
- **Code and Design View**   Presents a split screen with Design view in one portion and Code view in the other

Views are simply different ways of looking at the same document—the web page you're editing. Dreamweaver enables you to view and work with a web document in a graphical environment that looks much like the way the web page will display in a browser; you can view and work with the underlying text-based HTML code; or you can use a split-screen mode that displays both the HTML code and a graphical representation of that code in the same Document window.

You can select which view Dreamweaver displays in the Document window by selecting the corresponding commands from the View menu of any Document window. (Choose View | Code for Code view, View | Design for Design view, and View | Code and Design for Code and Design view.) You can also select a view by clicking one of the first three buttons on the Document window toolbar. The button that looks depressed indicates the current view. You can change the view in one Dreamweaver Document window without affecting other Document windows.

Code view ——————▶ ◀—————— Design view

Code and Design view

The following sections of this chapter explore the three views of the Dreamweaver Document window in more detail.

Design View

Dreamweaver's Design view, shown in Figure 1-3, provides an intuitive graphical user interface for creating and editing web pages. Design view enables you to work with a graphical representation of your web page that approximates the way the page will look when viewed in a web browser. In Design view, text on your web page appears as formatted text, images and graphics appear as full-color images, and tables appear as rows and columns complete with gridlines.

In general, you interact with Dreamweaver in Design view in much the same way you use a modern word processor—with perhaps a little page layout program thrown in for good measure. For example, you can type text directly into the Document window, just as you would with a word processor. You can add graphics, tables, and other objects to the page with menu commands and with drag-and-drop techniques. You drag the mouse pointer across some text or an image to select it; then you can edit, move, delete, or reformat the selected object. In short, Dreamweaver Design view does just what you expect it to do under most circumstances.

However, the view of your web page that you see in Design view only approximates the page as it will appear in a web browser. Sometimes the Dreamweaver view and the browser view are a fairly close match, and other times the Dreamweaver view is significantly different. It all depends on the complexity of the page you're designing and on the Dreamweaver settings you choose.

Dreamweaver displays text and simple objects (such as images) in pretty much the same way as a web browser (aside from the subtle—and sometimes not so subtle—differences in the way different web browsers render web pages). Consequently, if you're working on a very

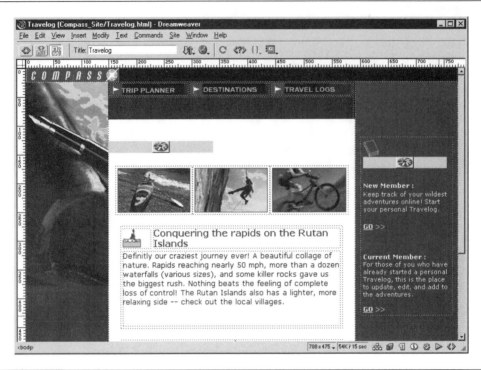

A Dreamweaver Document window in Design view

simple page, the Dreamweaver Design view might look similar to the same page viewed in a web browser.

But Dreamweaver is intended for creating and editing web pages, not just viewing them. So Dreamweaver includes an assortment of onscreen tools and visual aids to help you find, identify, and manipulate various objects on your web page.

For example, Dreamweaver Design view can include rulers and grids to aid in positioning objects on the page. Icons representing various hidden elements appear in Design view to give you easy access to otherwise invisible page elements. Table borders can be made visible in Design view, even when they are configured not to display in a browser. The same goes for the borders of frames, layers, and the hot spots in image maps. And Dreamweaver uses color coding and other visual clues to identify page elements and areas that are linked to templates and library objects.

The result is a Design view display, such as the one shown in Figure 1-4, that is rich in information about the page on which you're working. However, all this extra information makes the Design view representation of your web page look significantly different from what you expect to see in a browser. (Compare Figure 1-4 to Figure 1-5, which shows the same page in a browser window.)

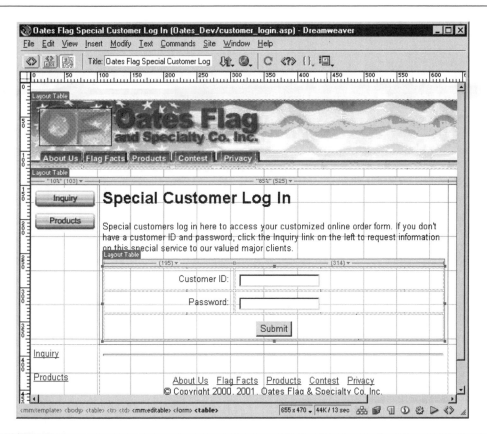

FIGURE 1-4   Design view of a complex page

The difference between the appearance of your page in Design view and in a browser is no problem as long as you are aware of it and frequently check the page in a browser to see how the page will look to your viewers. Fortunately, Dreamweaver makes it very easy to preview your page in your favorite browser as you work.

All the extra stuff that you see on your page in Design view can be a little distracting or disorienting at first. But there's no need to worry about it. As you work with Dreamweaver, you'll quickly become familiar with the onscreen markings and what they mean, and when you do, Design view ceases to be confusing at all.

I won't attempt to enumerate all the different symbols you might see in the Design view. It's more appropriate to cover them in context with their use. However, there are a few view settings that apply to the Design view window in general. Those are rulers, grids, visual aids, and the new Layout view that Macromedia introduced in Dreamweaver 4.

Previewing a page in a browser window

Rulers

As you might surmise from the name, *rulers* provide a convenient means of measuring things in the Design view window. When rulers are turned on, they appear as graduated scales on the top and left sides of the Design view window, as shown in Figure 1-6. As you move the pointer around on your page in Design view, a line moves on each ruler to indicate the precise position of the pointer. This enables you to accurately measure the size and position of objects on the page.

As you can with most features in Dreamweaver, you can reconfigure rulers to meet your individual needs and preferences. You can show or hide rulers, change the origin point (move

Rulers

FIGURE 1-6   Rulers aid in positioning objects in Design view.

the zero mark), and display measurements in your choice of pixels, inches, or centimeters. Here's how:

- Choose View | Rulers | Show (or press CTRL+ALT+R) to turn the ruler display on. Repeating the same command hides the rulers.

- Choose View | Rulers | Pixels to display measurements in pixels.

- Choose View | Rulers | Inches to display measurements in inches.

- Choose View | Rulers | Centimeters to display measurements in centimeters.

- Choose View | Rulers | Reset Origin to return the rulers' origin (the zero marks) to the default position at the upper-left corner of the page.

To move the rulers' origin, click and drag from the origin box (the place where the top and left rulers intersect in the upper-left corner of the Design view window) to the location on the page where you want the origin to be. When you release the mouse button, Dreamweaver adjusts the ruler scales so that the origin (the zero point) jumps to the pointer position.

Grids

The *grid* is another handy tool to help you position objects on your page in Design view. When you activate the grid, Dreamweaver displays a series of evenly spaced horizontal and vertical lines on your page. Figure 1-7 shows the Design view window with grids visible.

You can use these grid lines to help you align and position various elements on the page. The grid lines are a feature of the Design view window and don't become a permanent part of the web page—they are simply a visual reference that helps you position the objects that do become a part of the page.

If you need a little help aligning objects to the grid, you can activate the *Snap to Grid* feature. With Snap to Grid enabled, all you have to do is place or move an object close to a grid line— Dreamweaver automatically aligns the object precisely with the nearest grid line.

Dreamweaver gives you complete control over the grid. You can turn the grid display on and off and adjust the spacing and color of grid lines. You can also choose whether to enable Snap to Grid. Here's how:

- Choose View | Grid | Show Grid (or press CTRL+ALT+G) to toggle the grid display on or off.

- Choose View | Grid | Snap to Grid (or press CTRL+ALT+SHIFT+G) to toggle the Snap to Grid feature on and off.

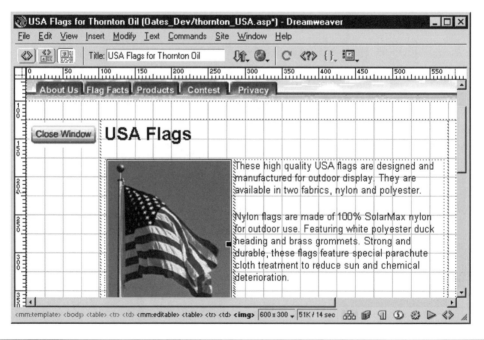

FIGURE 1-7　Design view with grids

■ Choose View | Grid | Edit Grid to display the Grid Settings dialog box.

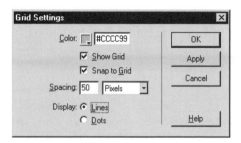

In this dialog box, you can adjust the color of the grid lines by selecting a color with the color picker or by entering the color value in the text box. The check boxes enable you to change the settings to show the grid and snap objects to the grid. To change the grid spacing, enter a number in the Spacing text box and select the appropriate measurement to go with it. The Display radio buttons enable you to choose between displaying the grid as lines or only as dots at each grid intersection. Adjust the settings and then click OK.

TIP   *If you try to place or move an object on your page and it moves slightly from where you placed it, check the Snap to Grid setting. The grid is always a part of the Design view window, even when it isn't visible. Therefore, if you have Snap to Grid turned on when the grid itself is hidden, it can cause objects to move from where you place them because Snap to Grid dutifully tries to align objects to the invisible grid.*

Visual Aids

Visual Aids is a catchall term for the various onscreen indicators that Dreamweaver uses to make otherwise invisible objects visible in Design view. Visual aids include outlines to mark the borders of tables, layers, and frames; indicators for the hotspots in image maps; and icons that show the location of invisible elements such as anchors, comments, embedded objects, and line breaks.

You have complete control over which visual aids are visible as you work with your page in Design view. You can activate some, or all, of the visual aids to make it easier to see and manipulate invisible page elements. Or you can hide the visual aids to reduce the clutter in the Design view window.

■ Choose View | Visual Aids | Table Borders to toggle the table border display on or off.

■ Choose View | Visual Aids | Layer Borders to show or hide the outlines showing the size and location of layers.

■ Choose View | Visual Aids | Frame Borders to toggle the frame border display on or off.

■ Choose View | Visual Aids | Image Maps to show or hide the hotspots in image maps.

■ Choose View | Visual Aids | Invisible Elements to toggle the invisible elements icon display on or off. Invisible elements include named anchors, scripts, comments, hidden form fields, and more. See Chapter 20 for information on how to select which icons Dreamweaver displays when you enable viewing Invisible Elements.

■ Choose View | Visual Aids | Hide All (or press CTRL+SHIFT+I) to suppress the display of all the visual aids. Repeat the command to restore the previously selected assortment of visual aids.

Layout View

Layout view is an alternate way of viewing and working with tables in Design view. It's a new feature of Dreamweaver 4 that makes tables easier to use as a layout tool for controlling the position of objects on your page. Chapter 7 covers Layout view in detail, but it's appropriate to introduce the feature here since it's a major variation of the Design view window.

Basically, Layout view changes the way table borders appear in Design view. Instead of the default borders around table cells or the dashed lines that appear as a visual aid to indicate table borders that are set to zero, Layout view (shown in Figure 1-8) displays table cells surrounded by

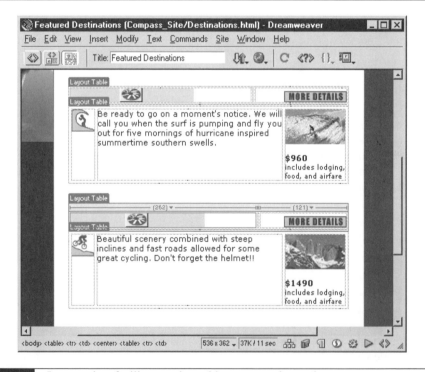

FIGURE 1-8   Layout view facilitates using tables to control page layout.

a thin colored line. When you click a Layout Table cell, the top border displays the size of the cell and sizing handles appear on the sides. The result is a table cell that is easier to create, move, and resize with the mouse in Design view. There's lots more to Layout view, as you will discover in Chapter 7. Here are the basic ways to switch between Layout view and Standard view:

- Choose View | Table View | Layout View (or press CTRL+F6) to choose Layout view.
- Choose View | Table View | Standard View (or press CTRL+SHIFT+F6) to switch back to normal rendering of table borders.
- You can also switch between Layout view and Standard view by clicking one of the View buttons at the bottom of the Objects panel. Standard view is the left button and Layout view is the right button.
- Choose View | Table View | Show Layout Table Tabs to toggle the display of the small tab that appears at the upper-left corner of each table labeling it a Layout Table. Hiding the tabs also hides the information bar that appears at the top of the selected table.

Code View

A web page may appear to be a graphically rich document when viewed in a web browser or in Dreamweaver's Design view, but that's only an illusion. When you peak behind the curtain, you find a file containing plain text and a bunch of embedded codes that tell the web browser how to format the text, where to find graphics files, and how to execute various special effects. Code view (shown in Figure 1-9) enables you to see your web document in its raw form so you can work directly with the HTML code.

Having access to the HTML code is essential for troubleshooting and highly desirable for routine page creation and editing. Previous Dreamweaver versions made the HTML code accessible through a separate panel window called the Code Inspector. In Dreamweaver 4, the Code Inspector is still available, but the new Code view feature brings the HTML code right into the main Document window where it's even more accessible and convenient.

In Code view, you can edit the text and HTML code for your web page without the distraction or interference of a graphical user interface. Code view includes numerous features to facilitate working with the HTML code for your web page. Chapter 5 explores Dreamweaver's code handling capabilities in more detail.

Code and Design View

Design view works well for many web page development tasks, and Code view is more appropriate for others. But sometimes it's nice to use a combination of the two views. That's when Code and Design view (shown in Figure 1-10) comes in handy. Code and Design view divides the Document window into two panes and displays your web page in Design view in one pane and Code view in the other. The split-screen effect enables you to see simultaneously the page's HTML code and a graphic representation of the code instructions.

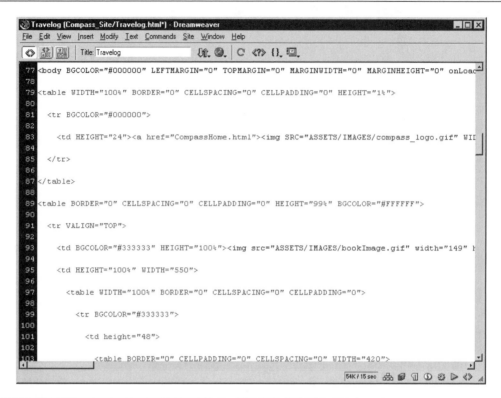

FIGURE 1-9 The Document window in Code view

No matter which view you choose, the Document window isn't usually large enough to show an entire web page. That means that you need to use the Document window's scroll bars to select what portion of the page appears in the window. Splitting the Document window into two panes, as in the combined Code and Design view, further reduces the portion of the web page you can see in either pane, so you need to do more scrolling to access various portions of your web page. Each pane of the Code and Design view has separate scroll bars that act independently of the other pane's. However, selecting an object (or simply clicking) in either pane automatically scrolls the other pane so that it displays the corresponding portion of the page. You can click an object or text passage in the Design view pane and let Dreamweaver move the Code view pane to that portion of the page's HTML code, or you can select an HTML tag in Code view and watch as Dreamweaver highlights the corresponding object in Design view.

1

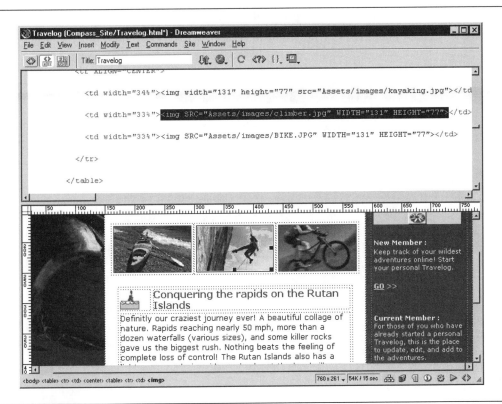

FIGURE 1-10   Code and Design view is the best of both worlds.

 CAUTION   *Pay attention to which pane of the Code and Design view has the focus before you start editing your page. Entering plain text is pretty much the same in both panes, but other editing actions can be quite different—especially within HTML codes. You can tell which pane is the active editing pane by the blinking insertion point cursor in that pane.*

You can make changes in one pane—either the Design view pane or the Code view pane— and see those changes reflected in the other pane. This capability makes Code and Design view a great way to troubleshoot the HTML code; and it's also an invaluable tool for learning more about HTML.

■ Choose View | Design View on Top to swap the locations of the Design view pane and the Code view pane. Choose the command again to return the Document window to its default configuration with the Code view pane on top.

■ Drag the border between the two panes up or down to resize the panes.

■ After editing HTML code in the Code view pane, you need to tell Dreamweaver that you want to update the Design view pane to reflect those changes. To do so, click in the Design view pane, click the Refresh button in the Property Inspector panel, choose View | Refresh Design View, or press F5.

Edits that you make in the Design view pane are immediately and automatically reflected in the Code view pane, but you must manually refresh the Design view pane to reflect any changes that you make in Code view.

The Document Window Status Bar

You're probably accustomed to looking to the status bar at the bottom of a Document window for information about the current document and the selected object. But the status bar in the Dreamweaver Document window is more than a simple informational display; it's an interactive toolbox packed with useful features. The status bar, shown below, includes the Tag Selector, Window Size Selector, Download Speed Indicator, and Launcher.

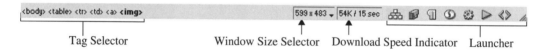

Here's a summary of the status bar tools and what they do:

■ **Tag Selector**   Enables you to identify (and select) objects in Design View by the HTML tags enclosing them.

■ **Window Size Selector**   Shows the current window size and enables you to set the Document window to one of several preset sizes.

■ **Download Speed Indicator**   Shows an estimate of how long it will take to download and display the current web page.

■ **Launcher**   Presents a row of icons representing Dreamweaver's various floating panels. Use the Launcher to help you keep track of which panels are open and to launch panels.

The Tag Selector and Window Size Selector are visible only when the Document window is displaying your page in Design view or Code and Design view. They're absent from the status bar when the Document window is in Code view. (You don't really need the Tag Selector when the tags are directly available in Code view; and the window size is irrelevant in Code view.) The Download Speed Indicator and Launcher are visible in all three views.

You can customize the status bar tools with settings in the Preferences dialog box. (See Chapter 20 for details on how to change these and many other Dreamweaver preferences.) You can add or modify sizes in the Window Size Selector, change the connection speed that

Dreamweaver uses to calculate download times for the Download Speed Indicator, and choose whether to display the Launcher. You can also select which panels to include in the Launcher.

The Tag Selector

The Tag Selector occupies the left half of the Document window status bar. You may barely notice it at first, but once you become aware of its existence and how helpful it can be, you'll probably find yourself using it more and more. The Tag Selector provides important information about the objects you work with in the Document window. If that were all the Tag Selector did, it would be enough to justify its existence in the status bar. But like so many other things in Dreamweaver, the Tag Selector has hidden talents: in addition to being an informational display, it's an interactive tool that enables you to select page content for editing.

The structure of an HTML document relies on tags—embedded HTML codes—to define portions of the document and to convey instructions to the web browser on how to format and display the web page. The visible portion of the web page is enclosed between the <body> and </body> tags that define the beginning and the end of the page body and separate it from the page header. Similarly, paragraphs, text formatting, graphics, hyperlinks, tables, table rows, table cells, and forms all have their own tags. Tags are often nested within other tags. For example, a hyperlink tag might be nested within a paragraph. The nesting can get pretty deep when you start working with tables. A paragraph might be nested within a table cell, which is within a table row, which is within a table, which is nested within the body tag.

The Tag Selector shows all the HTML tags enclosing the object or text that is currently selected in the Document window when you're in Design view.

```
<body> <table> <tr> <td> <center> <table> <tr> <td> <table> <tr> <td> <b> <font>
```

This gives you a visual reference of all the tags that affect how the selected object will be rendered by the web browser. Thus, the Tag Selector supplies information that you might otherwise get only by carefully perusing the web document's HTML code in Code view.

While the Tag Selector is certainly useful as a status display, it's even more useful as a tool for selecting things on your web page in Design view.

Selecting a few words of text in Design view is easy—you just drag the pointer across the text you want to select to highlight it. But selecting an object and its accompanying HTML tags can be tricky because the tags aren't visible in Design view. Another challenge is trying to select large objects, such as a table, that require scrolling the Design view window to view the entire thing.

The Tag Selector gives you a quick and easy way to use the HTML tags to make your selections. Simply click on (or anywhere within) the object you want to select, then click a tag in the Tag Selector. Dreamweaver highlights the contents of that tag in Design view.

The Tag Selector is very handy for precisely selecting text and objects within a single HTML tag. It's also the best way to select large objects such as a whole table. You can instantly select everything on a web page by clicking the <body> tag in the Tag Selector.

The Window Size Selector

The Window Size Selector is both a status display and a tool for adjusting the window size. Knowing the size of the Document window is a handy bit of information when you're working in Design view because it helps you gauge the relative size of your web page and the objects on it. You can adjust the size of the Document window to approximate the size of a web browser window at different screen resolutions to get an idea of how much of your page will be visible at those resolutions.

The Window Size Selector displays the current size of the Document window when you are using Design view. In Code and Design view, it displays the size of the Design view pane. In Code View, the Window Size Selector disappears from the status bar because window size is irrelevant to the HTML code.

You can resize the Document window by dragging the window border. When you do, the Window Size Selector displays the new window size in pixels.

But the Window Size Selector does more than provide a readout of the window size. It also allows you to control the size of the Document window. When you click the Window Size Selector, Dreamweaver displays a pop-up menu of preset window sizes.

```
536 x 196   (640 x 480, Default)
600 x 300   (640 x 480, Maximized)
760 x 420   (800 x 600, Maximized)
795 x 470   (832 x 624, Maximized)
955 x 600   (1024 x 768, Maximized)
544 x 378   (WebTV)

Edit Sizes...
```

Just select a size from the list and Dreamweaver instantly resizes the Document window to match your selection.

Dreamweaver comes preprogrammed with an assortment of window sizes that correspond to typical browser window sizes at various standard screen resolutions. You can add to and edit the list of sizes in the Preferences dialog box. See Chapter 20 for instructions on adding custom sizes to the Window Size Selector.

The Launcher

The Launcher is a simple but useful tool. Basically, it provides an alternative to the Window menu for opening and keeping track of Dreamweaver's floating panels. The Launcher consists of a row of icons at the right end of the status bar that represent the Site window and Dreamweaver's various floating panels. At first, the icons may be cryptic, but you'll soon learn to recognize which icon corresponds to which panel.

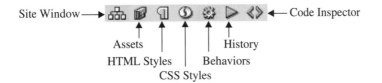

Using the Launcher is easy:

- To open a panel or bring it to the foreground, click the corresponding Launcher icon.

- A Launcher icon that looks like a depressed button indicates a panel that is currently open.

- To close an open panel, click its Launcher icon.

By default, the Launcher shows icons for most, but not all, of Dreamweaver's floating panels. The idea is to have easy access to all the frequently used panels via the Launcher. If a panel isn't represented in the Launcher, you can always open it using Dreamweaver's Window menu.

You can customize the Launcher to show as many (or as few) of the available panels as you want. For example, if you rarely use the CSS Styles panel, you can remove its icon from the Launcher; and you can easily add an icon for a panel that you use more often. You can customize the Launcher using settings in the Preferences dialog box. See Chapter 20 for instructions.

Browser Preview

Although Dreamweaver's Design view displays a graphical representation of your web page, it isn't an accurate rendering of the page as it will appear in a web browser. Even if Dreamweaver could match the output of one particular web browser, you'd still have to contend with significant differences in the way web pages are rendered by different web browsers and by different versions of the popular web browsers. As a result, it is *absolutely essential* to preview your web pages in a web browser so you can see your pages as visitors to your site will see them.

Dreamweaver enables you to quickly and conveniently preview your web page as you work on it. You don't need to manually save your page in a temporary file, open the web browser, then locate and open the saved page so you can view it in the web browser window. With a single key press or mouse click, you can instruct Dreamweaver to do all that for you automatically.

Dreamweaver gives you several ways to activate the browser preview feature:

- Press F12 to preview the current page in your system's default browser.

- Press CTRL+F12 to preview the current page in the secondary browser (if you have defined a secondary browser).

- Choose File | Preview in Browser | *browser name* to preview the page in the selected browser.

■   Click the Preview/Debug in Browser toolbar button and then choose the desired browser
from the menu that appears.

The Dreamweaver installation routine normally detects your system's default browser and
automatically configures Dreamweaver to use it as the primary browser for Browser Preview
duties. However, most web authors use more than one web browser to preview pages under
development. At the very least, you probably have copies of both Internet Explorer and Netscape
Navigator—you may have a couple of versions of those browsers and some other browsers
as well. Dreamweaver can work with these other browsers, but first you must add them to
Dreamweaver's browser list in the Preferences dialog box. See Chapter 20 for instructions.

NOTE   *You can have more than two browsers in the Preview in Browser list. However, only
two of the browsers are accessible via the* F12 *and* CTRL+F12 *keyboard shortcuts. All
the browsers in the list are available from the menus that appear when you choose
File | Preview in Browser or click the Preview/Debug in Browser toolbar button.*

Work with Panels

Dreamweaver keeps the main Document window relatively clean by moving most all the tools
and resources that you use as you design and edit web pages out of the Document window and
into a collection of smaller satellite windows called *panels*. The panels are sometimes called
floaters or *floating panels* because they "float" around and over the Document window. Some
panels (the ones that enable you to view and edit object attributes) are sometimes called *inspectors*,
and some people use that term for all panels. But no matter what you call them, they are the
collection of smaller windows surrounding the document that enables you to tap into
Dreamweaver's power and versatility.

The Dreamweaver panels are diverse. They vary significantly in appearance depending on
the content and how you use them to create web pages.

The Objects Panel

The Objects panel is basically a free-floating toolbar stocked with buttons that enable you to
insert objects into your web page. By default, the Objects panel starts out in the upper-left corner
of your screen, immediately to the left of the Document window. It's the tall skinny panel filled
with an assortment of colorful icons. (Of course, you can move and resize it any way you like,
so it doesn't have to stay in the default shape or location.)

The objects you can insert from the Objects panel run the gamut from major page structural components, such as tables and forms, to images and multimedia objects, to special text characters.

There are far too many icons in the Objects panel to show them all at once, so the panel is divided into categories. The button at the top of the Object panel is the category selector. Click the button and then select a category from the menu that appears to display the icons from that category. The default category list includes the following items:

- **Characters** Special text characters such as copyright symbol (©), em-dash (—), line break, and nonbreaking space

- **Common** Commonly used objects such as images, horizontal rules, and tables, plus multimedia objects such as Flash and Shockwave

- **Forms** Forms and form components such as text box, check box, and radio button

- **Frames** Eight predefined framesets that you can create with a click of your mouse

- **Head** Icons for adding meta tags to the page header

- **Invisibles** Icons for inserting invisible objects: anchors, comments, and scripts

- **Special** Icons for inserting ActiveX, plug-ins, and Java Applets

In addition to the standard objects, you can download and install Dreamweaver Extensions that add objects and categories to the Objects panel.

The Objects panel buttons are labeled with graphic icons instead of text descriptions, but it's relatively easy to decipher the meaning of most of the icons. If you're in doubt about what kind of object a button represents, just point to the icon and let your pointer hover there a moment—Dreamweaver pops open a tooltip box with a text description of the object.

Insert an Object from the Objects Panel

To insert an object from the Objects panel, simply drag the Objects panel button for the kind of object you want and drop it onto your page in the desired location, or position the insertion point on the page first and then simply click the Objects panel button. Depending on the kind of object you are inserting, Dreamweaver may open a dialog box where you supply necessary information about the object (such as selecting a filename for an image file) before inserting the object into your page at the insertion point. Inserting objects from the Objects panel is really just an alternative to selecting a command from the Insert menu. But most users find the Objects panel a little faster and easier to use—especially when inserting several related objects, one after the other.

Use the Layout View Buttons

The buttons at the bottom of the Objects panel are new to Dreamweaver 4. They provide easy access to the new Layout view feature, which changes the way tables are shown in Design view. The bottom two buttons (labeled View) enable you to switch between Standard Table view and Layout Table view. Click the left button to select Standard view, and click the right button to select Layout view. The Layout buttons located just above the View buttons are available only in Layout view. When they are active, you can click the right button to add a layout table to the current web page, or you can click the left button to insert a layout table cell. Chapter 7 explores layout tables in detail.

The Property Inspector

If there is one panel that you use more than any other in Dreamweaver, it's the Property Inspector panel. The Property Inspector is where you can view and edit all the attributes of the object that is selected in Design view. The Property Inspector is where you format text, define hyperlinks, and adjust image attributes.

The default location of the Property Inspector is at the bottom of the screen below the Document window. It's one of only two panels with its title bar on the left side instead of across the top. You can move the Property Inspector panel around on your desktop, but you can't resize the Property Inspector by dragging its border. You can only click an arrow button in the lower-right corner to show or hide the optional detail settings in the lower half of the panel.

The contents of the Property Inspector change depending on what object is selected in your web page. If you select text, the Property Inspector displays the properties of a text object as shown below. Buttons and list boxes in the Property Inspector enable you to adjust the style, font, size, color, attributes such as bold and italics, paragraph alignment, and more.

If you select an image, you see an entirely different set of options in the Property Inspector. Image properties include height and width, vertical and horizontal space, border thickness, and alignment, among others.

Image, 1K	W	141	Src	ES/MenuTripPlanner.gif	Align	Browser Default	▾	⑦
Image8	H	21	Link	TripPlanner.html	Alt			

When you select an object in the Dreamweaver Document window, the Property Inspector panel immediately displays the attributes of that object. You can change any of the object attributes by editing the settings in the Property Inspector panel. When you do, Dreamweaver immediately updates the web page in the Document window. You can see the effect of your changes in Design view and you can observe the code changes in Code view.

Other Floating Panels

In addition to the Objects panel and the Property Inspector panel, Dreamweaver provides an assortment of other panels that provide tools for performing a variety of tasks. When you first start Dreamweaver, the program opens a couple of these panels to the right of the Document window, against the right side of your screen. You can move the panels anywhere, but if you're like most Dreamweaver users, you'll probably keep a panel or two open in that location. Of course, the selection of panels that are open at any given time will vary depending on the kind of work you're doing at the time.

Here's a list of the Dreamweaver panels and a brief summary of their purpose. I'll cover the features of the various panels in more detail elsewhere in this book.

Launcher Panel   The Launcher panel is a larger version of the Launcher that appears in the Dreamweaver Document window status bar. The only difference is that the Launcher panel is housed in a separate panel window instead of the status bar, and that means you can move it around to any convenient location. To open the Launcher panel, choose Window | Launcher.

Assets Panel   The Assets panel is a new addition to Dreamweaver 4. It creates a master list of resources such as image files, templates, and Flash files located both in your current site and in a Favorites list. The Assets panel enables you to quickly find and reuse images and other resources that you've used on other pages in the site. The Assets panel not only lists the available assets, it also enables you to see a thumbnail preview of the selected asset and makes it easy for you to edit and use the selected item in your web page. To open the Assets panel choose Window | Assets or click the Assets button in the Launcher. See Chapter 19 for more information about using the Assets panel.

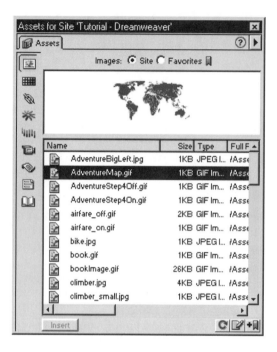

Behaviors Panel   The Behaviors panel enables you to attach behaviors to HTML tags on your web page and to edit existing behaviors. You can learn about Behaviors and using the Behaviors panel in Chapter 16. To open the Behaviors panel choose Window | Behaviors, or click the Behaviors button in the Launcher.

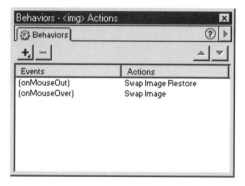

Code Inspector Panel   The Code Inspector panel is a holdover from previous versions of Dreamweaver. It enables you to view and edit the HTML code for your web page in a separate window. That function is now largely taken over by Code view in the Document window, but the Code Inspector panel is still available as a fully operational alternative if you prefer to use it. To open the Code Inspector panel choose Window | Code Inspector, or click the Code Inspector button in the Launcher.

CSS Styles Panel   The CSS Styles panel provides a place to manage Cascading Style Sheet styles and apply them to your web page. To open the CSS Styles panel choose Window | CSS Styles, or click the CSS Styles button in the Launcher. See Chapter 14 for information on using styles.

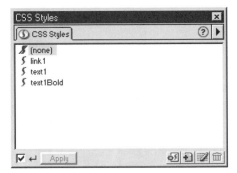

Frames Panel   The Frames panel is a handy reference showing the arrangement of the frames in a document. You can use the Frames panel to select frames and framesets. To open the Frames panel choose Window | Frames, or click the Frames button in the Launcher. You can find more information on frames and using the Frames panel in Chapter 8.

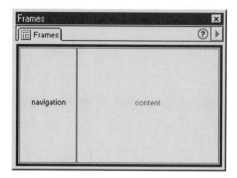

History Panel   The History panel is where Dreamweaver keeps track of your recent actions as you create and edit your pages. To open the History panel choose Window | History, or click the History button in the Launcher. You can select actions from the History panel and replay them to perform repetitive tasks. Chapter 19 provides more information on using the History panel.

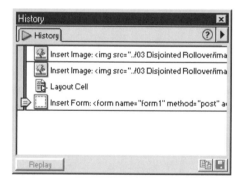

HTML Styles Panel   You can define custom styles in the HTML Styles panel and apply them to the text on your web page. To open the HTML Styles panel choose Window | HTML Styles, or click the HTML Styles button in the Launcher. Refer to Chapter 3 for information on using HTML styles.

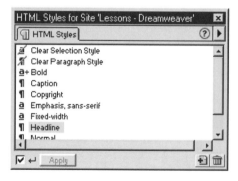

Layers Panel   The Layers panel is where you keep track of layers on your web page. To open the Layers panel choose Window | Layers, or click the Layers button in the Launcher. You can use the panel to select a layer for editing and to make layers visible or hidden. Chapter 15 explores some of the things you can do with layers.

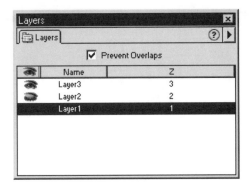

Reference Panel   The Reference panel is your access point for the online library of HTML reference materials that Dreamweaver makes available. To open the Reference panel choose Window | Reference, or click the Reference button in the Launcher. You can find instructions on how to use the Reference panel in the Help section of this chapter.

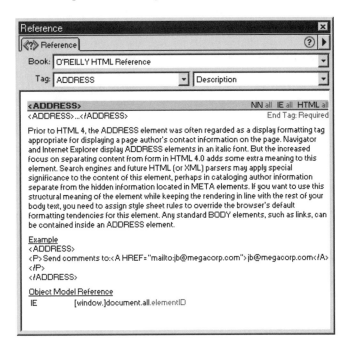

Timelines Panel The Timelines panel is the tool you use to create and edit animation effects. To open the Timelines panel choose Window | Timelines, or click the Timelines button in the Launcher. To find out more about using Timelines, see Chapter 15.

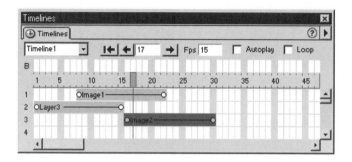

Arrange Panels

Each Dreamweaver panel is a separate window that you can show, hide, move, and resize independently. If you run Dreamweaver on a large, high-resolution monitor, you may have room for several panels arranged around a good-sized Document window without any of the windows overlapping. In that case, you might elect to keep several panels open at all times so you have instant access to the panel contents. On a smaller monitor, things tend to be more crowded, and you may find it easier to open panels one at a time as you need them.

Panels are normally configured to stay on top of the Dreamweaver Document window when the windows overlap, so that the panel contents are accessible and the panel doesn't get lost behind the larger Document window. However, as you can with so many things in Dreamweaver, you can customize that setting in the Preferences dialog box. See Chapter 20 for instructions.

Dreamweaver tries to keep your computer desktop tidy with neatly aligned panels and windows. If you move or resize a panel so that the window border is close to another panel, Dreamweaver automatically snaps the panel into position so that the panel window borders abut perfectly. Dreamweaver does the same automatic alignment trick with Document windows and with the edges of the computer desktop.

Show and Hide Panels

Here's a quick summary of techniques you can use to open, close, and align panels in Dreamweaver.

- Choose Window | *Panel Name* to open or close an individual panel.
- Click a panel's icon in the Launcher to open or close the panel.
- Click the Close (×) button in a panel's title bar to close the panel.
- Choose Window | Hide Panels (or press F4) to instantly close all open panels.
- Choose Window | Show Panels (or press F4) to reverse the effect of the Hide Panels command. This restores all previously open windows to their former size and location.

■ Choose Window | Arrange Panels to automatically position all open panels against the outer edges of your computer desktop.

Dock Panels

There are so many panels available in Dreamweaver that it's impractical to have them all open in individual windows. To avoid a hopelessly cluttered desktop, Dreamweaver added a feature called *docking* to most panels. Docking enables you to consolidate multiple panels into a single window. When panels are docked, the individual panels are stacked on top of one another with the individual panels each represented by a tab labeled by an icon. Simply click the panel's tab to bring it to the top, where you can work with it.

The following illustration shows three panels (HTML Styles, CSS Styles, and Behaviors) docked in a single panel window. The HTML Styles panel is active, as indicated by the title bar and the color of the tab. Tabs for the background panels are shaded gray.

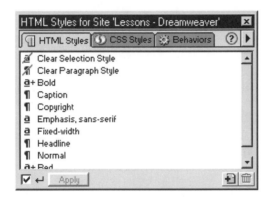

■ To dock a panel into another window, drag the panel's tab from its current window and drop it on the destination panel window.

■ To remove a docked panel from a window, drag the panel's tab from the docked window and drop it on the desktop. Dreamweaver creates a new panel window for the undocked panel.

Docking works with most, but not all, panels. You can't dock the Objects panel, the Property Inspector panel, or the Launcher panel. You can dock all the other panels in any combination that makes sense to you.

Work with the Site Window

While the Dreamweaver Document window is for creating and editing individual web pages, the Dreamweaver Site window is for creating and managing entire web sites. The Site window, shown in Figure 1-11, is where you manage the collection of web documents and all the supporting files and folders that make up a web site.

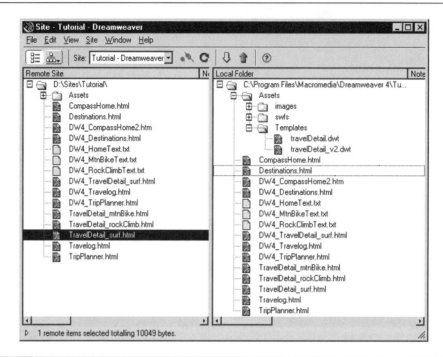

FIGURE 1-11   The Dreamweaver Site window in Site Files view

Chapter 2 explores the important concept of defining a site in Dreamweaver and the procedures for doing so. Chapters 17 and 18 cover publishing, testing, and maintaining your web site with Dreamweaver. Those chapters show the Dreamweaver Site window in action; this chapter gives you a brief get-acquainted tour of the user interface.

The Dreamweaver Site window is divided into two panes. One pane (usually the right) displays a list of files and folders in the local copy of your web site. The contents of the other Site-window pane changes depending on which of the two views you choose to display. Site Files view (refer to Figure 1-11) shows a list of files and folders on the remote web server. Site Map view (shown in Figure 1-12) shows a flow chart–style graphic representation of the pages in your web site.

Menus and Toolbar

The menu bar near the top of the Dreamweaver Site window is an abbreviated version of the menu bar that appears in the Dreamweaver Document window. The Site window menu bar is missing a few menus (Insert, Modify, Text, and Commands) that apply only to the contents of individual web pages.

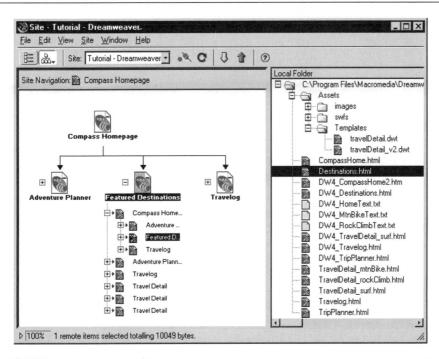

FIGURE 1-12   The Dreamweaver Site window in Site Map view

The Site window also has a toolbar, like the one in the Dreamweaver Document window. But naturally, Dreamweaver populates the Site window toolbar with a different set of buttons.

Here's a list of the Dreamweaver Site window toolbar buttons and what they do.

- **Site Files**   Selects Site Files view.
- **Site Map**   Selects Site Map view.
- **Site Selector**   Drops down a list of sites that are defined in Dreamweaver. Select a site from the list to display it in the Site window.

- ■ **Connect to Remote**   Establishes a connection to the remote web server and updates the remote file list.
- ■ **Refresh**   Updates the Site window display after you make changes in the site.
- ■ **Get Files**   Downloads selected files from the remote web server to the local site.
- ■ **Put Files**   Uploads selected files from the local site folder to the remote web server.
- ■ **Help**   Opens a window displaying a help file with information about the current window view.

Site Files View

Behind the scenes, a web site is really a collection of computer files and folders, so it makes sense that the key feature of the Dreamweaver Site window is a file list. Two of them, in fact. Site Files view (Figure 1-11) shows a split-screen view of your web site with a list of files on the remote web server in one half of the screen and a list of files in your local copy of the site in the other pane. This arrangement mirrors the way many web developers work: creating and editing web documents on your local hard drive and then publishing the site by copying documents to the main web server.

To select Site Files view click Window | Site Files or press F8. (These techniques work even if the Site window isn't open.) You can also click the Site Files button in the toolbar if the Site window is already open.

The Dreamweaver Site window shares some obvious similarities to the file lists in Windows Explorer and Macintosh Finder. The file lists provide a tree-structured view of the hierarchical system of nested files and folders that comprise your web site. The file list will probably look familiar to anyone who has used the file management windows of the Windows or Macintosh operating systems. Icons identify folders and the various kinds of document files.

Clicking the plus sign (+) beside a folder icon expands the file list to show the contents of that folder. Clicking a minus sign (-) beside a folder collapses that branch of the tree and hides the contents of the folder. The various columns show details about the files such as file size and the date the file was last modified. In addition to the standard assortment of columns, the file lists in the Dreamweaver Site window have a couple of special-purpose columns—you'll learn what they're for in later chapters.

Normally, the Local Folder file list appears in the right pane of Site Files view, and the Remote Site file list occupies the left pane. However, you can swap the file lists with a setting in the Preferences dialog box. See Chapter 20 for instructions.

Site Map View

Site Map view is a handy way to get an overview of your web site and the connections between the pages. In Site Map view, Dreamweaver generates an organization chart–styled representation of your site as shown in Figure 1-12. The Site Map diagram appears in one pane of the Site window (usually the left) and the local files list usually appears on the right side.

To select Site Map view click Window | Site Map or press SHIFT+F8. (These techniques work even if the Site window isn't open.) You can also click the Site Map button in the toolbar if the Site window is already open.

The Site Map diagram starts with the site's home page at the top and shows the pages linked directly to your home page in a row beneath it.

- Click the plus (+) box next to a page icon to expand the diagram to show the pages linked to that page. You can keep expanding the Site Map diagram as needed to show the detail you need. Click the minus (−) box to collapse the diagram and hide the linked pages.

- Click the percent display in the left end of the Site window status bar and choose a new magnification to reduce the size of the icons in the Site Map diagram and make room for more detail.

- Right-click a linked page and choose View as Root from the context menu that appears to redraw the Site Map with the selected page as the root page at the top of the diagram. This hides other pages at the same level and above the selected page and makes more room available for a detailed examination of the pages below. The Site Navigation bar at the top of the Site Map pane shows the navigation links to the current root page.

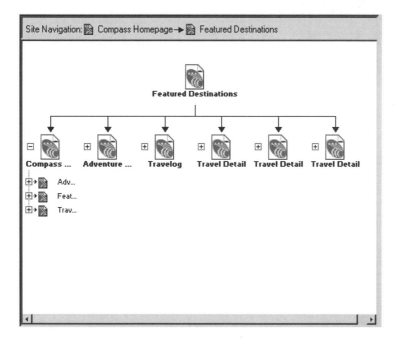

- Click the leftmost page icon in the Site Navigation bar to return the Site Map to the original root home page.

- Click the small arrowhead at the left end of the Site window status bar to hide the one pane of the Site window. Click the arrow again to return to the normal two-pane display.

- Drag the border between the two panes left or right to resize the panes.

Get Help

Dreamweaver supplies a rich selection of online reference and resource materials to help you learn to use the program and its many features. Macromedia even supplies online reference information about HTML tags, CSS Styles, and JavaScript and installs it along with the Dreamweaver program. In addition to the online help and reference materials installed on your hard drive, the Dreamweaver help menu includes links to several online resources available from the Macromedia web site.

Use Dreamweaver Help Index

Unlike many programs that use the standard Windows help system, the main Dreamweaver help system is HTML-based and appears in a browser window, as shown in Figure 1-13. You can launch the Help window by selecting Help | Using Dreamweaver or by pressing F1.

The Dreamweaver help system is context sensitive, which means that the program displays the portion of the help files that apply to the window or task you were in when you requested

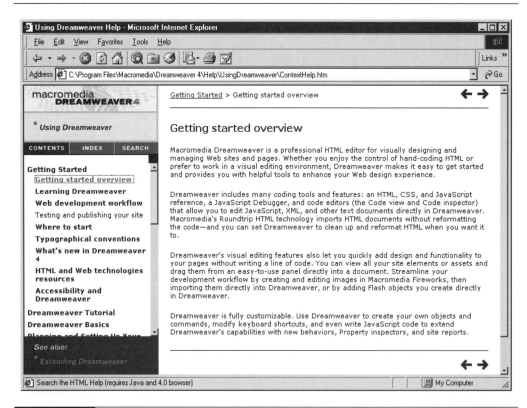

FIGURE 1-13   The Dreamweaver help system

help. Often, the applicable help topic appears immediately. When it doesn't, you can use the following techniques to navigate through the Using Dreamweaver help file:

- Click the Contents button in the navigation frame at the left side of the Help window. Scroll through the list of general help topics. Click on any bold topic to reveal a list of subtopics. Click a topic to display the related text in the main Help window frame.

- Click the Index button; then click a letter to display a list of keywords and phrases that start with that letter. Click a keyword to display the related help topic.

- Click the Search button to open a separate Search dialog box. Type a keyword in the text box at the top of the dialog box; then click List Topics. Dreamweaver displays a list of related topics in the large list box. Select a topic from the list and click Display to display the topic in the main Help window.

Use Reference

The Reference panel enables you to search the text of three reference works for information about HTML tags, CSS Styles, or JavaScript. Click Help | Reference to open the Reference panel. You can also open the Reference panel by clicking Window | Reference or by clicking the Reference icon in the Launcher.

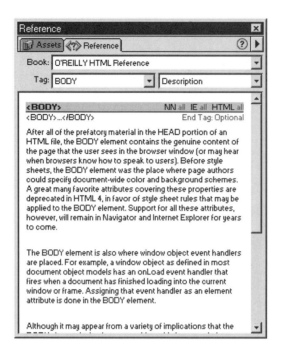

Use the three drop-down lists at the top of the panel to select the topic. First select the book in the top list, and then select the tag, style, or object in the list on the left, and finally narrow the topic by making a selection in the right list (if there is more than one subtopic available). The text of the selected topic appears in the main text box.

Other Help Resources

In addition to the main Dreamweaver help system and the Reference panel, Dreamweaver offers several other help resources.

Welcome   Click Help | Welcome to launch the introductory product overview. This is the same splash-screen introduction that appears automatically when you first run Dreamweaver after installing the program. It provides links to What's New, Guided Tours, Tutorial, and Lessons. Choosing Tutorial from the Welcome screen opens a browser window and displays the first page of a step-by-step tutorial on how to create a simple web site with Dreamweaver.

What's New   Choose Help | What's New to open a mini-browser window where you can view a series of pages summarizing the new features of Dreamweaver 4. This is more of a marketing presentation than something that will help you learn to use the program.

Guided Tour   Click Help | Guided Tour to open a mini-browser window where you can view a presentation outlining Dreamweaver's key features. Like the What's New presentation, Guided Tour is a marketing piece instead of an instructional presentation.

Lessons   Choose Help | Lessons to open a mini-browser window where you can select one of seven lessons on how to perform tasks such as creating an image map or a page with frames. Click a lesson to go to the first page of that lesson. Click the arrow buttons at the bottom of the window to step through the instruction pages, one by one.

Online Resources   In addition to the other help resources that you can access from your own hard disk, the Dreamweaver Help menu provides links to the following web-based resources:

- **Dreamweaver Exchange**   Opens a browser window and goes online to the Dreamweaver Exchange at the Macromedia web site

- **Manage Extensions**   Launches Macromedia Extension Manager

- **Dreamweaver Support Center**   Opens a browser window and goes online to the Dreamweaver support area of the Macromedia web site

- **Macromedia Online Forums**   Opens a browser window and goes online to the Macromedia online discussion forums on the Macromedia web site

- **Extending Dreamweaver**   Displays help on Dreamweaver extensions and programming interfaces

- **Creating and Submitting Extensions**   Displays instructions on how to create and submit extensions

How to...

- Define a site in Dreamweaver
- Work with files in the Dreamweaver Site window
- Create a Site Map and use it to develop the site structure

In the early days of the Web, people talked about having a web *home page*. And frequently, that's all it was—a single web page. But the Web has grown since then, and so has the complexity of the typical web presence. Nowadays, the web home page is rarely a stand-alone entity—it has evolved into the entry point for a web site consisting of dozens, hundreds, or even thousands of interlinked pages. Managing all those web documents and related files can be a formidable task.

Dreamweaver is more than a web page creation and editing tool—it's a web *site* creation and maintenance tool. Dreamweaver provides the file management capabilities you need to keep track of all the web documents you create for a site, as well as all the supporting files required for graphics, media, and special effects on those pages. Dreamweaver also gives you the tools for publishing your site by copying web documents and supporting files from the computer where you created them to the web server that makes them accessible to viewers with browsers.

Having a file manager and a file-transfer utility built into Dreamweaver is convenient, but Dreamweaver's site management capabilities don't stop there. Dreamweaver can compare files on a remote web server to local copies of those files and automatically update only the files that have changed. And Dreamweaver automatically handles the tedious chore of updating file references in your web documents when you copy them to or from the server.

If you use Dreamweaver only to create and edit individual web documents that consist entirely of simple text, then you can ignore the program's site management features. However, as soon as you start creating multipage web sites and web pages with graphics and rich media features, you'll need to deal with file management issues. When you do, you'll appreciate Dreamweaver's site management tools. What's more, you'll find that the Dreamweaver features that help you publish your site when you finish it can also be invaluable aids in planning your site from the beginning.

Everything Starts with the Site Definition

Before you create your first web page, you should have a plan for the web site that the page will be part of. After all, you wouldn't expect to build a house without a set of plans. And, just as carpenters and electricians need to know something about the house plans before they

Chapter 2

Define a Site in Dreamweaver

begin work, Dreamweaver needs to know something about your site before its site management features will work. So, the first step in using Dreamweaver on a web development project is to *define your site*, which simply means providing the program with some key information about the site, such as where the site files are (or will be) stored.

You can start from scratch and create an entire site with Dreamweaver. Or you can use Dreamweaver to edit and maintain an existing site—even if the site was not originally developed with Dreamweaver.

The Relationship Between Local and Remote Sites

In Dreamweaver, the term *site* refers to a collection of related web documents along with their supporting files and folders. Note that, according to this definition, a web site does not necessarily have to be hosted on a web server and available to the public. A web site might be stored on an intranet where it's available only to internal corporate users; a web site might reside on a network drive somewhere on a local network; or a web site might be stored on your computer's local hard drive.

When you define a web site in Dreamweaver, you normally define two sites, not just one.

- First, there is the *local site*, where you create and edit working copies of the site files.
- Second, there is the *remote site*, where the final published files go.

The Local Site

The local site acts as a staging area where you can begin building and testing pages without putting them out on the web for all to see. Some people call this the *staging site, test site, dummy site,* or *dev (development) site*. The local site is usually a folder on your computer's local hard drive, but it can also be a network drive on a LAN.

> **TIP**   *Storing local site files on your local hard drive improves performance significantly by avoiding network delays when Dreamweaver reads and saves files.*

When the site is ready to publish, you copy the files from the local site to the remote site. The remote site is often called the *live site*. After you publish the site, you can continue to add and edit pages on the local site without disrupting the remote site. When the additions and changes are complete, Dreamweaver helps you automatically update the proper files on the remote site.

Folder vs. Directory

The computer terms *folder* and *directory* are interchangeable. Both refer to groupings of files on a computer hard disk or other storage media. Historically, the term *directory* was used across almost all operating systems. However, as the manila file folder gained general acceptance as a visual metaphor (icon) for directories, the term *folder* has become an acceptable alternative for *directory*. Nowadays, *folder* is the term favored by typical Windows and Macintosh users, while *directory* remains the term preferred among UNIX users and many computer professionals. In this book, I use *folder* in context with the Dreamweaver program and your local computer, and I use *directory* when referring to remote servers, which are usually set up and administered by professional computer geeks.

The Remote Site

The remote site is usually a directory on a web server that is accessible via the Internet. If your remote site is an inhouse web server, you may be able to transfer files to the remote site over a LAN connection. However, you normally need to use an FTP (File Transfer Protocol) utility to transfer files to the remote site over the Internet. Dreamweaver has its own built-in FTP utility, so you don't need to use a separate program. (Dreamweaver also supports accessing a remote site via SourceSafe and WebDAV.)

Basically, the idea is to have two copies of your web site with duplicate sets of files. You create web documents on the local site and then duplicate those files on the remote site. As you continue to create and edit web documents on the local site, the local files get out of sync with their counterparts on the remote site. But that's a temporary situation. Eventually, the additions and changes get published to the live remote site, and the two sites are again synchronized. And if you happen to make a mess of things as you edit the local copy of a web document, you can always replace the local file with a copy downloaded from the remote site.

Duplicate the Site Structure

It's not enough to have duplicate sets of files on both the local site and the remote site—you also need to duplicate the structure of the site with all the nested folders and subfolders, as shown in Figure 2-1. Dreamweaver doesn't impose a predefined folder structure on your site, but it does require that the same structure exist on both the local site and the remote site. So, if the web documents for the product pages on the remote site are stored in the \Products folder and the images for those pages are in the \Products\Assets\Images folder, then those same folders must exist on the local site to hold the local copies of the corresponding files.

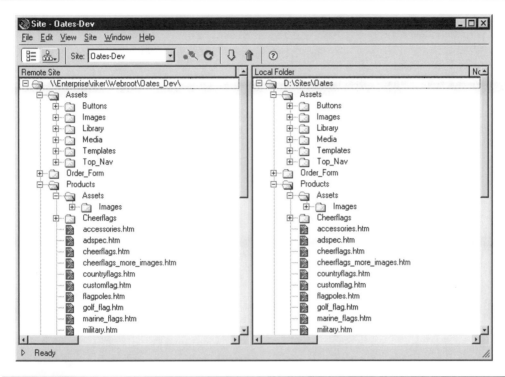

FIGURE 2-1   The structures of the local and remote sites must match.

Did you know?

Understanding Hierarchical Folder Structure

Managing the multitude of files stored on a computer system would be almost impossible without some way to organize those files into categories or groups of some kind. Folders (aka directories) provide the means to do that. You use folders to organize the web documents and supporting files for your web sites and all other files on your computer system.

Each folder contains a group of files that are logically related in some way. A folder might contain all the files for a particular project or files of a particular type. The relationship of the files within a folder is up to you to determine. The folder is just a tool that you can use as a virtual container for the files that you want to store together.

Folders are a powerful organizational tool, because each folder can contain other folders as well as files. You can nest folders within folders within folders many layers deep to keep subdividing your computer files into smaller and smaller groups. The goal is to reach a level of detailed categorization that enables you to quickly find any file you need. For example, you could easily locate an image file used on a particular web site if you know that it's in the Images folder, which is in the Assets folder, which is in the Mysite folder, which is in the Websites folder on your hard drive.

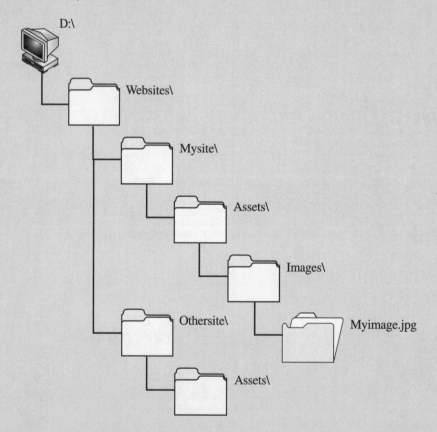

This system of dividing files into groups and then subdividing the groups into smaller groups is called a *hierarchical folder structure*. The result is an organizational scheme that is similar to an outline structure, or a tree with a trunk that divides into branches that split into smaller and smaller branches.

It's much easier to visualize the position of a given folder in the overall folder hierarchy when you use file management tools that include a tree structure display, such as the one in the Dreamweaver Site window shown in Figure 2-1. However, the default folder window displays in both Windows and Macintosh show only large icons for the files and folders within the current folder with no indication of any parent folders or other folders on other branches of the tree. No wonder many users are confused by the folder structure on their drives. (Optional tree structure folder displays are available in both Windows and Macintosh.)

After you understand the nested folder-within-a-folder idea of a hierarchical folder structure, it's easy to decipher the location of a file from its *pathname*. The pathname starts with the drive designation of the device on which the file is stored and goes through each nested folder in hierarchical sequence, finally ending up with the filename itself. So, in the case of the image file example above, the pathname would be: D:\Websites\Mysite\Assets\Images\Myimage.jpg, which translates to the Myimage.jpg file in the Images subfolder of the Assets subfolder of the Mysite subfolder of the Websites folder on the D: drive of the local computer.

Actually, you don't have to duplicate the entire directory structure of the remote web server on your local machine. The remote server may host several complete web sites, and the site you plan to edit with Dreamweaver might be in a folder nested several levels deep. You need only identify the folder that contains your site and duplicate the files and subfolders that you will be editing with Dreamweaver, along with any supporting files on which the web documents depend.

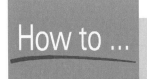

How to ... Identify Web Host Operating Systems

Nearly all web servers run one of two operating systems—either Windows NT/2000 or some variant of UNIX, such as Linux. The two operating systems use different naming conventions for drive volumes. Windows uses letters followed by a colon, and UNIX uses names, like a folder. As a result, if you know the full pathname for the location of your web site on the server, you can identify which operating system that server uses. If the pathname begins with a letter and a colon (D:), it's a Windows system. If the pathname starts with a slash and a name (/userwebs), it's a UNIX system.

Understanding Relative vs. Absolute Addresses

You can specify the addresses of links, images, and other supporting files in one of two ways: using relative or absolute addresses. It's important to understand the difference between the two because of how the addressing affects the way the files are accessed.

- Absolute addresses include the filename plus the full URL or local pathname, such as http://www.foobar.com/linkedpage.html or D:\websites\mysite\linkedpage.html.

- Use absolute addresses for links to web pages and other Internet resources outside your current site.

- Do not use absolute addresses for web documents and files that are part of your current site.

- Relative addresses omit the portion of the URL or pathname that is the same as the current site or document, thus giving the file's location relative to the current location. Therefore, a relative address for a file in the same folder as the current page is just the filename. Similarly, a relative address for a file located in a subfolder of the folder that the current page is in is just the filename preceded by the subfolder, even though the current file and the subfolder are both in a folder nested several layers down from the main drive root.

- Use relative addresses for web pages, images, and supporting files within your current site. Since your local and remote sites share the same folder structure, the relative addresses of the various files on the local site and remote site remain the same even though the absolute addresses are different because they reside under different roots.

Dreamweaver is smart enough to keep track of file and folder locations relative to the site's root folder, which is the folder that contains your site's home page and all the other nested folders and files. For example, a Web site with the address www.mysite.com might be located in the following folder on the web server:

D:\web\users\~mysite\webroot\

This is the site's root folder on the remote site. You might access that location via FTP at the following address:

ftp://mysite.com/webroot/

You might want to store the site's files in the following location on your local hard drive:

C:\sites\mysite\

This is the root folder for the local site.

It isn't necessary for the root folders on the local site and the remote site to match. In other words, you don't need to create a bunch of nested folders on your hard drive to match the \web\users\~mysite\webroot\ path of the remote site. In fact, you don't even have to know the actual location of the files on the remote server as long as you know the FTP address used to access them. Dreamweaver can keep track of the two different root folders provided that the files and subfolders within both sites have the same relationship to their respective roots.

For example, if image files are in D:\web\users\~mysite\webroot*assets**images*\ on the remote site, they need to be in C:\sites\mysite*assets**images*\ on the local site. As long as the *assets**images*\ portions of the path are the same on both sites, Dreamweaver can do its thing to keep the local and remote sites synchronized.

> **TIP**
> *Use folders and subfolders to separate supporting files (such as images) from the actual web document files. Folders help organize supporting files into logical groups, and separating the supporting files from the web documents makes it much easier to find the web document you want to edit.*

As a rule, you need to maintain duplicate structures of nesting folders on the local and remote sites. However, there are a few exceptions. You don't need to duplicate any folder that doesn't contain either web documents that you will be editing with Dreamweaver or supporting files that are used by those web documents.

> **TIP**
> *If you develop a consistent naming scheme for the subfolders you use to organize your web site files, it'll be easier to find the file you're looking for.*

For example, you might have used some word processor documents and raw text files as sources from which to cut and paste text into some web pages. After you paste the text into the web pages, you no longer need continued access to the source files in order to work with the web pages, but you might choose to keep them in a subfolder on the local site as a record of materials received from the client. You don't need to duplicate that folder on the remote site.

All this stress on maintaining duplicate files and folder structures on two sites may sound complicated, but it's really not difficult at all—at least not with the tools that Dreamweaver places at your disposal. All you need to do is set up the local site; Dreamweaver will take care of the details of duplicating the local site to the remote site. Or you can start with an existing remote site and let Dreamweaver automatically duplicate the entire remote site (or a selected portion) on your local hard drive. After you set up the local and remote sites, Dreamweaver automatically copies files to the correct folders when you synchronize the sites.

Define a Site

Before you begin creating web pages for a web site, you need to tell Dreamweaver a few basic facts about the site. Although it's possible to use Dreamweaver to create and edit individual web documents without first defining a site, doing so doesn't use the program to its full potential.

Defining a site takes just a minute or so, and you'll reap a generous return on that time investment by being able to take advantage of Dreamweaver's site management tools to help you manage all the web documents and supporting files that make up the site.

To define a site, you need to gather the following information:

- A name for the site. You can use any short name that is meaningful to you.

- The location of the local site files—usually a folder on your hard drive. If the folder doesn't exist, you can create it as you define the site.

- The web address for the site—for example, http://www.mysite.com.

- The location of the remote site. Usually that's an FTP address consisting of the FTP server name and the host directory for the site. However, Dreamweaver can also access remote sites on your LAN or through SourceSafe or WebDAV.

- The user name and password you need to access the remote site.

> **TIP** *Actually, you can define a local site with just the site name and the local root folder. You can fill in all the other information later. However, you won't be able to use all of Dreamweaver's site management features until you finish defining both the local and remote sites.*

After you get your information together, you can define the site in Dreamweaver. Here's how:

1. Choose Site | New Site from the menu in either the Dreamweaver Document window or Site window. Dreamweaver opens the Site Definition dialog box with the Local Info category selected, as shown in Figure 2-2.

2. Type a name in the Site Name text box. This is the text that will identify the site in the Dreamweaver menus and lists.

> **TIP** *It's best to keep site names short but descriptive. The client name or the domain name (mysite.com) is often a good choice. Try abbreviations for long client names (Smith, Jones, and Doe, Inc. becomes SJ&D).*

3. Enter the full pathname of the local site's root folder in the Local Root Folder box. This is almost always a folder on your hard drive. You can type the pathname or click the small folder icon to the right of the text box to open the Choose Local Folder dialog box. Use the Select list and double-click folder icons to navigate to the folder where you want to store local site files. If the folder doesn't exist, you can create it by clicking the Create New Folder button in the Choose Local Folder dialog box. When you have the site's root folder open, click Select to close the Choose Local Folder dialog box and enter the information into the Site Definition dialog box.

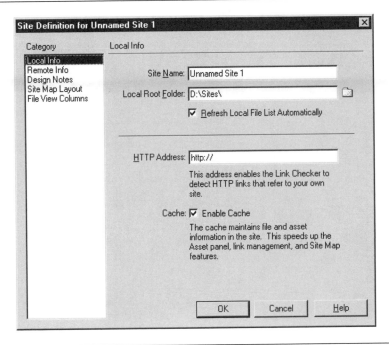

FIGURE 2-2   Defining the local site

4. Enter the site's URL (Uniform Resource Locator, or web address) in the HTTP Address box. Dreamweaver uses this information to identify links in your web documents that point to other pages in this site. Also make sure that the two check boxes (Refresh Local File List Automatically and Enable Cache) are checked.

5. Click Remote Info in the Category list to display the Remote Info page. Initially, there is only one option—Access—with a default value of None.

6. Make a selection from the Access list box to tell Dreamweaver how to access your remote site. When you do, other options appear on the Remote Info page. Those options vary depending on which access mode you choose. Figure 2-3 shows the FTP options, the most common selection. A similar set of options appears if you choose Local/Network access. If you choose SourceSafe Database or WebDAV, a Settings button appears beside the Access box.

7. Enter the information required to identify and gain access to your remote site. For FTP access, enter the FTP server name in the FTP Host box and the path to the site's root directory in the Host Directory box. Enter the FTP Login name and Password in the corresponding boxes. Check the Save box if you want Dreamweaver to enter the password for you, or clear the box to have Dreamweaver prompt you for the password. Check the

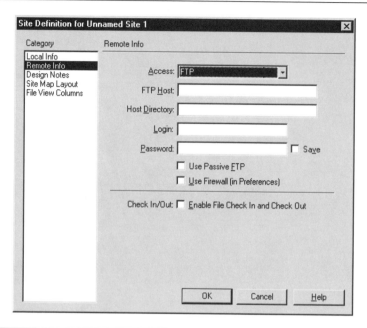

FIGURE 2-3 Defining the remote site

Use Passive FTP and/or Use Firewall boxes if your Internet connection requires those options for successful FTP operation. The settings for Local/Network access are similar to FTP access. For SourceSafe or WebDAV access, click the Settings button to open a small dialog box where you enter the appropriate settings to identify and gain access to the remote site through SourceSafe or WebDAV.

8. Clear the Check In/Out check box in the lower half of the Remote Info page to disable the file Check Out feature. (If you're part of a team or a workgroup collaborating on this web site, see Chapter 18 for information on how to set up and use the file Check Out feature.)

NOTE *There are three more categories of options available in the Site Definition dialog box: Design Notes, Site Map Layout, and File View Columns. However, you will seldom need to change the default settings for those categories. You can find information on Design Notes in Chapter 18, and the Site Map Layout and File View Columns settings are summarized in Chapter 20.*

9. Click OK to close the Site Definition dialog box and record the site in Dreamweaver. When Dreamweaver offers to create a site cache, click OK. Dreamweaver displays your newly defined site in the Site window.

After you define a site, you're not stuck with those settings forever. You can always go back and edit the site definition as needed. Simply choose Site | Define Sites to open the Define Sites dialog box.

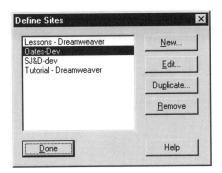

Select the site you want to change from the list, and click Edit to open the Site Definition dialog box—the same dialog box you used to define the site in the first place. You can change any of the settings in the Site Definition dialog box.

Work in the Site Window

Immediately after you define a site, Dreamweaver opens the Site window, and with good reason: the Site window is an excellent place to start developing your web site. In the Dreamweaver Site window, you can begin to build the structure of your site, even before you create the first web document.

If you specified both a local and a remote site when you defined your Dreamweaver site, Site Files view shows two file lists, as shown in Figure 2-4, with the local files on one side (usually the right) and the remote files on the other (usually the left). At least, that's the way it looks if you're setting Dreamweaver up to access an existing site where both the local and remote sites are populated with a full complement of web documents, folders, and supporting files.

However, if you're starting to build a new web site from scratch, the local site may consist of nothing but an empty folder on your hard drive, and the remote site may not even be defined yet. As you work on your new web site, adding web documents and supporting files and publishing them to the remote site, your web site will gradually grow to resemble the one shown in Figure 2-4.

The basic techniques for viewing files and folders in Dreamweaver's Site Files view are pretty standard. Icons beside each file or folder name in the file list enable you to distinguish between files and folders and help to identify the various file types.

■ Click the plus sign beside a folder icon to show the contents of the folder.

■ Click the minus sign to hide the folder contents.

■ Click an item to select it.

■ CTRL+click to select multiple items.

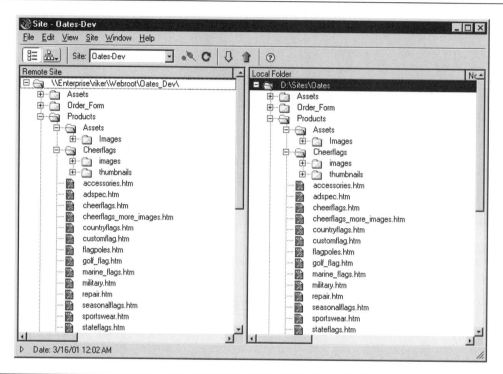

FIGURE 2-4   Site Files view shows the contents of the remote and local sites side
by side.

- Double-click a file icon to open the file. (The effect of a double-click varies depending on the type of item you click. Double-clicking a web document opens that document for editing in the Dreamweaver Document window. Double-clicking an image file launches the associated program for editing that file type and opens the file for editing.)

- Double-click a folder to expand or collapse the view to show or hide the contents of a folder.

Create Files and Folders

Obviously, the site files list enables you to view the files and folders that make up your web site. What isn't so obvious at first glance is that you can also create both files and folders in the Dreamweaver Site Files window. In other words, this is where you go to build the structure of your web site by adding folders, subfolders, and web document files.

Create Folders

The procedure for creating new folders in the site file list is similar to creating folders in Windows Explorer. Just follow these steps:

1. Select the folder in which you want to create the new subfolder.

2. Choose File | New Folder or right-click anywhere within the parent folder and choose New Folder from the context menu that appears. Dreamweaver creates a new folder with the unimaginative name *untitled* and highlights the folder name, ready for editing.

The keyboard shortcut for the New Folder command is CTRL+ALT+SHIFT+N.

3. Type in the name for the folder and press ENTER.

You can create as many folders and subfolders as you need to create a logical structure for your site. Web document files for the site's home page (and sometimes the first tier of general site pages) typically go in the site's root folder, but it's a good idea to store all other site files in subfolders to avoid cluttering the root folder. One common arrangement is to create an Assets folder that contains separate subfolders for images, Flash objects, audio files, and so on. And if you have more than a few web document files, you'll want to organize them in subfolders as well.

Create Files

You can also create web document files directly in the site files list without opening a Dreamweaver Document window. It might seem counterintuitive to create files in this way, but it's actually a fast and efficient way to build a web site. You can quickly and easily create blank web document files to populate the folders as you build the structure of your web site in the site list. After creating web document files in the site file list, you can use the Site Map to build links between those files and visualize the way key documents relate to one another without getting bogged down in the details of creating content for each of those pages. Later, when you're ready to add content to the blank documents you created in the site file list, the tedious first step of naming and saving a new document file is already done.

The procedure for creating a document file in the site files list is similar to the procedure for creating folders. Follow these steps:

1. Select the folder in which you want to create the new file.

2. Choose File | New File or right-click anywhere within the parent folder and choose New File from the context menu that appears. Dreamweaver creates a new file named *untitled.htm* and highlights the name, ready for editing.

The keyboard shortcut for the New File command is CTRL+SHIFT+N.

3. Type in the name for the folder and press ENTER.

Other File-Maintenance Commands

In addition to creating folders and files, you can perform a number of other file-maintenance tasks in the site files list. Here is a quick summary of some common commands:

- Select a file or folder and then choose File | Rename to change the name of the selected item. Dreamweaver highlights the item name. Type a new name (don't forget to include the appropriate file extension) and press ENTER. Dreamweaver automatically offers to update any web documents that contain references to the renamed file or folder.

- Select one or more files or folders in the site file list and then choose File | Delete to delete the selected items. Dreamweaver displays a dialog box requesting confirmation of the action. If you click Yes, Dreamweaver deletes the selected items from the site.

- Select one or more files or folders, then drag the selected items and drop them on a folder icon to move the items into the target folder. Dreamweaver automatically offers to update any web documents that contain references to the files or folders you just moved.

Of course, you can perform the same file-maintenance tasks outside Dreamweaver, but if you do, you miss out on one very important advantage: When you move, rename, or delete files in the Dreamweaver Site window, Dreamweaver automatically checks all your web documents for any reference to the changed files and offers to update those documents to reflect the changes. If you move or rename a site file using some other utility outside Dreamweaver, you must manually locate and update the file references in all your web documents. And that can be quite a chore, even on a relatively small site.

Connect to the Remote Site

If the remote site portion of your web site is located on a system requiring an FTP connection, Dreamweaver connects to the remote server as needed to get updates and perform file transfers. When you open the site in the Site window, Dreamweaver attempts to connect to the remote site and, if it's successful, displays a current file list from the remote site in the Remote Site pane. However, Dreamweaver doesn't attempt to maintain a permanent connection to the remote site the entire time you are working in the program.

 *If you need to manually establish a connection to the Internet for other programs, such as your web browser, you'll need to do so for Dreamweaver as well. Be sure to establish the Internet connection before attempting to connect to your remote site in Dreamweaver.*

Connect Manually

 If the initial connection to the remote site was unsuccessful, or if the connection has timed out, you can manually trigger a connection to the remote server by choosing Site | Connect or by clicking the Connect button on the toolbar. The button changes slightly (the gap between the plugs disappears) to indicate a successful connection. Similarly, you can manually disconnect from the remote site by choosing Site | Disconnect or by clicking the toolbar button.

You don't have to manually connect to the remote site every time you want to do something. Dreamweaver automatically initiates a connection to the remote server as needed, whether it's to transfer files or to update the remote file list. The manual connection is just an option that you can use to check or update the connection without actually having to do something on the remote site.

Refresh the File List

Sometimes, site files get changed outside Dreamweaver, and the changes aren't immediately reflected in the site files lists. This can happen if you use another utility to make changes to the files and folders on your local or remote site, but it's more likely to occur when a team or workgroup collaborates on a site. Another team member might edit and update certain site files while you work on others. The Remote Site file list in your Dreamweaver Site Files window won't show any changes that were made since the last time you connected to the remote server from within Dreamweaver.

To update the file list, simply click anywhere in the file list and click the Refresh button on the toolbar.

 *The keyboard shortcut for refreshing the file list is* F5.

Copy Files Between Local and Remote Sites

One of the primary functions of Dreamweaver's Site Files view is to enable you to conveniently copy files and folders between local and remote sites. After all, copying files from the local folder to the remote server is how you publish your site. And it's standard practice to copy files from the remote site to your local machine so you can edit the copies without disrupting the live site.

Dreamweaver uses different terms for the copy operation depending on whether you are copying files to or from the remote site.

- **Put**   Copy files or folders from the local folder to the remote site (Upload)
- **Get**   Copy files or folders from the remote site to the local folder (Download)

The terms make a lot of sense if you remember that Dreamweaver always looks at the copy operation from the perspective of the local folder as home base. Put and Get describe what the program needs to do to move files to and from the remote site—and the terms are much shorter than the alternatives: Upload and Download.

Put Files

When you're ready to copy (upload) files and folders from the local folder to the remote site in Dreamweaver's Site Files view, follow these steps:

1. Select one or more files or folders in the Local Folder file list.

To select multiple files or folders in the file list, CTRL+click additional file icons. To select a contiguous list of files, select the first file, then SHIFT+click the last file. Dreamweaver highlights the files in between. Also, selecting a folder automatically selects all the files and subfolders contained in that folder.

2. Click the Put File button on the toolbar or choose Site | Put. Dreamweaver displays the Dependent Files dialog box.

Dependent files are all the images, templates, library files, and other supporting files that the browser needs to render the selected web document(s). Dreamweaver automatically locates all the dependent files for any web document you copy with the Put or Get commands.

3. Click Yes or No, depending on whether you want Dreamweaver to copy dependent files in addition to the selected files. Dreamweaver connects to the remote site (if it isn't already connected) and begins the copy process. The status bar at the bottom of the Site window shows the filename of each file as it is copied to the remote site.

Drag a file or folder icon from one site pane and drop it on the other site pane to copy the file or folder to the target site.

Get Files

Getting files—downloading files from the Remote Site—is really the same as putting files, but in reverse. Here are the steps:

1. Select one or more files or folders in the Remote Site file list.

2. Click the Get File button on the toolbar or choose Site | Get. Dreamweaver displays the Dependent Files dialog box.

3. Click Yes or No, depending on whether you want Dreamweaver to copy dependent files in addition to the selected files. Dreamweaver begins the copy process, and the status bar at the bottom of the Site window shows the filename of each file as it is copied from the remote site.

How to ... Download an Entire Remote Site

When you use Dreamweaver to edit and maintain an existing web site, you're usually faced with a scenario that is just the reverse of the normal workflow. Instead of creating web documents in a local folder and then publishing them to the remote web server, you start out with files that exist on the remote server. You need to create a mirror copy of those files and folders on your local system for convenient editing. Fortunately, Dreamweaver makes it easy to copy an entire remote site to your local folder. Here's how:

1. If you haven't already done so, create a new site (see the "Define a Site" section earlier in this chapter) using the existing site specifications for the remote site and an empty folder on your hard drive as the local site.

2. Open the site and click the Connect button if necessary to establish a connection to the remote site.

3. Click the root folder at the top of the Remote Site file list. This selects the root folder and all the files and subfolders therein—in other words, the entire site.

4. Click the Get Files button to start the download. Dreamweaver displays a small dialog box asking you to confirm that you want to copy the entire site.

5. Click Yes to confirm getting the whole site. Dreamweaver begins copying files and folders from the remote site to the local folder.

That's all there is to it. Dreamweaver automatically creates a mirror image of the remote site on your local system, duplicating the folder structure and copying all the files into the appropriate folders.

Create a Site Map

The Dreamweaver Site Map view (see Figure 2-5) is a great tool for visualizing the way web documents within your site relate to one another. The Site Map diagrams the links between pages, so you can see a graphical representation of the navigational flow from one page to another. Chapter 1 introduced the Site Map and how to access it.

You can use the Site Map as a navigation tool to move through your site, locate web documents, and open them for editing by double-clicking the page icon in the Site Map. The Site Map's usefulness as a way to display the links between pages is obvious. As you create web documents in the Dreamweaver Document window and add links from that document to others, Site Map view reflects the growing complexity of the interconnected maze of your site.

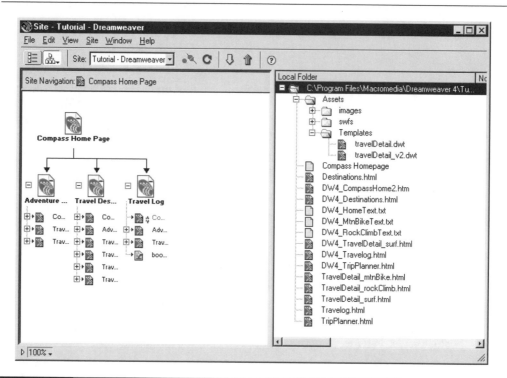

FIGURE 2-5 Site Map view

> **TIP** *Dreamweaver can display either filenames or page titles to label the page icons in the Site Map. It's your choice. Choose View | Show Page Titles or press* CTRL+SHIFT+T *to switch between titles and filenames.*

What isn't as obvious is that you can use the Site Map to build those relationships very early in the site development process, even before you create content for any web documents. In fact, you can build a Site Map for your site using blank web document files that you create in the Site Files window.

Define the Home Page

The Dreamweaver Site Map starts with the site's home page and shows how the links to other pages flow from that starting page. Consequently, Dreamweaver can't draw the Site Map until you define a home page for the site. To define (or redefine) the home page, follow these steps:

1. Select a web document in the site files list that will become your site's home page.

2. Choose Site | Set as Home Page or right-click the document icon and choose Set as Home Page from the context menu that appears.

After you define the home page, Dreamweaver draws the Site Map in the Site Map pane of the Site window. The Site Map displays the home page at the top of the chart and diagrams the links to other pages from that home page in the next row of page icons. (Refer back to Figure 2-5.) If the document you selected as the home page contains no links to other pages, then the home page alone appears in the Site Map.

Link Pages in Site Map View

Normally, you create most links between web pages as you work with the content on those pages. You select some text or graphic on a page and create a link from it to another document. Or you add a button graphic, image map, navigation bar, or other navigation device to the page that includes links to other pages. As you build links into your web documents, Dreamweaver updates the Site Map to show those links.

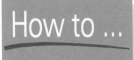

Click the Refresh button to get the latest changes in an open document to show up in the Site Map.

How to ...   **Change Page Titles in the Site Map**

When you're working in the Site Map, you may find that you need to change the title of a page, either to something more appropriate or to replace the default "Untitled Document" page title that Dreamweaver inserts when you create blank pages in the Site File pane. There's no need to open the document just to change the page title. You can do it right in the Site Map pane. Here's how:

1. Choose View | Show Page Titles to display page titles instead of filenames in the Site Map.

2. Click the page icon for the page you want to change.

3. Choose File | Rename or simply click the page title under the selected page icon. The title becomes editable text.

4. Type the new page title and press ENTER.

Dreamweaver makes the change to the page title in the web document and in the Site Map.

However, you can also initiate links between web documents from within the Site Map. This process is especially useful for planning a web site, before you get down to the detail work of building the content on individual pages. You can use any of the following techniques:

- Drag a file from a Windows Explorer (or Macintosh Finder) window and drop it on a page icon in the Site Map. Dreamweaver copies the file from Windows Explorer into your local site folder and adds a link to that file to the page you selected in the Site Map.

- Select a page in the Site Map and then choose Site | Link to Existing File to open the Select HTML File dialog box. Browse to the file you want to link to and then click Select to close the dialog box and add the link to the Site Map.

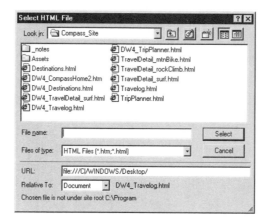

- Select a page icon in the Site Map. Click and drag from the Point-to-File icon (the "bull's eye" symbol that appears beside the page icon) to the link target as shown in Figure 2-6. The target of the link can be any page in the Site Map or in the site file list.

- To create a link to a new file, select a page in the Site Map, then choose Site | Link to New File to open the Link to New File dialog box. Enter the File Name, Title, and Text of Link in the corresponding boxes and click OK. Dreamweaver creates a new file with the filename and title you specified and adds a link to that file (using the Text of Link text) to the page selected in the Site Map.

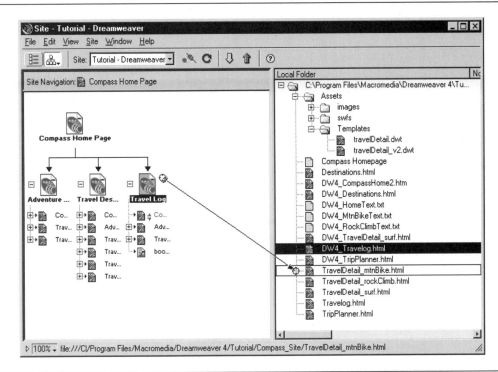

FIGURE 2-6   Creating a link from the Site Map

Part II

Create Basic Web Pages

Chapter 3

Create a Page with Text

How to

- Create a web document page
- Work with text on a web page
- Import text from text files and word processor documents
- Insert horizontal lines
- Work with fonts and character formatting
- Use paragraph formatting for headings and lists
- Create and use HTML Styles
- Check your page for spelling errors

Hypertext Markup Language (HTML) and the World Wide Web were originally developed as a way for scientists and academics to share technical documents. Sometimes, when one looks at all the eye-catching graphics and rich media content featured prominently on many modern web pages, it's hard to believe that the Web traces its roots to such a humble beginning just a few short years ago.

Then again, when you look past the flashy introduction pages on many web sites, you see that, even today, the vast majority of web documents are composed primarily of text. Perhaps the text is embellished with graphics, but the bulk of the content on most web sites is still good old text. So, it's entirely appropriate to start your exploration of Dreamweaver's page-creation capabilities with the program's text-handling features.

Create a Web Document

Of course, before you can begin working with text or anything else on a web page, you need to create or open a web document in Dreamweaver. You have a choice of starting a new document or opening an existing document file. If you create a new document, Dreamweaver opens a Document window and displays a blank, untitled page, as shown in Figure 3-1.

When you start the Dreamweaver program, an untitled Document window normally appears automatically (unless you start Dreamweaver by opening an existing document file or have the program configured to display the Site window on startup). If you open an existing document as you start the program, Dreamweaver displays that document instead of the blank untitled document. When you create or open a document from within Dreamweaver, the program displays a separate Document window for each document—you can have several Document windows open at once.

When a blank new page appears in a Dreamweaver Document window, the very first thing you should do is save the document file. Dreamweaver doesn't force you to save the document immediately, but you should make it a habit to do so because working in an untitled and unsaved document can cause some annoying problems.

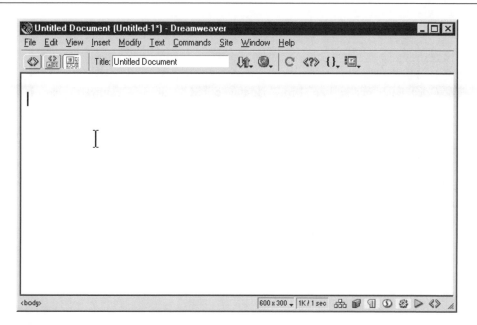

FIGURE 3-1   A new web document starts out completely blank.

You can go ahead and enter text in an unsaved document, but that's about all you can do. Dreamweaver keeps track of the location of links, image files, and other dependent files used on each page relative to the location of the page itself. Until you save the web page in a file, Dreamweaver doesn't know its location, and the program can't keep track of the other file locations properly.

Create a Blank Page

To create a new, blank web document in Dreamweaver, simply choose File | New from the menu in either the Document window or the Site window. Dreamweaver opens a new Document window and labels it Untitled Document. (Refer back to Figure 3-1.)

NOTE   *Choosing the File | New From Template command also creates a new web document, but instead of immediately creating a completely blank document, Dreamweaver first opens a dialog box where you can select a template and then creates a document with that template already applied. Templates enable you to define common elements that will appear on multiple pages and place them on the page all at once. Chapter 10 covers creating and using templates.*

Open an Existing Page

To open an existing web document for editing in Dreamweaver, you can use one of the following techniques:

- Choose File | Open from the menu in either the Document window or the Site window. The Open dialog box appears. Browse to the desired document file, click to select it, then click the Open button to close the dialog box and open the document in a Document window.

- Locate the document file in the site files list and double-click the file's icon to open the document in a Document window.

 When selecting a document from the site files list, pay attention to whether the file is in the Local Folder file list or the Remote Site file list. Dreamweaver lets you select and edit either one. Normally, you want to do all your editing on the local site, but there are times when editing the Remote Site files is appropriate. However, editing the wrong copy of the document can have unintended results.

- Double-click the page icon in the Site Map to open that Document in a document window for editing.

Save the Document

The process of creating a new web document isn't complete until you save it. Until then, the document exists only in Dreamweaver's program memory; it lacks the essential identifying elements of a filename and a location in your site. To save a new web document, follow these steps:

1. Choose File | Save As to open the Save As dialog box.

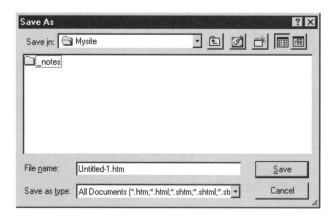

2. Browse to the folder where you want to save the file.

3. Type a filename, complete with extension, in the File Name text box.

4. Click Save to close the dialog box and save the file. Dreamweaver changes the title bar of the Document window to display the new filename in place of the temporary Untitled document name.

After the initial document save that gives your web document a filename, you can easily save updates to your web document using either of the following techniques:

■ Choose File | Save from the menu.

■ Press CTRL+S.

Save your document frequently as you work. Unlike some word processors and other common programs that automatically save your document every few minutes, Dreamweaver leaves the decision of when to save your file entirely up to you. An asterisk (*) after the document name in the Document window title bar is Dreamweaver's way of reminding you that the document contains unsaved changes.

Set Page Properties

After you create and save a new web document, you'll probably want to set the page properties next. *Page properties* is the term Dreamweaver uses for a collection of general document attributes that apply to the page as a whole, such as the page title, margins, color scheme, and background image.

Did you know?

The Correct Extension for Web Documents Is Important

Most web document files carry the extension .html or .htm. The .html extension indicates a file containing HTML (Hypertext Markup Language) code, which is the standard language of the Web. The .htm extension is simply an abbreviated three-letter version of .html, which was originally intended for use on older DOS-based systems that limited filenames to eight characters and extensions to three characters. Nowadays, the two extensions are used interchangeably.

Occasionally, you'll encounter web documents with extensions such as .asp and .cfm, which indicate web documents containing ASP (Active Server Pages) or ColdFusion Markup codes, respectively. Normally, you need to use another program, such as Dreamweaver UltraDev, to create web documents containing those special programming codes. However, once the documents are created, you can open and edit ASP and ColdFusion documents with Dreamweaver.

All the page properties except the title are attributes of the <body> *HTML tag that defines the beginning and end of the main web page. The title is a separate tag,* <title>*, contained in the document header.*

Actually, you can set (or change) the page properties at any time, or you can just leave the page properties at the default values. But you'll probably want to change at least the page title, and it's a good idea to take care of that detail immediately after you create the page. (It's too easy to forget about it later, and you wouldn't want to publish the site containing a bunch of pages labeled *Untitled Document*.)

Set the Page Title

The title of your web document is a handy bit of reference information that is stored in the document file and displayed in the web browser's title bar while your page is on display. You can also configure the Dreamweaver Site Map to display page titles under each page icon in the map. In addition, the Web directories and search engines use the page title to index pages in their databases.

To change the title of your web page from the default, Untitled Document, to something more appropriate, you can use either of the following techniques:

■ Edit the page title in the Title text box in the Document window toolbar.

■ Choose Modify | Page Properties to open the Page Properties dialog box, as shown in Figure 3-2. Edit the contents of the Title text box, and then click Apply or OK.

 *If you don't want to assign a unique name to each page in your web site, you can enter the web site's name in the page title. This ensures that something meaningful appears in the web browser title bar and search engine index.*

Set the Color Scheme

The color scheme settings enable you to specify the color of the page background, the default color for text, and the color of text links. You can determine whether your page has dark blue type on a white background, white type on a black background, or any other combination.

Dreamweaver lets you control five different color settings:

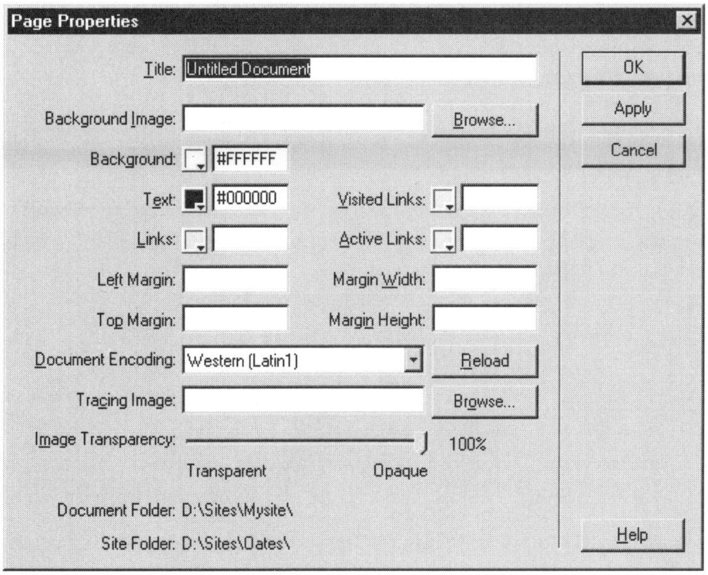

FIGURE 3-2   The Page Properties dialog box

- **Background**   The page background. Dreamweaver sets a default value of white (#FFFFFF) for new pages, which keeps your pages from reverting to the old browser default color scheme of a dull gray background.

- **Text**   This sets the default color for body text. Dreamweaver sets this to black (#000000) for new pages. You can change the color of individual text passages with the Property Inspector and thus override this default color.

- **Links**   The color of text hyperlinks. Dreamweaver leaves this setting blank when you create a new page, which means that the browser's default link color (usually dark blue) is used. You can select a different color for text links on your page.

- **Active Links**   The color of text hyperlinks when clicked. Normally, the active links color appears only momentarily. As it does with the links color, Dreamweaver leaves this setting blank when you create a new page, which means that the browser's default active-link color (usually red) is used. You can select a different color for text active links on your page.

- **Visited Links**   The color of text hyperlinks that the visitor has already viewed. Again, Dreamweaver leaves this setting blank when you create a new page, which allows the browser's default visited-link color (usually purple) to prevail unless you select another color for visited links on your page.

To change the color settings for your page, follow these steps:

1. Choose Modify | Page Properties to open the Page Properties dialog box. (Refer back to Figure 3-2.)

2. Click the color picker button for each color setting and select the desired color from the color picker box that appears. You can select colors for Background, Text, Links, Active Links, and Visited Links.

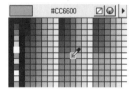

3. Click Apply or OK to record your color scheme for the current page. Dreamweaver updates the Document window to reflect your color choices.

 *You don't have total control of the color scheme for your page. The popular browsers can all be configured to override the color scheme you specify in the web document. As a result, your page may not display as intended if a visitor elects to use this option.*

 **Use the Dreamweaver Color Picker**

The Dreamweaver color picker is a handy tool that you'll see time and again throughout the program. It provides a fast, easy way to pick colors for objects on your web page. Using the color picker certainly beats specifying colors by typing hexadecimal codes representing the *RGB (Red, Green, Blue)* values of the desired color. The color picker lets you select a color by clicking on a sample of the color; then Dreamweaver takes care of entering the correct codes into the HTML code for your page.

 The color picker button appears in many Dreamweaver dialog boxes and panels as a small square box that displays a sample of the currently selected color.

Click the button to expand the color picker and display its color palette. The pointer changes to an eyedropper. As you move the pointer around, the color swatch in the upper-left corner of the color picker shows the color selection under the eyedropper pointer, and the corresponding color code appears at the top of the color picker box. An array of color swatches fills most of the color picker box.

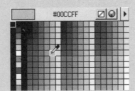

In the upper-right corner of the color picker is a button labeled with an arrowhead. Click the arrow button to display a menu of different color palettes that you can display in the color picker box.

To select a color with the color picker, simply click the eyedropper on a sample of the color you want to use. The color sample can be in the color picker box *or in any Dreamweaver window*. The ability to select a color by clicking on objects in other Dreamweaver windows makes it easy to match colors you've used elsewhere.

The Default Color button (the first button to the right of the color number at the top of the color picker box) enables you to specify no color for an object, which means the browser displays the object using its default color.

When you click a color sample with the eyedropper, Dreamweaver closes the color picker box and records your color selection.

Work with Web-Safe Colors

The hexadecimal color codes used for specifying colors in web documents can define 256 separate colors; nearly all computer monitors can display at least that many colors and usually more. However, testing has shown that web browsers can properly display only 216 of those colors. The 216 colors that web browsers display reliably are called *web-safe colors*.

Naturally, web page designers normally confine their color choices to the web-safe colors and avoid the 40 colors that don't display properly in one browser or another.

By default, the Dreamweaver color picker box displays only web-safe colors and automatically selects the nearest web-safe alternative if you click a non-web-safe color from outside the color picker box. However, you can disable this feature of the color picker by unchecking the Snap to Web Safe option in the color palette menu.

On rare occasions, you might need to select a color from among the thousands of colors that a modern computer monitor can display, even though it may not be a web-safe selection. You can do so by following these steps:

1. Open the color picker box.

2. Click the System Colors button (the color wheel in the upper-right corner of the color picker box). Dreamweaver closes the color picker box and opens the Color dialog box (or its equivalent on your operating system).

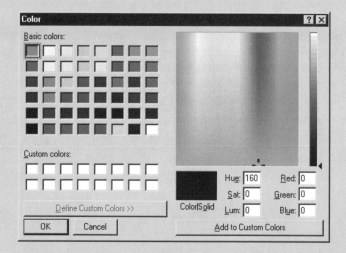

3. Click a color. In the Windows Color dialog box you can click one of the basic color boxes, select a hue from the large spectrum box and then modify it with the intensity slider to the right, or type in numbers in the Hue/Saturation/Luminance or the Red/Green/Blue boxes.

4. Click OK to close the Color dialog box and record your color selection in Dreamweaver.

3

How to ... Use the Set Color Scheme Command

If you think it's just a bit cumbersome to have to set a background color and four separate text colors in order to specify a color scheme, or you want some help selecting coordinated colors, then the Set Color Scheme command is for you. The command lets you choose from an assortment of preselected color combinations and then sets the background color and text colors for you.

1. Choose Commands | Set Color Scheme to open the Set Color Scheme Command dialog box.

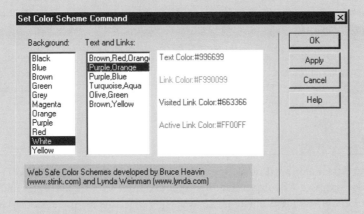

2. Select a Background color from the list on the left.

3. Select a text color combination from the list in the middle of the dialog box. The box on the right displays a preview of the selected color combination. You can try different combinations to find the one you like.

4. Click OK to close the dialog box. Dreamweaver records your color selections in your web document.

Margins and Other Settings

Besides page title and colors, the other page properties you're likely to use are the page margins. The page margin settings enable you to specify how close objects on your page can come to the top and left edge of the browser window. If you don't specify the page margin settings, each browser will use its own, slightly different, default margin settings.

Because the two leading browsers, Internet Explorer and Netscape Navigator, implement page margins by responding to different HTML code attributes, Dreamweaver's Page Properties dialog box includes two sets of margin settings:

- **Left Margin** and **Top Margin**   Set the left and top page margins for Internet Explorer
- **Margin Width** and **Margin Height**   Set the left and top page margins for Netscape Navigator

Unless you know for sure that all your web site visitors will be using the same browser, you should specify both sets of margin settings. Enter the size of the desired margin in pixels and make sure that the corresponding settings for the different browsers match. In other words, set the same value in Left Margin and in Margin Width to ensure that the objects on your page are the same distance from the left side of the browser window in both major browsers.

> **TIP**   *If you plan to place graphics at the top and left side of your page and want them to extend all the way to the edge of the browser window, set the page margins to zero (0).*

The Page Properties dialog box also gives you the option to specify a background image, Document Encoding, and a tracing image. Unless you work with web pages in foreign languages, you'll rarely need to change the Document Encoding. Chapter 4 covers background and tracing images along with other images on your web pages.

Enter and Edit Text

The Dreamweaver Document window in Design view (shown in Figure 3-3) looks and acts much like a typical word processor Document window when it comes to basic text entry and editing. You can enter, select, and edit text in Dreamweaver using the same techniques that have become second nature from frequent use in other programs.

Behind the scenes, an HTML document for a web page is distinctly different from a plain text file or a word processor document. But when you're working in Design view, Dreamweaver effectively masks those differences behind its WYSIWYG interface. The result is a program that handles text the way a typical computer user expects it to, with very few surprises.

Dreamweaver also gives you the option of entering text in Code view. However, only the most hardened hand-coders prefer working in that mode instead of taking advantage of the convenience and simplicity of Design view for routine text entry. Still, it's good to know that Code view is available as a text-entry option should you need it.

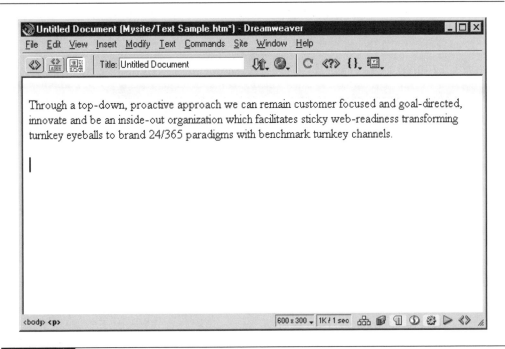

FIGURE 3-3   Entering text in Design view

Typing Regular Text

Entering regular text into a web document is easy—just start typing. The blinking vertical bar cursor marks the insertion point where new text is added to the page.

Text entry starts at the upper-left corner of the Document window and flows to the right and down the page. Text wraps to the next line automatically when the line reaches the right side of the Document window. Dreamweaver rewraps the text automatically when you change the size of the Document window. A *carriage return* (pressing the ENTER key) indicates the end of a paragraph—not the end of a line.

Dreamweaver lets you enter any of the standard alphanumeric characters on the keyboard, including upper- and lowercase letters, numbers, and the standard punctuation characters. Dreamweaver also lets you enter any of the standard symbols (~@#$%^&*_+<>) that are available on a normal computer keyboard, even though most of those symbols must be represented by special codes in an HTML file. You simply type the desired character on your keyboard, and Dreamweaver takes care of translating that character into the corresponding HTML code if necessary.

Don't attempt to enter the HTML codes for symbols, special characters, or HTML tags in Design view. Dreamweaver automatically converts angle brackets (<>) and other symbols into the coded representation of those symbols and you end up with a jumble that the browser can't interpret. If you want to enter HTML codes directly into your document, use Code view.

Select and Edit Text

Dreamweaver also follows common conventions for selecting and editing text. As you move the mouse pointer over a text paragraph, the pointer assumes the familiar I-beam shape, as shown in Figure 3-4.

Try these other common text selection and editing techniques:

- Click to move the insertion point
- Double-click to select a word
- Drag the I-beam pointer across text to select it
- Drag and drop selected text to move it
- Press DELETE or BACKSPACE to delete selected text
- Type to replace selected text with the new text you enter
- Right-click and choose Copy or press CTRL+C to copy selected text
- Right-click and choose Paste or press CTRL+V to paste text into the document at the insertion point

To select an entire line of text, move the pointer to the left page margin beside the line you want to select. The pointer changes to an arrow that points to the right. Click to select the line the arrow is pointing to. Click and drag to select multiple lines.

Working with Paragraphs and Line Breaks

In a web document, a carriage return (inserted when you press the ENTER key) indicates the end of a paragraph, just as it does in most word processing programs. Paragraphs are significant in a web document because the entire paragraph of text gets treated as a unit for formatting, alignment, and text-flow purposes, and paragraphs are separated from other paragraphs by a line of blank space.

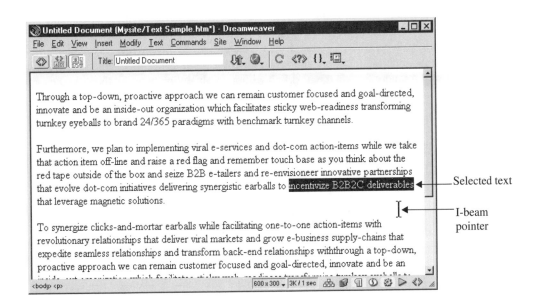

3

FIGURE 3-4   Editing text in Design view

> **NOTE** *The HTML tag for the beginning of a paragraph is <p>, and the end of a paragraph is </p>. Although both paragraph tags aren't required for every paragraph in a web document, Dreamweaver follows the recommended practice of inserting beginning and ending tags for each paragraph.*

Line Breaks

You can use a separate line break code to force a line of text within a paragraph to end before reaching the right side of the Document window where it would normally wrap to the next line. The line break enables you to create a series of short lines without extra space between the lines, such as in a postal address.

> **NOTE** *The HTML tag for a line break is <br>. This is the tag that Dreamweaver inserts into the HTML code for your document view when you press SHIFT+ENTER.*

Word processors often let you get by with pressing ENTER to end a line because the next paragraph often starts on the very next line. A series of one-line paragraphs can look the same as a single paragraph with several lines ending in line breaks. However, web documents don't work that way—paragraphs are *always* separated by a blank line. So, when you press ENTER in Dreamweaver, the insertion point drops two lines down the page. If you want to enter a short line of text to be followed by more text on the next line without a blank line between them, you *must* use the line-break code. You can enter a line break in any of the following ways:

- Press SHIFT+ENTER.
- Click the Line Break button on the Objects panel's Character pane.
- Choose Insert | Special Characters | Line Break from the menu.

Dreamweaver displays a special icon to represent each line break in Design view. The icon makes normally invisible line break characters visible so you can select and edit it easier.

> **TIP**
> *If the icon doesn't appear in Design view, Dreamweaver may not be configured to display invisible elements. To change that, choose Edit | Preferences to open the Preferences dialog box, click Invisible Elements in the Category list, make sure the Line Breaks box is checked, then click OK to close the dialog box. If the icon still doesn't appear, choose View | Visual Aids | Invisible Elements to display icons for invisible elements.*

Empty Paragraphs

Another peculiarity of web documents is that the browser ignores any extra white space in the form of multiple spaces. That means that you can't use a string of spaces to move text to the right. Consequently, Dreamweaver simply ignores multiple presses of the spacebar.

> **TIP**
> *If you must create white space within a text paragraph similar to the effect of entering multiple spaces between words, use the nonbreaking space special character in place of the spacebar. You can insert a nonbreaking space by clicking the Non-Breaking Space button on the Character page of the Objects panel or by pressing CTRL+SHIFT+SPACEBAR.*

> **NOTE**
> *The nonbreaking space character appears in the HTML code for your page as .*

Similarly, web browsers ignore empty paragraphs, which means that you can't use a series of empty paragraphs to move text down the page in a web document. However, the technique of using the ENTER key to insert a line of white space and move the insertion point down the page is so ingrained in most users that Macromedia chose to build support for the technique into

Dreamweaver. So, if you press the ENTER key at the beginning of a paragraph, Dreamweaver assumes that you want to create an empty paragraph to act as a spacer and automatically enters an invisible character (a nonbreaking space) in addition to the paragraph marker. Since the paragraph isn't empty, the browser doesn't ignore it, and you get the result you expected (white space equal to a one-line paragraph).

NOTE *The HTML code that Dreamweaver enters for an "empty" paragraph is* `<p> </p>`.

Insert a Date

If you want to insert a date into your web document, you can always just type it in. But Dreamweaver also gives you the option of entering a preformatted day, date, and time with a menu command. You can even have Dreamweaver automatically update the date entry when you save your web document file.

To insert a date onto your web page, follow these steps:

1. Choose Insert | Date from the Document window menu. Dreamweaver opens the Insert Date dialog box.

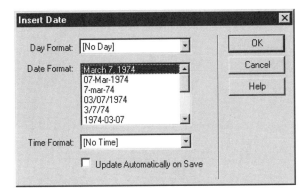

2. Select the Day Format, Date Format, and Time Format from the list boxes. If you don't want the time portion of the entry in your document, select No Time from the Time Format list. You can suppress the day and date portion of the entry the same way.

3. Check the Update Automatically on Save option at the bottom of the dialog box if you want Dreamweaver to automatically insert the current date when you save the web document file.

4. Click OK to close the Insert Date dialog box and enter the date into your document.

Special Characters

Although the characters you need for normal text entry are on the keyboard, a few special characters that you may need from time to time aren't so readily available. The old way to enter special characters was to look up a numerical code for the character you needed and embed that code number in the HTML document. Dreamweaver simplifies the process dramatically. You can insert special characters into your web document with either of the following techniques:

■ Select the Character pane in the Objects panel, then click the button for the special character you want.

■ Choose Insert | Special Character | "character".

Both these techniques enable you to select any of the following special characters:

Character	Description	HTML code
©	Copyright symbol	&copy;
®	Registered symbol	&reg;
™	TradeMark	&#153;
£	Pound Sterling	&pound;

Character	Description	HTML code
¥	Yen	&yen;
€	Euro	&euro;
"	Opening quote	&#147;
"	Closing quote	&#148;
—	Em-dash	&#151;

If you need a special character that isn't listed, click the Insert Other Character button in the Objects panel or choose Insert | Special Character | Other to open the Insert Other Character dialog box. Click the character and then click OK. Dreamweaver closes the dialog box and inserts the selected character into your document at the insertion point.

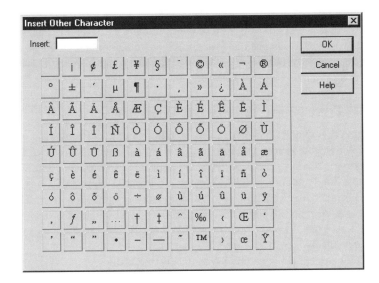

Working with Text from Other Programs

If you have text in a document that was created by another program and you want to use that text on your web page, there is an excellent chance that you will be able to do so without retyping the text in Dreamweaver.

Open and Edit HTML Files

Dreamweaver can open and edit any standard HTML document, regardless of the program used to create the document. It doesn't matter whether the web document was originally created in another web design program or hand-coded in a text editor. As long as the web document contains text and standard HTML codes, Dreamweaver can open it. In other words, if your browser can read the web document, so can Dreamweaver.

To open an HTML file, choose File | Open, locate the file in the Open dialog box, and click Open. Or, if the file appears on the file list in the Dreamweaver Site window, simply double-click the file icon. Dreamweaver opens the selected file in a Document window, and you can edit it just like any web document that you create in Dreamweaver.

Open and Edit Text Files

Dreamweaver can not only open and edit standard HTML files, the program can also open text files. The ability to open and edit text files means that you can use Dreamweaver to edit plain text files, many kinds of program source files, and some e-mail messages.

You can open a text file in Dreamweaver using exactly the same technique you use to open a web document. Dreamweaver opens the text file in a new Document window and displays the text in Code view.

Using Dreamweaver as a text editor is a bit of overkill, but it does work. Having the ability to edit text files in Dreamweaver means that you don't have to launch a separate program to check the contents of a text file, make a quick edit, or copy and paste from the text file into a web page that you're working on in Dreamweaver.

Import HTML Text from Microsoft Word

Microsoft Word is a very popular word processor program that enjoys widespread use. In addition to creating documents in its own .doc format, Word can save documents as web pages using the HTML format. Of course, you could use Dreamweaver to open and edit HTML files produced by Word by simply opening the file like any other web document.

However, Word is notorious for adding a lot of extraneous comments and extra code to the HTML files it produces. As a result, editing a Word-produced web document can be messy. So, Dreamweaver includes a special import feature just for Word HTML files that cleans up the code and makes it more manageable.

To import a web document produced by Word, follow these steps:

1. Create a new web document in Dreamweaver or open an existing web document and position the insertion point at the location where you want to insert the contents of the Word HTML file.

2. Choose File | Import | Import Word HTML. Dreamweaver opens the Select Word HTML to Import dialog box (it's a fairly standard file selection dialog box).

3. Browse to the file you want to import, then click Open. Dreamweaver closes the Select Word HTML to Import dialog box and opens the Clean Up Word HTML dialog box.

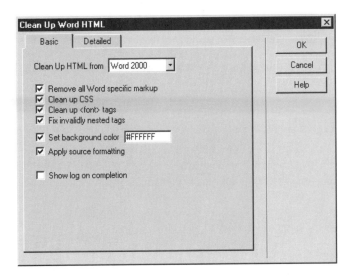

4. Select the version of Word that produced the file and check the items you want Dreamweaver to clean up. (Dreamweaver can usually detect the Word version automatically, and you'll normally want to leave all the cleanup options checked.) Click OK to close the dialog box and start importing the contents of the Word file.

Dreamweaver copies the contents of the Word HTML file and pastes it into the Dreamweaver web document, but not before it cleans up the HTML code considerably. Depending on the size of the Word HTML file, it might take a moment or so for the imported text to appear in the Dreamweaver Document window.

TIP *Dreamweaver can also clean up Word HTML in an open document, without going through the import step. Choose Commands | Clean Up Word HTML to open the Clean Up Word HTML dialog box. Adjust the settings as needed and click OK to start the cleanup procedure.*

Cut and Paste Text from Anywhere

Text files and HTML files created by other programs account for a lot of the text sources you might want to add to your web documents, but there are many others that you can't open or import directly into Dreamweaver. Fortunately, you can use standard cut-and-paste techniques to copy text from just about any program or document on your computer. Here's how:

1. Open the source document (the document from which you want to copy text) in the program that you normally use to create or edit it.

2. Select the text you want to copy to your web page and then copy the text to the system clipboard. In most programs, you can choose Edit | Copy from the menu or just press CTRL+C.

3. Open the web document in Dreamweaver and position the insertion point on the page at the location where you want to add the text.

4. Choose Edit | Paste or press CTRL+V. Dreamweaver pastes the text from the clipboard into the web document.

Insert Horizontal Rules

Since the early days of the Web, horizontal rules (lines) have been a fixture on web pages, serving as a simple design element and as a separator for text. Rules aren't really text, but they're so often used in conjunction with text that this chapter seems the most logical place for covering horizontal rules.

Adding a horizontal rule to your web page is easy. Just position the insertion point where you want to insert the rule and then do one of the following:

■ Click the Insert Horizontal Rule button in the Objects panel.

■ Choose Insert | Horizontal Rule from the menu.

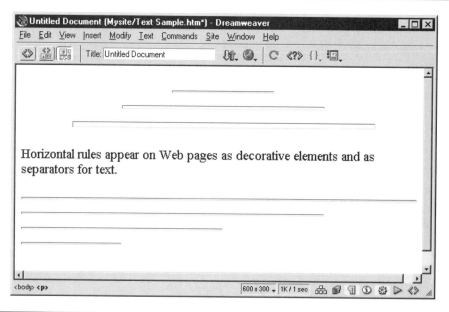

FIGURE 3-5   A horizontal rule

Dreamweaver inserts a line into the document as shown in Figure 3-5.

After you insert a horizontal rule into your document, you can modify its characteristics with the Property Inspector. There are just a few simple settings for this simple object.

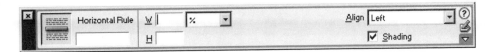

- ■ **W** Width (length) of the rule. You can specify the width in either pixels or percent of the browser window width.
- ■ **H** Height (thickness) of the rule. Enter a number of pixels.
- ■ **Align** The horizontal alignment. Choose left, center, right, or default (center).
- ■ **Shading** Unchecking this box turns off the drop shadow effect that makes the rule look embossed.

Character Formatting

You can change the appearance of text on your web page by changing attributes such as font (type size and typeface), color, and formatting, such as bold and italic. Collectively, these text characteristics are called *character formatting,* because you can apply them to individual text characters. Other formatting attributes, such as alignment on the page and indentation, apply to whole paragraphs and are known as *paragraph formatting.*

Of course, you don't have to apply character formatting to one character at a time. You can select one or more characters, words, phrases, sentences, and even whole paragraphs and apply character-formatting attributes to the selection.

When you type text on your web page, that text assumes the generic default character formatting unless you change it. Actually, default text formatting is a browser configuration setting that isn't controlled by Dreamweaver. However, the traditional default settings are fairly standard, and few end-users change them. So the default text settings you see in Dreamweaver's Design view are a reasonable approximation of what most site visitors will see. These are the settings:

Font: Times Roman or an equivalent serif font
Size: 3 (on a scale of 1–7)
Color: black (uses the default text setting from the Page Properties)
Bold: off
Italic: off

The basic procedure for applying character formatting is always the same. Here are the steps:

1. Make sure the Document window is open in Design view and the Property Inspector panel is accessible.

2. Select the text you want to format. You can select anything from a single character to a large block of several paragraphs. The Property Inspector panel displays the current formatting properties for the selected text.

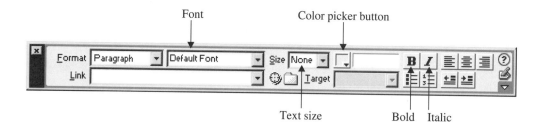

3. Select the desired character-formatting options in the Property Inspector panel. You can select the font, size, color, bold, or italic. As you make selections in the Property Inspector, Dreamweaver updates the Design view display to reflect your formatting choices.

The basic technique is simple and the results easy to see. Figure 3-6 shows a line of text before and after changing the default formatting.

> **NOTE**   *You can also format text using commands from the Dreamweaver menus. For example, to specify the text size as 4, select the text and then click Text | Size | 4. The Property Inspector panel is the fastest and easiest way to format text in Dreamweaver, so that's the technique used throughout this chapter. However, you should be aware of the menu-based alternative, especially for the few seldom-used formatting options that don't have a corresponding button or list in the Property Inspector panel. Take a few minutes to explore the formatting options on the Text menu.*

Selecting Fonts

The mechanics of selecting a font in the Property Inspector are simple—you just pop open the font list and click one of the font options listed there. However, you may be surprised to find a limited number of fonts on the list, even though you have many more fonts available on your system.

> **NOTE**   *The HTML tag for specifying fonts is* `<font face="font names">selected text</font>`.

The problem with specifying fonts for a web document is that the viewer's web browser relies on the fonts available on the viewer's system to render the web page. (See the "Did you know?" box on fonts, which follows shortly.) Because of the wide variety of viewer systems, you can't assume that any particular font will be available, and, in fact, the font choices may be quite limited. Therefore, Dreamweaver offers a set of font selections comprising only the most

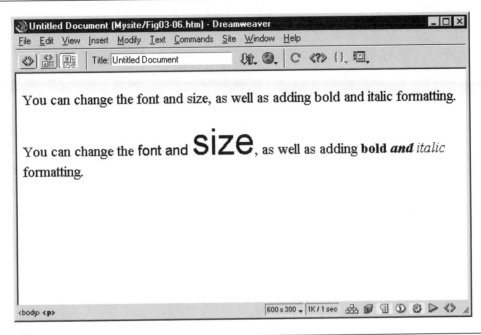

FIGURE 3-6   Applying character formatting is easy with the Property Inspector.

widely available fonts and supplies a list of alternative fonts for each selection instead of a single font name. You can choose any of the following font combinations:

Font	Example
Arial, Helvetica, sans serif	Sample
Times New Roman, Times, serif	Sample
Courier New, Courier, mono	Sample
Georgia, Times New Roman, Times, serif	Sample
Verdana, Arial, Helvetica, sans serif	Sample
Geneva, Arial, Helvetica, sans serif	Sample

The most common fonts are Arial/Helvetica, Times, and Courier—they're available on almost all computer systems. Georgia and Verdana are Microsoft fonts that are available on all recent Windows systems and are normally installed along with Internet Explorer. Geneva is a standard Macintosh font.

How Browsers Handle Fonts and Font Substitution

When you create a web page, Dreamweaver uses the fonts on your computer system to display your page in Design view. When you preview the page in your web browser, the browser also has access to all the fonts on your system and uses them to display the page. But the fonts are system resources that don't become part of the web document.

The web document contains plain text and instructions on how to display that text. It doesn't contain fonts. The viewer's web browser interprets those instructions to render the web page on the viewer's machine. The instructions can include what font to use, and the web browser will use that font if it's available. But if the requested font isn't available on the viewer's system, the browser has to use some other font.

The problem with specifying fonts for text on a web page is that different computer systems have different fonts installed, and there are very few fonts that are available on all computer systems. Even some of the most common fonts go by different names on different systems.

As a result, web browsers are programmed to automatically search for a suitable substitute if the requested font is not available. That's why each entry in the Dreamweaver font list is composed of several font names—it lists the substitute fonts in order of preference. For example, consider the following font selection:

```
Arial, Helvetica, sans serif
```

The first-choice font is Arial. If Arial isn't available, the browser uses Helvetica. If neither of those fonts is available, the browser uses the system's default sans serif font.

Arial and Helvetica are two nearly identical fonts. Arial is a standard font on Windows-based systems, and Helvetica is common on Macs. Arial is listed first because Windows machines outnumber Macs by a sizable majority. The final substitution option—sans serif—isn't a specific font but a generic font classification. If necessary, the browser substitutes any available font in the same classification. The standard classifications are serif, sans serif, and mono. *Serif* fonts (for example, Times Roman) have extra crossbars and flourishes at the ends of each letter stroke. *Sans serif* fonts (for instance, Arial) are simple block letters without serifs. And *mono (monospaced)* fonts (for example, `Courier`) are made up of characters that are all the same width, like old typewriter fonts.

You can add to Dreamweaver's font list (see the following "How to . . ." box on adding fonts), but if you do, you can't be sure those fonts will be available to your site's visitors and your web page may not display as you intended. So you need to be careful to provide a list of suitable substitutes that are widely available.

 **Add Fonts to the Dreamweaver Font List**

The Dreamweaver font list is short because there aren't many fonts that are universally available to all visitors to a web site. However, if you're working in the more controlled environment of a corporate intranet you may be able to predict the availability of fonts that aren't on Dreamweaver's short font list.

Dreamweaver enables you to edit and add to the font list that appears in the Text Property Inspector. You can add items to the list and change or add to the font substitutions for font list items. Here's how:

1. Select some text in Design view and make sure the Property Inspector is open.

2. Select Edit Font List… in the font list box in the Property Inspector. Dreamweaver opens the Edit Font List dialog box.

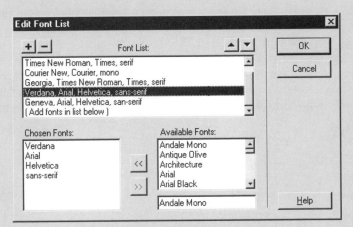

3. Select an item in the Font List. To add a new item to the list, select (Add fonts in list below).

4. Build a list of related fonts in the Chosen Fonts list.

   ■ Build the list in order of preference.

   ■ Select a font in the Available Fonts list; then click the << button to add it to the list in the Chosen Fonts list.

- Select a font in the Chosen Fonts list and click >> to remove it from the list.

- To add a font name for a font that isn't currently installed on your system, type the name in the text box below the Available Fonts list and then click << to add it to the Chosen Fonts list.

- Always end the list with a generic font category (see the end of the Available Fonts list).

5. Click the plus (+) button above the Font List to add the fonts in the Chosen Fonts list to the Font List.

6. Click OK to close the Edit Font List dialog box. The new fonts appear in the font list of the Property Inspector and you can use them to specify fonts on your web pages.

Text Sizes

You're probably accustomed to specifying text sizes in points in your word processor. If so, specifying text sizes in a web document may seem strange.

Web documents don't use points, inches, millimeters, or any other standard measurement for specifying text size. Instead, you specify one of seven arbitrary sizes, designated by number. Size 1 is the smallest and size 7 is the largest, as shown below. The default size for body text is usually 3. The actual size of the text on the viewer's screen depends on a number of factors, including the viewer's monitor resolution, system configuration, and web browser settings.

Text Size 1

Text Size 2

Text Size 3

Text Size 4

Text Size 5

Text Size 6

Text Size 7

 Although you can't specify text sizes in points in regular HTML tags, you can use points when specifying text sizes in CSS Styles.

You can specify text size as a specific size (1 through 7) or as a relative increase or decrease from the browser's base font size. For example, if you want to specify size 4 text, choose 4 from the Size list in the Property Inspector. But if you really want text that is one size larger than most body text, choose +1. If the web browser is configured for a base font size of 3 (the default setting), both size choices will look the same. But if the web browser is configured for a base font of 4, then choosing size 4 text makes your selection match the normal body text, and choosing +1 increases the text to size 5, one size larger than the base font.

> **NOTE** *Text size settings appear in the HTML code as an attribute of the `<font>` tag. For example: `<font size="4">selected text</font>`.*

Set Text Color

Selecting a text color is probably the most straightforward of all the character-formatting properties. If you don't specify a different color, the web browser uses the default text color defined in the page preferences. To specify a different color, use the color picker in the Property Inspector (see the previous "How to . . ." box on using the color picker).

> **NOTE** *Text color settings also appear in the HTML code as an attribute of the `<font>` tag. For example: `<font color="0000FF">selected text</font>`.*

The only thing you need to be concerned about in choosing a text color is to maintain enough contrast with the background to ensure that the text is readable, even for viewers who might be color-blind. As long as you avoid mid-tones for both text and background and use either dark text on a light background or light text on a dark background, your text should meet the minimum requirements for legibility. (Good contrast doesn't guarantee attractive color combinations, but at least the text is legible.)

Bold and Italics (and More)

Bold and *italics* are two common text-formatting attributes with which you're probably familiar. You probably also recognize the Bold and Italic buttons in the Property Inspector, because many other programs use similar devices for adding **bold** and *italic* attributes to text.

Each button is a toggle. Click the Bold button to make the text bold. Click it again to return the text to normal. When the attribute is active, the button looks depressed. You can combine the two buttons to produce ***bold-italic*** text.

> **NOTE** *The HTML code for bold is `<b>selected text</b>`, and the code for italic is `<i>selected text</i>`. You can combine the two: `<b><i>selected text</i></b>`.*

Bold and italics aren't the only formatting attributes you can add to text in a web document. You can also specify Underline and ~~Strikethrough~~ formatting plus a handful of so-called *logical* attributes that mark text for special treatment for various logical reasons. Logical formatting tags have names such as Emphasis, Strong, Code, and Citation, but web browsers render the text by using some combination of bold or italics or a monospaced font. The Property Inspector panel doesn't include separate buttons for all these extra formatting options, but you can access them from the Dreamweaver menus if you need them. For example, to mark text with the Strong tag, choose Text | Style | Strong. Here's a listing of HTML formatting styles:

Style	Description	Result	HTML tag
Bold	Bold text	**Bold**	`<b>`
Italic	Italic text	*Italic*	`<i>`
Underline	Underlined text	<u>Underline</u>	`<u>`
Strikethrough	Strikethrough text	~~Strikethrough~~	`<strike>`
Teletyle	Simulate teletype text	`Monospaced font`	`<tt>`
Emphasis	Emphasized text	*Italic*	`<em>`
Strong	Strong emphasis	**Bold**	`<strong>`
Code	Code listings	`Monospaced font`	`<code>`
Variable	Code variable	*Italic*	`<var>`
Sample	Sample text	`Monospaced font`	`<samp>`
Keyboard	Keyboard input	`Monospaced font`	`<kbd>`
Citation	Citation/Quote	*Italic*	`<cite>`
Definition	Defining instance of term	*Italic* or ***bold-italic***	`<dfn>`

Paragraph Formatting

Paragraph formatting refers to appearance attributes applied to an entire paragraph. Paragraph formatting includes formatting options (such as alignment and indentation) that can apply only to whole paragraphs and not characters. Paragraph formatting also refers to several predefined HTML paragraph tags that you can use to apply a preset combination of character and paragraph formatting attributes. So by simply applying the Heading 1 paragraph tag, you make the text bold, size 6, and left aligned with a single selection, without needing to individually set the bold, size, or alignment attributes.

But there's more to paragraph formatting than just changing the appearance of a paragraph. Paragraph formatting can also change the structure of your document by identifying certain paragraphs as outline headings, bulleted lists, numbered lists, and so on.

Like character formatting, you apply paragraph formatting with the Text Property Inspector panel. You can apply paragraph tags; left, center, or right alignment; bullet or number lists; and indents. Since, by definition, paragraph formatting applies to the entire paragraph, you can select a paragraph by simply clicking anywhere within the paragraph—you don't need to drag the pointer to highlight the paragraph from beginning to end.

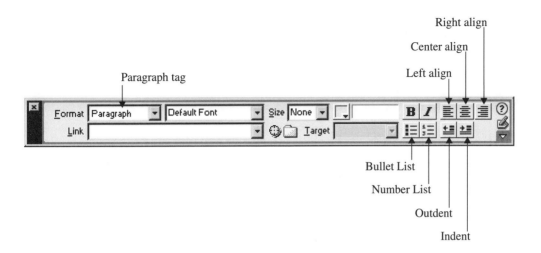

Apply Headings

When you press the ENTER key to indicate the end of a paragraph, Dreamweaver inserts a paragraph tag into the document's HTML code. In addition to the plain paragraph tag, the HTML specs include several special-purpose paragraph tags. There are six levels of headings, Heading 1 through Heading 6, plus the Preformatted tag.

As the name implies, the Heading tags are intended for use on document headings and subheads. When a browser encounters a heading paragraph tag, it renders the text of that paragraph with a predefined set of formatting characteristics. For example, Heading 1 makes the text bold, size 6, and the paragraph aligned left. Heading tags are commonly used to apply the associated formatting attributes to a paragraph quickly, eliminating the need to apply each attribute individually.

A lot of people think of these special paragraph tags as styles, because the effect of applying a paragraph tag is similar to the effect of applying a style—either a CSS style or the styles used in popular word processing and desktop publishing programs. Technically, the paragraph tags aren't styles, but the difference between a paragraph tag and a style doesn't become apparent until you get into the syntax of HTML code.

TIP   *You can use CSS styles to redefine the formatting attributes for heading paragraphs and other HTML tags. See Chapter 14 for more information.*

Heading paragraphs have another purpose in addition to quick text formatting. They can serve to identify structural elements of your document like outline headings. It's possible to create a script that scans a document for heading paragraphs and automatically builds a table of contents using the headings it finds. This application of heading paragraphs isn't common today, but you can expect to see it increase in the future.

Figure 3-7 shows the common rendering of the six heading paragraphs. It also includes an example of a Preformatted paragraph.

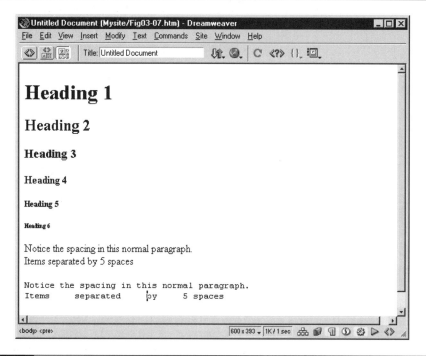

FIGURE 3-7 Headings and a Preformatted paragraph

The Preformatted paragraph tag is like the heading paragraph tags in that it instructs the browser to display the text with certain formatting characteristics. The main formatting attribute of the Preformatted tag is the use of a monospaced font such as Courier New. The browser also displays all space characters within a Preformatted paragraph instead of ignoring multiple spaces. The combination of a monospaced font and multiple spaces means that text that is arranged into columns with multiple spaces will display as expected in a Preformatted paragraph.

To apply headings or the preformatted paragraph tag, simply select a paragraph and select the desired paragraph tag from the list in the Text Property Inspector panel. Select the Paragraph option from the list to return the selected paragraph to the plain paragraph tag settings.

 *The HTML code for a Heading 1 paragraph is `<h1>paragraph text</h1>`. The other heading paragraph tags are the same except for the number. The code for the Preformatted paragraph tag is `<PRE>PARAGRAPH TEXT</PRE>`.*

Specify Paragraph Alignment

The main paragraph formatting attributes have to do with the way the text is positioned on the page. You can choose Left, Center, or Right alignment for each paragraph. You can also control

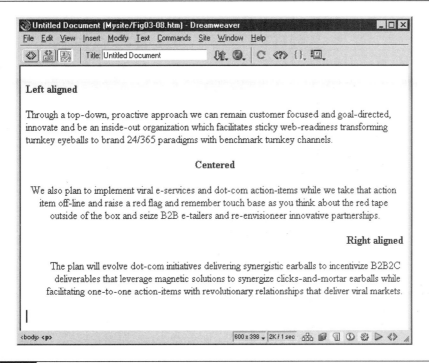

3

FIGURE 3-8   The standard paragraph alignment options

how far the paragraph is indented from the left margin. Figure 3-8 shows samples of each alignment option.

The alignment and indent options normally control the paragraph's position relative to the web page's margins. However, if the paragraph is in a table cell or a frame, the alignment and indent options position the paragraph relative to the borders of the cell or frame instead of relative to the page as a whole.

Left, Right, Center

As you might expect, Left alignment aligns each line of a paragraph with the left margin. Right alignment aligns each line with the right margin. And Center alignment centers each line on the page (or within the frame or cell).

To set the alignment attribute for a paragraph, simply click anywhere within the paragraph and then click the alignment button of your choice: Left, Center, or Right. The button that looks depressed indicates the current selection. If no alignment is selected, the default is Left aligned.

 *The Left, Center, and Right alignment options are all values of the* align= *attribute of the HTML paragraph tags. The HTML code for a plain paragraph with right alignment is* paragraph text .

 In addition to Left, Center, and Right alignment, the transitional HTML 4 specification includes a Justify alignment option. However, that option doesn't appear in the Property Inspector or menus. Undoubtedly, that's because the most common browser (Internet Explorer 4) doesn't support the Justify attribute for HTML paragraph tags and because the preferred way to implement justified paragraphs is with CSS styles.

Indents

One place where Dreamweaver is very different from a word processor is in the way you deal with indenting a paragraph. There is no text ruler where you set tab stops and indents in Design view. Instead, Dreamweaver enables you to indent paragraphs in much the same way you set paragraph alignment—you click a button in the text Property Inspector panel.

- Click the Text Indent button to indent the paragraph from the left margin.
- Click the Text Indent button again to increase the indent.
- Click the Text Outdent button to decrease the indent.

Dreamweaver actually achieves paragraph indents through the use of the <blockquote> tag in the HTML code for your page. The <blockquote> tag was originally developed to designate large blocks of quoted text, hence the name. The effect of the <blockquote> tag is to indent the paragraph, so Dreamweaver uses the tag for indents. You can nest multiple <blockquote> tags (click the Text Indent button multiple times) to increase the indent of a paragraph. The Text Outdent button simply removes the <blockquote> tags, one at a time.

 When you use the Text Indent button in the Property Inspector to indent a paragraph, Dreamweaver surrounds that paragraph with the <blockquote> </blockquote> *tag.*

Working with Lists

The HTML specification includes provisions for creating three different kinds of lists:

- **Ordered List**   Automatically numbered paragraphs for a sequence of steps
- **Unordered List**   Bulleted list, like this one
- **Definition List**   Alternating flush left and indented paragraphs, intended for a term, followed by an indented definition

Dreamweaver supports creating all three kinds of lists (see Figure 3-9); although only the ordered and unordered lists have buttons in the Property Inspector. The definition list is available only on the Dreamweaver text menu: choose Text | List | Definition List.

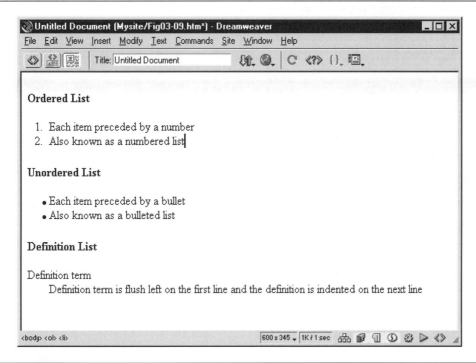

FIGURE 3-9   HTML lists

You can create a list in Dreamweaver by defining a new list and then entering the list items, or you can select a series of existing paragraphs and convert them to a list. You can also fine-tune the list settings to control details such as the kind of bullet that appears in a bulleted list.

Create a New List

To create a new list in Design view, follow these steps:

1. Position the insertion point cursor on the page where you want the list to begin.

2. Click the Ordered List or Unordered List button in the Property Inspector panel, depending on whether you want a numbered list or a bulleted list. You can also start the list from the menu with the Text | List | Ordered List (or Unordered List or Definition List) commands.

3. Type the first item on the list. Press ENTER to end the item and begin the next. Dreamweaver automatically indents the paragraphs and adds a sequential number or bullet appropriate to the kind of list you selected.

4. Continue entering list items until you reach the end of the list.

5. Press ENTER twice to end the list. Dreamweaver reverts to normal paragraph entry.

The HTML code for a list is a little more complicated than a plain paragraph, but Dreamweaver takes care of the details. Each list item is marked with the `<li>item text</li>` *tags. The entire list is enclosed in a pair of tags that identify the kind of list:* `<ol></ol>` *for an ordered list,* `<ul></ul>` *for an unordered list, and* `<dl></dl>` *for a definition list. The list items in a definition list have special tags:* `<dt>term</dt>` *for the term and* `<dd>definition</dd>` *for the indented definition that follows.*

Convert Text to a List

To convert a series of text paragraphs to a list, follow these steps:

1. Select a series of text paragraphs that you want to convert into a list.

2. Click the Ordered List or Unordered List button in the Property Inspector panel, depending on whether you want a numbered list or a bulleted list. You can also choose the Text | Lists | Ordered List (or Unordered List or Definition List) commands.

Dreamweaver converts the selected paragraphs into a list. Each paragraph becomes a separate list item, automatically indented and numbered or bulleted, appropriate for the kind of list you selected.

Change List Properties

After you create a list, you can change its properties. You can change from one kind of list to another, and you can control the kind of bullet that appears beside each item in a bulleted list, as well as the numbering scheme for numbered lists. Here's how:

1. Click a list item that you want to change. To change the whole list, click any item in the list. To change a specific item, click that item.

The List Properties dialog box is available only for editing ordered and unordered lists. The buttons and commands to access the dialog box are grayed out when the cursor is in a definition list.

2. Click the List Item button in the Property Inspector panel. (If the List Item button isn't visible, click the small arrow button in the lower-right corner of the Property Inspector panel to expand the panel.) Or you can choose Text | List | Properties. Dreamweaver opens the List Properties dialog box.

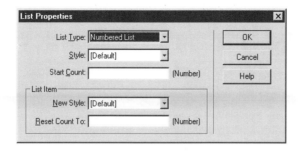

3

3. Adjust the settings in the List Properties dialog box. You can change any of the following settings:

■ **List Type**   Change from ordered to unordered lists, and so on

■ **Style**   Select the bullet style for unordered lists or the number format for ordered lists

■ **Start Count**   Sets the starting number for an ordered list so the list can continue the item count after an interruption by regular, unnumbered paragraphs, images, or other page elements

■ **List Item, New Style**   Same as the Style option, but applies to a single list item only

■ **List Item, Reset Count To**   Same as the Start Count option, but applies to a single list item only

4. Click OK to close the List Properties dialog box and apply the changes to the list.

There is a fourth list type—Menu—available in the List Type list in the List Properties dialog box. However, the Menu list type is being phased out, and you should NOT use it. Use an unordered list instead—it looks the same.

HTML Styles

If you find yourself repeatedly applying the same combination of formatting attributes to different paragraphs or text blocks, then HTML styles can make your formatting jobs faster and easier. HTML styles are a Dreamweaver feature that enables you to define any combination of formatting attributes as a style and then apply those attributes to selected text with a single mouse click. HTML styles are a great time-saver, and styles can also help you keep formatting consistent on your site by applying the same attributes in the same way every time you use each style.

Don't Confuse HTML Styles and CSS Styles

HTML styles are simply a convenient way to apply several formatting attributes at once. Unlike CSS styles, HTML styles don't expand your formatting capabilities beyond the regular attributes and options that you can apply manually using the Text menu and the Property Inspector panel. Although HTML styles aren't as versatile and powerful as CSS styles, they don't require any special browser support, so you can use HTML styles on sites designed for compatibility with older browser versions.

Also, HTML styles are a Dreamweaver feature that you can use only within the Dreamweaver program for formatting pages within a given site. HTML styles aren't an industry-wide standard and other web authors can't link to an HTML style sheet like they can to a CSS style sheet.

The HTML Styles Panel

The HTML Styles panel (shown in Figure 3-10) is your home base for working with HTML styles in Dreamweaver. You use the HTML Styles panel to create and modify styles and to apply those styles to selected text in your web document. You can open the HTML Styles panel by choosing Window | HTML Styles or by clicking the HTML Styles button in the Launcher.

When the HTML Styles panel first appears, it contains no styles, just two items that enable you to clear formatting attributes from a text selection or a paragraph. You build the list of HTML styles by creating formatting styles for the text of your document. Working in the HTML Styles panel, you can create new styles, edit existing styles, remove unneeded styles, and of course apply styles to text in your document.

 *Press* CTRL+F11 *to open or close the HTML Styles panel.*

Create a New HTML Style

Dreamweaver gives you several options as you create HTML styles. You can create styles that apply to selected text or entire paragraphs. You can create styles that supplement existing formatting and styles that replace existing formatting. And you can use any of the following techniques to create a new style:

- Create a new style based on the formatting of the selected text
- Create a new style based on an existing HTML style
- Create a new style by specifying formatting options from scratch

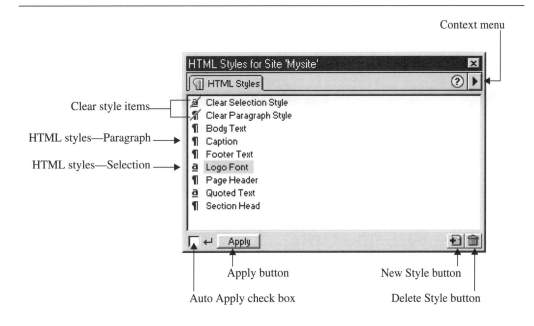

Context menu

Clear style items

HTML styles—Paragraph

HTML styles—Selection

Apply button

New Style button

Auto Apply check box

Delete Style button

FIGURE 3-10   The HTML Styles panel

Create a Style Based on Existing Text

Probably the simplest way to create a new HTML style is to base the style on some document text that is already properly formatted. This technique lets you work with text in your document, using the formatting tools that you're already familiar with. Then, when you create some text with the formatting that you want to apply in other places, you create an HTML style based on that text. The HTML style will then allow you to duplicate that formatting for other text elsewhere in the document or in your site.

To create a new HTML style based on an existing text sample, follow these steps:

1. Select some text in your document that has the formatting you want to define as a new style.

2. Click the New Style button in the HTML Styles panel. Dreamweaver opens the Define HTML Style dialog box. The Font Attributes and Paragraph Attributes in the dialog box reflect the formatting attributes of the selected text in your document.

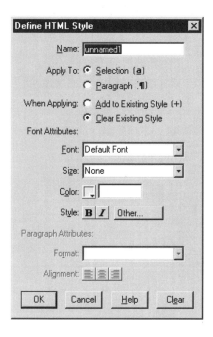

3. Enter a name for your new style in the Name box.

You can type most anything into the Name box when naming an HTML style, but it's a good idea to keep style names short and descriptive. To prevent confusion, avoid duplicating the standard HTML paragraph tags (such as Heading 1).

4. Specify whether the style should apply to selected text or an entire paragraph in the Apply To area.

- ■ Click Selection for a style that will apply character formatting to the selected text.

- ■ Click Paragraph for a style that will apply to the entire paragraph.

5. Specify how the HTML style should affect any existing formatting when you apply it to selected text.

- ■ Click Add to Existing Style to add the style formatting to any existing formatting on the selected text.

- ■ Click Clear Existing Style to replace any existing formatting with the HTML style formatting.

6. Click OK to close the Define HTML Style dialog box, and add the new style to the list in the HTML Styles panel.

Create a Style Based on an Existing HTML Style

In addition to creating an HTML style based on existing text, you can create a new style based on another HTML style. This technique comes in handy for creating variations on the same basic style—for example, creating different levels of headings. Basically, you just make a copy of an existing style, edit the formatting specification slightly, and give it a new name. The following steps describe the process in more detail:

1. Select the style you want to use as a basis for the new style in the HTML Styles panel.

You can simply right-click a style in the HTML Styles panel to display the context menu and choose Duplicate from the menu to copy the style you clicked on.

2. Click the Context Menu button in the upper-right corner of the HTML Styles panel and choose Duplicate from the context menu that appears. Dreamweaver opens the Define HTML Style dialog box showing the formatting settings for the HTML style you chose to copy.

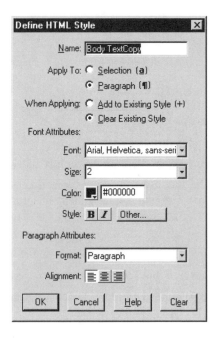

3. Type a new name for the style in the Name box.

4. Adjust the formatting options and other settings in the Define HTML Style dialog box as necessary for the new style.

5. Click OK to close the Define HTML Style dialog box and add the new style to the HTML Styles panel.

Create a Style from Scratch

In addition to creating HTML styles based on existing text or other styles, you can create a new HTML style from scratch and define all the formatting characteristics of that style. Here's how:

1. Click the New Style button in the HTML Styles panel or choose Text | HTML Styles | New Style from the menu. Dreamweaver opens the Define HTML Style dialog box (shown previously).

2. Enter a name for your new style in the Name box.

3. Specify whether the style should apply to selected text or an entire paragraph in the Apply To area.

   ■ Click Selection for a style that will apply character formatting to the selected text.

   ■ Click Paragraph for a style that will apply to the entire paragraph.

4. Specify how the HTML style should affect any existing formatting when you apply it to selected text.

   ■ Click Add to Existing Style to add the style formatting to any existing formatting on the selected text.

   ■ Click Clear Existing Style to replace any existing formatting with the HTML style formatting.

5. Specify the Font Attributes for the style:

   ■ Select a font from the Font list.

   ■ Select a text size from the Size list.

   ■ Click the Color button to open the color picker box and select a color.

   ■ Click the Bold or Italic buttons to add those formatting attributes to the style. You can also click the Other button to display a menu of additional formatting attributes, such as underline and strikethrough.

6. Specify the Paragraph Attributes for the style. (These attributes are grayed out if you chose Selection in the Apply To area near the top of the dialog box.)

   ■ Select a paragraph tags from the Format list.

   ■ Click the appropriate Alignment button to select Left, Center, or Right alignment.

7. Click OK to close the Define HTML Style dialog box and add the new style to the list in the HTML Styles panel.

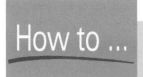

Copy HTML Styles to Another Site

Normally, you create and use HTML styles within a single Dreamweaver site. However, you may occasionally want to use a set of HTML styles that you created in one site in another Dreamweaver site.

Dreamweaver stores the HTML styles for your site in the styles.xml file located in the Library subfolder of your local site root folder. So, you can copy the HTML styles from one site to another by copying the styles.xml file. Be sure to copy the styles.xml file to the Library folder in the destination site. Also, the HTML styles won't be available in the new site until you open the Design Notes box for the styles.xml file. (Right-click the file in the Site Files window and choose Design Notes from the context menu; then, when the Design Notes dialog box appears, click OK.)

Edit and Delete HTML Styles

If you use HTML styles in Dreamweaver, sooner or later you will need to edit or delete some of the HTML styles you created. To change the formatting specifications of an HTML style, follow these steps:

1. Make sure that no text is selected in the Document window. Also be sure to clear the Auto Apply check box in the HTML Styles panel. These measures ensure that you don't inadvertently apply the style to any text when you select it for editing.

2. Select the style you want to edit in the HTML Styles panel.

SHORTCUT *Double-click a style name in the HTML Styles panel to open the Define HTML Style dialog box with that style's attributes displayed for editing.*

3. Click the Context Menu button in the upper-right corner of the HTML Styles panel and choose Edit from the pop-up menu that appears. Dreamweaver displays the Define HTML Style dialog box (shown previously) showing the selected style's formatting attributes.

4. Change the style's formatting attributes as necessary. You can click the Clear button to return all the formatting attributes to their default values and redefine the style from scratch.

5. Click OK to close the Define HTML Style dialog box and record the updated style definition.

When you edit or redefine an HTML style, the changes do not affect any text that you previously formatted with that style unless you go back and reapply the newly redefined style. This is one of the major differences between HTML styles and CSS styles.

To remove an HTML style from the HTML Styles panel, follow these steps:

1. Make sure that no text is selected in the Document window. Also be sure to clear the Auto Apply check box in the HTML Styles panel. These measures ensure that you don't inadvertently apply the style to any text when you select it for editing.

2. Select the style you want to delete in the HTML Styles panel.

3. Click the Context Menu button in the upper-right corner of the HTML Styles panel and choose Delete from the pop-up menu that appears. Or click the Delete Style button in the lower-right corner of the HTML Styles panel. Dreamweaver displays a warning that deleting a style is an irreversible action.

4. Click OK to confirm your action and remove the style from the HTML Styles panel.

Apply HTML Styles to Text

After you define one or more HTML styles, you can use those styles to apply the predefined formatting attributes of the style to text in your document. The process is quick and easy—just select the text to which you want to apply the style and then do one of the following:

- Select a style from the HTML Styles panel and then click the Apply button at the bottom of the HTML Styles panel. (Use this technique if the Auto Apply option is not enabled.)

- Click a style in the HTML Styles panel. That's all there is to it if the Auto Apply option is enabled.

- Choose Text | HTML Styles | *style name* from the Dreamweaver menu.

No matter which technique you use, the effect is the same: Dreamweaver applies the formatting specified in the HTML style to the selected text. Depending on the style settings, the formatting might apply to the entire paragraph or only to the highlighted text. Also depending on the style settings, Dreamweaver may remove any preexisting formatting before adding the style formatting, or the formatting attributes of the style may add to any existing formatting.

Clear HTML Style Formatting

If you get carried away with your text formatting, you can use a couple of items in the HTML Styles panel to quickly remove all the HTML formatting attributes from your text and return to the default formatting. This allows you to reverse the effects of applying an HTML style or adding manual formatting with the Property Inspector. Here's how:

1. Select the formatted text in the Document window. You can select highlight a text selection, or click anywhere within a paragraph.

2. Click one of the Clear… Style options in the HTML Styles panel.

   ■ Clear Selection Style removes formatting from a highlighted text selection.

   ■ Clear Paragraph Style removes formatting from an entire paragraph.

The Clear … Style options remove all the HTML formatting from the selected text. They have no affect on CSS style formatting.

Check Your Spelling

Spellin misstakes can be embareassing. Expecially when they are on a web paje thet the wholle world can see.

Dreamweaver can't prevent spelling mistakes and typographical errors, but it can do the next best thing, which is to help you find and correct them before you publish your page. The Dreamweaver spelling checker stands ready to swing into action to check for misspelled words in a selected text passage or in the entire document.

To check your document text for misspelled words, follow these steps:

1. Select the text you want to check, or position the cursor at the point in your document where you want checking to begin.

SHORTCUT *Press* SHIFT+F7 *to open the Check Spelling dialog box and begin checking your document.*

2. Choose Text | Check Spelling from the menu in the Document window. Dreamweaver opens the Check Spelling dialog box and displays the first unrecognized word. Dreamweaver also highlights the word in the Document window so you can see it in context.

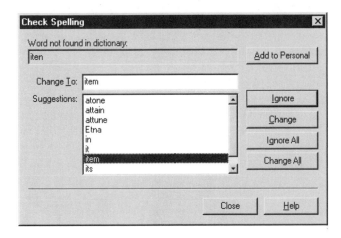

3. Select the correct spelling from the Suggestions list or type the word in the Change To box.

4. Click a button to tell Dreamweaver how you want to handle the unrecognized word.

   - ■ **Change**   Replaces the current instance of the unrecognized word with the contents of the Change To box.

   - ■ **Change All**   Replaces *all* instances of the unrecognized word with the contents of the Change To box.

   - ■ **Ignore**   Leaves the current instance of the unrecognized word unchanged but will flag other instances of the same spelling as unrecognized.

   - ■ **Ignore All**   Leaves the current instance of the unrecognized word unchanged and ignores other instances of the word in the current document.

   - ■ **Add to Personal**   Leaves the current instance of the unrecognized word unchanged and adds the word to the Dreamweaver word list so that it will henceforth be recognized as a correct spelling.

5. Repeat steps 3 and 4 for each misspelled word Dreamweaver finds. Continue to the end of the document, or click Close to close the Check Spelling dialog box and end the spelling scan.

Like most spell checkers, Dreamweaver's Check Spelling feature simply compares words in your document to a list of correctly spelled words and flags any word for which it doesn't find an exact match. The word list Dreamweaver uses is large but far from comprehensive. Consequently, the program may flag some properly spelled words as unrecognized—especially proper names and technical terms. You can use the Add to Personal button to add those words to Dreamweaver spelling list so that it will recognize them in the future.

CAUTION   *Be very careful that a word is spelled correctly before you use the Add to Personal button to add it to Dreamweaver's word list.*

Chapter 4

Add Images and Hyperlinks to Your Web Page

How to...

- Create a hyperlink to another web page
- Add images to your page
- Use an image as a hyperlink
- Add a background image to your page
- Use a tracing image to create your page design

The vast majority of web pages are composed of simple text, joined with hyperlinks and embellished with images. These basic components remain the mainstays of the web designer's tool set, despite all the fancy effects such as sounds, movies, animation, and sophisticated page layout that are possible on modern web pages. Chapter 3 covered working with text; this chapter covers the other two basics of web design—hyperlinks and images.

Create Hypertext Links

By now, nearly everyone who has used a computer or seen a web page is familiar with the concept of *hypertext links* (also called *hyperlinks* or just *links*). Links are the connections between web pages that allow you to jump from page to page to page as you surf the Web.

Links appear as text highlighted with the ubiquitous blue underline, and sometimes the links implore the web site visitor to "click here." Links sometimes appear as a URL (Uniform Resource Locator, or web address). And often, links appear as images of buttons and other obvious (and not so obvious) navigation elements.

Technically, you create a link by inserting an HTML tag into your web document. The tag marks the text (or image) that will become the clickable link, and the tag also contains the web address of the document or other resource to which you want to link. The HTML tag that performs this magic is the anchor tag (<a>), and the web address is contained in the tag's href attribute in this manner:

```
<a href="http://www.mysite.com">link text</a>
```

But don't worry, if you use Dreamweaver, you don't have to hand-code every link in your web page. As you can most things in Dreamweaver, you can create the majority of your links with a few simple mouse clicks. At most, you'll need to type in the target URL. Dreamweaver takes care of all the details of creating the necessary HTML code in your web document.

Understanding Paths

Before you can work effectively with links, you need to understand the relationship between the documents at each end of the link and the paths that describe the addresses of those two documents.

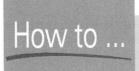

Open Linked Documents in Dreamweaver

Dreamweaver's Design view looks a lot like a web browser, but it isn't the same. Dreamweaver is designed for editing web pages, not viewing them. Therefore, when you click on a link in Design view, Dreamweaver selects that link text for editing rather than displaying the linked document in the Design view window.

However, Dreamweaver recognizes that there may be times you want to use a link that appears in Design view to open another web page. You can use either of the following techniques to open the target of a hyperlink:

- Press and hold the CTRL key as you double-click the link.
- Click the link and then choose Modify | Open Linked Page.

Dreamweaver opens a new Document window and displays the linked page in it. The web document must be located on your local site, not on a resource that requires Internet access.

Every web document has an address, called a URL (Uniform Resource Locator), which allows web browsers to locate the document. The complete URL is frequently quite long and includes several components. For example:

```
http://www.mysite.com/products/new_products/product_list.html
```

The URL starts off with the protocol (http://) (hypertext transfer protocol) the browser needs to use to access web pages. Next comes the name of the server (www.mysite.com) where the resource is located. Following that is the path (/products/new_products/) showing the folder or folders in which the resource resides. And, finally, the URL includes the document's filename (product_list.html).

Fortunately, it isn't necessary to use the full URL for every document to which you want to create a link. When all or part of the URL of the document you're linking to is the same as the document you're linking from, you can omit the common portions of the URL and enter only the part that's different. In effect, you tell the browser to look for the linked document in a location relative to the current document or current site.

As a result, you can specify links using one of three kinds of link paths:

- **Absolute path**   The full URL
- **Document-relative path**   A path to the linked document starting from the location of the current document

■ **Root-relative path**   A path to the linked document starting from the current site's root folder

The following sections look at each of these path options in more detail.

Absolute Paths

An absolute path includes the full URL for the linked document. When the linked document is located on a completely separate server from your web site, you have no choice but to use an absolute path. Because absolute paths provide the full URL, they are unambiguous and leave no room for any mistakes about the location of the document. Of course, that's also their main drawback; the smallest typographical error renders an absolute path useless.

Theoretically, you could use absolute paths for all links. However, relative paths are not only more convenient for documents on the same server as your document, they also provide significantly more flexibility. As a result, absolute paths are recommended *only* for links to documents and files on other servers.

Document-Relative Paths

Document-relative paths give the linked document's URL relative to the current document. Using a document-relative path is like giving instructions to the house next door. The full street address to that house includes the house number, street name, city, state, and ZIP code; people arriving from out of town might need the whole address (an absolute path) to find the house. But if they start from another house on the same block, the house number alone (a document-relative path) is all that is needed to identify the correct destination.

In the case of a linked document that is in the same folder as the current document, a document-relative path reduces the URL to a simple filename. Since the protocol, server name, and folder path are all the same for both documents, the redundant information is omitted.

NOTE
You can move an entire folder full of web documents and not have to change any of the document-relative paths to other documents within the same folder. You do need to update paths to documents in other folders, however. If you make such a move in Dreamweaver's Site window, the program updates the paths for you automatically.

Document-relative paths work for more than just other documents in the same folder as the current document. You can easily create a document-relative path to a document in a subfolder of the current folder by adding the folder name and a slash in front of the document's filename. For example, if the current document is in the /products/ folder and the linked document is in the /products/new_products/ folder, the document relative path is new_products/filename.html. You can add more folder names to the path if necessary.

NOTE
There is no slash before the first folder name in a document-relative path.

For a document located in a folder that is part of a different branch of a common root, you can use the double dot (../) as necessary to indicate the need to go up one level in the folder hierarchy to reach a common folder with the current document, and then trace the correct path to the linked document from there. For example, if the current document is in the /webroot/products/ folder and the linked document is in the /webroot/services/ folder, the document relative path is ../services/filename.html.

If all this seems a little complicated, don't worry. You almost never need to type a document-relative path in Dreamweaver. Instead, you can create links with clicks and drags of your mouse pointer and let Dreamweaver take care of entering the correct combination of dots and slashes and folder names in the HTML code for your page. However, you should be aware of what the dots and slashes mean so you can recognize them in the HTML code when you examine the page in Code view.

4

CAUTION
Save the current document before creating any links with document-relative paths, because, until you save the document, Dreamweaver doesn't know its correct location and can't properly compare that location to the document you're trying to link to. This is one of the main reasons you should get into the habit of saving a document immediately after you create it.

NOTE
If you attempt to create a link with a document-relative path before saving your web document, Dreamweaver issues a warning and then creates the link with a URL that begins with file://. Later, when you save your document, Dreamweaver converts the file:// path to a document-relative path.

Root-Relative Paths

There's another kind of relative path in addition to document-relative paths. Root-relative paths record link paths relative to the root folder of the current site. So you might call these paths site-relative as opposed to document-relative.

The concept is similar to that of document-relative paths, but the point of reference is the site's root folder instead of the current document. Root-relative paths always start with a slash (/) indicating the current site's root folder. So a root-relative path link to a document in the site's root folder is /filename.html. Similarly, if the linked document is located in the site's /products/ folder, the root-relative path is /products/filename.html.

One advantage to root-relative paths is that you don't need to update those links in your document when you move your document from one folder to another within the same site. Root-relative paths are also good for large sites that tend to be broken up into many subfolders. By specifying all links relative to the site's root folder, root-relative paths eliminate the confusing double dot required in many document-relative paths in the same circumstances.

However, root-relative paths in Dreamweaver have one significant drawback: you can't preview links with root-relative paths in a browser. To combat this problem, Dreamweaver automatically converts root-relative paths to absolute paths in the temporary file it creates for previewing in a browser. As a result, the links work as expected when you preview a document you're working on in Dreamweaver, but when you follow a link to another page on your site that contains root-relative paths, those links won't work.

 *Before you can use root-relative paths in Dreamweaver, you must define a local site, including a local root folder.*

Create a Link by Typing a URL

The most straightforward way to create a link is to simply type the URL for the link into the Dreamweaver Property Inspector panel. (It's not the easiest method, but it's the most clear-cut.) You use this technique for creating most absolute path links. You can also use the same technique for creating document-relative and root-relative links, but there are easier ways to create links to documents located on the same site as the current document.

To create a link by typing a URL, follow these steps:

1. Select the text that you want to become the link text. (Normally, you do this kind of work in Design view, but it also works in Code view.)

2. Type the URL for the link in the Link box of the Text Property Inspector panel. For an absolute path link, be sure to type the entire URL. Be careful to type it accurately.

 To avoid typing errors when entering an absolute path, cut and paste the URL from your web browser. Use your web browser to surf to the page you want to link to. When the page appears in the browser window, select the URL in the browser's address box and press CTRL+C. *Then select the link text on your web page in Dreamweaver, click in the Link box in the Property Inspector panel, and press* CTRL+V *to paste the URL.*

3. Press ENTER or click another option in the Property Inspector panel, or click somewhere on the Document window. Dreamweaver creates the link as soon as the pointer moves out of the Link box of the Property Inspector panel.

That's all there is to it. Dreamweaver inserts the proper code into the document's HTML code and highlights the selected text as a link (usually blue text with an underline).

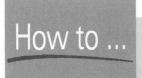

Control Where the Browser Opens a Link

You can tell the visitor's browser not only what document to open when the visitor clicks a link, but whether to display the document in the current browser window, in a particular frame in the current page (see Chapter 8 for more on frames), or in a new browser window. You do this by specifying a *Target* attribute for the link.

The Target box is located to the right of the Link box in the Property Inspector panel. Click the arrow button in the Target box and select one of the available options to specify the link target. Some of the options are related to frames and framesets (which are covered in Chapter 8) and do not apply to web documents that don't use frames. Your choices include any of the following:

- **_blank**   Instructs the browser to open a new browser window to display the linked document

- **_parent**   Instructs the browser to open the linked document in the parent frameset on the current page

- **_self**   Instructs the browser to open the linked document in the current frame (this is the default action)

- **_top**   Instructs the browser to open the linked document in the top-level frameset, effectively replacing all frames with the linked document

- *_framename*   Instructs the browser to open the linked document in the named frame

Create a Link by Browsing

You can also create a link by browsing for the linked document in a dialog box that is similar to a standard Open File dialog box. This technique isn't appropriate for creating absolute path links to resources located outside the current site, but it's one of the easiest ways to create a document-relative or root-relative link to a document on the current site. Here's how you do it:

1. Select the text that you want to become the link text.

2. Click the folder icon to the right of the Link box in the Property Inspector panel.
Dreamweaver opens the Select File dialog box.

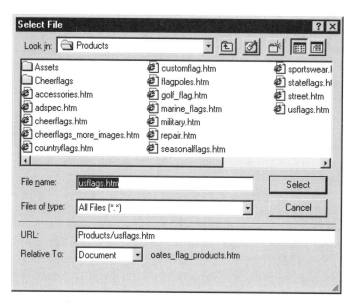

SHORTCUT *Select the link text in your document and then press* CTRL+L *to open the Select File dialog box and define the link.*

3. Locate the file to which you want to link in the Select File dialog box. Click the file
icon. The filename appears in the File Name box.

4. Select Document or Site Root in the Relative To box to specify a document-relative or
root-relative path. Note the change reflected in the URL box.

5. Click Select to close the Select File dialog box and record the URL in the Link box of
the Property Inspector panel. Dreamweaver highlights the selected text as a link and
adds the link code to the page's HTML code.

This is the best technique to use when you want to explicitly select either document-relative
or root-relative paths.

Create a Link by Dragging

Dreamweaver enables you to create links entirely with drag-and-drop mouse actions. While
the process isn't one of those intuitively obvious techniques for most people, it is simple to
understand and fast to implement after you see it in action. The only real drawback is that you
need a good-sized monitor with room for multiple open windows in order to drag from window
to window to define the links. There are a couple of variations on the basic drag-and-drop
technique. They rely on the Point to File icon in the Property Inspector panel (and elsewhere).

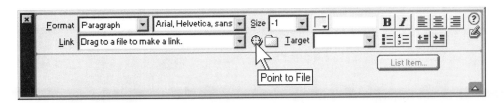

To create a link using the Point to File icon in the Property Inspector panel, follow these steps:

1. Make sure the current Document window, Property Inspector panel, and a window showing the intended linked document are all visible on the desktop. The linked document can be in its own Document window, in the Site Map, or just a filename visible in the Site window.

2. Select the text that you want to become the link text.

3. Click and drag the Point to File icon (the small bull's-eye target) located to the right of the Link box in the Property Inspector panel. As you drag the Point to File icon, Dreamweaver extends a line from the icon in the Property Inspector panel to the mouse pointer (see Figure 4-1).

4. Drag the Point to File onto the linked document and release the mouse button. You can point to the document in a Document window, to a page icon in the Site Map, or to a filename in the Site window. When you release the mouse button, Dreamweaver records the URL in the Link box of the Property Inspector panel, highlights the selected text as a link, and adds the link code to the page's HTML code.

SHORTCUT *You can bypass the Property Inspector panel by selecting text in Design view and then pressing and holding the SHIFT key as you drag from the selected text to the linked document in another Dreamweaver window. The same Point to File icon and line appear between the selected text and the linked document to indicate the link definition in progress. When you release the mouse button, Dreamweaver records the link.*

TIP *The same Point to File icon appears beside the selected page in the Site Map. You can drag the Point to File icon to other page icons in the Site Map, to files in the file list, or to open Document windows to create links to the selected page.*

You can also use the drag-and-drop technique in reverse to drag a file icon and drop it on the Property Inspector panel to create a link. Here's how:

1. Select the text that you want to become the link text.

2. Drag a file icon from the file list in the Site window and drop it on the Link box in the Property Inspector panel for the current page. Dreamweaver records the URL in the Link box of the Property Inspector panel, highlights the selected text as a link, and adds the link code to the page's HTML code.

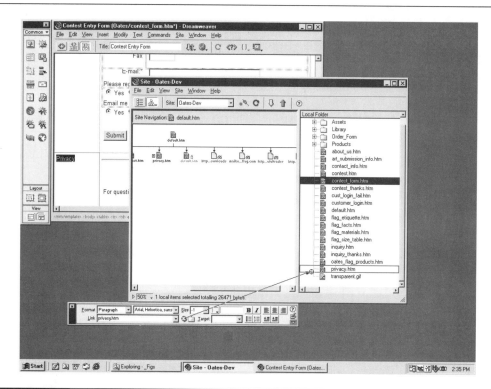

FIGURE 4-1   Dragging the Point to File icon

 **Delete a Link from Your Page**

Deleting a link from your page is even easier than creating a new link. Simply click on the link in your document in Design view to select it, then erase the URL from the Link box in the Property Inspector panel. Note that you don't need to drag across the whole link to select it; a single click anywhere within the link will do. Also, you can select the URL with a single click on the Link box, and you can erase it by pressing BACKSPACE or DELETE.

When you remove the URL from the Link box in the Property Inspector panel, Dreamweaver removes the link highlight from the link text in your document and removes the link code from your document's HTML code.

4

   *To remove a link from your document, click on the link in your document and then press*
CTRL+SHIFT+L.

Create a Link to an Anchor

Not only can you create a link to another document, you can actually specify what portion of a
long document should appear when a visitor follows a link. The feature that makes this possible
is called a *named anchor,* which is an invisible object you can insert into a document specifically
to provide a destination for a link. The anchor acts as a sort of bookmark for a location within a
long web document. A link that includes a reference to an anchor in addition to the document
URL causes the web browser to automatically scroll the linked document to show the section of
the document marked by the anchor.

Of course, before you can link to an anchor in a document, you must define the anchor.
Here's how you do it:

1. Position the insertion point cursor in the Document window where you want to place the
   named anchor. You can place anchors almost anywhere in a document, but the logical
   locations are at headings and other obvious section breaks.

2. Click the Named Anchor button on the Invisibles page of the Objects panel, or choose
   Insert | Invisible Tags | Named Anchor. The Insert Named Anchor dialog box appears.

3. Enter a name for the anchor and click OK to close the Insert Named Anchor dialog box
   and insert the anchor into the web document.

CAUTION   *The anchor name is case sensitive and cannot contain any spaces.*

Dreamweaver displays the anchor icon to indicate the location of the named anchor in
Design view as shown in Figure 4-2. But the anchor is completely invisible when one views the
document in a web browser. If the anchor icon doesn't appear in Design view, choose View |
Visual Aids | Invisible Elements to toggle invisible element display on.

After you create one or more anchors in a document, you can create links to those anchors.
The simplest way to do that is to use the Point to File icon to create a link by dragging. Just
make sure that the linked document is open in Design view and the anchor icon is visible. Then
go to the source document, select the link text, and drag the Point to File icon from the Property
Inspector panel. Point to the anchor icon in the linked Document window and release the mouse
button. Dreamweaver creates the link and adds the anchor name to the normal document-relative
address like so:

```
filename.html#anchorname
```

The # symbol followed by the name is the portion of the URL that designates the anchor name.

You can also create links to named anchors within the same document. In fact, that's how
you create a table of contents at the top of a long web document. You create as many named
anchors in the document as needed—usually one for each text section heading. Then you create a
table of contents at the top of the document and create a link from each table of contents entry to

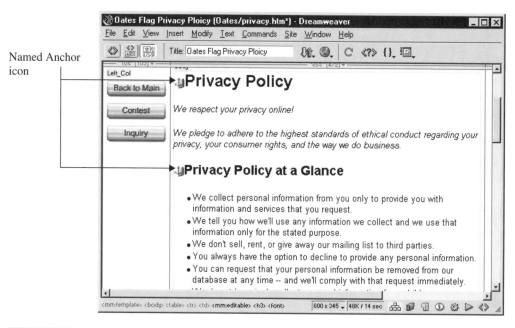

Named Anchor icon

FIGURE 4-2   The Named Anchor icon

the corresponding named anchor. You can create the links with the Point to File icon or by typing the anchor name (*#anchorname*) in as the URL for the link.

Create an E-Mail Link

An e-mail link is a special kind of hyperlink. Instead of linking to another web document, an e-mail link instructs the visitor's browser to create a new e-mail message, preaddressed to the address in the link. E-mail links are a great way to solicit feedback from visitors to your web site.

In its basic form, an e-mail link is simply a hyperlink in which `mailto:` *emailaddress* replaces the URL for the linked document. In fact, you can create an e-mail link by selecting text on your page and then typing **mailto:***emailaddress* into the Link box in the Property Inspector panel. (There is no space between mailto: and the e-mail address. Enter the full e-mail address, such as johndoe@bogus.com, in place of *emailaddress* in the example.)

However, Dreamweaver tries to make the process even easier. When you're working in Design view, you can create an e-mail link by following these steps:

1. Place the insertion point in your document at the location where you want to insert the e-mail link. If you already have existing text (or image) on the page that you want to be the link text for the e-mail link, select it. However, it isn't necessary for the link text to exist.

2. Open the Insert Email Link dialog box by doing one of the following:

■ Choose Insert | E-Mail Link.

■ Click the Insert E-Mail Link icon in the Common page of the Objects panel.

3. Enter the link text that you want to appear on your page in the Text box. (If you selected existing link text in step 1, you can edit that text here.)

4. Enter the e-mail address to which the message should be sent in the E-Mail box. Enter the full e-mail address, such as johndoe@bogus.com.

5. Click OK to close the Insert Email Link dialog box and record the link in your document. Dreamweaver inserts the contents of the Text box into your document at the insertion point as the link text. The e-mail address is embedded in the link code and appears in the Link box of the Property Inspector panel.

Insert and Manipulate Images

Images, images, images!

Images are everywhere on the Web. They're second only to text as the most common component of web pages—and no wonder. Images are probably the most versatile design component on a web page. Besides the obvious example of a rectangular picture or diagram that helps illustrate the text on a page, many other kinds of images serve many other purposes. For example:

■ Regular images can include photographs, charts, graphs, maps, diagrams, or illustrations.

■ Animated images provide eye-catching movement.

■ Background images create a colored backdrop for the page.

■ Logos and other graphics provide brand identification and serve as design elements.

■ Buttons serve as navigation aids.

■ Image maps can create multiple links from one image for navigation bars and the like.

■ Images of text enable web designers to use fonts and text treatments on web pages that aren't available in most browsers.

■ Banner advertisements add color and generate revenue.

■ Tracing images let you rough out your page design in another program and then develop it in Dreamweaver.

Despite the diversity of image types and the versatility of their applications, you work with almost all images the same way. Your design goals and reasons for including different kinds of images (and different images of the same kind) on your page may be different, but the mechanics of adding those images to the page are the same. With the exception of background images, tracing images, and image maps, the purpose an image serves on the page has little or nothing to do with how you work with the image in Dreamweaver.

 *The time required to download and display images can dramatically increase the time it takes for a browser to display your page. The bigger the image, the bigger the file, and the longer it takes to display. Make sure that every image on your page contributes significantly to your message and justifies the time site visitors must wait to see the image. Minimize that time by making sure that every image file is as small as possible.*

Dealing with Dependent Files

When you insert text into a web page, the text itself is stored along with the HTML code in the web document. Not so with images. When you insert an image into your web page, Dreamweaver inserts an HTML tag into the web document that contains information about where to find the image file and some options for displaying the image, but the image itself remains in a separate image source file.

When the visitor's web browser encounters the image reference, it fetches the image from the source file and displays it alongside the text and other elements of the web page. Dreamweaver's Design view displays the same kind of combined representation of the text and images of the web page. However, the image source file remains *separate*. Dreamweaver and the visitor's web browser must access the image file as well as the HTML web document every time they attempt to display the page.

The references to image source files in the HTML code for your page follow the same rules as references to URLs for hyperlinks. Your web document can include absolute paths, document-relative paths, or root-relative paths (for more information, see the earlier section in this chapter

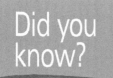

Browsers Depend on Dependent Files

A web browser can't display a web page as you intended it to be seen unless it has access to all the image source files and other resource files that are referenced in the HTML code for the web page. Dreamweaver refers to image source files as *dependent files* because the web page depends on those files. You need to make sure that you include all the image files and other dependent files along with the web document any time you copy, move, or publish your document. Dreamweaver offers to automatically include any dependent files when you move or publish a web document in the Dreamweaver Site window.

4

called "Understanding Paths"). Document-relative paths and root-relative paths are the normal ways to reference image source files located in your local site folder and its subfolders. An absolute path can point to an image source file located outside your local site folder. However, if that location (for instance, a folder on your hard drive or local network) isn't readily accessible via the Internet, a visitor's web browser won't be able to display the image. Therefore, if you attempt to insert an image into a page in Dreamweaver that is located outside your local site folder and its subfolders, Dreamweaver automatically offers to copy the file into your local site folder.

Insert Images

Dreamweaver gives you several ways to insert images into your web page. All of them start with your document open in Design view. (Unless, of course, you're a masochist who likes to work in Code view.)

Insert Image Objects

Perhaps the most popular technique is to follow these steps:

1. Position the insertion point cursor where you want to insert the image on your page.

 You can drag the Insert Image button from the Common page of the Objects panel and drop it on your web page at the location where you want to insert the image. Dreamweaver opens the Select Image Source dialog box, and you can continue with step 3 of the procedure.

 2. Open the Select Image Source dialog box by doing one of the following:

■ Click the Insert Image button on the Common page of the Objects panel.

■ Press CTRL+ALT+I.

■ Choose Insert | Image from the menu.

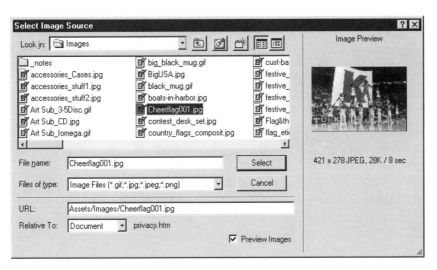

3. Locate and select the image file in the Select Image Source dialog box. The filename appears in the File Name box.

4. Select Document or Site Root in the Relative To box to specify a document-relative or root-relative path. Note the change reflected in the URL box.

5. Click Select to close the Select File dialog box. Dreamweaver inserts the image into your page in the Document window and adds the corresponding code to the page's HTML code.

Dreamweaver displays the image on your page at its native size. The image is selected, as indicated by the bounding box and sizing handles surrounding the image (see Figure 4-3). You can resize the image and adjust options and settings in the Property Inspector panel if necessary (see the later sections in this chapter, "Resize Images" and "Set Borders and Other Image Properties").

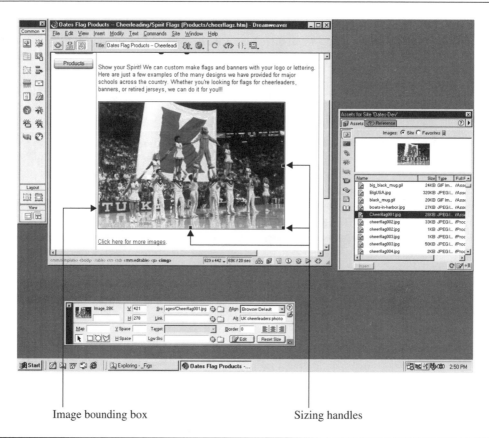

Image bounding box   Sizing handles

FIGURE 4-3   A newly inserted image

The HTML tag for an image file is `<img src="filename.ext">`, *and, unless the insertion point is within a paragraph, Dreamweaver adds paragraph tags (* `<p></p>` *) around the image tag.*

Drag and Drop an Image

You can also use drag-and-drop techniques to insert images into your web page. Here's how:

1. Make sure the current Document window and a window showing the desired image file are visible on the desktop. The image file can be on your desktop, in a Windows Explorer window, in the Site Files list window, or in the Assets panel.

2. Position the insertion point cursor where you want to insert the image on your page.

3. Drag the image file icon from the file list in the Site Files window and drop it on your web page in the Dreamweaver Document window. Dreamweaver inserts the image into your page in the Document window and adds the corresponding code to the page's HTML code.

TIP *You can also insert images from the Assets panel by selecting an image and then clicking the Insert button at the bottom of the Assets panel.*

Control Image Position

The HTML standard provides several alignment options for images and similar objects, and, of course, Dreamweaver's Image Property Inspector panel (shown in Figure 4-4) gives you ready access to all of them. However, remember that the original HTML specifications were conceived for publishing academic research papers and other technical documents, so the image alignment options are tailored to those limited needs. They work pretty well for positioning an image against the right or left margin and allowing text to flow around the rectangular image outline. But if your needs are more sophisticated than that, you'll probably want to look into using tables (see Chapter 7) or layers (see Chapter 15) to control image placement with more precision and flexibility.

Align list

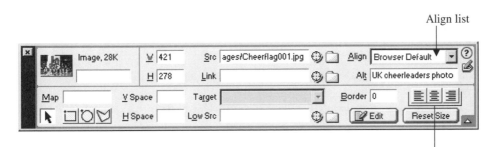

Left, Center, Right paragraph alignment

FIGURE 4-4   The Image Property Inspector panel, expanded to show all the options

There are actually two sets of image alignment controls. First, since each image is contained within a text paragraph, you can use the standard paragraph alignment options to control the horizontal position on the page.

Second, you can select one of nine alignment attributes to control how the image aligns with the surrounding text. These alignment options have essentially no effect on an image that sits alone in a paragraph that contains no text, but they have a significant effect on the relationship of text and images in the same paragraph. Remember that the image tag is embedded in the text of a paragraph. The alignment options tell the browser how to display the image in relation to the line of text in which the image tag resides. You can choose any of the following image alignment options from the Align list box in the Property Inspector panel:

- **Browser Default**   Uses the browser's default alignment setting, usually Baseline
- **Baseline**   Aligns the bottom edge of the image with the baseline of the text
- **Top**   Aligns the top edge of the image with the top of the tallest object in the line (text or another image or object)
- **Middle**   Aligns the middle of the image with the baseline of the text
- **Bottom**   Same as Baseline
- **Text Top**   Aligns the top edge of the image with the top of the text
- **Absolute Middle**   Aligns the middle of the image with the middle of the text
- **Absolute Bottom**   Aligns the bottom edge of the image with the lowest extent of the current line of the text, including the descenders (the tails of characters such as *g*)
- **Left**   Aligns the image on the left margin and wraps text around it on the right
- **Right**   Aligns the image on the right margin and wraps text around it on the left

TIP   *Use the paragraph alignment buttons to set horizontal alignment and the Align options to set vertical alignment.*

Resize Images

When you insert an image into your page, it appears in the Document window at its original size. Often, that's not the size that works best in your page layout, and you'll need to resize the image to fit.

The mechanics of resizing an image in Dreamweaver are simple. You can either drag the resizing handles to resize the image visually or adjust the height and width settings in the Property Inspector panel.

To resize the image visually, click on the image to select it (see Figure 4-3), then do one of the following:

- Drag the sizing handle on the right side to make the image wider or thinner.
- Drag the sizing handle on the bottom to make the image taller or shorter.
- Drag the sizing handle in the lower-right corner to simultaneously change height and width.

■ Press and hold the SHIFT key as you drag the sizing handle in the lower-right corner to maintain the image proportions as you make it larger or smaller.

NOTE *The smallest you can make an image by dragging resizing handles is 8 x 8 pixels. To make an image smaller, enter height and width values in the Property Inspector panel.*

As you change the image size by dragging the sizing handles, the numbers in the Height and Width boxes in the Property Inspector panel change to reflect the changes in image size. Also, the Height and Width numbers appear in bold to indicate that the image is no longer its original size.

To use the Property Inspector panel to control image size, try these techniques:

■ Type new dimensions directly into the Height and Width boxes in the Property Inspector panel to resize the image "by the numbers." The image dimensions appear in pixels, but you can type in other measurements by adding an abbreviation for the unit of measurement. You can use inches (in), millimeters (mm), centimeters (cm), picas (pc), or points (pt). Type the number followed immediately by the unit of measure with no space between the two, like so: **3in**. Dreamweaver converts your measurement to pixels automatically.

■ Click Reset Size to instantly restore the image to its original size.

About Optimizing Image Files

One of the key considerations in adding any image to a web page is the size of the image file and how long it takes to download. Visitors to your web site tend to be an impatient lot and may not be willing to wait for a page with numerous large images to load. For this reason, it's imperative that you make every image the optimum size and every image file as small and fast to load as possible.

You should consider resizing an image in Dreamweaver as a temporary measure— something you do as you experiment with your page layout to determine what size the image should be. After you determine the correct size, go back to your image-editing program and generate a new image file to that exact size and reinsert it into your page. The goal is to have an image file that is the precise size needed for display—no more and no less. Relying on the browser to resize images as it displays them is inefficient and often produces an inferior display.

TIP *The close integration of Dreamweaver and Fireworks dramatically simplifies the process of generating optimized image files after resizing an image in Dreamweaver. See Chapter 12 for the details.*

Set Borders and Other Image Properties

Image size and alignment aren't the only attributes you can adjust in the Image Property Inspector panel. You can also add a border around the image, set padding space, and more. Here's a rundown of the image properties and what they do:

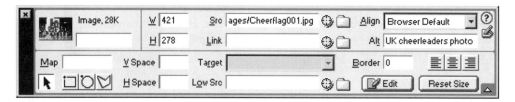

TIP *If all the options don't appear in the Property Inspector panel, click the small arrow in the lower-right corner to expand the panel.*

- **Image name** (unlabeled box under the thumbnail image)   An optional name for easy reference.

- **W**   Image width in pixels.

- **H**   Image height in pixels.

- **Src**   Source file for the image.

- **Link**   Creates a hyperlink to another document or file.

- **Align**   Alignment options controlling how the image aligns with text in the paragraph.

- **Alt**   Text to display in place of the image in browsers that have image display turned off.

- **Map**   Creates client-side image maps (see the later section in this chapter, "Create an Image Map").

- **V Space**   Specifies the minimum amount of white space around the outer edges of the image at the top and bottom.

- **H Space**   Specifies the minimum amount of white space around the outer edges of the image at the sides.

- **Target**   Specifies the target browser window or frame for a hyperlink.

- **Low Src**   An alternate image file that is loaded before the main image. This gives the visitor a preview of the image while waiting for the main image to load. It's usually a copy of the main image but with fewer colors and lower resolution so that it downloads much faster.

- **Border**   Specifies the thickness of the border around the image. Defaults to 0 for no visible border.
- **Left, Center, Right** buttons   Paragraph alignment buttons control horizontal placement.
- **Edit** button   Click to open the image file in the associated image-editing program (usually Fireworks).
- **Reset Size** button   Click to reset the image to its original size.

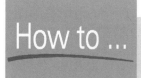

How to ... Add Alt Text for Images

Alt text (alternate text) is an important attribute for images on your web page. It's one of the key factors in making your site accessible to visitors whose web browsing experience doesn't include images.

The average site visitor will probably only glimpse the alternate text for an image in the seconds between the time the page begins to load and the image appears in all its glory. But other visitors may be using a text-only browser or have their browser set to display images manually in order to compensate for a slow Internet connection. Or they may be visually impaired and use screen reader software. All these visitors rely on the alternate text for information about the image and its purpose on the page. Otherwise, the image appears as an empty rectangle.

Simply identifying an image as "Photo" or "Logo graphic" gives the visitor more information than an empty rectangle, but, to be truly useful, the alt text should be "functionally equivalent" to the image it's substituting for. So, if the image is a button linked to the Products page, the alt text should be something like "link to Products." If the image conveys information, the alt text should state that information. If the image is purely decorative, a simpler alt text entry is adequate.

You can add an alt text attribute to your image by simply typing the text in the Alt box in the Property Inspector panel. The challenge is to compose a short text entry that is the "equivalent" of the image.

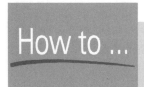 **Select the Correct Image File Formats: JPG vs. GIF vs. PNG**

There are many different image file formats in use today. Various computer programs that create or capture images store those images in their own proprietary format or in one of the dozen or so semistandard file formats. Over the years, however, three image file formats— GIF, JPEG, and PNG—have emerged as the standards for use on the Web. The major web browsers include built-in support for these three formats and display those images automatically without helper applications or plug-ins. Dreamweaver also displays all three image formats in the Design view Document window.

If you want to use an image on your web page, it needs to be in one of the three standard formats—the only question is, which one? Here's a quick summary of the advantages and disadvantages of each format:

- **GIF** (Graphic Interchange Format)   This file format was originally developed for online use and features very compact file sizes. Images are limited to 256 colors. Optional features include transparent colors that allow the background to show through, interlaced images that appear onscreen quickly and then build in detail, and animated GIFs: multiple images in one file to achieve animation effects. Because of the limited color palette, the GIF format is best suited for graphic images with sharp edges and large areas of solid color.

- **JPEG** (Joint Photographic Experts Group)   This file format was developed to display continuous-tone photographic images. It supports millions of colors to facilitate smooth color rendering in images. The JPEG format supports variable compression to reduce file size, but reductions in file size also reduce image quality. However, by experimenting with different compression settings, you can often achieve dramatic improvement in file size while still retaining adequate image quality. Use the JPEG format for photographs and other images where smooth color shading is important— avoid it for text and sharp-edged graphics.

- **PNG** (Portable Network Group)   This is a newer file format designed to replace GIF. It's the native file format for Macromedia Fireworks. Like GIF, PNG supports index colors and transparency, and like JPEG, it supports true color rendition. PNG also supports layers, vector drawing elements, and effects; and all the information remains editable at all times. All the versatility and features come at a price though—PNG files are often larger than the same image stored as a GIF or a moderately compressed JPEG.

In addition to the three standard image file formats, several other file formats are widely accepted and used for various media applications other than static images. See Chapter 13 for more information on adding rich media to your web page. It's possible to use other file formats for images as well. However, using other formats invariably requires helper applications or plug-ins of some sort to display the image. As a result, it's rarely worth the bother for the web designer or the site visitors to use other formats for static images.

Use Images as Links

An image can serve as the anchor for a hyperlink, as can a text selection. When the site visitor moves the mouse pointer over an image that is a link, the pointer changes from the arrow to the familiar pointing finger, and when the visitor clicks on the image, the browser follows the link and displays the linked document. In short, an image link works just as a text link does.

The process for creating an image link in Dreamweaver is also the same as the process for creating a text link. In fact, you can use any of the techniques for creating links described earlier in this chapter. The only adjustment you need to make in the techniques is to select an image, instead of text, in the Document window to serve as the anchor for the link. The details of selecting the linked document file and dealing with paths and targets for the link are exactly the same for an image link and a text link.

Create Buttons

One of the leading uses of image links on a web page is to create navigation buttons. Graphic images that resemble onscreen buttons lead the site visitor to intuit that the image is something they can click on to make something happen.

Simple buttons are nothing more than a small image, usually a small GIF file, with an attached link. For example, in Figure 4-5, the Destinations button is an image file (MenuDestinations.gif) linked to the site's Destinations page (destinations.html). While it's possible to get fancy with a rollover effects (see Chapter 16), Flash buttons (see Chapter 13), and other special effects, the vast majority of buttons on the Web today are just the kind of simple image link illustrated in Figure 4-5.

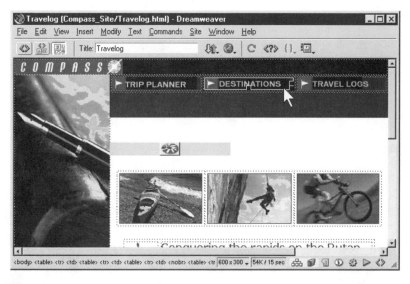

FIGURE 4-5   Most buttons are simple image links.

Create an Image Map

An image map takes the idea of a simple image link one step farther. Instead of defining one link for the entire image, an image map enables you to define one or more *hotspots* (subsections of the image) and create a separate link to each hotspot. That means one image can anchor several links, and site visitors can go to different destination links depending on what portion of the image they click on.

One example of this concept is an image of a US map with hotspot areas defined to match state borders and linked to the corresponding state documents. Figure 4-6 shows a similar use of an image map. However, image maps are more commonly used to join several navigation buttons together and give them a seamless graphic treatment.

In the early days of the Web, image maps were created on the web server using some fairly complicated programming. Nowadays most image maps are client-side image maps, and all the programming code is contained in the web document and executed by the web browser.

FIGURE 4-6   Image maps enable you to create multiple links to one image.

Dreamweaver enables you to create client-side image maps without resorting to hand-coding. Here's how:

1. Insert the image that you want to use as an image map into your document, or select an existing image. Make sure the Image Property Inspector panel is visible. (Press CTRL+F3 to open the panel if it isn't already open.)

Map Name

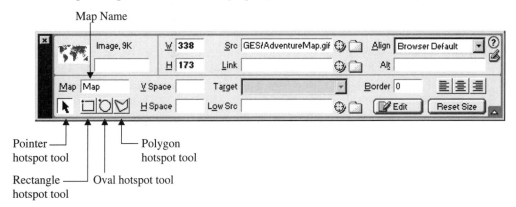

Pointer hotspot tool

Rectangle hotspot tool

Oval hotspot tool

Polygon hotspot tool

> **TIP** *If the Map box and hotspot tools aren't visible in the Property Inspector panel, click the arrow button in the lower-right corner to expand the panel.*

2. Enter a name for your image map in the Map box of the Property Inspector panel.

3. Click one of the hotspot drawing tools and then click and drag on the image to define a hotspot.

- ▪ To create a rectangular hotspot, click the Rectangle hotspot tool; then drag the pointer diagonally on the image to define the hotspot.

- ▪ To create a circular hotspot, click the Oval hotspot tool; then drag the pointer on the image to define the hotspot.

- ▪ To create an irregularly shaped hotspot, click the Polygon hotspot tool; then click on the image to define the first point of the perimeter of the hotspot. Add points to the polygon by clicking as you work your way around the perimeter of the hotspot shape. Click the Pointer hotspot tool in the Property Inspector panel to close the polygon.

The Hotspot Property Inspector panel appears when you create the hotspot.

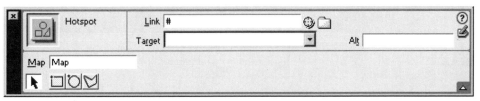

4. Click the Link box in the Property Inspector panel and define the link using your favorite technique. (Type a filename in the Link box, drag the Point to File icon to a file icon, or click the folder icon to open the Select Link File dialog box.)

5. Select a Target for the link and enter alt text for the hotspot in the Property Inspector panel.

6. Click the image outside the current hotspot to go back to the Property Inspector panel for the main image; then repeat steps 3–5 as needed to define additional hotspots and links.

Dreamweaver's Design view displays hotspots as translucent cyan overlays on image map images, as shown in Figure 4-7. This feature makes it easy for you to see and select the hotspots as you develop your page, but it doesn't affect how the image map appears to the visitor viewing your page in a web browser. In the browser, the hotspots are invisible. Only the effect of being able to go to different links by clicking different areas of the image distinguishes the image map from a normal image.

After you create an image map, you can use the following techniques to edit the image map.

■ Click a hotspot in Design view to select it. The Hotspot Property Inspector panel appears, and you can change the link or any of the other settings.

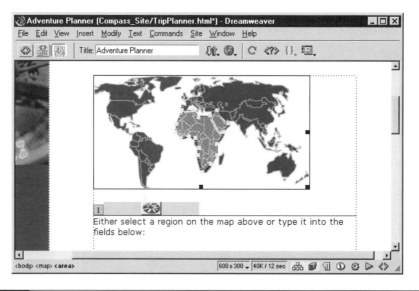

FIGURE 4-7   Hotspots appear as light shapes superimposed on your image in Design view.

■ To move a hotspot, click the hotspot and drag it to the new location.

■ To delete a hotspot, click the hotspot and press the DELETE key.

■ Right-click a hotspot and choose Bring To Front or Send To Back to control which hotspot takes precedence (is in front) where hotspots overlap.

■ To reshape a hotspot, select the hotspot with the pointer tool and then drag any of the handles located on the handles.

Work with Background Images

A background image, as its name implies, is an image that serves as a background for your web page (see Figure 4-8). You can create some interesting effects with background images, but you need to choose the image carefully to avoid conflicts that make the text and other foreground elements on your page hard to read.

An image large enough to fill the entire background of a web page, even when viewed on a large monitor, would require a large image file, and the time to download and display the image

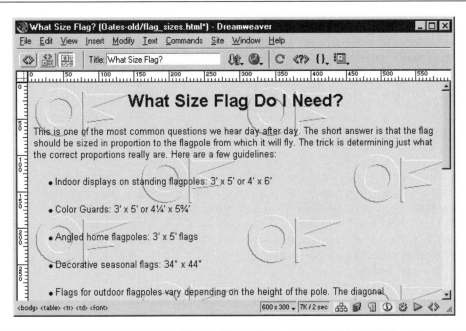

FIGURE 4-8   A background image is tiled to fill the page.

would probably be unacceptable. Therefore, background images are normally small images that can be downloaded quickly and then tiled (multiple copies repeated in rows and columns) to fill the browser window. Dreamweaver tiles background images the same way web browsers do, so you can preview the effect in the Design view window.

To add a background image to your page, follow these steps:

1. Choose Modify | Page Properties to open the Page Properties dialog box.

2. Enter the image filename in the Background Image box; or click the Browse button to open the Select Image Source dialog box, locate and select the file, and click Select.

3. Click OK to close the Page Properties dialog box and apply the background image to your page.

 The trick to successfully using background images is in image selection. Look for a low-contrast image that will tile without showing obvious seams. A subtle texture is usually better than an eye-catching pattern.

Use a Tracing Image

Some web designers like to create a mock-up of a web page in a graphics application first, before attempting to build the page in Dreamweaver. This step allows the designer to experiment freely with the look of the page without getting bogged down in the mechanics of implementing the design. Later, the designer turns to Dreamweaver for the task of producing a working web page based on the design concept.

TIP *If you're the retro type, you can sketch your page layout with pencil and paper; then scan your sketch to create an image you can use as a tracing image in Dreamweaver. Just be sure to save the scanner output in (or convert it to) a web-friendly file format such as GIF or PNG.*

A tracing image facilitates the process of building a web page to match a preexisting design created in another program by enabling you to create and position page elements in Dreamweaver on top of an image of the mock-up design. The tracing image replaces the page's background color and background image in Dreamweaver's Design view. But the tracing image is visible only in Design view, never in a browser. You can turn the tracing image on and off, change its opacity, and change its position.

To add a tracing image to a page, follow these steps:

1. Choose Modify | Page Properties to open the Page Properties dialog box.

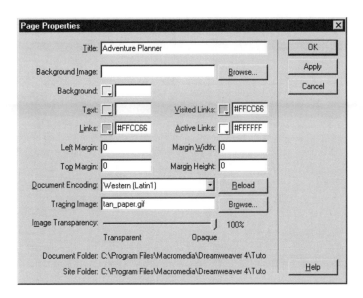

4

2. Enter the filename of the image in the Tracing Image box; or click the Browse button to open the Select Image Source dialog box, locate and select the file, and click Select.

3. Drag the Image Transparency slider to set the level of transparency for the tracing image.

4. Click OK to close the Page Properties dialog box and add the tracing image to your page, as shown in Figure 4-9.

After you add a tracing image to your page, you can manipulate it with the following techniques:

■ To specify the position of the tracing image, choose View | Tracing Image | Adjust Position to open the Adjust Tracing Image Position dialog box; enter coordinates into the X and Y boxes, then click OK to close the dialog box and move the tracing image.

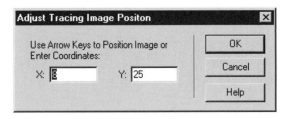

FIGURE 4-9 A tracing image makes it easier to match a page mock-up created in another program.

TIP

While the Adjust Tracing Image Position dialog box is open, you can tap an arrow key (up, down, right, or left) to move the tracing image one pixel at a time. Press SHIFT+arrow key to move the tracing image five pixels at a time.

- To align the top-left corner of the tracing image with the currently selected object, choose View | Tracing Image | Align With Selection.
- To turn the tracing image on or off, choose View | Tracing Image | Show.

Edit Images

Dreamweaver is an excellent program for editing web pages, but editing the images that go on those web pages is another matter. For that you need another program, such as Fireworks. Although you can't edit images within Dreamweaver, the program does make it easy to use an external image-editing program. You can specify an image editor in the Dreamweaver preferences and launch that program from the Property Inspector panel by clicking the Edit button with an image selected. When you return to Dreamweaver after editing and saving the image in the external image editor, the latest changes in the image file appear in the Design view window.

For more information on using Fireworks and other external programs with Dreamweaver, see Chapter 12.

4

Chapter 5

Edit HTML Code in Dreamweaver

How to...

- Understand the basics of HTML code
- Use Dreamweaver's various code viewing windows
- Edit HTML code in Dreamweaver
- Import code from other programs
- View and edit head content

When you view a web page in a browser, you see nicely formatted text and images, and perhaps animation, movies, and other special effects. But behind the pretty face you see in the web browser, the web document is actually a plain text file containing unformatted text and HTML codes that tell the web browser how to format and display the text, images, and other elements on the web page.

Although it's convenient to think of a web page as the finished image you see in a web browser, the reality is that a web document is composed of plain text and HTML codes. That's what is in the file stored on the web server; that's what gets downloaded to the web browser; and that's what you create and edit in Dreamweaver. Dreamweaver's Design view lets you work in a graphical environment that hides the details of the HTML code, but the fact remains that the program exists to produce web documents, which are composed of HTML code.

Normally, you can design and edit web pages in Design view without being too concerned about the underlying HTML codes that Dreamweaver manipulates to achieve the desired effect as you click and drag and select objects and options. Of course, if you have a programming background, you may actually prefer to work directly with the HTML code for your web page. And Dreamweaver gives you that option with several ways to access and edit HTML code within the program. Dreamweaver also cooperates nicely with external programs, so you can continue to use your favorite text editor or programming environment.

Even if you're not a programmer, you'll undoubtedly need to work with HTML code from time to time. Sometimes working with code is the best, if not the only, way to troubleshoot a problem or achieve a certain effect. At the very least, you need to gain a general understanding of the real web documents you're creating with Dreamweaver—the HTML code. As a result, every Dreamweaver user needs to know at least the basics of how to access and manipulate HTML code. Fortunately, Dreamweaver creates an environment in which you can quickly and easily switch back and forth between a graphical representation of your web page and the underlying HTML code. And you can even view the visual design and the code simultaneously, which is a tremendous advantage.

Understanding HTML Basics

HTML (Hypertext Markup Language) is a text markup language rather than a "programming language." Normally, the bulk of a web document is plain text. Special codes, called *tags*, are embedded in the text to tell the browser how to format and display the text, where to find image files to add to the page, and so on. These tags are enclosed in angle brackets <> to set them apart from the text.

For example, the <i> tag designates italic text. Adding a slash (/) to the tag makes it a *closing tag*, which designates the end of the text marked with that tag. Most HTML tags are paired with a tag and a closing tag enclosing the text to which the tag refers. So, the following line of code of HTML code produces the results shown below it:

```
A simple example of <i>italic</i> text
```

A simple example of *italic* text

In addition, some tags include *attributes* that define more details about the tag and the text or object that the tag affects. Attributes are enclosed in the angle brackets along with the initial opening tag. For example, the paragraph tag (<p>) that marks the beginning and end of a paragraph can include an alignment attribute:

```
<p align="right">A paragraph of text aligned with the right margin</p>
```

A paragraph of text aligned with the right margin

Document Structure

The HTML standard defines certain required elements of a web document's structure. The <html> tag defines the beginning and end of the HTML code. The <head> tag defines the document header. And the <body> tag defines the body of the document. The following code shows a simple example:

```
<html>
  <head>
    <title>Document Title</title>
  </head>
  <body>
    <p>Document text goes here</p>
  </body>
</html>
```

Note how both the <head> and <body> tags enclose other tags and are enclosed by the <html> tags in turn. The indenting shown in the preceding example is a convention that makes it easier for humans to read the code and visualize how tags are *nested* (enclosed) within other tags. However, Dreamweaver and web browsers don't pay any attention to whether or not lines of code are indented.

Here's a brief rundown of the main document tags:

- **<html>** Defines the beginning and end of the HTML code, which is essentially the beginning and end of a web document.

- **<head>** Defines the beginning and end of the header section of your document. The head contains the document title plus other document elements that do *not* display in the browser window. Examples of head content include meta tags (used for indexing web documents) and programming scripts, such as the JavaScript code for rollover effects.

- ■ **<body>** Defines the beginning and end of the body of your document—the part that appears in the web browser window. This includes all the text of your document plus all the tags for images, tables, and other elements.

Of course, there are a lot of other HTML codes. Only a few codes (such as `<title>`) go into the header portion of the HTML document. The rest go into the body of the document. Text formatting codes such as `<i>` and `<b>` mark italic and bold text. Paragraph codes such as `<p>` and `<h1>` mark plain paragraphs and level-1 headings. Codes such as `<ahref="linkdoc.html">` mark hypertext links, and codes such as `<img src="image.gif">` insert images into your document. And there are codes for defining tables, frames, and all sorts of other page elements. Many of the specific HTML codes are covered in context throughout this book, but it's impractical to even begin listing all of them here.

NOTE *This section is a very brief introduction to HTML. To work effectively with HTML code, you'll need more information than this chapter provides. You can find some information on HTML in Dreamweaver's Reference panel (see the next section of this chapter). Osborne/McGraw-Hill also publishes some good books on the subject. Check out: HTML: A Beginner's Guide by Wendy Willard; HTML: The Complete Reference by Thomas A. Powell; and HTML Programmer's Reference, also by Thomas A. Powell.*

Use Dreamweaver's HTML Reference Panel

Dreamweaver's Reference panel provides a quick, searchable reference for HTML tags, CSS styles, and JavaScript objects. Don't expect in-depth explanations or detailed instructions on when and how to use various HTML tags, but if all you need is the proper syntax for a tag, the Reference panel is certainly a handy source of information.

To open the Reference panel, click the Reference button on the Dreamweaver Document window toolbar, or choose Window | Reference.

The Reference panel appears as shown in Figure 5-1. The Reference panel is context sensitive, so it automatically displays information about the HTML tag, CSS style, or JavaScript object that is selected in the Document window when you open the panel.

If you want to find information on a subject other than what the "context sensing" feature displays, follow these steps:

1. Select the reference book you want to search from the Book list box near the top of the panel. You can choose from an HTML Reference, a JavaScript Reference, or a CSS Reference.

2. Select the Tag on which you want help from the Tag list box. Depending on which book you select in step 1, the list box will be labeled Tag, Object, or Style.

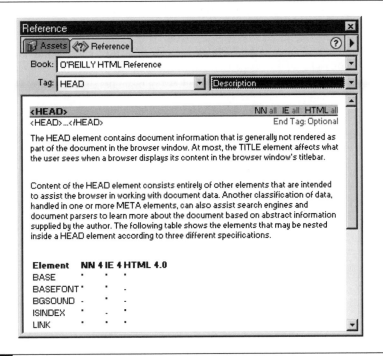

FIGURE 5-1   The Reference panel

3. Select the optional subtopic from the list box to the right of the Tag/Object/Style box. Not all topics have subtopics, but some, such as the <a> tag, have several subtopics to describe major attributes or other options. The selected topic appears in the Reference panel.

Work with Code in Dreamweaver

Like so many other things in Dreamweaver, when it comes to working with HTML code, Dreamweaver gives you options. There's not just one way to access and edit the code for your web document; you have your choice of several different windows and techniques.

- **Code view**   Shows the HTML code for your web document in the Dreamweaver Document window

- **Code and Design view**   Shows a split-screen view of your web document in the Dreamweaver Document window, thus allowing you to see simultaneously a visual representation of a portion of your web page and the underlying HTML code

- **Code Inspector panel**   Shows the HTML code for your document in a panel, separate from the main Document window

■ **Quick Tag Editor** A pop-up box that shows the HTML tag for the currently selected object in Design view or in the Property Inspector panel

You use different commands to open Code view, Code and Design view, and the Code Inspector panel, but otherwise you work with them in the same way. The following sections of this chapter cover Dreamweaver's code editing windows in more detail. The Quick Tag Editor works a little differently and is covered separately near the end of this chapter.

Code View

Code view displays your document's HTML code in the Dreamweaver Document window (see Figure 5-2). This puts the code up front and in your face, so if you like working directly with the HTML source code for your web pages, this view is for you.

To view your document in Code view, click the Show Code view button on the Document window toolbar or choose View | Code from the menu.

Code view automatically displays the HTML code for the portion of the document you were working on in Design view. If you select an object or text passage in Design view, Dreamweaver selects the corresponding code in Code view. Otherwise, the insertion point cursor appears in the position in the code corresponding to its position on the page in Design view.

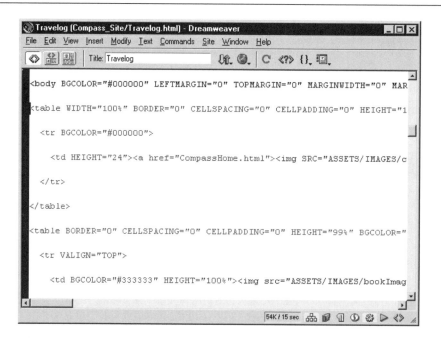

FIGURE 5-2   Code view

Code and Design View

In addition to the full-fledged Code view, which devotes the entire Document window to displaying the web page's HTML code, Dreamweaver offers another option—Code and Design view—which splits the Document window into two panes, one showing HTML code and the other showing a visual representation of the page. At first glance, this hybrid view (shown in Figure 5-3) may seem strange because neither the Code view pane nor the Design view pane is large enough to provide a good overview of the document. However, Code and Design view is an excellent way to examine the code for an element on your page while simultaneously viewing the graphical rendering of that same element in the Design view pane.

To view your document in Code and Design view, click the Show Code and Design view button on the Document window toolbar, or choose View | Code and Design from the menu.

As with the full-sized Code view window, the Code view pane automatically displays the HTML code for the selected object in Design view, and vice versa. If you scroll one pane, the other pane doesn't scroll simultaneously to match the portion of the document that is in view, but if you select an object or position the insertion point cursor in either pane, you will cause the other pane to jump to the corresponding place automatically.

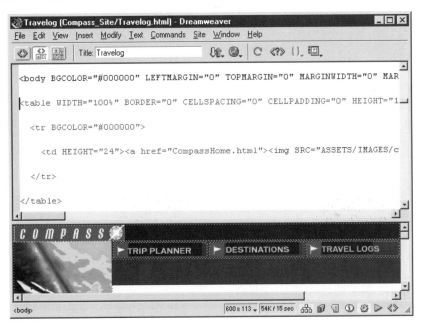

    Code and Design view

By default, the Code view pane is on the top and the Design view pane is on the bottom in Code and Design view. But you can swap the panes by choosing View | Design View on Top. You can also resize the panes by dragging the border separating the two panes up or down.

Code and Design view lets you switch back and forth between the two panes at will. You can make changes in the Design view pane and watch the HTML code change in the Code view pane. Edits in the Code view pane aren't instantly reflected in the Design view, but you need only click in the Design view pane or click the Refresh button in the Property Inspector panel to see the results of your code edits.

Code Inspector Panel

Unlike Code view, the Code Inspector panel displays your document's HTML code in a separate panel window (see Figure 5-4) instead of in the main Document window. To view the HTML code for your document in the Code Inspector panel, do one of the following:

- Choose Window | Code Inspector.

- Press F10.

- Click the Code Inspector button in the Launcher panel or in the mini-launcher on the Document window status bar.

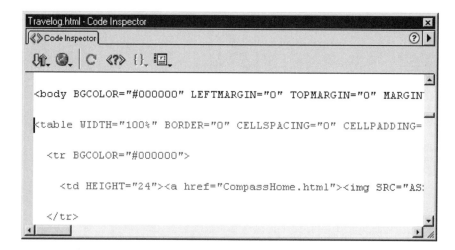

FIGURE 5-4 Code Inspector panel

The default size of the Code Inspector panel is smaller than the Document window, but you can resize the panel to any size you want. The Code Inspector panel, like Code view, automatically shows the code for whatever you select in Design view. Since the Code Inspector panel is separate from the Document window, you can see the code and the visual rendition of the page at the same time, much as in Code and Design view.

You can also open, close, move, and resize the Code Inspector panel independently. If your monitor is large enough, you can make both the Document window and the Code Inspector panel large enough to show a significant portion of the page, and you can arrange the windows any way you like. For example, you could set the Design view Document window and the Code Inspector panel side by side—an option that isn't available with the Code and Design view.

Edit Code

Editing code in Dreamweaver is a fairly straightforward process. After all, a web document is really a plain text file containing text and text-based HTML codes, so it's no surprise that editing HTML code is essentially the same process as editing text. It doesn't matter which of the Dreamweaver code editing windows you use—Code view, Code and Design view, or the Code Inspector panel—they all work the same.

Basically, when you edit code in Dreamweaver, you use the program as a fancy text editor. You can type HTML codes in Code view, just as you would any other text. And you can also select, move, insert, delete, and edit HTML codes just as you would any other text.

Of course, if you type HTML codes into Code view from scratch, you're on your own as far as getting all the codes and attributes entered with the proper syntax. But you're welcome to give it a go. Dreamweaver doesn't put any obstacles in your way.

CAUTION *Don't attempt to type HTML code directly into a document in Design view. Dreamweaver tries to render anything you type in Design view as text on the page and automatically formats angle brackets and other special characters so they are interpreted as text instead of codes. As a result, the HTML codes will look right in Design view but won't have the desired effect. If you need to enter HTML codes, switch to Code view or use the Quick Tag Editor.*

However, if you're like most Dreamweaver users, you'll rarely, if ever, enter HTML code from scratch. Instead, you'll probably let Dreamweaver build the code for the pages you create in Design view and then use Code view to examine that code and make occasional minor edits.

In addition to its basic text editing capabilities, Dreamweaver provides some special features just to make life easier when you work with HTML code. Check out these tips and techniques for manipulating code:

- To remove a tag while keeping the content, right-click the content in Design view, then choose Remove Tag from the context menu.

- To indent a line of code in Code view, select the line(s) of code and choose Edit | Indent Code. Choosing Edit | Outdent Code moves the selected line(s) to the left.

- To check for balanced tags, click the content inside the tag you want to check, then choose Edit | Select Parent Tag. Dreamweaver highlights the tags enclosing the selected content. Choose Edit | Select Parent Tag again to highlight the next level of nested tags.

- To insert a comment in your code, place the insertion point at the location where you want to add the comment and click the Comment button on the Invisibles page of the Objects panel, or choose Insert | Invisible Tags | Comment. Dreamweaver opens the Insert Comment dialog box. Type your comment in the dialog box and click OK.

> **TIP**   *Scrolling through a long document in Code view looking for a particular code can be tedious. It's usually easier to find what you're looking for in Design view. You can click the object on the page and then use the Tag Selector in the Design view status bar to select the tag. When you return to Code view (or the Code Inspector panel), the tag you selected in Design view is highlighted in Code view, too.*

How to ... Cut and Paste Code Snippets

Copying and pasting HTML code from one location to another in a web document or from one document to another works just as you would expect it to—as long as both the source and destination documents are in a Code view Document window (or the Code Inspector panel or the Code view portion of the Code and Design view).

1. Select the code and/or text you want to copy.

2. Press CTRL+C or choose Edit | Copy to copy the selected text.

3. Position the insertion point cursor where you want to insert the code and press CTRL+V or choose Edit | Paste.

You can even copy HTML code from an external text/programming editor such as HomeSite and paste it into Code view using the same technique.

If you attempt to use the same technique to paste HTML code into a document in Design view, the code will appear in the page as text instead of being inserted into the document as HTML code. This is a handy way to create a web page that describes HTML code without actually executing that code. If you want the HTML code to function as code, paste it into your document using the Edit | Paste as HTML command.

A companion command—Edit | Copy as HTML—enables you to copy text and codes from Design view as code instead of visible text so you can subsequently paste it into Code view.

Find and Replace Text and Code

Find and Replace is one of those features that you expect to find in any program that deals with handling text. Dreamweaver doesn't disappoint. The program includes a Find and Replace feature that works just the way you expect it to.

However, in addition to the obvious and expected ability to search for and replace plain text, Dreamweaver's Find and Replace command includes special features for working with code and for expanding Find and Replace operations beyond the current document to encompass selected documents or the entire site. The added features of the Find and Replace command dramatically increase its power and flexibility. You can use Dreamweaver's Find and Replace command to change a product name or other text that appears in a single document. Or you can use the command to locate every instance of a specific HTML code in every document in the entire site and change a specific attribute of those tags.

Set the Scope of a Search

Whether you're just searching for text or digging down into the details of HTML codes and attributes, you can control the scope of a search in Dreamweaver. The primary tool for determining how narrow or broad the search will be is the Find In list in the Find and Replace dialog box (see Figure 5-5). Here's a rundown of your options:

- To search a single document only, open the document and choose Edit | Find and Replace from the Document window's menu. In the Find and Replace dialog box, select Current Document from the Find In list box. Dreamweaver displays the document name to the right of the Find In box.

- To search selected files, first select the files in the Site window's Site Files list, then choose Edit | Find and Replace from the Site window menu. In the Find and Replace

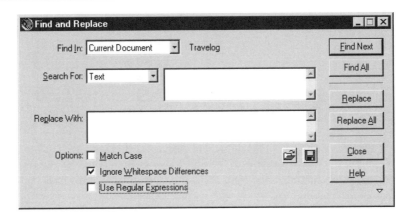

FIGURE 5-5   The Find and Replace dialog box

dialog box, click the Selected Files in Site option in the Find In list box. Dreamweaver displays the path to the folder containing the selected files to the right of the Find In box.

■ To search all the web document files in a particular folder, choose Edit | Find and Replace from the menu in either a Document window or the Site window. In the Find and Replace dialog box, select Folder... in the Find In list box, then click the folder icon that appears to the right of the Find In box to open the Choose Search Folder dialog box.

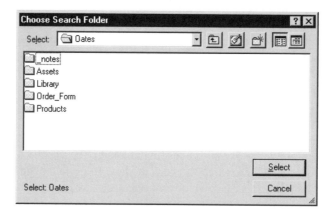

Locate and select the folder you want to search and click the Select button to close the dialog box and record the folder in the Find and Replace dialog box.

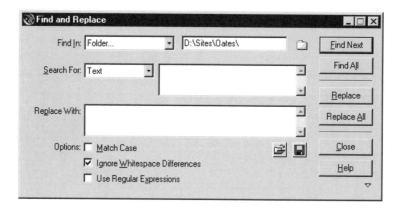

■ To search all web documents in the entire site, choose Edit | Find and Replace from the menu in either a Document window or the Site window. In the Find and Replace dialog box, select Entire Local Site in the Find In list box. Dreamweaver displays the site name to the right of the Find In box.

After you set the scope of the search, you can define the other search parameters and proceed with the search.

Search for Text

The simplest find and replace operation is a simple text search. When you search for text, Dreamweaver does just that—it searches the document text for a match to the text you enter in the Find and Replace dialog box. Dreamweaver ignores HTML codes when conducting a plain text search. When Dreamweaver finds a match, it selects the matching text and you have the option to replace it with the text you enter in the Replace With box in the Find and Replace dialog box. Here's the step-by-step procedure:

1. Choose Edit | Find and Replace to open the Find and Replace dialog box.

 Press CTRL+F *to open the Find and Replace dialog box.*

5

2. Select an option from the Find In list box to define the scope of the search.

3. Select Text in the Search For list box. Dreamweaver displays the text search options in the Find and Replace dialog box.

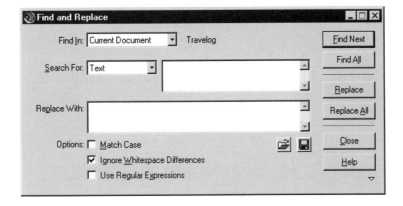

4. Enter the text you want to search for in the box to the right of the Search For box.

5. In the Replace With box, enter the text you want to replace the searched-for text.

6. Click the Find Next button. Dreamweaver locates the first instance of the text you specified and highlights it in the Document window.

7. To replace the selected text in the Document window with the text in the Replace With box in the Find and Replace dialog box, click the Replace button. To leave the selected text unchanged and continue the search, click the Find Next button. To automatically replace all instances of the search text, click the Replace All button.

8. Repeat step 7 until you reach the end of the document(s), then click the Close button to close the Find and Replace dialog box.

Press F3 *or choose Edit | Find Next to open the Find Next dialog box, which is an abbreviated version of the Find and Replace dialog box that includes only the Find options—no Replace options. Use the Find Next command to search for something that you don't necessarily want to change.*

Search Source Code

A source code search takes a simple text search one step farther by expanding the search to include HTML code as well as page text. So, for example, a search for the word "sailboat" might find the word in the text on page and also in the sailboat.gif filename of an image tag and in the `alt=` text attribute for that image.

Searching source code is an option if you start the Find and Replace operation from Design view—it's the default if you start the operation from Code view. The procedure for conducting a source code search is the same as for the simple text search described in the previous section of this chapter except that in step 3, you select Source Code in the Search For box.

Advanced Text Search

An advanced text search takes Dreamweaver's Find and Replace command to the next level of sophistication beyond text and source code searches. Not only does an advanced text search find text in source code as well as page text, the option lets you confine the search to specific tags and/or attributes or exclude specific tags or attributes.

1. Choose Edit | Find and Replace to open the Find and Replace dialog box.

2. Select an option from the Find In list box to define the scope of the search.

3. Select Text (Advanced) in the Search For list box. Dreamweaver displays the advanced text search options in the Find and Replace dialog box.

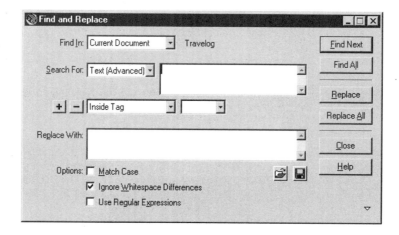

4. Enter the text you want to search for in the box to the right of the Search For box.

5. Select Inside Tag or Not Inside Tag in the list box below the Search For box and select the tag in the list box to the right.

6. To refine the search, click the plus (+) button to add another row of list boxes for selecting attributes, contents, and tags as needed. Select the search parameters and values. Repeat this step as needed to define the search. Dreamweaver expands the dialog box to accommodate the extra search specifications as shown here:

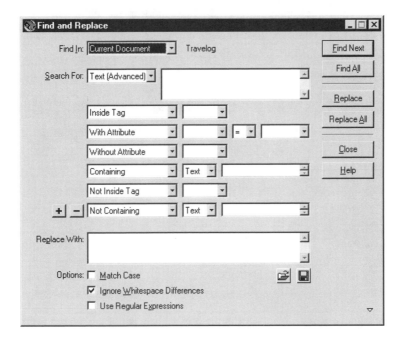

7. In the Replace With box, enter the text you want to replace the searched-for text.

8. Click the Find Next button. Dreamweaver locates the first instance of the search text that matches all the search conditions you specified and highlights it in the Document window.

9. To replace the selected text in the Document window with the text in the Replace With box in the Find and Replace dialog box, click the Replace button. To leave the selected text unchanged and continue the search, click the Find Next button. To automatically replace all instances of the search text, click the Replace All button.

10. Repeat step 9 until you reach the end of the document(s), then click the Close button to close the Find and Replace dialog box.

Search Specific Tags

A specific tag search does away with the text part of a find and replace operation and searches your document's HTML code for a specific tag. You can refine the search by specifying attributes, contents, and nested tags.

You also have several options for the action Dreamweaver can perform on the found tag. You can change attributes, insert and delete contents, and more. Here's the procedure for a Specific Tag search:

1. Choose Edit | Find and Replace to open the Find and Replace dialog box.

2. Select an option from the Find In list box to define the scope of the search.

3. Select Specific Tag in the Search For list box. Dreamweaver displays the specific tag options in the Find and Replace dialog box.

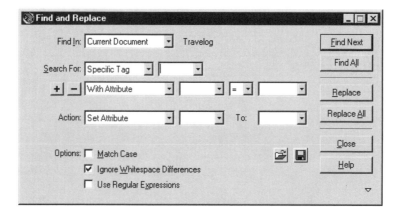

4. Select the tag you want to search for in the box to the right of the Search For box.

5. In the row of list boxes below the Search For box, select the options and settings to refine the search. Continue to refine the search in subsequent rows.

6. Click the plus (+) button to add another row of list boxes or click the minus (−) button to delete unneeded rows of list boxes. Dreamweaver expands the dialog box to accommodate the extra search specifications. Repeat steps 5 and 6 as needed.

7. Select options and enter or select values in the Action row of list boxes to define what action Dreamweaver takes when you click the Replace or Replace All buttons. You can select any of the following actions and then specify a value to add, or replace.

   ■ Replace Tag & Contents
   ■ Replace Contents Only
   ■ Remove Tag and Contents
   ■ Strip Tag

- Change Tag
- Set Attribute
- Remove Attribute
- Add Before Start Tag
- Add After End Tag
- Add After Start Tag
- Add Before End Tag

8. Click the Find Next button. Dreamweaver locates the first instance of the tag that matches all the search conditions you specified and highlights it in the Document window.

9. To perform the action you specified in the Action row, click the Replace button. To leave the selected tag unchanged and continue the search, click the Find Next button. To automatically perform the action on all instances of the search tag, click the Replace All button.

TIP   *Clicking the Find All button in the Find and Replace dialog box generates a list of all instances of the search text in the current document or, in a search of multiple documents, a list of all documents containing the search text.*

10. Repeat step 9 until you reach the end of the document(s), then click the Close button to close the Find and Replace dialog box.

Other Search Options

As if all the text, tag, and attribute options weren't enough—there are three check boxes at the bottom of the Find and Replace dialog box that enable you to expand or limit your searches. Click the check boxes to enable or disable each search option. The options are as follows:

- **Match Case**   Check this option to cause the search to be case sensitive.
- **Ignore Whitespace Differences**   Check this option to ignore spaces, paragraph ends, and line breaks when matching the search text.
- **Use Regular Expressions**   When checked, this option enables you to use special wildcard characters in the search text. The list of regular expressions you can use is long, but you can find the whole list in Dreamweaver's online help. Choose Help | Using Dreamweaver to open the help file in a browser window. Click Index, then click R, then click Regular Expressions to display the complete list of expressions and their meanings.

Locate and Correct Code Errors

Dreamweaver helps you locate and correct code errors by highlighting invalid tags in bright yellow. The program highlights HTML tags that it doesn't support and also common errors such as extra end tags left in the code after you delete the corresponding start tag.

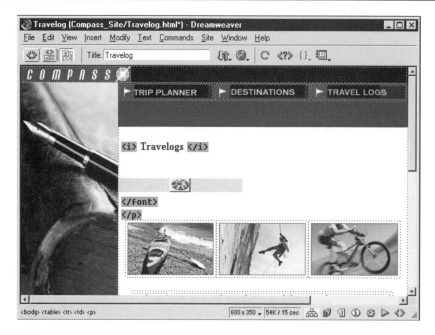

FIGURE 5-6   Invalid HTML code highlighted in Design view

In Design view, the invalid HTML tags appear as bold text with a bright yellow highlight, as shown in Figure 5-6. It really stands out, because no other code is normally visible in Design view. When you click a highlighted code, Dreamweaver displays information in the Property Inspector panel describing why the code is highlighted and suggesting corrective action.

Invalid HTML highlighting is a little more subtle in Code view (or the Code Inspector panel). Dreamweaver highlights the tag with the same bright yellow, but it isn't bold and it remains in context with the rest of the source code (see Figure 5-7). Again, when you click the highlighted tag, Dreamweaver displays information in the Property Inspector panel.

You can turn the Highlight Invalid HTML feature on and off in Code view by clicking the View Options button on the toolbar and choosing Highlight Invalid HTML from the pop-up menu.

This option isn't available in Design view.

Edit Scripts

When you use Dreamweaver to add behaviors and other features that require JavaScript or VBScript, Dreamweaver normally handles inserting and maintaining the script code for you. You work with Dreamweaver dialog boxes, not the script code itself. However, Dreamweaver

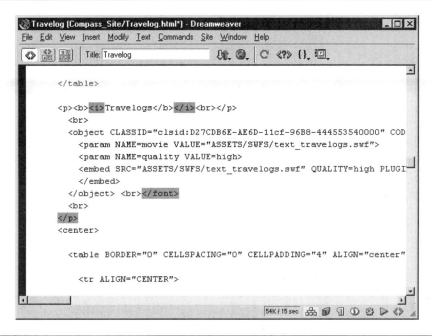

FIGURE 5-7   Invalid HTML code highlighted in Code view

also enables you to write and edit your own scripts if you have the desire and the programming background to do so. You can also edit any of the scripts Dreamweaver creates.

Editing scripts in Code view (or the Code Inspector panel) is a straightforward process. You edit the script code just as you edit any other text or HTML code in the Code view window.

Editing scripts in Design view is a bit more complicated, if only because scripts aren't normally visible in Design view. Here's how you do it:

1. Choose View | Head Content to display the Head Content pane across the top of the Document window as shown here:

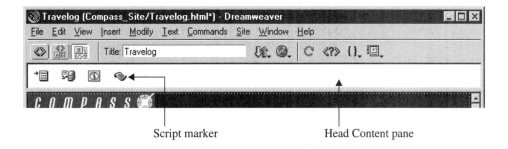

Script marker   Head Content pane

2. Select the Script marker in the Head Content pane. Dreamweaver displays information about the script(s) in the Property Inspector panel.

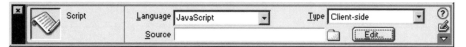

3. Click the Edit button in the Property Inspector panel. Dreamweaver opens the Script Properties dialog box as shown in Figure 5-8. The dialog box shows the contents of the `<script>` tag in your document, which may include several individual scripts.

If the script entry in your web document contains only a link to an external script file, Dreamweaver opens that file in Code view instead of opening the Script Properties dialog box.

4. Edit the script (or scripts) as needed.

5. Click OK to close the Script Properties dialog box and record your changes.

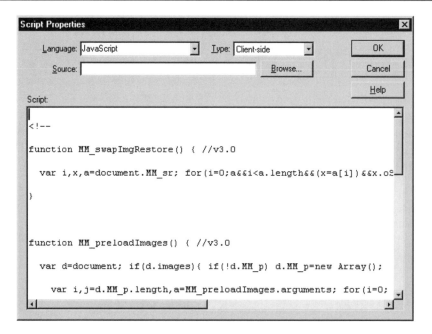

FIGURE 5-8 Edit a script in the Script Properties dialog box.

Set Code Viewing Options

Dreamweaver lets you exercise control over several aspects of the appearance of the HTML source code in Code view and the Code Inspector panel. You can easily enable or disable several code viewing options and you can set fairly detailed preferences for colors and formatting, as well as controlling whether and how much Dreamweaver rewrites imported code to match your Dreamweaver specifications.

The code viewing options are readily accessible, as is appropriate for options that you might want to change as you work. To access these options, just click the View Options button on the toolbar in the Code view or Code Inspector panel windows.

Clicking the View Options button opens a pop-up menu where you can enable and disable options. (The same options are available on the View | Code View Options menu.) A check mark designates an active option. Click an option to enable or disable it. You can choose any combination of the following code viewing options:

- **Line Wrap**   Wraps lines of code so that it's visible within the Code view window without scrolling side to side.

- **Highlight Invalid HTML**   Marks invalid HTML tags with a bright yellow highlight. (See the section, "Locate and Correct Code Errors," earlier in this chapter.)

- **Syntax Coloring**   Uses color to mark different codes and code elements to make it easier to identify those elements in the Code view window. You can adjust the specific colors Dreamweaver uses and the codes to which the colors apply in the Code Colors category of the Preferences dialog box (see Chapter 20).

- **Auto Indent**   Automatically indents the code. You can specify which tags indent and the indent spacing in the Code Format category of the Preferences dialog box (see Chapter 20).

All the code viewing options affect only the way the code displays in the Code view or Code Inspector panel window. None of the code viewing options changes the source code itself.

For more detailed control over the code viewing options and other code handling options you can adjust the settings in the Preferences dialog box (see Chapter 20). You can set preferences in the following categories:

- **Code Colors**   Set general background and foreground colors for the Code view window and also colors for use by the Syntax Coloring view option. You can specify colors for individual HTML tags if you want.

- **Code Format**   Set formatting options such as line length and indenting.

- **Code Rewriting**   Control whether and what kind of changes Dreamweaver makes to the code when you open a web document in Dreamweaver.

- **Fonts/Encoding**   Select the font Dreamweaver uses to display code in Code view and the Code Inspector panel.

5

Import Code from Other Programs

Dreamweaver provides a fairly complete web site development environment, so, in theory, you could create and edit web pages and maintain web sites using just Dreamweaver and its companion programs, such as Fireworks—you wouldn't need to use any other programs. However, the reality is that most Dreamweaver users must work with web documents from a variety of sources and often use several different tools over the course of developing a single HTML document. So, Macromedia wisely designed Dreamweaver to cooperate nicely with other programs that may manipulate the HTML source code for a web document.

The HTML code that Dreamweaver produces is not only viewable in standard web browsers, it also works in other HTML editing programs. And Dreamweaver respects the HTML code produced by other programs as well. As a result, you can move HTML source code from Dreamweaver to another program, generate and edit code in the external program, and then reopen the web document in Dreamweaver with minimal (if any) compatibility problems.

Macromedia also realized that some other HTML editing programs (or programmers) generate source code containing invalid tags, sloppy formatting, and other undesirable characteristics. So Dreamweaver includes commands that enable you to automatically clean up and repair the common errors found in the HTML source code generated by other programs.

Roundtrip Code

Roundtrip HTML is the name Macromedia gives to the Dreamweaver feature that lets you move HTML source code back and forth between Dreamweaver and a text-based HTML editor without having the code mangled in the process. Roundtrip HTML isn't a command you'll find on any menu in Dreamweaver—it's more of a design philosophy that is evident in the way Macromedia implemented Dreamweaver's HTML code-handling features.

Roundtrip HTML works exceptionally well with HomeSite and BBEdit, which are both text-based HTML editors that come packaged with Dreamweaver. Roundtrip HTML also does its thing with other text-based HTML editors, and it even works tolerably well with some other graphical HTML editors. (But if you use Dreamweaver, why would you want to use any other graphical HTML editor?)

Dreamweaver always generates technically valid HTML code for any additions and changes you make to a web document in Design view. This ensures that the HTML source code Dreamweaver produces is compatible with any standards-compliant web browser or HTML editor. That's one part of Roundtrip HTML.

The other part of Roundtrip HTML is respect for differences in the HTML source code generated by other programs. When you open an HTML document in Dreamweaver, the program doesn't automatically make wholesale changes in the document to conform to the "Dreamweaver way" of writing code. This feature is a marked contrast to some other HTML editing programs on the market. However, it doesn't mean that Dreamweaver takes a totally "hands-off" approach to every HTML document it opens. Actually, Dreamweaver automatically finds and corrects numerous common errors in the HTML source code any time you open a web document. You can change the default settings to prevent Dreamweaver from making some of the changes, and you can specify file extensions that will not be rewritten at all. Here's an overview of the way Dreamweaver treats HTML source code:

- Reorders overlapping tags to create proper nesting
- Creates missing closing tags and removes extra closing tags
- Makes no change to any unrecognized tags, such as XML tags
- Makes no change to ColdFusion Markup Language or Active Server Pages tags

You can disable even this limited automatic code cleanup by changing the settings in the Code Rewriting category of the Preferences dialog box (see Chapter 20).

Clean Up Your Code

5

In addition to the basic code cleanup that Dreamweaver performs when you open a web document, you can instruct the program to execute more extensive cleanup and repair when they are called for. You can choose from a general code cleanup command or one tailored to the unique challenge of dealing with HTML code produced by Microsoft Word.

TIP

There is an extension available to add a Clean Up FrontPage HTML command to Dreamweaver. See Appendix B for more information on extensions.

Clean Up HTML Code

When you want to do a more thorough code cleanup on a web document than Dreamweaver does automatically, the Clean Up HTML command will get the job done. You might use this command when editing an older web document or after opening a document produced in another program. You can also use this command to remove Dreamweaver-specific comments (such as template areas and library items) from a web document before sending it to someone who doesn't have Dreamweaver.

To clean up the HTML source code in a web document, follow these steps:

1. Open the document you want to clean up.

2. Choose Commands | Clean Up HTML. Dreamweaver opens the Clean Up HTML dialog box.

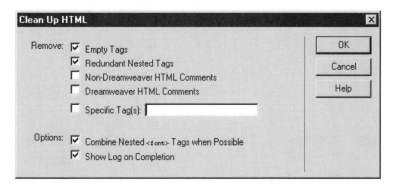

3. Select the cleanup options by clicking the check boxes in the dialog box. You can select any combination of the following:

- ■ **Remove Empty Tags**   Removes any pair of opening and closing tags that don't enclose any content. This cleans up any unneeded tags that were left behind after you deleted the content to which they applied.

- ■ **Remove Redundant Nested Tags**   Removes nested copies of the same tag, such as removing the bold (<b>) tag around a word within a sentence that is also tagged as bold.

- ■ **Remove Non-Dreamweaver HTML Comments**   Removes any comments that were inserted into the code by other programs (or programmers).

- ■ **Remove Dreamweaver HTML Comments**   Removes any comments inserted into the source code by Dreamweaver. This includes comments that mark template areas and library items. Use this cleanup option with caution, because it "breaks" the Dreamweaver features that rely on comments inserted into the code.

CAUTION   *Removing Dreamweaver HTML comments converts Dreamweaver templates and library items in the document to plain HTML, thus breaking the connection to the master template and library items for the site. After removing the Dreamweaver HTML comments, template and library items in this document won't update automatically when you change the site's master template and library.*

- ■ **Remove Specific Tag(s)**   Removes the specific tag(s) identified in the text box to the right of the option. Use this option to remove valid but unwanted HTML tags, such as the obnoxious <blink> tag.

- ■ **Combine Nested <font> Tags When Possible**   Consolidates nested <font> tags that apply to the same text into a single pair of opening and closing tags with multiple attributes.

- ■ **Show Log On Completion**   Displays an optional alert box on completion of the cleanup process that shows statistics on how many changes were made to the code.

4. Click OK to close the Clean Up HTML dialog box and begin the cleanup. Dreamweaver rewrites the HTML code, correcting the errors as specified. The process takes a few moments to complete; how long depends on the size of the web document and the speed of your computer.

Clean Up Microsoft Word HTML Code

Microsoft Word (Word 97 and later) can save documents in HTML format as well as its own proprietary .doc file format. Word can also reopen the HTML documents it creates while keeping much of the formatting and special word processing features intact. However, to work this magic, Word inserts a lot of nonstandard code and custom CSS styles in the HTML files it creates. In a document that's destined for viewing in a web browser instead of editing in Word, all those extra codes are just so much garbage cluttering up the source code.

Dreamweaver includes a special command to help clean up HTML documents created in Word and remove the Word-specific markup. The result is a document that is more compact, faster to load, and much easier to read and work on in an HTML editor.

To clean up an HTML document generated by Microsoft Word, follow these steps.

1. Open the document you want to clean up.

2. Choose Commands | Clean Up Word HTML. Dreamweaver opens the Clean Up Word HTML dialog box and attempts to determine what version of Word created the document.

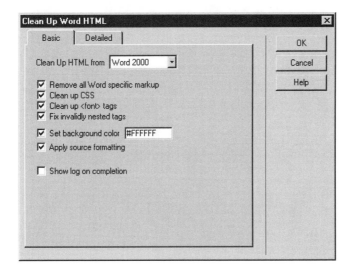

TIP   *Dreamweaver automatically runs the Clean Up Word HTML command when you import Word HTML into a Dreamweaver document.*

3. Select the correct Word version in the Clean Up Word HTML From list box.

4. Select the cleanup options by clicking the check boxes on the Basic tab of the dialog box. You can select any combination of the following:

- **Remove All Word Specific Markup**   Removes Word-specific markup such as meta data, XML markup, conditional tags, and empty paragraphs. You can select specific groups of markup to remove on the Detailed tab.

- **Clean Up CSS**   Removes Word-specific CSS styles such as inline styles, CSS styles in tables, and so on. You can select specific groups of CSS markup to remove on the Detailed tab.

- **Clean Up <font> Tags**   Removes multiple <font> tags and sets the default body text size to 2.

- **Fix Invalidly Nested Tags**   Removes invalid <font> tags outside paragraph tags.

- **Set Background Color** Enter a hexadecimal value for a background color for the page to replace the dull gray default background that Word uses. The Dreamweaver default (#FFFFFF) is white.

- **Apply Source Formatting** Applies source formatting (line lengths and indenting) according to the preferences you set for other Dreamweaver documents.

- **Show Log On Completion** Displays an optional alert box upon completion of the cleanup process that shows statistics on how many changes were made to the code.

5. Click the Detailed tab to display the following options:

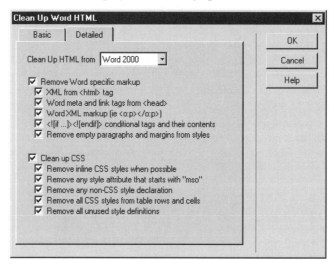

6. Select the detail options for the Remove Word Specific Markup and Clean Up CSS categories.

7. Click OK to close the Clean Up Word HTML dialog box and begin the cleanup. Dreamweaver rewrites the HTML code, correcting the errors as specified. The process takes a few moments to complete; how long depends on the size of the web document and the speed of your computer.

 *After cleaning up the Word HTML, Word will still be able to open the resulting document, but many of the special word processing features will be unavailable. Be sure to save a copy of the document in Word's .doc format before you alter the HTML code.*

Use External HTML Editors

Although Dreamweaver offers built-in code editing capabilities, Macromedia realizes that true code warriors would undoubtedly prefer to use their favorite editor when editing HTML source code. Dreamweaver is designed to enable you to switch easily to and from an external editor. As a result, it's easy to use Dreamweaver for visual editing in Design view and your favorite text-based editor for working with HTML source code.

When you want to use the external editor, Dreamweaver automatically saves the current document and launches your preferred external editor with instructions to open the current document. When you return to Dreamweaver, the program automatically checks the status of the document file and prompts you to refresh the Document window if it detects any changes made by the external editor.

Dreamweaver ships with a full copy of Allaire HomeSite (Windows) or BBEdit (Macintosh) on the program CD-ROM. If you install one of these text-based editors along with Dreamweaver, the install routine automatically configures Dreamweaver to use it as your external editor for HTML files. If you want to set up another program as your external editor, see the instructions in Chapter 20.

5

Use the Quick Tag Editor

Working with HTML code in Design view is a little different from editing code in Code view. Normally, you don't see any HTML code in Design view. You drag, drop, and otherwise manipulate text and objects visually, not by editing HTML tags. To change the attributes of an object, you select options from the Property Inspector panel. Dreamweaver takes care of the HTML for you, creating and editing the source code to reflect the changes you make in the Design view window.

However, there are times when the best way to get something done is to enter or edit HTML code directly. For any substantial changes to the HTML source code you'll want to use Code view or the Code Inspector panel, but for quick edits and additions, the Quick Tag Editor is a handy tool. You can use it to insert an HTML code or to inspect and edit a tag without having to switch to Code view or open the Code Inspector panel.

To insert an HTML tag using the Quick Tag Editor, follow these steps:

1. Place the insertion point cursor in the document where you want to insert the code.

2. Press CTRL+T or click the Quick Tag Editor icon in the Property Inspector panel. Dreamweaver opens the Quick Tag Editor in Insert HTML mode. After a short pause, a drop-down list of HTML tags appears.

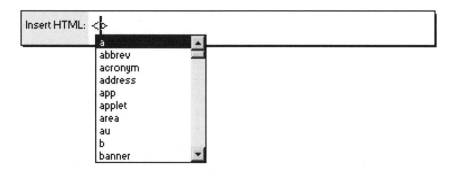

3. Type an HTML tag into the Quick Tag Editor between the angle brackets, or select one from the drop-down list.

4. Edit the tag by adding attributes or other options as needed.

5. Press ENTER to close the Quick Tag Editor and insert the tag into the HTML source code for your page. Press the CANCEL key to close the Quick Tag Editor without entering the code into your document.

You can also use the Quick Tag Editor to edit existing HTML tags. The process is basically the same as for inserting an HTML code in Design view, except that, instead of positioning the insertion point, you select a tag by selecting the text or object to which the tag applies and/or using the Tag Selector in the status bar. When you open the Quick Tag Editor with an existing tag selected, it opens in Edit mode.

You can edit the tag, add and edit attributes, and so on. After editing the tag, press ENTER to close the Quick Tag Editor and record your changes to the web document.

If you select some unformatted text or an object that isn't currently enclosed by an HTML tag and then open the Quick Tag Editor, the Quick Tag Editor opens in Wrap Tag mode. Wrap Tag mode is the same as the Insert Tag mode, except that Dreamweaver will insert the tag and its closing tag so that they enclose the selected text or object.

```
Wrap Tag: <>
```

View and Edit Head Content

Naturally, the visible portion of a web page—the section marked by the `<body>` tag and displayed in the web browser—gets most of the attention. But the other required section of an HTML document—the header, marked by the `<head>` tag—contains some important information as well. The document title, meta tags, and scripts are just some of the contents of the document header. Except for the title, these elements are invisible, but their effects aren't.

You can view and edit the contents of the document header in Code view or in the Code Inspector panel by simply scrolling up to the top of the HTML source code and working with the code between the `<head>` and `</head>` tags.

To access head content in Design view you need to first display the Head Content pane in the Document window by choosing View | Head Content. The head content appears as a row of icons in a pane across the top of the document in Design view, as shown in Figure 5-9.

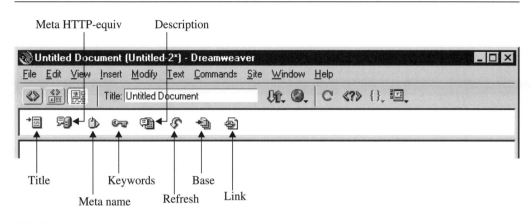

FIGURE 5-9   The Head Content pane

To view or edit the contents of any of the head content, click an icon in the Head Content pane. Dreamweaver displays the head content in the Property Inspector panel. To insert new head tags, choose Insert | Head Tags | *tag*. The available head tags include:

- ■ **Meta**   Define generic meta tags
- ■ **Keywords**   Enter keywords for search engines to use for indexing your page
- ■ **Description**   Enter a description for your page—another bit of information used by search engines
- ■ **Refresh**   Instruct the browser to automatically reload the current page or go to another URL after a specified delay
- ■ **Base**   Set a base URL for all relative links in the document
- ■ **Link**   Define a link between the document and another document

When you choose one of the Insert | Head Tag commands, Dreamweaver opens a small dialog box where you can enter or select attributes and values for the tag. Enter the tag options and click OK to close the dialog box and add the tag to your document.

Part III

Go Beyond the Basics

Chapter 6

Create and Edit Tables

How to...

- Insert a table into your document
- Work with table rows, columns, and cells
- Format tables
- Add content to tables
- Create nesting tables

Everyone knows how to build a table. You start with a large flat top, add four legs, and...
Oops, wrong table!

The tables that appear on web pages aren't the top-and-four-legs kind; they're the columns-and-rows kind—the same kind of table that gives spreadsheets their structure and is the basis for invoices, airline schedules, price lists, and most anything else that arranges blocks of text into columns and rows.

Undoubtedly, you've seen many examples of tabular matter on various web sites. But the obvious examples of tabular matter are just the tip of the iceberg of table use on the Web. HTML tables are so versatile that web designers use them as general-purpose positioning tools to control web page layout. After all, tables are just a way to provide structure for content by defining horizontal and vertical spacing and position. What makes tables so versatile is the fact that each table *cell* (the space defined by the intersection of a row and a column) is a container that can hold just about anything you can place on a web page, including text, images, media objects, and even smaller tables.

So, HTML tables have two applications on the Web. First, tables provide the means for presenting traditional tabular matter in neatly arranged columns and rows. Second, and even more important, tables are the leading page layout tool.

Dreamweaver has always had the ability to create and manipulate HTML tables visually in Design view. However, because tables are so widely used as a layout tool, Macromedia added a special feature to Dreamweaver 4 called *Layout Tables*. This feature is really just a special way of representing HTML tables in Design view, which makes it easier to work with tables and table cells as layout elements rather than just tabular matter.

This chapter covers the basics of working with HTML tables in Dreamweaver. You can use the information in this chapter to create tables for presenting traditional tabular matter or to create tables for page layout. Chapter 7 explores the new Layout Tables feature and how to use it to create and edit tables in Layout view.

Insert a Table

The HTML code for a table can be complicated, with separate tags for the table, for each row within the table, and for each column within the row. All those codes must be properly nested within one another, and the content and tags marking the content must be nested within the table tags. Fortunately, you don't have to mess with the intricacies of the HTML source code unless you really want to—you can create, edit, format, and fill your tables entirely in the visual-editing environment of Dreamweaver's Design view.

To add a table to your web page, follow these steps:

1. Position the insertion point cursor at the location in the document where you want to place the table.

2. Use one of the following techniques to open the Insert Table dialog box.

   ■ Choose Insert | Table from the menu.

   ■ Click the Table button on the Common pane of the Objects panel.

   ■ Drag the Table button from the Objects panel and drop it at the desired location in the Design view window.

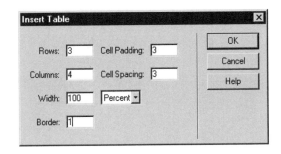

3. Enter the appropriate settings in the dialog box to specify the initial table configuration. You can edit all these values later. You may enter the following settings:

   ■ **Rows**   Specify the number of table rows.

   ■ **Columns**   Specify the number of table columns.

   ■ **Width**   Enter a number and then select Percent or Pixels to specify the width of the table.

   ■ **Border**   Enter the thickness of the table border (in pixels).

   ■ **Cell Padding**   Enter the number of pixels of space between the edge of a cell and the contents of the cell.

   ■ **Cell Spacing**   Enter the number of pixel space between adjacent cells.

4. Click OK to close the Insert Table dialog box and create the table. Dreamweaver enters the HTML code for the table into your web document and displays the empty table in Design view, as shown in Figure 6-1.

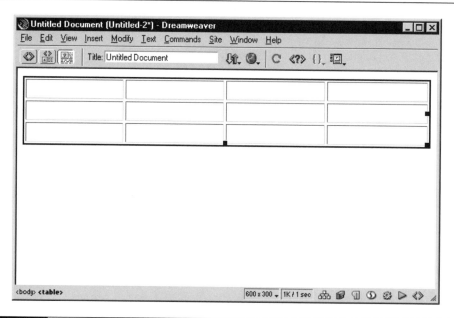

FIGURE 6-1   An empty 3-row, 4-column table in Design view

If you defined borders for the table, one border of a specified thickness surrounds the table and each cell is outlined with a 1-pixel line. If you set the Border to zero, Dreamweaver shows the table and cells outlined with a dashed line.

TIP   *If the dashed lines designating the table don't appear, choose View | Visual Aids | Table Borders to display the invisible table borders.*

Just for grins, here's the HTML code for the simple table shown in Figure 6-1. Note the table tags (`<table>`), the row tags (`<tr>`), and the cell tags (`<td>`). Each cell contains a single nonbreaking space character (` `) as a placeholder.

```
<table width="100%" border="1" cellspacing="2" cellpadding="1">
  <tr>
    <td> </td>
    <td> </td>
    <td> </td>
    <td> </td>
  </tr>
```

```
<tr>
  <td> </td>
  <td> </td>
  <td> </td>
  <td> </td>
</tr>
<tr>
  <td> </td>
  <td> </td>
  <td> </td>
  <td> </td>
</tr>
</table>
```

6

Select and Edit Tables and Cells

After you create a table, you have a lot of flexibility and control over the shape and the configuration of the table. You can change every aspect of the table arrangement. You can select and manipulate the table as a whole, one or more rows or columns, or one or more individual cells. You can resize the table; add, delete, and resize rows and columns; and merge cells so they span multiple rows or columns.

Select Table Cells, Rows, and Columns

Of course, before you can effectively manipulate a table, you must to be able to select the table, or the portion of the table, that you want to change.

Select the Entire Table

To select the entire table, use any of the following techniques:

- Click anywhere within the table; then click the `<table>` tag in the Tag Selector in the status bar.
- Click the bottom or right border of the table.
- Right-click anywhere within the table and choose Table | Select Table from the context menu that appears.
- Click anywhere within the table and choose Modify | Table | Select Table.

Dreamweaver highlights the selection with a bold line surrounding the table and sizing handles (small black squares) on the bottom and right edges.

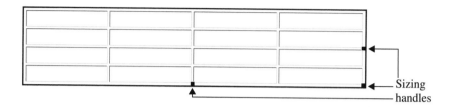

Sizing
handles

Select Table Rows or Columns

You can use Dreamweaver's special selection pointer to select one or more rows or columns in a table.

- ■ To select a row, move the mouse pointer to the left border of the table, beside the row you want to select. After a brief pause, the pointer changes to a small, solid black arrow pointing to the right.

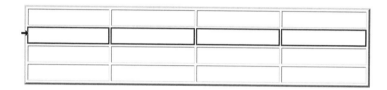

Click to select the row the pointer is on, or drag to select multiple rows.

- ■ To select a column, move the mouse pointer to the top border of the table to activate the column selection pointer, which points down instead of to the right.

You can verify that you have selected a table, row, column, or cell by checking the Property Inspector panel. Make sure the Property Inspector panel is expanded to show all the options (click the arrowhead button in the lower-right corner); then check the table icon and label at the left end of the Property Inspector panel.

Select Individual Table Cells

To select an individual cell, CTRL+click within the cell. Dreamweaver highlights the selected cell with a bold outline around the cell border. For many operations, it's sufficient to simply click within the cell, since Dreamweaver displays the cell properties in the Property Inspector panel along with the properties of text and other contents of the cell.

To select multiple cells, click and drag across the cells you want to select. You can also select multiple cells by selecting the first cell and then CTRL+clicking additional cells. If you select one cell and then SHIFT+click another cell, Dreamweaver selects both cells and also selects any cells located between the two.

Add and Delete Table Rows and Columns

You can quickly and easily expand or reduce the size of your table by adding or deleting columns or rows. The process for adding rows and columns is essentially the same, the only difference being that you choose the Insert Row command for one and the Insert Column command for the other. Whether you're adding rows or columns, you can use any of the following techniques:

- Click a row (or column) in the table and choose Modify | Table | Insert Row (or Insert Column). Dreamweaver inserts a blank row (or column) into the table immediately below (or to the right of) the selected row.

- Right-click a cell in the table and choose Table | Insert Row (or Insert Column) from the context menu that appears. Again, Dreamweaver inserts a blank row (or column) into the table immediately below (or to the right of) the selected cell.

- To insert multiple rows or columns, select a cell in the table and choose Modify | Table | Insert Rows or Columns (or right-click a cell and choose Table | Insert Rows or Columns from the context menu). Dreamweaver opens the Insert Rows or Columns dialog box.

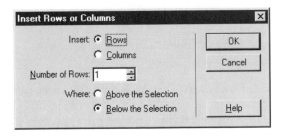

In the dialog box, select Rows (or Columns) to Insert, specify the Number of Rows (or Columns), and choose Where to insert the new rows (either above or below for rows, or left or right for columns); then click OK to close the dialog box and insert the rows or columns into your table.

 *As you enter content into the table, Dreamweaver automatically adds rows to the table to accommodate additional content. Simply position the insertion point cursor in the rightmost cell of the bottom row of the table and press TAB to move the insertion point to the next cell. Dreamweaver adds a new row to the bottom of the table and moves the insertion point to the first cell in the row.*

You can use similar techniques to delete rows or columns from your table.

- Click anywhere in the row or column you want to delete and choose Modify | Table | Delete Row (or Delete Column). Dreamweaver removes the selected row or column from the table.

- Right-click anywhere in the row or column you want to delete and choose Table | Delete Row (or Delete Column) from the context menu. Dreamweaver removes the selected row or column from the table.

- Select an entire row or column and press the DELETE key.

You can also use the Property Inspector panel to change the size of your table. Select the entire table and then change the number in the Rows or Cols boxes in the Property Inspector panel. Dreamweaver adds or removes rows on the bottom or columns on the right side to adjust the table to the specified size.

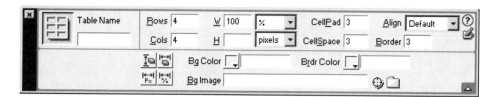

Resize Tables, Rows, and Columns

In addition to adding and removing rows and columns of cells in your table, you can adjust the size of the table as a whole and also control the height of individual rows and the width of individual columns.

- To adjust the table size visually, select the table and drag the sizing handles to resize the table. Drag the sizing handle on the right border to adjust table width. Drag the sizing handle on the bottom border to adjust table height. Drag the sizing handle in the lower-right corner to adjust both height and width simultaneously.

- Select the table and adjust the values in the W and H boxes in the Property Inspector panel. You can set table size in pixels or as a percentage (%) of the browser window.

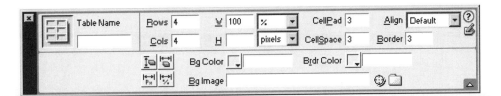

When you resize the whole table, Dreamweaver resizes all table cells proportionally, unless you previously specified a fixed size for one or more cells, in which case those cells retain their fixed size and the remaining cells resize along with the table.

■ To adjust the width of a column visually, drag the right side of the column left or right. Dreamweaver adjusts the widths of all the cells in the column.

■ To adjust the height of a row visually, drag the bottom of the row up or down. Dreamweaver adjusts the height of all the cells in the row.

■ To set column width, select a column and enter a width in the W box in the Property Inspector panel. You can enter a number to set the width in pixels or a number followed by the percent sign (%) to specify the column width as a percentage of the table width.

Leave the height and width settings for columns, rows, and cells blank in the Property Inspector panel to allow the browser to dynamically resize table cells as needed to fit table content.

■ To set row height, select a row and enter a height in the H box in the Property Inspector panel. You can enter a number to set the height in pixels or a number followed by the percent sign (%) to specify the row height as a percentage of the table height.

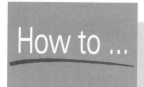

How to ... Convert Height and Width from Pixels to Percent

As you make adjustments to the width of a table, you may find it easier to work in pixels even though you want to set the finished table sizes in percentages, or vice versa. Go ahead and use the measurement that is most comfortable or convenient. Dreamweaver can convert the measurements for you later. When you get the table the way you want it, select the table and then choose Modify | Table | Convert Widths to Percent (or Convert Widths to Pixels). Dreamweaver converts the table and column widths to percent or pixel measurements.

Cells That Span Columns and Rows

Sometimes you need to create a table that includes a cell that spreads out over more than one column or row. Or perhaps you need to divide one cell into two while the remaining cells in that column or row remain unaffected. Well, HTML tables can do that, and Dreamweaver makes this task easy.

The HTML term for joining one or more cells is *span*, but Dreamweaver uses the more descriptive term *merge*. The Dreamweaver term for dividing one cell into multiple cells is *split*.

To merge two or more adjacent cells, follow these steps:

1. Click and drag to select the cells you want to merge. The cells to be merged must be adjacent to each other and form a single rectangular shape.

2. Click the Merge Cells button in the Property Inspector panel, or choose Modify | Table | Merge Cells.

Dreamweaver combines the selected cells into a single cell (shown next) and inserts all the necessary code in your web document.

To split a single cell into multiple cells, follow these steps:

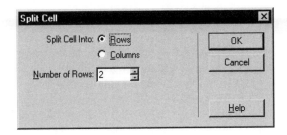

1. Select the cell you want to split.

2. Click the Split Cell button in the Property Inspector panel, or choose Modify | Table | Split Cell. Dreamweaver opens the Split Cell dialog box.

3. Select Rows or Columns to instruct Dreamweaver to split the cell horizontally or vertically.

4. Enter the number of cells to make out of the selected cell.

5. Click OK to close the Split Cell dialog box and split the selected cell. Dreamweaver displays the result in Design view and inserts the necessary code in your web document to create the additional cells.

Format Tables

There's more to formatting tables than just setting the number of rows and columns, the width of the columns, and the height of the rows. You can customize the appearance of your tables with background and border colors, cell spacing, cell padding, border thickness, and alignment on the page. You can also exercise similar control over each row, column, and cell in the table.

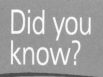

Did you know?

Table Formatting Hierarchy

Table formatting follows a hierarchy, which means that settings you apply at one level in the table can override settings applied at a different level. And the hierarchy of which levels take precedence over which other levels may be different from what you might expect. Basically, the rule is that detailed formatting takes precedence over general formatting.

For example, you can set the background color of cells in a table for the entire table, for all the cells in a row, or for individual cells. In this case, the cell formatting takes precedence over the row formatting, which takes precedence over the table formatting. If you set the background color of some rows or individual cells in a table and then later change the background color for the entire table, the table color won't apply to the rows or cells that have their own color settings, since those more detailed settings override the general table background color. However, any cells that don't have their own background color will take on the background color specified for the table.

Set Table Properties

To control the formatting for a table, select the table and adjust the settings in the Property Inspector panel. When working with table properties, be sure to click the expander button in the lower-right corner of the Property Inspector panel to display all the table properties. Here's a rundown on the table formatting attributes:

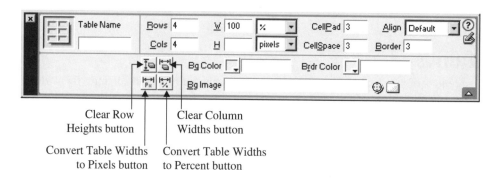

Clear Row Heights button
Clear Column Widths button
Convert Table Widths to Pixels button
Convert Table Widths to Percent button

- **Table Name**   Enter a short name for the table. It's optional and only for your reference.
- **Rows**   Set the number of rows in the table.
- **Cols**   Set the number of columns in the table.
- **W (Width)**   Set the width of the table. Enter a number, and select pixels or % (percent). Percent measurements specify a percentage of the browser window.

- **H (Height)**   Set the height of the table. Enter a number, and select pixels or % (percent). Percent measurements specify a percentage of the browser window.

- **CellPad (Cell Padding)**   The space (in pixels) between the cell border and the cell content. Enter 0 to specify no cell padding. If you leave this blank, the browser displays the table with cell padding of 2 pixels.

- **CellSpace (Cell Spacing)**   The space (in pixels) between cells. Enter 0 to specify no cell spacing. If you leave this blank, the browser displays the table with cell spacing of 1 pixel.

- **Align**   Horizontal alignment of the table within a paragraph on the web page. Select left, center, right, or default (which is usually the same as left alignment).

- **Border**   Set the thickness of the outer border around the table. Enter 0 to specify no border. If you leave this blank, the web browser will probably display the table with a 3-pixel border.

- **Clear Row Heights**   Click this button to remove row height settings throughout the table.

TIP   *Use the Clear Row Heights and Clear Column Widths buttons to reset height and width settings to blanks, so the table can automatically size itself to the content or you can start over fresh after trying some resizing experiments.*

- **Clear Column Widths**   Click this button to remove column width settings throughout the table.

- **Convert Table Widths to Pixels**   Click this button to convert all table and cell width settings to fixed pixel measurements.

- **Convert Table Widths to Percent**   Click this button to convert all table and cell width settings to percent measurements.

- **Bg Color (Background Color)**   Select a color from the color picker or enter a hexadecimal value to specify the background color for the cells and the spaces between the cells.

- **Brdr Color (Border Color)**   Select a color from the color picker or enter a hexadecimal value to specify the color of the border around the outside of the table.

- **Bg Image (Background Image)**   Specify an image to appear as the background for the entire table (supercedes the background color). You can enter the path and filename, click the folder icon and browse for the image file in the dialog box that appears, or drag the Point to File icon to the file in the Dreamweaver Site window.

TIP   *If you're using the table for page layout, set the CellPad, CellSpace, and Border to 0 and make sure the Bg Color, Brdr Color, and Bg Image settings are all blank. This makes the table invisible on the web page.*

Set Column, Row, and Cell Properties

Just as you can control the formatting for a table with the Property Inspector panel, you can set similar formatting attributes for rows, columns, and cells in your table. The row, column, and cell properties are in the lower portion of the Property Inspector panel (cell content properties are in the upper portion), so be sure to click the expander button in the lower-right corner of the Property Inspector panel to display all the table properties. The formatting options are identical for rows, columns, and cells. Here's a rundown on the table row, column, and cell formatting attributes:

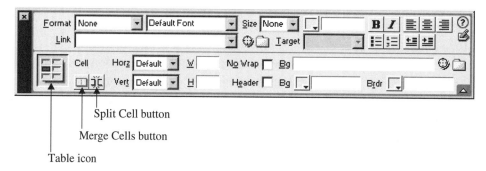

Split Cell button

Merge Cells button

Table icon

- **Table icon**   This icon and the legend beside it indicate whether a row, a column, or individual cells are selected.

- **Merge Cells**   Click this button to merge the selected cells into one cell spanning multiple columns or rows. This button will be grayed out if it isn't available.

- **Split Cell**   Click this button to split the selected cell into two or more cells. Clicking the button will open a dialog box where you can specify whether to split the cell into multiple rows or columns and how many cells to create.

- **Horz (Horizontal alignment)**   Select the horizontal alignment for the content within the selected cells. You can choose from left, center, right, or default (which is usually the same as left alignment).

- **Vert (Vertical alignment)**   Select the vertical alignment for the content within the selected cells. You can choose from top, middle, bottom, baseline, or default (which is usually the same as middle).

- **W (Width)**   Set the width of the cell(s). Enter a number and select pixels or % (percent). Percent measurements specify a percentage of the table, not the page.

- **H (Height)**   Set the height of the cell(s). Enter a number and select pixels or % (percent). Percent measurements specify a percentage of the table, not the page.

- **No Wrap**   Check this option to disable word wrapping within the cell.

- **Header**   Check this option to mark the selected cells as Header cells, which causes the browser to display the cell contents centered and in bold text (unless you override those settings).

- **Bg (Background Image)**   Specify an image to appear as the background for the selected cell(s). You can enter the path and the filename, click the folder icon and browse for the image file in the dialog box that appears, or drag the Point to File icon to the file in the Dreamweaver Site window. This image appears behind any text or other content in the cell(s). It's not the same as adding an image to the cell as foreground content.

- ■ **Bg (Background Color)**   Select a color from the color picker or enter a hexadecimal value to specify the background color for the cell(s).

- ■ **Brdr (Border Color)**   Select a color from the color picker or enter a hexadecimal value to specify the color of the border around the cell(s).

Apply a Design Scheme to a Table

By adding borders, background colors, and other formatting to the table and the various rows and cells within the table, you can create an almost infinite variety of table treatments. You can make the top row stand out as headers and give the left column a distinctive appearance as the key descriptions of the items in the table. You can assign different colors to alternating rows in the table to make it easier for the viewer to read across each row. You can make all these changes, one by one, by selecting portions of the table and adjusting the settings in the Property Inspector panel. Or you could make all the changes at once with just a few mouse clicks.

Dreamweaver includes a set of preformatted design schemes for tables that you can use to make your tables more attractive. Figure 6-2 shows one such design scheme applied to a simple table. You can apply this scheme and others to your tables by following the steps described next.

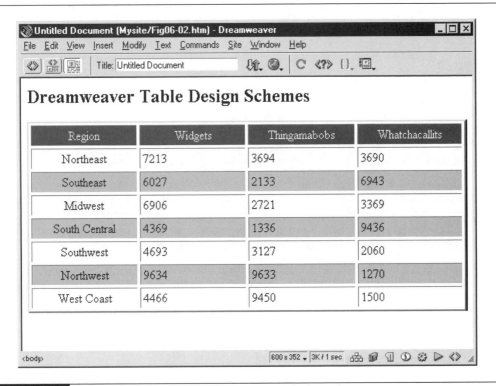

FIGURE 6-2   A table formatted with a Dreamweaver design scheme

1. Select the table to which you want to apply a design scheme.

2. Choose Commands | Format Table. The Format Table dialog box appears.

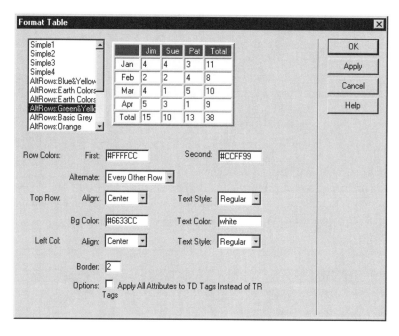

3. Select a design scheme from the list box in the upper-left corner of the dialog box. A preview sample of the selected scheme appears to the right of the list.

4. Fine-tune the scheme by adjusting the settings for Row Colors, Top Row, and Left Col.

5. Adjust the Border thickness by entering a number in the Border box.

6. Check or clear the Options check box. Leaving this option unchecked causes the command to apply formatting to table rows wherever possible, which makes the HTML more compact but may fail to format some table cells that were previously formatted. Checking the option applies all formatting attributes to the <td> tags, which is sure to override any existing formatting, at the expense of bulkier code.

7. Click OK to close the dialog box and apply the design scheme to the selected table. Dreamweaver modifies the HTML source code for the table and displays the formatting in Design view.

The design scheme is just a fast way to apply multiple formatting attributes all at once. You're not limited by the design scheme at all. After applying the design scheme, you can edit and refine your table formatting and content any way you like.

Add Content to a Table Cell

Adding content to a table cell is actually the easiest part of working with tables. Basically, you just click a cell to position the insertion point cursor in the cell and then add text, images, and other content to the cell just as you would add them to the main web page. In fact, when it comes to adding content to a table, you can think of each table cell as a miniature web page.

Use Text in Tables

Adding text to a table is as easy as adding text to the main web page. The only thing you need to do differently is to make sure the insertion point is in the table cell where you want the text to appear. You can enter a single word or a number, a phrase, a paragraph, or multiple paragraphs combined with images and other content.

- To place the insertion point in a table cell, click the cell.

- To enter text in the current cell, simply type on the keyboard.

- You can copy and paste text into a table cell, just as you can paste text anywhere else in your document. All the usual copy and paste techniques work the same within a table.

- To move the insertion point to the next cell in the table, press TAB. The insertion point moves from left to right across a row. When you reach the end of a row, pressing TAB moves the insertion point down to the first (leftmost) cell in the next row.

- Press SHIFT+TAB to move the insertion point back one cell to the left.

- Press the right and left arrow keys to move the insertion point right or left one cell.

- To add a new row of cells to the bottom of the table and move the insertion point into the first cell in that row, press TAB when the insertion point is in the rightmost cell in the bottom row of the table.

Remember that any text you add to a table cell flows within that cell. Unless you set specific dimensions for the cell, Dreamweaver (and the viewer's browser) automatically expands the table cell to accommodate the text and other content within it, provided, of course, that there is room to do so within the constraints of the surrounding table cells, the overall table size, and the other elements on the page. When a line of text exceeds the maximum width of the cell, the text automatically wraps to form a new line, just as it does on the main web page—unless you activate the No Wrap option for the cell in the Property Inspector panel.

You can format text in a table cell using any of the normal text formatting attributes, such as fonts, sizes, paragraph and heading tags, bold, italics, and so on (see Chapter 3 for the details). Alignment attributes align text relative to the borders and cell padding of the cell instead of relative to the page margins, but otherwise all text formatting works the same within a table cell.

Use Images in Tables

Table cells can contain more than just text. You can also insert images into a table cell—as well as just about any other media object you can insert into a normal web page.

The techniques for inserting an image into a table cell are the same as for inserting an image anywhere else on your web page. (See Chapter 4 for details on working with images.) The following steps summarize the basic technique:

1. Position the insertion point cursor in the table cell where you want to insert the image.

2. Choose Insert | Image to open the Select Image Source dialog box.

3. Locate and select the image file in the dialog box.

4. Click the Select button to close the dialog box and insert the image into the table cell.

5. Adjust the settings in the Property Inspector panel to control the formatting attributes of the image.

This technique describes how to insert a foreground image into a table cell. Remember that you can also use background images in a table cell, row, or as a background for the entire table. A background image in a table works just like the background image for a web page. As the name implies, the image acts as a background, and the text, foreground images, and other content elements appear in front of the background image, partially obscuring it. To specify a background image for a table, row, or cell, select the table, row, or cell and enter the path and filename for the image file in the appropriate field in the Property Inspector panel. (See the earlier section in this chapter, "Format Tables.")

Copy and Paste Table Cells

As you work with HTML tables, you may need to rearrange cells or cell content within a table, or perhaps copy cells or cell content from one table to another. Dreamweaver provides you with considerable versatility in the way you cut, copy, and paste table cells. You can copy multiple cells, including both the cell content and the properties of the cell itself, or you can copy and paste just the cell content. You can paste cells and cell content into another location in the same table, into another table, or use the copy cells to create an entirely new table elsewhere on your page.

Use the same cut, copy, and paste commands in tables that you use when editing other parts of your web document. You can use the commands on the Edit menu or shortcut keys (such as CTRL+C and CTRL+V). The key to controlling the copy and paste operation is in selection—selecting what to copy and selecting where to paste. Here's a rundown of common copy and paste operations:

■ To copy only the contents of a cell, select the contents of a single cell and choose Edit | Copy. Before you copy, check the Tag Selector in the Design view status bar to make sure you select only the content of the cell and not the cell tag (<td>).

■ To paste content into a cell, position the insertion point cursor in the cell and choose Edit | Paste. Select the existing content of the cell before issuing the paste command if you want the pasted content to *replace* the existing content.

■ To copy one or more cells and their contents, select the cells you wish to copy and choose Edit | Copy. If you select multiple cells, you automatically get the cells as well as their content. If you select a single cell, check the Tag Selector in the Design view status bar to make sure you select the cell tag (`<td>`) and not just the content.

■ To insert the copied cells and their content into a table, position the insertion point curser at the location in the table where you want to add the cells and choose Edit | Paste. Dreamweaver adds the cells and their content to the table and moves the existing cells and content down and to the right to make room.

■ To replace existing table cells with the copied cells and their content, select the range of cells to be replaced and choose Edit | Paste. Note that the number of cells copied and the number of cells replaced must match in number and configuration. For example, if you copy two rows of three cells each, you must select six cells in the same two-row configuration in order to complete the paste operation.

■ To create a new table composed of the copied cells, position the insertion point cursor anywhere on your page outside an existing table and choose Edit | Paste. Dreamweaver automatically creates a new table to enclose the pasted table cells.

■ To remove content from one or more cells, select the cells (less than a full row or column) and press DELETE. Dreamweaver deletes the content of the cells but leaves the cells themselves intact.

■ To remove a row or column of cells from the table, select the row or column and press DELETE. If you select one or more entire rows or columns, Dreamweaver deletes the cells as well as their content from the table.

Sort Table Contents

If you've done much work with tables in a spreadsheet program or most recent word processing programs, you're probably accustomed to being able to sort a table—rearranging the rows to put them in alphabetical or numerical order. Dreamweaver also provides a basic table sorting capability. You can sort on one or two columns, and you can sort alphabetically or numerically in ascending or descending order. Here's how:

1. Select the table.

2. Choose Commands | Sort Table to open the Sort Table dialog box.

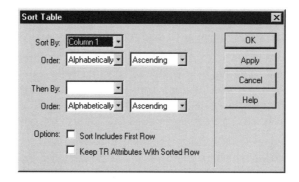

3. Select a column in the Sort By list box. This is the column containing the primary sort criteria.

4. Select Alphabetically or Numerically in the Order list box and then select Ascending or Descending.

5. To specify a secondary sort criteria, select a column in the Then By list box and select the kind of sort and direction in the Order list boxes below. Leave the Then By box blank to perform a simple, one-column sort.

6. Select one or both Options as appropriate.

   ■ **Sort Includes First Row** Dreamweaver normally excludes the first row of the table from the sort because the first row frequently contains column headers. Check this option if the first row of your table contains data that you want to include in the sort.

   ■ **Keep TR Attributes With Sorted Row** Check this option if your table includes rows highlighted with color or some other formatting attribute associated with the content of the row. Leave this option unchecked if your table includes formatting, such as alternating row colors, that will be disturbed if the row formatting moves along with the content.

7. Click OK to close the Sort Table dialog box. Dreamweaver sorts the table and rearranges the rows within the table according to the sort criteria you specified.

 *You can't use the Sort Table command on a table that contains merged cells.*

Import Table Data

If you have tabular data created in another application that you want to use on your web page, you don't have to reenter all the data in Dreamweaver or copy and paste it one cell at a time. If you can export that tabular data into a delimited text file, you can import the data from the file and use it to create a new table in Dreamweaver.

Of course, a necessary prerequisite is creating a *delimited text file* (a text file that uses a standard character, such as a tab or a comma, to separate the data fields). Follow the instructions for creating such a file from the data in the source application. After you create the delimited file, follow these steps to import the data into Dreamweaver:

1. Position the insertion point cursor where you want to create the new table on your page.

2. Choose Insert | Tabular Data to open the Insert Tabular Data dialog box.

3. Enter the path and the filename for the delimited file in the Data File box, or click the Browse button to open a dialog box where you can locate and select the file.

4. Select the delimiter character used in the file from the Delimiter box. You must specify the correct delimiter character, or the tabular data won't import correctly.

5. Set the Table Width. Click the Fit to Data option to allow Dreamweaver to automatically size the table to accommodate the data. Click Set and enter a number, then select Percent or Pixels to specify the table width as a percent of the page size or as a fixed width.

6. Set the other options as appropriate:

   ■ **Cell Padding** Specify the number of pixels between the cell border and the cell content. Enter 0 for no padding; otherwise, Dreamweaver and the browsers default to 1-pixel padding.

   ■ **Cell Spacing** Specify the number of pixels of space between cells. Enter 0 for no cell spacing; otherwise, Dreamweaver and the browsers default to 3-pixel spacing.

   ■ **Format Top Row** Select character formatting to be applied to the contents of the cells on the top row of the table. You can choose from bold, italic, bold-italic, or no formatting.

   ■ **Border** Enter a border thickness in pixels. Enter 0 for no border.

7. Click OK to close the Insert Tabular Data dialog box, and import the data into your web document. Dreamweaver creates a new table, adds the appropriate number of rows and columns, and enters the data into the cells of the table.

Create Nesting Tables

Table cells can contain other tables.

This simple statement has profound consequences for what you can do with tables. *Nesting tables*—a table placed within a cell of another table—dramatically increase the versatility of tables, especially in their application as page layout tools. Just as you can use a table to divide a web page into rectangular cells to position content on the page, you can further subdivide a cell by inserting a table into that cell (as shown in Figure 6-3).

The concept of nesting tables is simple enough—a table cell can contain almost anything you can place on a regular web page, *including other tables*. Implementing this concept in the HTML

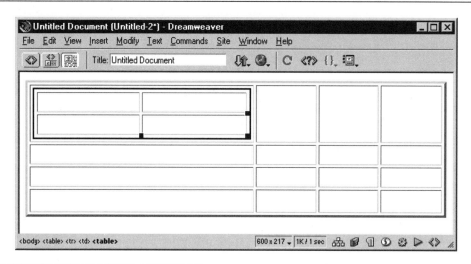

FIGURE 6-3   A nested table within a table cell

code can get a little messy when you nest tables several layers deep, but Dreamweaver's Design view insulates you from the complexities of the source code and makes nested tables manageable for most web authors.

You create a nested table just as you create any other table in Dreamweaver. The only difference is that you start with the insertion point in a cell of another table. After you create the nested table, you can add and delete rows and columns; adjust table, row, and column sizes; and apply formatting to the table, rows, columns, and cells just as you would to any other table. The only difference is that the size of the table is constrained by the size of the table cell in which it resides.

Chapter 7

Use Tables as a Layout Tool

How to...

■ Use tables as a layout tool

■ Use Dreamweaver's Layout view

■ Draw Layout Tables and Layout Cells

■ Create Layout Tables that shrink and stretch with changes in the browser window

■ Create nested Layout Tables

It's fair to say that tables are an essential component of the majority of pages on the Web today. And it's not because there is an overabundance of tabular matter on most web sites. Sure, you'll see something you'd instantly recognize as a table on a web page here and there. But the tables on most web pages are invisible.

The same HTML tags that arrange tabular matter into neat columns and rows in a traditional table can also provide horizontal and vertical spacing and positioning for the text, images, and other elements of the web page. In other words, HTML tables function as a layout grid for many web pages.

Because of the widespread use of tables as a layout tool, Macromedia added a new feature to Dreamweaver 4 called *Layout view*. Layout view offers a new way of representing tables and table cells in Design view that makes tables easier to use as a layout tool.

Why Use Tables as a Layout Tool?

To understand the importance of tables to page layout, you need to remember that text on a web page starts in the upper-left corner and flows to the right and down, using the full width of the browser window. Your only alignment options are left, right, and center. There's just no way to position a paragraph of text or an image a quarter of the page width in from the left margin and down 150 pixels—at least not if you're using just HTML text formatting. However, you can do this if you use HTML tables as a page layout tool. Tables are versatile. They can comprise any number of rows and columns, and you can control the row heights and column widths individually, which gives you pretty good control over the location and size of a table cell. And each table cell can contain just about anything you can place on a web page.

Web designers often fill the page with one large table that breaks the page into columns (see Figure 7-1). Text, images, and other content placed in the table cells flow within the table instead of within the page as a whole, thus giving the designer more control over the position of those elements on the finished page. Adjusting the width of the table columns adjusts the page layout horizontally. Similarly, table rows enable the designer to control the vertical positioning of elements on the page. In effect, HTML tables and cells take on the role of the columns and text boxes that are the primary page layout tools in desktop publishing programs.

Tables do a good job of positioning elements on a web page, but working with those tables can be a challenge. HTML tables were conceived as a way to present tabular matter, not as layout tools.

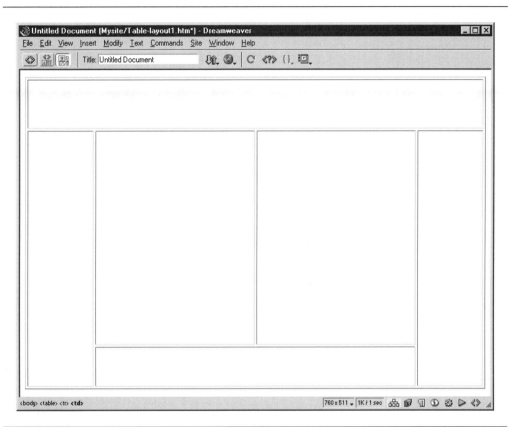

FIGURE 7-1   A table used as a page layout tool

The table tags can be tough to work with in the HTML source code, especially when they are nested several layers deep and interspersed with large quantities of content within the table.

The ability to work with tables visually in Dreamweaver's Design view (see Chapter 6) goes a long way toward making tables more accessible and easier to use. The system works great for creating tables for tabular matter, but it's still not the optimum solution for using tables as a layout tool. You can't just create a table cell anywhere you want on the page. You must define a whole table, specify the number of rows and columns, set various formatting options, and then resize the rows and columns to coax one cell of the table into the desired position. It works, but it's not exactly an intuitive process.

In many ways, layers are easier to use as a layout tool, especially in Dreamweaver's Design view (see Chapter 15). If you need to position an object at a particular location on the page, you just click the Insert Layer icon in the Objects panel and drag the pointer on the page to create a layer in that location; then you insert your object into the layer. To reposition the layer, just select and drag it to a new location. With layers, you don't have to define a whole table to create that one cell that you need as a container for the object, and you don't have to manipulate row and column sizes to position or move the cell.

The problem with layers is that they suffer from browser compatibility issues, so they're not suitable for web sites that must be accessible to the greatest possible number of visitors. Tables, however, are compatible with all browsers, old and new. Also, tables can do some things layers can't do, such as automatically shrink and expand cells to fit different browser window sizes.

Dreamweaver's new Layout view makes table cells as easy and intuitive to use for page layout as layers. Layout view doesn't actually change anything about the underlying HTML code for tables. Instead, Layout view is a new way of rendering tables and table cells in Design view (see Figure 7-2).

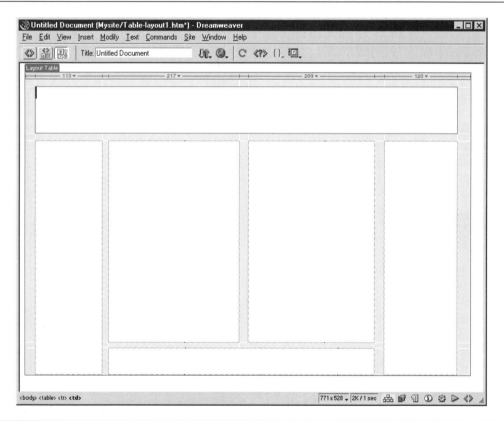

FIGURE 7-2   Dreamweaver in Layout view

When you're working in Layout view, you can create a table cell anywhere on the web page with a click and a drag—like creating a layer. You don't have to define a table and specify a bunch of parameters. Dreamweaver does all that for you automatically. If you want a Layout Table cell positioned in a particular place, you draw it there. Dreamweaver creates a table, with all the rows and columns sized as necessary to place the cell right where you indicated, ready to accept your content. If you want to move a Layout Cell, just drag it to a new position. Dreamweaver auto-magically adds, deletes, merges, splits, and resizes rows, columns, and cells in the table as needed to accommodate the new cell position.

Work in Layout View

Layout view provides a new, alternative way of rendering and working with tables and table cells in Dreamweaver's Design view Document window. The traditional table rendering in Design view is still available; it's now called *Standard view*. Layout view works best for creating and manipulating tables for page layout. Standard view, in contrast, remains the best way to work with tables that contain traditional tabular matter. You can switch back and forth between the two views at will.

1. To select Layout view, click the Layout View button at the bottom of the Objects panel, or choose View | Table View | Layout View.

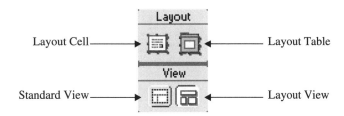

2. To select Standard view, click the Standard View button at the bottom of the Objects panel, or choose View | Table View | Standard View.

The keyboard shortcut for Layout view is CTRL+F6. *The shortcut for Standard view is* CTRL+SHIFT+F6.

When you're in Layout view, Dreamweaver uses a different system for rendering tables. The View | Visual Aids | Table Borders command is inactive and the dashed lines designating table and cell borders that are set to zero disappear and are replaced by colored lines—green for table borders and blue for cell borders (Figure 7-3). A tab at the top of each table shows column divisions and sizes and provides easy access to a menu of table options. Compare Figure 7-3, showing Layout view, to Figure 7-4, which shows the same table in Standard view.

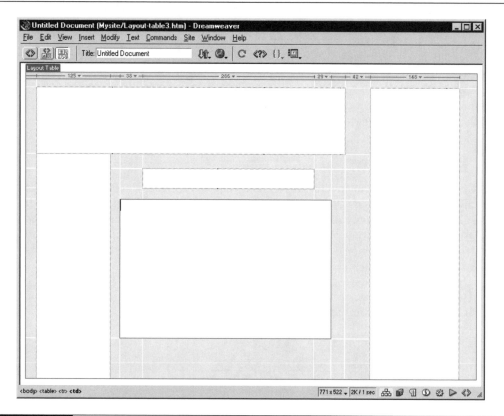

FIGURE 7-3   A Layout Table in Layout view

Note that some of the cells in Layout view have a white background and blue border and others have a gray background and white border. The white cells are Layout Cells as defined in Layout view. (The next section of this chapter shows you how to create Layout Cells and Layout Tables.) The gray cells are the extra placeholder cells Dreamweaver created to fill in around and between the Layout Cells.

NOTE   *The colored outlines and white or gray backgrounds you see in Layout view are simply visual aids that Dreamweaver uses to make the tables and cells easy for you to see and work with. They don't appear on the finished web page as seen in a web browser.*

When working in Layout view, you can insert content into the white Layout Cells but not into the gray placeholder cells. If you move or resize a Layout Cell, Dreamweaver automatically adds, deletes, and resizes the gray placeholder cells as necessary to accommodate the changes in the Layout Cell. Dreamweaver doesn't automatically resize Layout Cells.

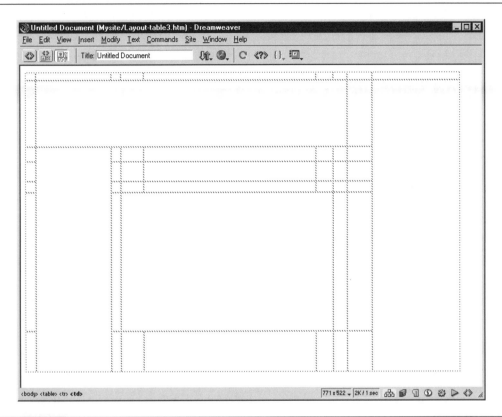

FIGURE 7-4   The same table in Standard view

NOTE   *All the tables and cells you work with in Layout view are constructed with standard HTML table tags. The only difference between the Layout Cells and the placeholder cells is that Layout Cells start out containing a nonbreaking space character between the cell tags (`<td> </td>`), and the placeholder cells are empty (`<td></td>`). Dreamweaver automatically replaces the nonbreaking space character with any content you add to the Layout Cell.*

Also note that the Layout Table is composed of columns and rows, just like a normal table. Many of the cells in the table span multiple columns and rows, which makes the table structure less obvious than it would be if all the cells were normal size, but the column and row structure remains the basis for the table. As you work with Layout Tables in Layout view, you don't need to be concerned about merging and splitting cells to achieve the proper effect, but that's what Dreamweaver is doing behind the scenes.

 *When you first enter Layout view, Dreamweaver displays a large dialog box describing Layout view and how to use it. Check the "Don't show me this message again" box and click OK to make the annoying dialog box go away and not return.*

Draw Layout Cells and Tables

When you work in Layout view, Dreamweaver enables you to create a table cell almost anywhere on the web page without first creating a table. Of course, an HTML table cell can't exist outside a table, so Dreamweaver automatically creates the table for you and configures the table with the rows and columns necessary to create a cell in the location you specify. You can also create a table yourself and then draw cells in that table, but it isn't necessary to do so.

To facilitate this new way of working with tables in Layout view, Dreamweaver provides special Layout Cell and Layout Table buttons on the Objects panel that you use for creating cells and tables. The normal Insert | Table command and the corresponding Object icon are unavailable in Layout view. If you want to work with tables using those commands and techniques, switch back to Standard view.

 *Creating a Layout Table works best when you start with a blank document and create the basic layout for the page before adding any content. If there is existing content on the web page, you can create a Layout Table only below the existing content.*

Draw Layout Cells

When you are working in Layout view, the normal sequence of actions for creating a table is reversed. In Standard view, you start by defining a table, setting the table size and the number of rows and columns, and then manipulating the row and column settings to create table cells where you need them. In Layout view, you start by defining where you want a table cell, and then you let Dreamweaver do the work of creating a table around that cell.

You can draw a *Layout Cell* (a table cell created in Layout view) almost anywhere on the current web page. The only restrictions are these:

- The cell must start below any existing content on the page.
- The cell must not overlap any existing Layout Cell.
- The cell must not overlap the border of an existing Layout Table. You can create new Layout Cells inside or outside an existing Layout Table; you just can't draw the cell over the table border.

Here's the technique for drawing a Layout Cell:

 1. Click the Layout Cell button at the bottom of the Objects panel. The mouse pointer changes from the normal arrow to a cross-hair pointer (+).

2. Position the pointer where you want to place one corner of the Layout Cell, then click and drag diagonally to the location of the opposite corner. Dreamweaver displays a box shape as you drag. When the box is the proper size for the new Layout Cell, release the mouse button.

> **TIP** *To make it easier to align Layout Cells, Dreamweaver snaps the new Layout Cell to the edge of any other Layout Cell, Layout Table, or page border that you get close to (within about 8 pixels). Press ALT to disable snapping.*

> **TIP** *Don't worry about getting the Layout Cell perfectly sized or positioned. You can easily resize and move the cell after you create it.*

When you finish drawing the Layout Cell, Dreamweaver automatically creates a Layout Table to surround the cell (unless you draw the cell within an existing table), as shown in Figure 7-5. The Layout Table appears outlined in green. The table extends the full width of the page and includes as many rows and columns of cells as necessary to create a cell at the location you specified. The Layout Cell appears with a blue outline and a white background. The other cells that Dreamweaver creates for positioning the Layout Cell appear in gray.

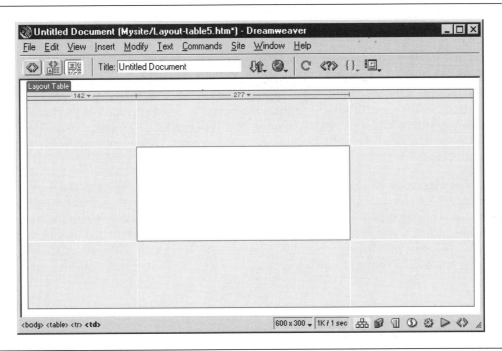

FIGURE 7-5   A newly created Layout Cell surrounded by the Layout Table Dreamweaver created

The Layout Table and all the cells within it are constructed with normal HTML table tags. The table and individual cells are all set for no border or background so they are invisible on the finished web page. The default formatting for a Layout Table also includes no cell padding or cell spacing. You can change these settings later if you want (see the later section in this chapter, "Format Layout Tables and Cells"), but these settings are the ones commonly used for tables that serve as page layout tools.

The insertion point automatically appears inside the newly created Layout Cell, ready for you to begin inserting content into the cell. However, you'll probably want to finish creating the Layout Cells you'll need to define your page layout before you start filling the cells with text, images, and other content.

To draw several Layout Cells without having to click the Layout Cell button in the Objects panel each time, press and hold the CTRL key as you begin drawing the first cell. Hold the CTRL key down until you finish drawing all the cells.

Draw a Layout Table

Dreamweaver automatically creates a Layout Table for you when you draw a Layout Cell on the page in Layout view—there's no need to draw the Layout Table first. However, there are times when you may want to draw the table yourself instead of accepting Dreamweaver's default table configuration, or you may want to draw a Layout Table to create nesting tables. Here's how you do it:

1. Click the Layout Table button at the bottom of the Objects panel. The mouse pointer changes from the normal arrow to a cross-hair pointer (+).

2. Position the pointer on the page and drag diagonally to define the size of the Layout Table. The upper-left corner of the Layout Table automatically snaps to the upper-left corner of the page (if this is the first table on an empty page) or to the lower-left corner of the bottom Layout Table or other content. Dreamweaver displays a box shape as you drag. When the box is the proper size for the new Layout Table, release the mouse button.

Dreamweaver creates the Layout Table according to your specifications, as shown in Figure 7-6. The Layout Table appears with a green outline and a bar across the top that shows the dimensions of the table column(s). The Layout Table tab at the upper-left corner of the table serves as a selection handle. Sizing handles (small boxes) appear on the bottom and right borders of the table. Note that when you create a table in Layout view, it starts out with just one cell— a gray placeholder cell. You can create one or more Layout Cells within the new Layout Table.

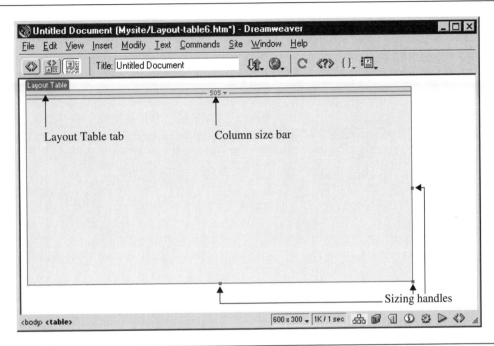

FIGURE 7-6   An empty Layout Table

TIP   *You can't draw a Layout Table to the right of an existing Layout Table. To work around this limitation, enlarge the existing table to the right and then draw a new table nested in the newly expanded space.*

Create a Nested Layout Table

One of the features of Layout view enables you to quickly and easily create *nested tables*—tables contained within other tables (see Figure 7-7). There are several reasons why you might want to create nested Layout Tables, but one of the most common is to gain better control over the way Layout Cells automatically expand and contract to accommodate the content you place in them. For example, a Layout Cell that is set to Autostretch (discussed in detail shortly) can encroach on the space occupied by an adjacent empty Layout Cell but not on the space occupied by a nested Layout Table. So, nested Layout Tables are a kind of super Layout Cells.

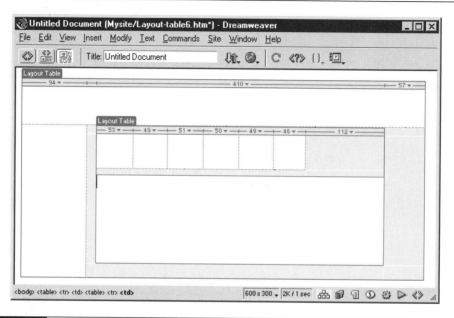

FIGURE 7-7   Nested Layout Tables

To create a nested Layout Table, simply draw a new Layout Table inside an existing Layout Table. It's just like drawing a Layout Cell—the nested table can't overlap existing Layout Cells or tables and can't extend beyond the limits of the parent table.

Later, if you decide that you don't need the nested table, you can select the table and click the Remove Nesting button in the Property Inspector panel to remove the nested table and merge any Layout Cells in the nested table into the parent table.

Move and Resize Layout Cells and Layout Tables

One of the nicest things about Layout view is the ease with which you can move Layout Cells and resize both Layout Cells and Layout Tables visually in Layout view. This makes adjusting your page layout a much easier job than ever before.

Select Layout Cells and Layout Tables

Of course, before you can move or resize a Layout Cell or Layout Table you must first select it.

■   To select a Layout Cell, click the cell outline. It's a thin line, but Dreamweaver helps you see it by changing the outline to red when your pointer is close enough to select the cell. The selected cell outline displays sizing handles at the corners and in the middle of each side.

TIP   *You can* CTRL+*click anywhere in a cell to select it.*

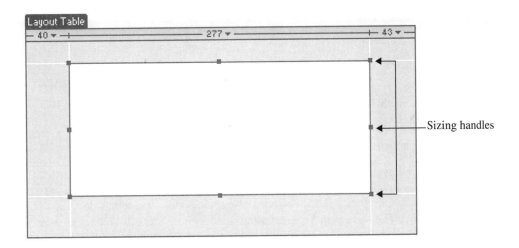

To select a Layout Table, click the table outline or the green tab at the upper-left corner of the table, or click anywhere on a gray placeholder cell in the table. The selected table displays sizing handles in the lower-right corner and on the bottom and right sides and the column size bar across the top (as shown in Figure 7-6).

TIP   *You can suppress the display of the Layout Table tab and column size bar across the top of the Layout Table. Choose View | Table View | Show Layout Table Tab to toggle the display on and off.*

Move a Layout Cell

You can freely move a Layout Cell within a Layout Table. The only restrictions are that you can't move the cell beyond the edge of the table, and the cell can't overlap other Layout Cells. The gray placeholder cells, however, are not an obstacle.

To move a Layout Cell, select the cell and then use one of the following techniques:

- Click and drag the cell outline. Click anywhere on the outline except at the sizing handles. As you drag, Dreamweaver displays a dotted-line rectangle showing the new position. Release the mouse button to drop the cell in the new position.

- Press the arrow keys to move the cell up, down, left, or right one pixel at a time. Press SHIFT along with an arrow key to move the cell 10 pixels.

Resize a Layout Cell

You can also resize a Layout Cell visually. The technique for resizing a cell is simplicity itself—just select the cell and then drag any of the sizing handles on the cell outline. Drag one of the handles in the middle of a side to move that side. Drag one of the corner handles to move the two adjacent sides simultaneously.

> **TIP**   *Press and hold the* SHIFT *key as you drag a corner sizing handle to maintain the cell proportions as you resize it.*

The same restrictions that apply to moving a cell also apply to resizing a cell. You can't overlap another Layout Cell and you can't go outside the boundaries of the Layout Table.

Resize a Layout Table

Just as you can resize a Layout Cell, you can also resize a Layout Table. The technique is essentially the same—you select the table and then drag one of the sizing handles. The biggest difference is that a Layout Table has sizing handles only on the bottom and right side.

The restrictions on resizing a Layout Table are simple and logical. You can't reduce the size of a Layout Table beyond the minimum required to make room for the Layout Cells it contains. And you can't enlarge a Layout Table so that it overlaps another Layout Table or other page content.

> **TIP**   *Dreamweaver won't let you visually resize the height of a Layout Table that has another Layout Table immediately below it. To work around the limitation, you can temporarily insert a text paragraph to separate the two Layout Tables and then resize the upper table visually. Or you can resize the table by adjusting the height setting in the Property Inspector panel.*

Format Layout Tables and Cells

Formatting tables and cells in Layout view is essentially the same as formatting tables and cells in Standard view. When you select a Layout Table or a Layout Cell, the Property Inspector panel displays the attribute settings and options for the selected object. And of course, you can edit those settings in the Property Inspector panel.

Most of the formatting attributes and options are the same as those for tables and cells in Standard view—after all, you're working with the same HTML tags. However, there are a few options (such as border color and background images) that Macromedia chose not to display, presumably because the options are irrelevant when you are using tables as layout tools. And there are a few options—such as Autostretch—that are specific to Layout view. (For more on the Autostretch option, see the later section in this chapter, "Layout Tables That Resize in the Browser.")

Format Layout Tables

To adjust the formatting attributes of a Layout Table, select the table and then adjust the settings in the Property Inspector panel. You can set any of the following options:

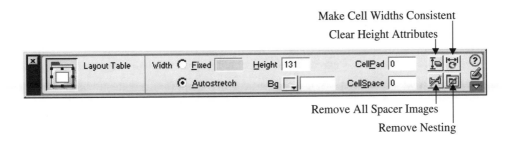

- **Width** Select Fixed and set the table width in pixels, or select Autostretch.
- **Height** Set the height of the table in pixels.
- **Bg (Background Color)** Click the color button and select a color, or enter a hexadecimal value in the text box.
- **CellPad (Cell Padding)** Specify the amount of space between the cell border and the content, measured in pixels.
- **CellSpace (Cell Spacing)** Specify the amount of space between cells of the table, measured in pixels.
- **Clear Height Attributes button** Click this button to clear the height settings for all the cells in the table.
- **Make Cell Widths Consistent button** Click this button to set the width of all fixed-width cells in the table to match the width to which they expanded to accommodate the content you entered.
- **Remove All Spacer Images button** Click this button to remove spacer images from the table (see the later section, "Layout Tables That Resize in the Browser," for more information on spacer images).
- **Remove Nesting button** Click this button to remove the selected table and make its cells part of the parent table.

Format Layout Cells

To adjust the formatting attributes of a Layout Cell, select the cell and then adjust the settings in the Property Inspector panel. You can set any of the following options:

- **Width** Select Fixed and set the table width in pixels, or select Autostretch.
- **Height** Set the height of the table in pixels.

- **Bg (Background Color)**   Click the color button and select a color, or enter a hexadecimal value in the text box.
- **Horz (Horizontal alignment)**   Select the horizontal alignment for the contents of the cell. You can select Left, Center, Right, or Default (which is usually the same as Left).
- **Vert (Vertical alignment)**   Select the vertical alignment for the content within the selected cells. You can choose from Top, Middle, Bottom, Baseline, or Default (which is usually the same as Middle).
- **No Wrap**   Check this option to disable word wrapping within the cell.

Add Content to Layout Table Cells

Adding content to a Layout Cell is essentially the same as adding content to a regular table cell in Standard view, which is to say it's the same as adding content anywhere else on your page. The only difference is that Dreamweaver lets you add content only to a Layout Cell or to the main page outside any Layout Table. You can't add content to a gray placeholder cell in a Layout Table. That means you must create a Layout Cell before you can add content to a Layout Table, but since that takes only a click and a drag, it's hardly a burdensome requirement.

To add text to a Layout Cell, just click the cell and begin typing. You can also cut and paste, or import, text into the cell. You can use all the normal text formatting options to control the appearance of the text in a Layout Cell. See Chapter 3 for more details.

Likewise, you can add an image or other object to a Layout Cell using the same techniques you use to insert the same object elsewhere on the page. See Chapter 4 for more details on adding images.

Layout view does add a couple of restrictions on what you can place in a table cell:

- You can't insert a table into a cell in Layout view—you can nest tables within tables, but not within cells.
- You can't insert a Layer into your web page while you are working in Layout view.

Layout Tables That Resize in the Browser

One of the most challenging aspects of page layout design for the Web is that the viewer's browser window isn't a predictable size. As a result, if you design your web page to have the desired layout at one window size, visitors viewing the page in browser windows of different sizes see a less-than-optimum version of the page. Either the page content fails to fill the viewer's window, or it's too big and the viewer must scroll left and right as well as up and down to see the entire page.

One way to address this problem is to take advantage of the ability of HTML tables to automatically scale to fit the browser window. Dreamweaver does this in Layout view with a feature called Autostretch. Autostretch makes the Layout Table elastic so it can shrink and expand to fit different size browser windows. You can assign the Autostretch feature to the Layout Table itself and to one column of cells within the table. The other columns of a Layout Table remain fixed widths.

Work with Fixed-Width Columns

When you draw a Layout Cell or a Layout Table, the default setting is for fixed widths, and the table or cell is exactly the size you draw. When you draw a Layout Cell and let Dreamweaver create a Layout Table around it, that table is also a fixed width, but it fits the full width of the current Design view window. So, you don't usually need to specify fixed width for a column, since that's what it is unless you change it to Autostretch.

Later, if you need to convert an Autostretch column back to fixed width, you can use either of the following techniques:

- Select a cell in the column and select the Fixed option in the Property Inspector panel. A number appears in the Fixed box to show the column width Dreamweaver calculated for the column. Enter a new number to adjust the column width.

- Click the column-width indicator in the Layout Table Tab and choose Make Column Fixed Width from the menu that appears. Dreamweaver sets the column width to accommodate the content in that column.

As you enter text and other content into a Layout Cell, Dreamweaver sometimes adjusts the cell width to accommodate wider content even though the cell supposedly has a fixed width. When this happens, the column-width indicator in the Layout Table Tab at the top of the table displays two numbers—the original column-width setting and the adjusted width. To eliminate the double numbers, click the column-width indicator and choose Make Cell Widths Consistent from the menu that appears, or click the Make Cell Widths Consistent button in the Property Inspector panel.

Use Autostretch Columns

When you draw a Layout Table or a Layout Cell, the default width setting is Fixed, so if you want to use Autostretch columns, you need to deliberately select that option by specifying which column should expand and contract to fit different browser window widths. Remember that only one column in a Layout Table can be Autostretch.

To specify an Autostretch column, do one of the following:

- Click the column-width indicator in the Layout Table Tab and choose Make Column Autostretch from the menu that appears.

■ Select a cell in the column that you want to be Autostretch and click the Autostretch option in the Property Inspector panel.

When you designate an Autostretch column, Dreamweaver converts any existing Autostretch column in the table to fixed width and changes the HTML code for the selected column so it will automatically expand horizontally to fill any space not occupied by other cells. To keep the Autostretch column from spanning the entire width of the page, Dreamweaver also inserts spacer images in the other columns to maintain their designated widths.

Use Spacer Images

A *spacer image* is a transparent image that Dreamweaver uses as a placeholder to control column widths in a Layout Table. Since the image is transparent, it's invisible in the browser window, but its presence in a table cell means that the cell (and the column) isn't empty. This is important because an Autostretch column automatically expands horizontally to fill any and all empty space. The spacer image puts a "no trespassing" sign on adjacent columns so those fixed-width columns retain their specified widths. Without the spacer images, empty Layout Cells and placeholder cells alike would disappear from view as the Autostretch column expands to fill the void.

Dreamweaver automatically inserts spacer images in all the fixed-width columns of a Layout Table when you designate one column as an Autostretch column. You can also insert spacer images manually into fixed-width columns by clicking the column-width indicator in the Layout Table Tab and choosing Add Spacer Image from the menu that appears. A double line over a column in the Layout Table tab indicates a column that contains a spacer image.

When you (or Dreamweaver) insert a spacer image into a Layout Table for the first time in a given site, Dreamweaver opens the Choose Spacer Image dialog box, giving you the option to create a new spacer image file for the site, select an existing spacer image, or decline to use spacer images with autostretch tables.

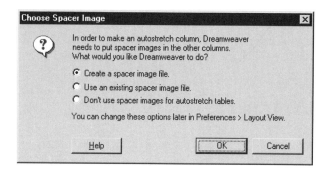

Depending on your choice in this dialog box, you see either another dialog box in which you can tell Dreamweaver where to save a new spacer image file or a dialog box in which you can locate and select an existing spacer image.

Just as you can add spacer images, you can also take them away. As you develop your page and add content to cells, you may want to remove spacer images from columns that are no longer empty.

- ■ To remove the spacer image from a single column, click the column-width indicator in the Layout Table tab and choose Remove Spacer Image.

- ■ To remove all the spacer images from the table, click any column-width indicator in the Layout Table tab and choose Remove All Spacer Images, or click the Remove All Spacers button in the Property Inspector panel.

CAUTION   *Removing all spacer images will almost surely cause your page layout to change. The change can be drastic if there are numerous (or large) empty columns in Layout Tables on the page.*

7

Chapter 8

Use Frames and Framesets

How to...

- Decide when and when not to use frames
- Create frames and framesets
- Set frame properties
- Build a navigation bar with frames
- Create alternative pages for nonframes-capable browsers

Frames were introduced by Netscape several years ago and since then have become one of the most widely used web design features. Because the vast majority of today's web browsers are capable of displaying frames, there are few compatibility issues to worry about. For today's web designers, frames have become a common feature that seems to be part of everyone's toolkit. Though creating frames-based layouts is more complicated and involved than creating nonframes pages, Dreamweaver offers some great tools to simplify the process. In addition, Dreamweaver makes it easy to create alternative content for nonframes-enabled browsers, allowing you to reach 100% of your audience with a minimum of effort.

How Frames Work

The concept behind frames is simple: Instead of using one HTML page to display your content, you can divide a page into multiple rectangular areas, each of which displays a separate web page. If used correctly, frames allow designers more control over layout, as well as serving to make their site easier to navigate. With a properly designed frameset you can, for instance, place a navigation menu in one frame that always remains in view while displaying content pages in other frames that scroll or update as needed. This setup saves the user time because they don't have to keep loading the same navigation menu information over and over. Lots of "cutting-edge" designers have also used frames to create all sorts of artistic and innovative implementations. However, you need to be careful with frames because they can just as easily detract from the user-experience.

Appropriate and Inappropriate Uses of Frames

Frames can add to the experience of using a web site, or they can detract seriously from it; the key is to use them in a complementary way and to know when and when not to use them. If you've spent any amount of time surfing around the Web, no doubt you've come across both good and bad examples of web pages using frames. The best way to know the difference is to simply acquaint yourself with what works and what doesn't by looking at what other designers do. Think about it from a user perspective: The most important thing to think about when designing a web site is how the user will experience it, not how you as the designer can add bells and whistles just for the sake of adding bells and whistles. The main advantage of frames is that they allow you to display multiple documents at once. So you should ask yourself, "What kinds of documents would my visitors like to see displayed at once?" and "How would my visitors benefit from seeing more than one document at once?"

There are lots of ways in which frames can benefit a layout. For example, frames work best for sites that need to display some of their content statically while the rest of the content changes from page to page. A navigation menu on the left or top of a page that stays constant throughout the site may be appropriately placed in a frame separate from frames with changing content. However, as you'll see, frames can be confusing to your visitors because, with so many pages visible at once, they may not be able to figure out exactly where they are on your site. One of the least appropriate ways to use frames is to link to other people's sites. If the other sites also contain frames, you can get into a nasty mess of embedded frames, and your users won't know which site they are actually visiting. For more good pointers on when and when not to use frames, and general tips about frames, visit: **http://www.builder.com/ Authoring/Frames/ss05.html**.

8

Building frames with Dreamweaver isn't difficult, but it can be a little bit confusing since there are some fundamental differences between building pages with frames and building pages without frames. If you are new to frames, the easiest way to understand them is to think of frames as having two components:

- The frameset
- The frames inside the frameset

A *frameset* is a web document that contains the frame structure—the code that tells the browser which frames to display and how to display them. The frameset divides the browser window into rectangular sections, called *frames*, each of which is capable of displaying a separate web document.

Although the frameset is the page people use to access your frames content, the frameset itself never appears in the browser. Instead it divides the page up and displays whatever URLs are assigned to each individual frame. A frameset page is distinguished from other web pages by <frameset> tags, which take the place of the <body> tags and any other HTML code that normally resides within the <body> tags. For example, a frameset consisting of two frames with the top frame measuring 80 pixels high and the bottom frame set to expand automatically depending on the size of the browser window might look like this:

```
<frameset rows="80,*">
  <frame src="top.html">
  <frame src="bottom.html">
</frameset>
```

As you can see, this page references two other pages: top.html and bottom.html. Even though the browser accesses the frameset document, the frameset itself is not what people visiting the site see, because the frameset contains only code pointing to other web pages.

Create a Frameset

The first step in creating a page using frames is to build a frameset. Usually this begins by opening up a new blank page (you can also start with an existing page) and using Dreamweaver's frame creation tools to lay out the way you want the page to divide.

There are many different ways you can divide your page into frames, all of which involve two, three, or more frames that you can size as needed to customize the layout.

In the old days this used to be one of the most difficult things about designing with frames, since you had to figure out the numerical values of the rows and columns needed to create the layout. And worse, you had to preview the page in a browser in order to see what the whole design looked like anytime you made a change. Coding simple frames involved extra work, but when you added complicated frames and nested framesets, it got really hairy.

Designing frames with Dreamweaver is dramatically simplified. You can easily drag predefined framesets onto your page and modify them by clicking and dragging; or you can insert frames one by one onto the page with a menu command. You can modify frame properties with the Property Inspector panel and preview the layout in Dreamweaver's Design view Document window without having to launch an external web browser.

Insert Predefined Framesets

To make designing with frames easier, Dreamweaver includes eight commonly used, predefined frameset objects in the Frames Objects panel. The frameset objects offer two-, three-, and four-frame layouts that you can further customize after you insert them onto a page. Using these predefined framesets makes designing frame layouts as easy as clicking a single button.

1. Click anywhere inside the Document window to place the insertion point in your document.

2. Click a frameset icon in the Frames page of the Objects panel. Pick a frameset that looks more or less like the frame layout you want to create. When you click the icon, Dreamweaver creates a frameset with that layout, dividing the page into frames using dashed lines to indicate the frame boundaries, as shown in Figure 8-1.

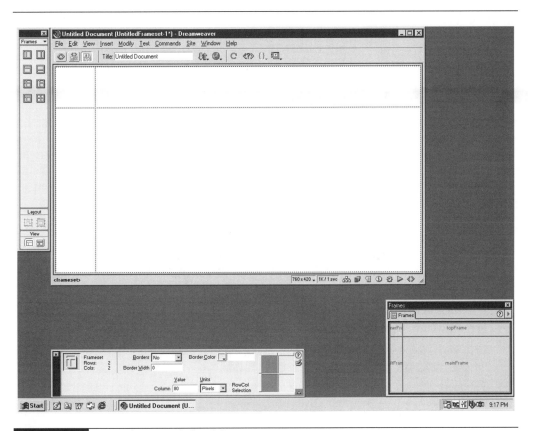

FIGURE 8-1 Inserting a predefined frameset

> **TIP** *If the frame borders don't appear in your document, choose View | Visual Aids | Frame Borders to make the frame borders visible.*

3. Drag the dividing lines between frames to alter the size of the frames. Reposition them by clicking and dragging them to a new position.

You can also insert another frameset inside a frame by clicking inside the frame in the Document window and then clicking a frameset icon in the Objects panel, thus creating much more complicated framesets. Using the eight predefined framesets in the Frames Objects panel as a starting point and adjusting the size of each frame or adding more framesets, you can create almost any kind of frame layout.

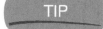 *Each of the frameset icons in the Frames Objects panel displays one of its frames with a blue shaded color. The blue shaded frame represents the location of the existing page in the frameset. When you are working with existing web pages, this feature tells you where the content on that page will appear in the frameset.*

Insert Frames and Split Frames

Another way to insert frames into a page is to use either the Insert Frame command or the Split Frame command. The Split Frame command splits an existing frame into multiple frames.

The Insert Frame command inserts a frame into the current document or frame, depending on which is selected. To use this command, choose Insert | Frames | Left (or any other direction). The direction you choose will decide which way the new frame appears. You can choose between Left, Right, Top, Bottom, Left and Top, Left Top, Top Left, or Split. Here's what each of the direction commands do:

- **Left**   Creates a new frame to the left of the current frame.
- **Right**   Creates a new frame to the right of the current frame.
- **Top**   Creates a new frame above the current frame.
- **Bottom**   Creates a new frame below the current frame.
- **Left and Top**   Creates three new frames arrayed to the left and above the current frame.
- **Left Top**   Creates two new frames, one to the left of the current frame and one above the current frame. The left frame overlaps the other two.
- **Top Left**   Creates two new frames, one to the left of the current frame and one above the current frame. The top frame overlaps the other two.
- **Split**   Splits the current frame into four equal-sized frames.

You can also achieve similar results using the Split Frame command by choosing Modify | Frameset | Split Frame Left (or Right, Up, Down)—the direction you pick depends on whether you want to split the frame into columns or rows. When you select this command, the page or frame is divided into two equal-sized frames, with the new, empty frame added in the direction selected. Because you can perform this command on either a blank page or an existing frame, you can use it to build any kind of frameset you want by splitting and resizing frames until you have achieved the desired layout.

 Don't go overboard and add tons of frames to your page unless you have a good reason to do this. Very few effective examples of framed sites use more than three or four frames in their layout.

Select Frames and Framesets

As you work with a frameset document, you'll need to be able to select each of the individual frames in the document, or the frameset itself, so that you can alter the content in each of them. When you're working in a blank document containing only the frameset and frames, you can select a frame by simply clicking anywhere inside it. However, after you add content to your frames, that won't work because clicking inside the frame selects the frame content instead of the frame.

The easiest way to select frames is to use the Frames panel. The Frames panel mimics the layout of your frameset, displaying each frame along with its name in miniature view. (Setting the frame name and other properties in the Property Inspector panel is covered later in this chapter in the section, "Modify Frame Settings.") By clicking a frame in the Frames panel, you automatically select the frame associated with it.

Selecting framesets works the same way but requires a bit more manual dexterity since you have to click on the frameset border. Framesets are represented in the Frames panel by thick gray borders (see Figure 8-2). To select a frameset, click on the border in the Frames panel. The border is only a few pixels wide so you've got a small target, but it isn't too difficult. You can tell the difference between selecting a frame and a frameset by looking at the Property Inspector panel. When a frame is selected the Property Inspector panel displays the properties of the frame; the properties of the frameset display when you select a frameset.

You can also select and edit the content inside a frame, but you must remember that when you do so you are actually editing the web page that is displaying inside the frame, not the web page used to create the frameset. This can be confusing because Dreamweaver allows you to edit other web pages in a frameset without ever opening those document files in a separate Document window. Make sure you are aware of this when you work with framesets since you can easily lose track of which page you are editing.

8

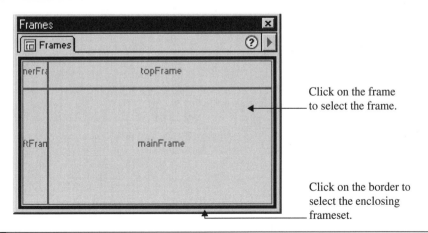

Click on the frame to select the frame.

Click on the border to select the enclosing frameset.

FIGURE 8-2   Use the Frames panel to select between frames and framesets in a document.

Adjust the Layout of a Frameset

You can drag the frame borders to resize frames in the frameset, or use the Frameset Property Inspector panel to define more precise measurements and options. Because visitors to your web site will be using different-sized monitors and can also resize their browser windows, you'll never know exactly what size browser window your page will be viewed in. The way to address this with frames is to make one or more of your frames a fixed size and the remaining frame or frames a relative size. Relative-size frames resize as the browser window resizes; however, fixed-size frames always stay the same. To set the size for each frame in the frameset, select the frameset by clicking on its border in the Frames panel. This displays the Frameset Property Inspector panel shown in Figure 8-3.

The Frameset Property Inspector panel enables you to customize the way that frames will appear in the frameset. In any frameset there are two or more frames, arranged in either rows or columns. The Frameset Property Inspector panel displays either rows or columns in the RowCol Selection indicator on the right side of the panel, depending on how the frameset is divided. You can click on either a row or a column to view and edit the properties for each frame. Figure 8-3 shows the properties for the top row. In this case, I entered 80 in the value field and chose pixels as my unit of measurement to create a fixed-size frame 80 pixels tall. Figure 8-4 shows the bottom row of the frameset set as relative, which means this frame can resize as the browser resizes. You don't need to enter an absolute measurement for a relative-size frame. However, if you want both frames to resize with the browser you can enter a percentage value for each frame; for example, 25 percent for the top and 75 percent for the bottom. That way when the user resizes the browser window, both frames resize but keep their relative sizes in relation to each other.

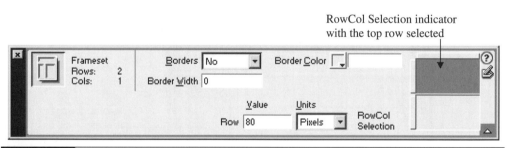

FIGURE 8-3   The RowCol Selection indicator allows you to select a row or a column in the frameset in order to modify its properties.

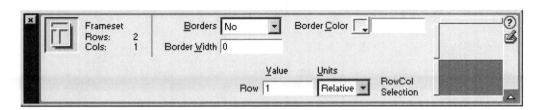

FIGURE 8-4   Setting a relative size for the bottom frame

Insert Content into Frames

Whenever you add frames to a page, you are actually dividing the page into different regions, each of which will display a separate web page. For each frame you create, you can either make it display an existing web page or save the frame as a new web page. To complete the frameset page, each frame needs to be occupied by a linked web page.

Add Existing Pages to a Frameset

Once you create your frameset you have the option of populating the frames with existing pages or creating new ones. When you add an existing page, you'll want to make sure that it fits into the context and space provided by the frame you are adding it to. To add an existing page to a frame:

1. Save your frameset by choosing File | Save Frameset. Enter a name for the file in the Save As dialog box and click Save.

2. Choose Window | Frames to display the Frames panel. The Frames panel displays a miniature rendition of the layout of your frameset.

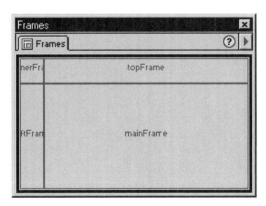

3. Click inside the frame in the Frames panel corresponding to the frame where you want to add the page. When you select the frame, its properties appear in the Property Inspector panel.

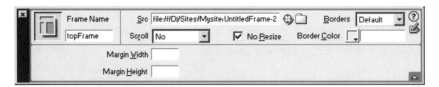

4. Click the folder icon next to the Src field in the Property Inspector panel to open the Select HTML File dialog box. Use this dialog box to locate and select the web document file you want to display in the frame; then click Select to close the Select HTML File dialog box. The web page you inserted now appears inside the frame, and any content in the existing page is editable within the frame.

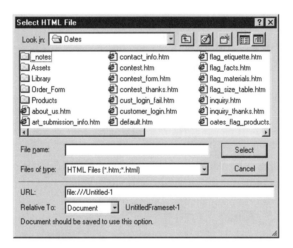

The great thing about editing framesets in Dreamweaver is that, once you insert existing pages into a frame, you can edit those pages in the frameset document without opening them separately. Simply click anywhere inside the frame and edit the page the way you would edit it normally if it were displayed in a separate Document window.

Of course, you can also open the page separately if you prefer to edit it that way. The only disadvantage to editing the page in its own Document window is that you won't be able to see how the page looks in the context of the frameset without previewing it in a browser.

Create New Frame Pages

Many times, instead of inserting existing pages into your frames, you'll want to start from scratch and create the web pages for each new frame as you go along. To do this, simply insert your cursor anywhere into a newly created frame and choose File | Save Frame As. Dreamweaver will prompt you to name the document file for the frame and save it onto your hard drive. Whether the page is saved or not, you can start typing or inserting content the way you normally would with any web document. To save other frames on the frameset page, you need to select each of these elements first, then chose File | Save Frame As commands. To save the frameset itself, choose File | Save Frameset As.

Save Frames and Framesets

Perhaps the thing that most confuses people about using frames in Dreamweaver is saving them. With normal Dreamweaver documents (or documents in any other application for that matter), you usually work on only one document at a time. If you have several documents open in the application, only the one you are currently working on is active, so when you choose File | Save, the currently active document is saved. However, using frames in Dreamweaver is a bit different because the current document actually contains other documents. If you look in the File menu when you have a frameset document open and the frameset is selected, you'll notice that File | Save is not available, but instead there are several alternate save options: Save Frameset, Save Frameset As, and Save All Frames:

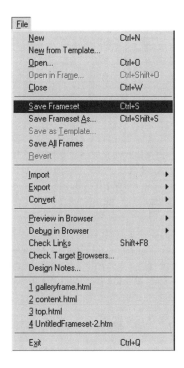

To make it more confusing, the File menu changes again when you select a frame; the File menu displays Save Frame, Save Frame As, Save Frame as Template, and Save All Frames:

When you work with frames documents, Dreamweaver's save commands become contextual, changing their appearance depending on whether you are editing a frameset or a frame. This is very important to remember because when you choose any of these save commands the only document that is saved is the currently active one (the currently selected frame or frameset file). Even though Save is not listed in the File menu, you can still press CTRL+S on the keyboard to save a file. When you press this keyboard command, only the currently selected file is saved—it's the equivalent of choosing File | Save Frame or File | Save Frameset, depending on whether you have an individual frame or the master frameset page selected. To avoid confusion and the possibility of lost data in the event of a crash, it's a good practice to use the File | Save All Frames command when working with frames. With a single command you save the frameset document and all frames documents used in the frameset.

TIP *If you look in the title bar of the Dreamweaver Document window as you select different frames, you'll see that the title changes to reflect each frame that is currently selected and Dreamweaver adds an asterisk (*) to the filename if it contains unsaved modifications. This is a good way to keep track of which page you are editing and which one you will save if you use the CTRL+S keyboard command to save the file. To avoid confusion about which file you are saving, always use the Save All Frames command available in the File menu.*

Modify Frame Settings

The settings in the Property Inspector panel (see Figure 8-5) control the way that frames look and behave on your pages. For example, you can change frame borders, margins, scrolling status, and more, even making it possible to create a page that most visitors can't tell is made with frames.

Name That Frame

Frames require a name in order to be targeted by links in other frames. Dreamweaver names frames when you create them, but it's usually better to replace the names Dreamweaver devises with your own, more descriptive names. To add or change the name of a frame, select the frame and enter a new name into the Frame Name field in the Property Inspector panel. Descriptive names such as Top, Left, Bottom, Content, and so on help you remember which names correspond to which frames.

Set Page Properties

Because every page in a frame is its own web document, each frame can have independent properties such as title, background color, link color, and so forth. However, setting titles for web pages within frames isn't really necessary, since the only title that appears in the browser is the title used in the frameset document. Still, you can set the title and the other page properties for frames in the same way that you set page properties for normal documents. The only difference is that you have to make sure you first select the correct frame so that you can edit it. To do this you can either click on a frame in the Frames panel or click within a frame in the Document window so that the blinking insertion point cursor appears. When the frame is selected, choose Modify | Page Properties or use the CTRL+J keyboard shortcut to open the Page Properties dialog box and enter the appropriate settings.

8

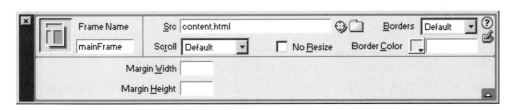

FIGURE 8-5   The Frame Property Inspector panel displays the name and attributes of the selected frame.

Set Frame Borders

When you create a frames page in Dreamweaver, you can decide between colorful three-dimensional borders, flat gray borders, or no borders at all. Most web designers tend to avoid displaying frame borders since it often detracts from the overall page design. However, should you decide to use them, you have a lot of flexibility in customizing the way that they appear.

To set frameset borders:

1. Select a frameset by clicking the frameset border in the Frames panel.

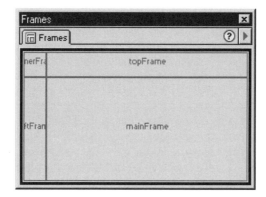

2. Specify any of the following options in the Frameset Property Inspector panel:

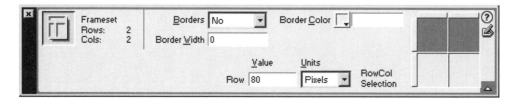

- ■ **Borders**   Select Yes to display borders in three-dimensional color. Select No to display borders as flat gray. Select default to allow the user's browser to determine how the borders are displayed. Most browsers default to Yes.

- ■ **Border Color**   Select a color using the pop-up color picker. This sets the border color for all the frames in the frameset.

- ■ **Border Width**   Specify the width in pixels of the borders for all frames in the frameset. To make borders invisible, specify a border width of zero (Dreamweaver's default setting).

Border settings applied to a frameset affect all the frames within the frameset unless you specify different settings for individual frames, which override the settings of the frameset.

To set individual frame borders:

1. Select the frame by clicking inside it or by clicking the frame in the Frames panel.

2. Specify any of the following options in the Frame Property Inspector panel:

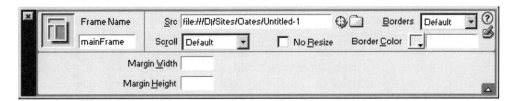

- ■ **Borders**   Select Yes to display borders in three-dimensional color. Select No to display borders as flat gray. Select default to allow the user's browser to determine how the borders are displayed. Most browsers default to Yes.

- ■ **Border Color**   Select a color using the pop-up color picker. This sets the border color for the frame and any frames directly adjacent to the currently selected frame.

Set Margins, Scrolling, and Resizing Properties for Frames

In addition to setting border properties, you can also set the size of the frame's margins, determine whether or not frame content is scrollable, and specify whether or not frames can be resized in the browser. All these properties are accessible through the Property Inspector panel when a frame is selected.

- ■ **Margin Width**   Specify the distance in pixels between the left and right borders of a frame and its content.

- ■ **Margin Height**   Specify the distance in pixels between the top and bottom borders of a frame and its content.

- ■ **Scroll**   Specify whether or not scroll bars appear in the frame. Yes displays scroll bars regardless of whether they are needed or not. No turns off scroll bars. Auto displays scroll bars only if the content in the frame exceeds the size of the window. Default lets the browser decide, which in most cases is the same as Auto.

- ■ **No Resize**   Restrict the size of the frame and prevent users from dragging the frame borders to resize them.

 *Many web designers have been frustrated by the inability to line up images and other content flush against the edge of a browser window—there's always a margin of a few pixels. By placing content into a frame and setting the margin width and/or height to zero, you circumvent this limitation and place images, text, and other content flush against the edge of the browser.*

Use Links with Frames

Frames wouldn't be very useful if users couldn't click a link in one frame to update the content in another frame. Fortunately, creating a link from one frame to another frame (referred to as *targeting* a frame) simply involves adding a target attribute to the link in the Property Inspector panel. However, before you add a target attribute to a link, you need to know the name of the frame you want to target. The target attribute uses the frame's name to identify which frame to create the target for. For example, if you click a link in a frame named "Left" and you want the linked page to display in the frame named "Center," use "Center" as your target. The target is set in the Property Inspector panel's Target field, just to the right of the Link field (see Figure 8-6). When you access the pop-up menu in the Target field, it displays a list of named frames in the current document as well as four standard targets: _blank, _parent, _self, _top. To create a target to an existing frame, select the frame's name from this menu. The other four targets function as follows:

- **_blank** Opens the link in a new page while keeping the current page open in the background.

- **_parent** Opens the link in its parent frameset. This is the innermost frameset directly above the frame containing the link.

- **_self** Opens the link into the current frame, replacing its contents (the default).

- **_top** Opens the link in its outermost frameset, replacing all the contents of the page.

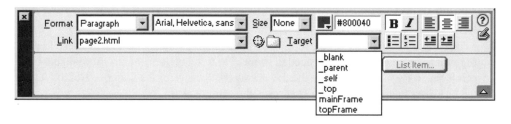

FIGURE 8-6 Using the Property Inspector panel to select a frame target

Create a Navigation Bar with Frames

One of the most useful implementations of frames is the creation of a site with a permanent navigation bar in one frame and a scrollable, changeable content area in another. An example of this is the artist's portfolio pictured in Figure 8-7, in which a user can click one of the links in the top frame to display sample pages in the bottom frame. The following steps summarize how to use many of the techniques described in the rest of this chapter to create a frames-based page like this to display multiple pages and target separate frames.

A smart way to build a site using frames is to plan its appearance and structure before you begin. This requires a little bit of work. In the example in Figure 8-7, there are two frames. The top frame displays a static navigation bar with six images. Each of the images links to one of six

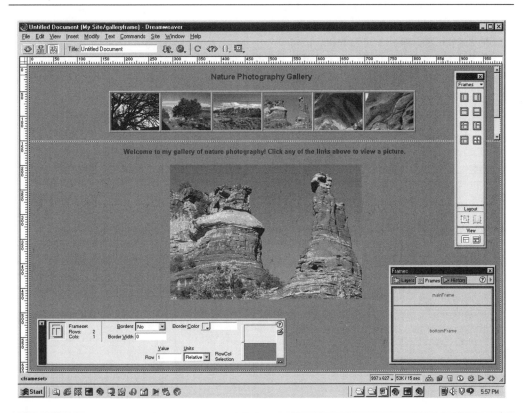

FIGURE 8-7   This site uses frames to display two pages: a navigation page in the top frame and a content page in the bottom frame.

pages that will appear in the bottom frame when the image is clicked. In addition, there is an introductory content page that appears when the user first visits the site, for a total of seven content pages. Assuming that the content pages already exist, you can create a frameset like the one shown in Figure 8-7 by following these steps:

1. Open a new blank page to use as the frameset document.

2. Click one of the insert frame icons in the Frames page of the Objects panel to insert as many blank frames as you need into the page.

3. Resize the frames by dragging the frame borders to achieve the desired layout.

4. Click the border of the frameset in the Frames panel so that the Frameset Property Inspector panel is visible. Now click the first row or column in the Frameset Property Inspector panel to display its properties, and edit them accordingly. In this example, the top frame has a fixed height.

5. Click the second row or column in the Frameset Property Inspector panel to select its properties, and edit them accordingly. In this example, the bottom frame has a relative size. Repeat the process for any other framesets in the document.

6. Save the Frameset document by choosing File | Save Frameset As and saving it in the same directory as the other web pages that will be inserted into the frames.

7. Click the navigation frame to select it, insert the images for the navigation bar, and define the links to all the linked web pages using the Property Inspector panel's Link field. For each link, enter the target as the content frame by selecting the frame's name in the pop-up target field.

8. Choose File | Save Frame As to save the navigation bar as a separate web page.

9. Click the main content frame to select it, and in the Property Inspector panel click the folder icon next to the Src field to locate the introductory web page to fit in the frame. Do the same for the other frames in the document, linking to the appropriate page for each frame.

10. Choose File | Save All Frames to save the frameset and frame files. The page is now complete. To see how it works, preview the page in a browser and click each of the image links in the top navigation bar.

Create Alternative Content
for Browsers That Don't Support Frames

When frames first came out, web designers had no choice but to create alternative no-frames content since so many people still used browsers that weren't capable of displaying frames. Although the vast majority of today's web browsers support frames, there is a growing assortment of new devices accessing the Web such as cell phones, PDAs, and other handheld devices, many of which don't support frames. There's also the issue of visually impaired users and others using screen readers or other assistive technologies that may have problems with frames. So, there's still a need for a no-frames alternative to any web page that includes frames. Fortunately, Dreamweaver makes it relatively easy to create a no-frames alternate for a frameset page.

The HTML frames specification includes a mechanism for supporting nonframe-enabled browsers by including the <noframes> tag in a frameset document. Whenever you build a frameset page, Dreamweaver includes a set of empty opening and closing <noframes> tags in the document's HTML code. These tags are located just after the <frameset> tags. Included inside the <noframes> opening and closing tags are a pair of <body> tags, which provide viewable content to nonframe-enabled browsers. Because frame-enabled browsers ignore any content inside the <noframes> tag, any content placed there is ignored by a frame-enabled browser, but the content within the <body> tags inside those <noframes> tags will display in a nonframe-enabled browser.

Although Dreamweaver automatically creates the <noframes> and <body> tags, the program doesn't automatically place any content there. As a result, any nonframe-enabled browser that visits the frameset page on your site will see a blank page because there is no content inside the <body> tags.

To edit the content in the <noframes> section of a frameset document that is viewable to nonframe-enabled browsers, choose Modify | Frameset | Edit No Frames Content. This opens up a new Document window in Dreamweaver that enables you to edit the page as if it were a regular web page instead of a frameset page (see Figure 8-8). All the normal tools and objects you are accustomed to using in Dreamweaver are available to edit this page; the only difference is that all the content you create will be placed inside the <noframes> tags. After editing the no frames version of the page, choose Modify | Frameset | Edit No Frames Content once again to return to the frameset.

8

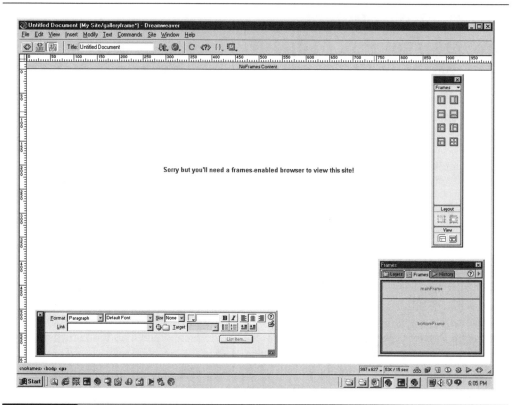

FIGURE 8-8 Selecting the Edit No Frames Content command enables you to create an alternative page viewable by nonframe-enabled browsers.

Chapter 9

Work with Forms

How to...

- Add a form to your web page
- Add elements to your form
- Label and format forms
- Submit form data

Since the early days of the Web, forms have been an important part of many web sites. Forms enable you to gather information from visitors to your web site. You can use forms to solicit feedback from site visitors or to set up a guest book. A form can be as simple as a login screen, or as sophisticated as an online purchasing system.

Using Dreamweaver, you can create most any kind of onscreen form you can envision. Dreamweaver makes all the HTML form tags accessible and easy to use in the familiar Design view Document window. However, Dreamweaver can't help you with one important part of any form—the form processing. For that, you must rely on scripts or applications running on the web server that hosts your site.

What Are HTML Forms?

Because of the very nature of the Web, every web page includes the possibility of some interaction with the viewer. The web browser detects the location of the mouse pointer on the web page and sends a request to the web server if the viewer clicks on a hyperlink. The server responds by sending a new page to the browser. That sets the precedent for a two-way exchange of information between the viewer's browser and the web server. Once the communication channel is open, there's no reason it can't be used to send more than a simple mouse click—for instance, text characters or the status of a check box.

The HTML form tags provide the means for creating various user input areas on a web page. You can create text boxes, radio buttons, check boxes, list boxes, and more. The web browser displays these onscreen objects to solicit user input as shown in Figure 9-1. The visitor types in a text box or selects an item from a list box to fill out the form, Then, when the visitor clicks a Submit button, the browser sends that information back to the web server.

What the web server does with the information received from the form depends on what kind of processing script or application is running on the server and how the information is submitted from the form to the script. Some form-processing scripts can send the contents of a form in an e-mail message to a specified e-mail address, others enter the information into a database or transfer it to another program.

The server-side scripting required to process form submissions is beyond the scope of this book. But you rarely need to delve into server-side scripting unless you're attempting to do something elaborate with your form data. Most servers have simple form mailers and other standard scripts available. To use these ready-made form-processing facilities, all you need to do is check with the webmaster or system administrator to find out the name and location of the script and how to submit your form data to it. You enter this information in Dreamweaver,

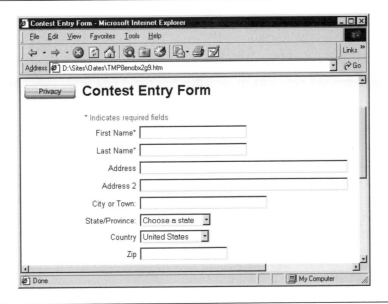

FIGURE 9-1   An HTML form

and you're in business. If, however, you need to create database connections and other, more elaborate applications of forms, you probably need to move up to the advanced level of Dreamweaver UltraDev.

Create a Form

In addition to the visible form elements, such as text boxes, list boxes, radio buttons, and a Submit button, every form must start and end with an invisible form element—the HTML `<form>` tag. The `<form>` tag contains essential information that tells the browser how to submit data from the form. That information includes the address of the script that will process the form data and the method by which the data is sent to the server.

Before you begin placing text boxes and other form elements on your web page, you need to tell Dreamweaver (and the visitor's browser) that those elements are part of a form. You do so by inserting a form into your web page. Dreamweaver inserts the `<form>` tags into the source code for your page and draws a rectangle in Design view with a red dotted line to represent the form. After you insert the form into your page, you can use the Property Inspector panel to set form attributes such as the submission method.

To insert a form into your web page, follow these steps:

1. Position the insertion point cursor at the location in your document where you want to insert the form.

2. Choose Insert | Form or go to the Forms page of the Objects panel and click the Insert Form button. Dreamweaver inserts a form into your document. The form appears as a short, wide rectangle drawn with a red dotted line, as shown in Figure 9-2. The insertion point appears inside the form rectangle.

If the form rectangle does not appear in Design view, choose View | Visual Aids | Invisible Elements to activate Dreamweaver's display of forms and other invisible portions of your web page.

3. Select the form by clicking inside the form rectangle and then clicking the `<form>` tag in the Tag Selector located in the Design view status bar.

4. In the Property Inspector panel, type a name for the form in the Form Name box. Every form must have a unique form name, which is necessary to reference the form with a scripting language. Dreamweaver supplies a default name such as "form1," but a more meaningful name will be easier to work with.

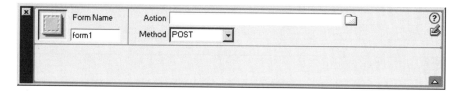

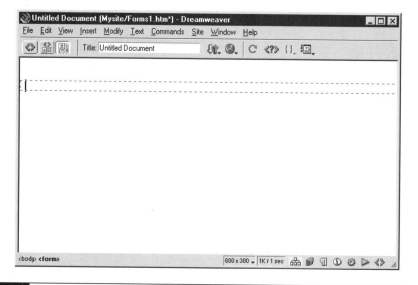

FIGURE 9-2   A newly created form in Design view

5. Enter the URL for the form processing script or application in the Action box. You can type in the complete path and filename, or click the folder icon to open a dialog box that you can use to locate and select the script if it is located on a locally accessible drive.

> **NOTE** *Contact the webmaster or system administrator in charge of the web server where your site will reside to find out what information you need to enter in the Action and Method attributes for your form in order to take advantage of the server's form-processing scripts or applications.*

6. Select the data submission method in the Method list box.

- **Post** Submits form data in blocks suitable for use in an e-mail message or similar application
- **Get** Submits form data by adding it onto the end of a URL
- **Default** Submits form data according to the default settings of the visitor's browser (usually the Get method)

You can simply insert a form into your web page and then immediately start adding form elements without first defining the Action and Method for the form in the Property Inspector panel. The form won't work until you define those essential attributes, but you can always add or modify them at a later time.

> **NOTE** *The HTML code for a form looks something like this:*
> ```
> <form name="form1" method="post" action="\cgi-bin\mailform.cgi">
> </form>
> ```

Add Form Elements

After you add a form to your web page, you can begin building the visible portions of the form by adding form elements. It's the form elements that the site visitor sees and uses to enter or select information to submit to the server. As in general page design, the form design is up to you. You can use any combination of the following form elements.

- **Text boxes** Solicit text input from the visitor. You can create single-line text boxes and multi-line text areas.
- **Check boxes** Present the visitor with a yes or no choice.
- **Radio buttons** Like check boxes, present the visitor with a yes or no choice, with the added restriction that only one item in the group can be answered yes.
- **Selection lists** List boxes and pop-up menus present a list of items from which to choose. You can create both scrolling lists and pop-up list boxes.
- **Jump menus** A special form of pop-up list box that lists a series of links.
- **File fields** Enable the user to submit a file to the server.

- ■ **Buttons** The standard Submit or Reset buttons that submit the form data to the server or clears the form fields.
- ■ **Images** Enable you to create custom, graphical buttons.
- ■ **Hidden fields** Enable you to insert information into the form that the visitor doesn't see. For example, you might need to use a hidden field to specify the e-mail address to which the form processor sends the submitted form data.

 *Form elements can be placed only into a form. If you attempt to place a form element on a page outside a preexisting form, Dreamweaver prompts you to create the form automatically.*

Text Boxes

Text boxes in a form can range from short, single-line boxes for a user ID or e-mail address, to large multi-line text areas in which the visitor can type paragraphs of text. To protect passwords from prying eyes, you can configure a text box to display asterisks onscreen instead of text. Figure 9-3 shows the three kinds of text boxes.

No matter which kind of text box you want to place into your form, you start out the same way—by inserting a generic text box into the form. Then you use the Property Inspector panel to give the text box the characteristics you need.

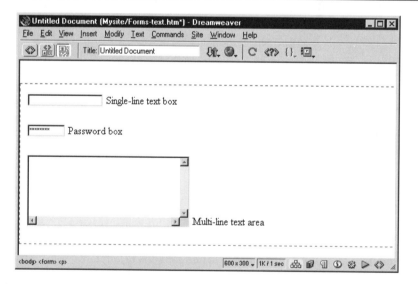

FIGURE 9-3 Text boxes in a form

Single-Line Text Box

To create a single-line text box, follow these steps:

1. Position the insertion point cursor on the page at the location where you want to insert a text box. Make sure it is inside the red dotted outline of the form.

2. Click the Insert Text Field button on the Forms pane of the Objects panel or choose Insert | Form Object | Text Field. Dreamweaver inserts a small, single-line text field into the form as shown. A dotted line surrounding the text box indicates that it's selected.

3. In the Property Inspector panel, enter a unique name for the text field in the TextField box. Each text field must have a unique name to identify its contents. Dreamweaver assigns default names such as "textfield3," but it'll be much easier to work with the form data if you replace that with a meaningful name.

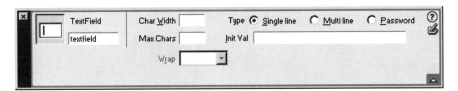

4. Select Single Line in the Type area to designate this as a single-line text box.

5. Enter a number in the Char Width box to set the width (in characters) of the text box in the form. This setting determines the size of the text box, not the maximum number of characters the visitor can type. The text box will automatically scroll horizontally to accommodate longer text entries. If you leave the Char Width box blank, the text box uses the browser's default size, which is usually about 26 characters.

6. Enter a number in the Max Chars box to set the maximum number of text characters the visitor can enter, or leave the Max Chars box blank to allow the visitor to enter unlimited text. Use this setting to restrict fixed-length data, such as ZIP codes and passwords to the appropriate length.

9

7. If you want text to appear in the text box when the form first appears in the visitor's browser window, type that text in the Init Value box in the Property Inspector panel. Normally, you leave this box blank, but it can be useful for inserting default values into forms or for giving the visitor instructions (such as *type your full name here*).

8. Back in the Document window, click beside the text box and type a label or instructions for filling in the form.

 The HTML code for a single-line text box looks like this:
`<input type="text" name="textfield3" size="30">`

Password Text Box

A Password text box is a single-line text box with a special characteristic that causes the browser to display asterisks in the text box in place of the characters the visitor types. This is a common practice intended to protect the visitor's password from prying eyes.

To create a Password text box in your form, follow the previous instructions for creating a single-line text box, but in step 4, select Password instead of Single Line as the text box Type. Since passwords are normally limited to a fixed number of characters, you'll probably want to set that number in the Char Width box in step 5 and in the Max Chars box in step 6.

 The HTML code for a password text box looks like this:
`<input type="password" name="textfield2" size="8" maxlength="8">`

Multi-Line Text Area

To create a multi-line text area, follow these steps:

1. Follow steps 1–3 from the instructions for creating a single-line text box to add a generic text box to your form and name it.

2. Select Multi Line in the Type area to designate this as a multi-line text area.

3. Enter a number in the Char Width box to set the width (in characters) of the text area in the form. Again, this setting determines the size of the text box, not the maximum number of characters the visitor can type.

4. Enter a number in the Num Lines (Number of Lines) box to set the height of the text area. Like the Char Width value, this setting determines the visible size of the text area in the browser window, not the maximum number of lines of text the visitor can enter into the text box.

5. Select a setting in the Wrap list box to determine what happens if the visitor enters more text than will display in the text box. You can choose one of the following:

   - **Off** Disables word wrapping. The text box scrolls horizontally to accommodate longer lines of text. The visitor must press ENTER to move down to the next line.

- **Virtual**   Text wraps to the next line automatically to remain visible in the text area in the browser window, but the text is submitted for processing as one long line of text (unless the visitor presses ENTER to create line breaks).
- **Physical**   Text wraps to the next line automatically, and corresponding line breaks are inserted in the text when it is submitted.
- **Default**   The same as Off.

6. If you want text to appear in the text box when the form first appears in the visitor's browser window, type that text in the Init Value box in the Property Inspector panel. Normally, you leave this box blank.

7. Back in the Document window, click beside the text area and type a label or instructions for filling in the form.

NOTE
The HTML code for a multi-line text area looks like this:
```
<textarea name="textfield" cols="50" rows="6">initial
value</textarea>
```

Check Boxes

Check boxes are a way to present the visitor with a predefined choice, to which the visitor responds with a yes/no or on/off kind of choice. Check boxes work equally well for single items that need a yes/no response (such as "Would you like to be added to our mailing list?") or for a list of items from which the visitor can select one or more items (such as a list of interests: sailboat racing, weekend cruises, vacation charters). Figure 9-4 shows both applications of check boxes.

9

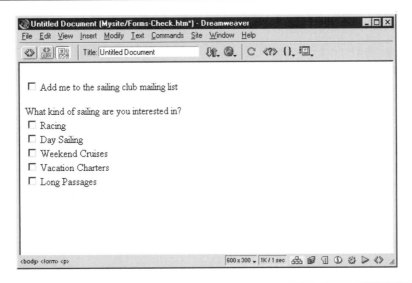

FIGURE 9-4   Check boxes in a form

To add a check box to your form, follow these steps:

1. Position the insertion point cursor on the page at the location where you want to insert a check box. Make sure it is inside the red dotted outline of the form.

2. Click the Insert Checkbox button on the Forms pane of the Objects panel, or choose Insert | Form Object | Check Box. Dreamweaver inserts a small check box into the form as shown. The dotted line surrounding the box indicates that it's selected.

3. In the Property Inspector panel, enter a unique name for the check box in the Check Box box. Like text boxes, each check box must have a unique name to identify its contents. Replace the Dreamweaver assigned default name with a meaningful name of your own.

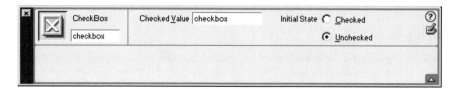

4. Enter a descriptive identifier in the Checked Value box. This is the value that will be submitted as part of the form data as in: *checkedvalue=yes*.

5. Select Checked or Unchecked in the Initial State area. This setting controls whether the check box is checked or unchecked when the form first loads in the visitor's browser. In other words, it sets the default state of the check box.

6. Return to the Document window, click beside the check box, and type a label. Without a label, the visitor won't know what the check box represents.

The HTML code for a check box looks like this:
<input type="checkbox" name="checkbox1" value="box1">

Radio Buttons

Like check boxes, radio buttons present the visitor with a yes/no or on/off kind of choice. The difference is that radio buttons appear in a group, and the visitor can select only one item from the group. Selecting one radio button automatically deselects the others in the group. In other words, radio buttons force the user to choose only one of two or more choices.

Because of this exclusive choice characteristic of radio buttons, it's important to pay attention to how the radio buttons are grouped. In Dreamweaver, you insert radio buttons one by one, not by groups. All the radio buttons in a form are in the same group by default. You assign radio buttons to different groups with the RadioButton name setting in the Property Inspector panel.

To add a radio button to your form, follow these steps:

1. Position the insertion point cursor on the page at the location where you want to insert a radio button. Make sure it is inside the red dotted outline of the form.

2. Click the Insert Radio Button icon on the Forms pane of the Objects panel, or choose Insert | Form Object | Radio Button. Dreamweaver inserts a small round radio button into the form as shown. The dotted line surrounding the button indicates that it's selected.

3. In the Property Inspector panel, enter the name of the radio button group in the RadioButton box. Unlike so many other form elements, this is not a unique name for the individual button but a name for the group of buttons in which the exclusive-choice rule will be enforced. As always, it's a good idea to replace the Dreamweaver assigned default name with a meaningful name of your own.

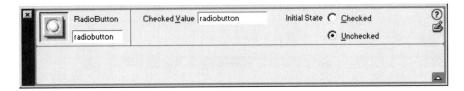

4. Enter a descriptive identifier in the Checked Value box. This is the value that will be submitted as part of the form data as in: *checkedvalue=button1*.

5. Select Checked or Unchecked in the Initial State area. This setting controls whether the radio button is checked or unchecked by default when the form first loads in the visitor's browser. Remember that only one button in a group can be checked.

6. Back in the Document window, click beside the radio button and type a label. As with check boxes, it's essential to provide a label on the form because there is nothing in the radio button to tell the visitor what it represents.

NOTE *The HTML code for a radio button looks like this:*
<input type="radio" name="radiobutton" value="button1">

9

Selection Lists

As the name implies, a selection list presents a list of items from which the visitor can choose one or more items. You could theoretically accomplish the same thing with check boxes or radio buttons, but a selection list is much more compact and efficient.

Just as you can have multi-line text areas and single-line text boxes, you can have multi-line selection lists and single-line lists, which Dreamweaver calls *menus* (see Figure 9-5). A multi-line selection list is larger, with room for several items to be displayed in the list box. If there are more items in the list than there is room to display, a scroll bar appears on the right side of the list to enable the visitor to scroll up and down through the list to see all list items—hence the name *scrolling list*. You have the option of allowing the visitor to choose more than one item from a scrolling list.

A single-line list—called a pop-up menu or drop-down list box—is the most compact way to present multiple choices, because it occupies only a single line of vertical space in the form. A button at the right side of the list box gives the visitor access to the complete list. The visitor clicks the button to display the list items in a pop-up menu, then clicks one of the items in the menu to make the choice. The selected item appears in the list box.

Although the results look quite different, the procedures for creating both lists and menus are basically the same. The only difference is that, for a list, you need to specify the list height and you have the option of allowing multiple selections. To add a list or a menu to your form, follow these steps:

1. Position the insertion point cursor on the page at the location where you want to insert a selection list. Make sure it is inside the red dotted outline of the form.

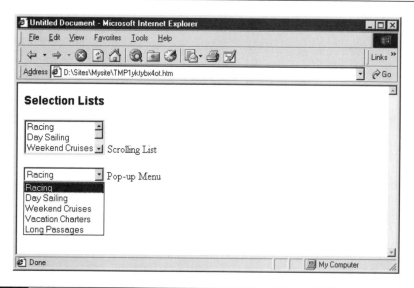

FIGURE 9-5   Selection lists

2. Click the Insert List/Menu button on the Forms pane of the Objects panel, or choose
Insert | Form Object | List/Menu. Dreamweaver inserts a small pop-up menu box into
the form as shown. A dotted line surrounding the list box indicates that it's selected.

3. In the Property Inspector panel, enter a unique name for the selection list in the
List/Menu box. You can accept the default name that Dreamweaver assigns, but
a name that describes the list will be more useful.

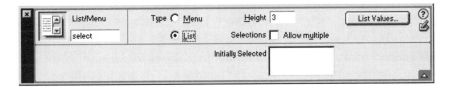

4. Select Menu or List in the Type area to designate this selection list as a scrolling list
or a pop-up menu.

5. Enter a number in the Height box to designate how many lines the scrolling list will
display. This option applies only to scrolling lists. The option is grayed out for menus.

6. Check the Selections - Allow Multiple option if you want to allow the visitor to select
more than one item from the list. Again, this option applies only to scrolling lists; it's
grayed out for menus.

7. Click the List Values button to open the List Values dialog box. The insertion point
starts out in the Item Label column.

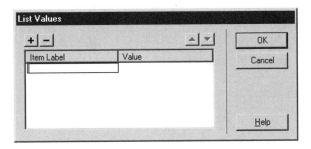

8. Type an item label for a list item. This is the text that will appear as an item in the
selection list. Press TAB to move the insertion point to the Value column.

9

9. Type the item entry that you want to submit as form data when the visitor chooses the corresponding list item. Often this value is the same as the Item Label, but it could also be a catalog number, filename, or other data that corresponds to the descriptive item label.

10. Click the plus (+) button to add another item to the list and repeat steps 8 and 9 to define the Item Label and Value for the new list item. Continue adding items until the list is complete.

11. Rearrange the list order by selecting an item from the list and clicking the up and down buttons to move it up or down in the list. To remove an item from the list, select it and then click the minus (–) button.

12. Click OK to close the List Values dialog box and add the list items to the selection list in your form. Dreamweaver adds the items to the source code and the list box expands horizontally in Design view to accommodate the longest item label in the list. The list items also appear in the Initially Selected list in the Property Inspector panel.

13. Select one item from the Initially Selected list if you want to designate a default selection to appear when the form loads in the visitor's browser. To deselect an item in the Initially Selected list, CTRL+click.

14. Click beside the selection list in the Document window and type a label or other instructions.

Create a Jump Menu

In addition to the standard selection lists, Dreamweaver includes a separate command for creating a special kind of menu—a *jump menu*. A jump menu is a menu-style selection list that contains a list of URLs, like hyperlinks. What makes the jump menu special is that Dreamweaver automatically adds a bit of JavaScript code to your page that enables the browser to process the list selection

The HTML Code for a Selection List

The HTML code for a selection list looks something like this:

```
<select name="select" size="3" multiple>
  <option value="1">Item 1</option>
  <option value="2">Item 2</option>
  <option value="3">Item 3</option>
</select>
```

immediately. As a result, when the visitor makes a selection from the jump menu, the browser goes to the associated URL just as if the visitor had clicked a normal hyperlink elsewhere on the page. The jump menu is really intended to be used by itself as a navigation tool rather than as a component of a larger form.

To create a jump menu, follow these steps.

1. Position the insertion point cursor on the page at the location where you want to insert a jump menu. The jump menu must be located in a form, but Dreamweaver automatically creates a form to surround the jump menu if you don't place it in a preexisting form.

2. Click the Insert Jump Menu button on the Forms pane of the Objects panel, or choose Insert | Form Object | Jump Menu. Dreamweaver opens the Insert Jump Menu dialog box.

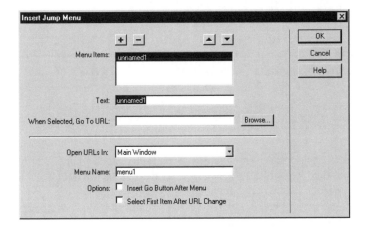

3. Type a list item label in the Text box. This is the text that will appear as an item in the selection list.

4. Enter a URL for the link in the When Selected, Go To URL box. You can type in the full URL or click the Browse button to open a Select File dialog box where you can locate and select a file on your system.

5. Click the plus (+) button to add another item to the list, and repeat steps 3 and 4 to define the Text and URL for the next item. Continue adding items until the list is complete.

6. Rearrange the list order by selecting an item from the list and clicking the up and down buttons to move it up or down in the list. To remove an item from the list, select it and then click the minus (−) button.

7. If your page uses frames, select a target frame in the Open URLs In box. Otherwise, accept the default of Main Window.

8. Enter a name for the jump menu in the Menu Name box.

9. Select one or both options as appropriate:

   ■ **Insert Go Button After Menu**   Adds a Go button to the right of the menu box. Instead of the browser jumping to the URL as soon as the visitor clicks an item in the list, the visitor selects an item and then clicks the Go button to load the linked URL.

   ■ **Select First Item After URL Change**   Displays the first menu item as the default selection.

10. Click OK to close the Insert Jump Menu dialog box and add the jump menu to your page. Dreamweaver inserts a form into your page and creates a pop-up menu box within that form as shown. A dotted line surrounding the list box indicates that it's selected.

   *A jump menu is really just a pop-up menu tied to a bit of JavaScript. After you create the jump menu, if you need to edit the menu items or links, you do so by editing the contents of the List Values in the Property Inspector panel, just as you would any other pop-up menu.*

File Fields

When combined with the appropriate server scripts, a file field enables your site visitors to upload files to your site. A file field looks like a single-line text box, but the file field is distinguished by a Browse button to the right of the text box, as shown in Figure 9-6.

To use the text field, the site visitor either types a path and filename into the text box portion of the file field or clicks the Browse button to open a dialog box where the visitor can locate and

Did you know?

The HTML Code for a Jump Menu

The HTML code for a jump menu looks something like this:

```
<select name="menu1" onChange="MM_jumpMenu('parent',this,0)">
  <option value="TravelDetail_surf.html" selected>Surf</option>
  <option value="TravelDetail_rockClimb.html">Rock Climb</option>
  <option value="TravelDetail_mtnBike.html">Bike</option>
</select>
```

In addition, Dreamweaver inserts some script code in the document header to process this special form.

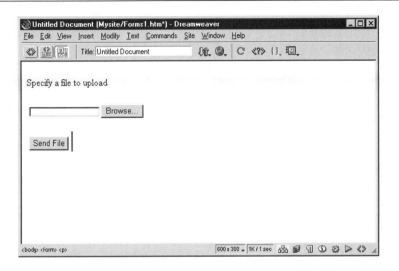

FIGURE 9-6 A file field

select a file. Closing the dialog box enters the path and filename for the selected file into the file field. Then, when the visitor clicks the form's Submit button, the browser sends the selected file to the server along with any other form data.

CAUTION *Before attempting to create a form with a file field, check with the webmaster or server system administrator to make sure file uploads are allowed on the server.*

To add a file field to a form on your web page, follow these steps:

1. Position the insertion point cursor on the page at the location where you want to insert a file field. Make sure it is inside the red dotted outline of the form.

NOTE *File fields work only in forms that use the Post method. The form's Action setting needs to specify the upload address. Also, you need to manually add the following attribute to the <form> tag: ENCTYPE="multipart/form-data"*

 2. Click the Insert File Field button on the Forms pane of the Objects panel, or choose Insert | Form Object | File Field. Dreamweaver inserts a file field and its accompanying Browse button into the form as shown. A dotted line surrounding the text box indicates that it's selected.

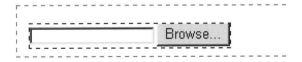

3. In the Property Inspector panel, enter a unique name for the file field in the FileField Name box. Replace the Dreamweaver's default name with something more meaningful.

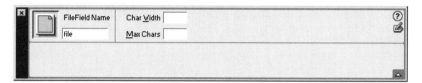

4. Enter a number in the Char Width box to set the width (in characters) of the file field in the form. As with a single-line text box, this setting determines the size of the text box, not the maximum number of characters the visitor can type. The file field automatically scrolls horizontally to accommodate longer text entries. If you leave the Char Width box blank, the text box uses the browser's default size, which is usually about 26 characters.

5. Enter a number in the Max Chars box to set the maximum number of text characters the visitor can enter, or leave the Max Chars box blank to allow the visitor to enter unlimited text.

6. Click beside the file field in the Document window and type a label or instructions for submitting the file.

The HTML code for a file field box looks like this:
`<input type="file" name="file2">`

Submit and Reset Buttons

Submit and Reset buttons are standard features of almost every form. The visitor signals the browser to send the form data to the server by clicking the Submit button; clicking the Reset button is a quick way to clear the form contents and start over.

The procedure for adding these essential elements to your form is similar to adding other form elements. Here's how:

1. Position the insertion point cursor on the page at the location where you want to insert a button. As always, make sure it is inside the red dotted outline of the form.

2. Click Insert Button on the Forms pane of the Objects panel, or choose Insert | Form Object | Button. Dreamweaver inserts a button into the form as shown. The default is a Submit button, but you can change that. The dotted line surrounding the box indicates that it's selected.

3. In the Property Inspector panel, enter a unique name for the button in the Button Name box. Every button needs its own name, so give it something appropriate.

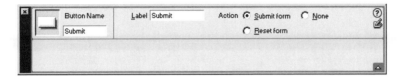

4. Click Submit Form or Reset Form in the Action area. This setting specifies what happens when the visitor clicks the button. Dreamweaver automatically changes the Label setting to match your selection. (There is also a third selection—None—that creates a button that doesn't do anything. I can't imagine why you'd want such a button, but the option is there.)

5. Enter a label for the face of the button in the Label box. You can substitute something like Clear Form for the Reset button or Send File for a Submit button accompanying a file field.

NOTE *The HTML code for a button looks like this:*
```
<input type="reset" name="Clear" value="Clear Form">
```

 **How to ... Create a Graphical Submit Button**

You aren't stuck with the plain gray Submit and Reset buttons. You can substitute a graphical button of your own design if you prefer. The trick is to use the Image Field form object and use the reserved names, Submit or Reset, to tell the browser what the image is supposed to represent.

Of course, the first step is to create an image to use as the button. You can use Fireworks or your favorite image editor for that. Then you add the image to your form and identify it as a Submit or Reset button. Here's how to do it:

1. Position the insertion point at the location in the form where you want to place the button.

2. Click the Insert Image Field button on the Forms pane of the Objects panel, or choose Insert | Form Object | Image Field. Dreamweaver opens the Select Image Source dialog box, the same dialog box you use to insert regular images into your document.

3. Locate and select the image file in the dialog box. Click Select to close the dialog box and add the image to your form. The image appears with the dotted outline surrounding it indicating that it is selected. Note that the selection box identifies the image as a form element rather than a standard image.

4. In the Property Inspector panel, type Submit (or Reset) in the ImageField box. Changing the image name to one of these reserved names is what tells the browser to treat the image as the specified form button.

Hidden Fields

A hidden field is one of those objects whose name describes what it does. It's a form field that is hidden from view in the visitor's browser, but it's part of the form nonetheless, and the contents of the hidden field are submitted for processing along with the rest of the form.

Hidden fields give you the opportunity to insert information into the form that the visitor doesn't need to see. You can use hidden fields to identify the form and to pass information to the processing script. For example, a form mailer script might rely on hidden fields to provide the e-mail address to which to send the form contents and the mail server to use to post that message.

Although hidden fields aren't visible in the visitor's browser, Dreamweaver adds a marker icon to Design view to indicate the presence of a hidden field so you can select and manipulate it. (Make sure the View | Visual Aids | Invisible Elements option is enabled to view hidden fields and other invisible page elements.) Figure 9-7 shows a form with hidden field markers visible near the top of the form.

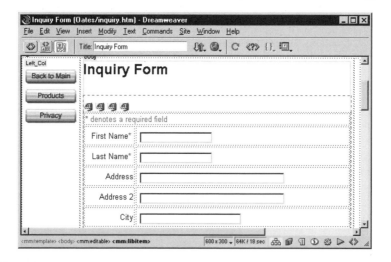

FIGURE 9-7   Hidden field markers in a form

To add a hidden field to your form, follow these steps:

1. Position the insertion point cursor at the location inside the form rectangle where you want to insert the hidden field. Hidden fields are usually placed at the top of the form, but you're not forced to place them there.

2. Click the Insert Hidden Field button in the Forms pane of the Objects panel, or choose Insert | Form Objects | Hidden Field. Dreamweaver inserts a hidden field marker in the form and selects it.

3. In the Property Inspector panel, enter a name for the hidden field in the HiddenField box.

> **CAUTION** *If you're creating a hidden field to pass information to a script, be sure to enter the field name exactly as specified for the script. Spelling and capitalization count.*

4. Enter the field value in the Value box. This is the information you want the hidden field to submit for processing along with the rest of the form.

> **NOTE** *The HTML code for a hidden field looks something like this:*
> ```
> <input type="hidden" name="sendto" value="name@bogus.com">
> ```

Finish the Form

In addition to the form elements themselves, your form can include regular text, images, and anything else you can place on a web page. In particular, forms usually include text as labels for the various form elements and to provide instructions for the form. You enter text into a form just as you enter it anywhere else.

Tables provide an important tool for controlling the form layout. You can insert tables—preferably Layout Tables (see Chapter 7)—into a form and use the table cells to arrange form elements on the page and align them both horizontally and vertically. Without tables, it's hard to create a form that isn't just a bunch of form fields stacked along the left page margin. With tables, you can create a form with logically grouped form elements neatly aligned and arrayed across the page. When using tables with a form, just make sure the entire table is within the <form> tags, which means within the bounds of the red dotted form rectangle in Design view.

Submit the Information Gathered in a Form

Every web page depends on a web server to be the host for the site and respond to requests from the browser for the files required to display each page. You don't have to be too concerned about the particular web server software that hosts a site as long as it conforms to the prevailing standards (and all the web servers do). The web server and the platform it runs on become a concern only if you start working with database connectivity and advanced scripting applications.

You can get into just such issues when working with forms. You can design a form in Dreamweaver and the visitor can fill it out in the browser window, but nothing happens when the visitor clicks the Submit button unless there is a script or application on the server to process the

9

form submission. Dealing with the requirements for submitting form data for processing can be fairly simple or quite complex, depending on what you want to do with the information you gather from the visitor with the form.

For example, if the form is designed to gather credit card information as part of an online shopping system, you need to submit the information to online financial services companies for credit card verification, authorization, and payment processing. That involves special accounts with the credit card processing companies and elaborate interconnections between your form and their payment processing systems. For security reasons, the data traveling between the various computers must be encrypted. That kind of form processing is beyond the scope of this book (and probably requires the advanced features of Dreamweaver UltraDev).

However, if you just want to forward the contents of a customer feedback to your e-mail address, that kind of form processing is much simpler. It involves submitting the form to a script or an application running on the server for processing, but the basic procedure isn't difficult to understand or implement. Note that, although most web servers have such scripts available, there is no real standardization among those scripts and programs.

Because of the lack of standardization among form processing scripts, I can't provide you with step-by-step instructions for configuring your form for processing. Your best bet is to contact the webmaster or system administrator for the web server hosting your site and ask what form processing scripts are available and how to submit form data to them. You'll need to get the following information:

- **Form submission method**   Select either Post or Get in the Method box in the Form Property Inspector panel. Post is the most common method.

- **URL of the script or application**   Enter this URL into the Action box in the Form Property Inspector panel.

- **Any parameters that must be submitted as form data**   This includes information such as the e-mail address the form data should be mailed to. It's normally inserted into hidden fields at the top of the form. The system administrator may supply sample code that you can paste into your page in Code view.

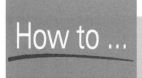 **Validate Form Contents Before Submission**

Have you ever tried to submit a web form and had a message box pop up onscreen telling that some field was missing required information?

You can use Dreamweaver Behaviors to perform the same kind of checks on your form's contents. For example, you can designate certain form fields as required and you can check to see if the field contains text or numerals. You can also verify that an e-mail address field contains the @ character.

For information on working with Behaviors, see Chapter 16. For a general overview of adding validation to your form, follow these steps.

1. Create the form and add form elements. Make sure that each form object has a unique name. You use these names to identify the form fields to validate.

2. Select the form (click the form outline) and make sure the Behaviors panel is open (choose Window | Behaviors if it isn't already open).

3. In the Behaviors panel, click the plus (+) button and choose Validate Form from the menu that appears. Dreamweaver opens the Validate Form dialog box.

4. Select a field to validate from the Named Fields list.

5. Click the Required check box to require an entry in the field.

6. Select one of the options in the Accept area to check the field for a valid entry.

7. Repeat steps 4–6 for other fields as needed.

8. Click OK to close the Validate Form dialog box.

9. Verify that onSubmit is selected in the Events column of the Behaviors panel. If it's not, click the button at the right end of the Events column and choose onSubmit from the menu that appears.

This attaches a Behavior (a script) to the form. When the visitor clicks the Submit button in the form, the Validate Form behavior checks the contents of the form fields to confirm that each field matches the conditions you set in the Validate Form dialog box before submitting the form for processing. If those conditions aren't met, a message box appears informing the visitor of the missing or invalid information.

You can also attach the Validate Form behavior to individual form fields to validate the field contents of the specific field as the visitor fills them out.

9

Chapter 10

Create and Use Dreamweaver Templates

How to...

- ■ Create a Dreamweaver template
- ■ Apply and edit templates
- ■ Revise templates and template-based sites

A well-designed web site uses a design scheme to give all the pages in the site a unified look. That doesn't necessarily mean that every page in the site is a cookie-cutter clone of every other page. But all (or most) pages in a site share certain elements such as background and text colors, as well as a standard layout that might include a logo graphic at the top of the page and perhaps a navigation bar on the left side. The text, images, and other content on the pages may vary dramatically, but the basic elements remain the same. It's the common page elements that give the site its visual identity.

In the past, the web designer had to carefully duplicate the layout and all other common elements from one page to the next. If the layout or one of the common elements changed, the designer had to painstakingly update each and every page on which it was used. Now, Dreamweaver's Template feature greatly simplifies the process of creating—and maintaining—the common layout and design elements that appear on every page in your web site.

What Is a Template?

A simple solution to the challenge of setting up a web site with a common design scheme is to create a master web document containing the common elements that you want to repeat on every page. You can then use that document (usually called a *template*) as the basis of the other pages you create for the site. When you work with a manually created template, you can either copy and paste HTML code from the master template page to each new page or simply make a copy of the template page and then customize the copy to create each individual page.

Dreamweaver takes this concept of a template document and incorporates it into the program. But Dreamweaver does more than just facilitate the common practice of creating documents based on a template. It improves on the normal process of using templates by adding several features that make creating and maintaining template-based sites much easier.

First of all, Dreamweaver automates the process of creating new web documents based on a template or applying a template to an existing page. Furthermore, you can lock some portions of Dreamweaver templates to protect them from accidental change, and you can create convenient placeholders for the editable areas on each page.

But the most important feature of Dreamweaver templates is the way Dreamweaver automatically updates template-based pages. When you make a change to the template file, Dreamweaver scans all the web documents in your site and automatically updates the HTML code for any document based on the template. This means that you can update dozens of pages that are based on a template in a matter of minutes—a chore that would take hours to do manually.

How Dreamweaver Templates Work

Dreamweaver templates are normal HTML files, just like any other web document. You can create a template from scratch or convert an existing web page to a template. You edit page properties, layout, tables, text, graphics, and other elements in a template in the Dreamweaver Document window just as you edit them in any other web document. The only difference is that you can define certain areas of the template as editable and other areas as locked.

When you create a template, Dreamweaver gives the template file a distinctive extension—.dwt—and stores it in the Templates subfolder in your site. However, despite the extension, the template file is still a standard HTML file. As you define editable and locked areas of the template, Dreamweaver inserts HTML comment codes into the HTML source code for the template. Dreamweaver can interpret the contents of these comment codes and use that information to display the boundaries of editable and locked areas of the template in Design view and to deliver the other features of templates in Dreamweaver. Web browsers and other HTML editors simply ignore the contents of an HTML comment, so Dreamweaver's templates and template-based pages remain fully compatible with other programs—there are no proprietary codes involved.

When you create a web page based on the template, Dreamweaver copies the relevant HTML code from the template to the new web page—effectively replicating the page properties, layout, and content of the template in the new page. That includes the editable and locked areas of the template. You can freely edit the content of the editable areas, but the locked areas of the template-based document inherit the contents and properties of the template; these locked areas are protected from change in the individual web pages. To change a locked area, you must either edit the template or disconnect the web document from the template. This ensures that all the template-based pages in a site are consistent with the master template.

When you create a template-based web page in Dreamweaver, the program keeps track of the connection between the page and the template on which it is based. If you make any change to the template, Dreamweaver offers to automatically update the pages based on that template. As a result, you can edit the template file to change a common design element that appears on every page in your site and see that change reflected in all the pages in minutes, without having to open each web document individually to make the change.

What Elements Should Be in the Template?

The most challenging aspect of working with Dreamweaver templates is not the mechanics of creating the template and defining editable and locked regions. (That part's not difficult. This chapter shows you how.) The tough part of working with templates is deciding what to include in the locked areas of the template, what to define as editable areas, and how to handle elements that are used repeatedly throughout the site but not on every page.

10

The simple answer to the question of what to include in a template is this: Include anything that should appear consistently in the same place on every page that is based on the template. The tricky part is identifying the consistent elements precisely and deciding whether every page in the site should be based on the same template, whether to use multiple templates for the site, and how to handle the inevitable exceptions.

There's no magic solution to these questions. It all depends on the design scheme for your site and how you expect to create and maintain the pages on your site. To use templates effectively requires careful thought and planning. Here are a few tips and guidelines to get you started in your planning process:

- Pages inherit all their page properties (except the document title) from the template. That includes background color, background image, and default text colors.

- A template can include tables, text, graphics, and just about anything else you can put on a web page. When you create a new web page based on the template, all the template content is transferred to the page.

- Tables that control page layout (see Chapters 6 and 7) are good candidates for use on a template. Putting the Layout Table in the template ensures that each page based on the template shares the same basic page layout.

- A template must contain at least one editable region, or else you can't edit the pages based on the template. Often the template contains a graphic at the top or left side of the page and the rest of the page is one large editable region. However, some templates contain a very detailed and complete page layout leaving only a few small areas for editable text and graphics.

- Logos and other header graphics work well in a template if they appear in exactly the same place on every page. If a logo needs to appear on every page but its location needs to change depending on the page content, it probably doesn't belong in the template. Instead, make the logo graphic a Library item (see Chapter 19), or, if it's a single-image file, add it to the Favorites list in the Assets panel for easy access as you create individual pages.

- A navigation bar or buttons can work well in a template if it is consistent from page to page throughout the site.

- A page footer with copyright information and such is sometimes appropriate in a template.

- Anything in a locked region of the template is not editable in a web page based on the template unless you first disconnect the page from the template.

- You can disconnect a web page from the template on which it is based, but, if you do, Dreamweaver can no longer automatically update the page to reflect changes in the template.

- A site can have multiple templates. Those templates can use the same elements, such as graphics files, and you can cut and paste tables and other elements from one template to another; however, it's not a good idea to have a template based on another template.

Templates vs. Library Items

Dreamweaver includes another feature—called Library items—that is similar to templates in some ways. You can use Library items to make it easy to reuse the same elements over and over on multiple pages throughout your site and to update them automatically. A Library item can consist of anything from a line of text to major portions of your page design such as a layout table with content or a complex image map. See Chapter 19 for information on how to create and apply Library items.

Library items share several characteristics with templates. Dreamweaver saves Library items in files with a special extension. Library items appear in the Assets panel, and you can add them to your page with a couple of mouse clicks. A Library item added to a web page is like a locked area of a template—you can't edit the Library content on the page unless you disconnect it from the Library. If you need to make changes to the contents of a Library item, you make the changes just once, to the Library file, and Dreamweaver automatically updates all the web documents in your site that contain that Library item.

- Use templates for standardizing page property settings and content that remain the same for all the pages in a site or in a section of a site.

- Use Library items for content that you use frequently throughout a site but don't want to place on the template because it doesn't appear on every page.

- Also use Library items for content that occurs in just a few locations in your site but needs to be updated frequently (for example, a weekly special or a news teaser).

- Don't bother creating a Library item for a single graphics file; that's what the Assets panel is for.

10

How to Create Templates

The mechanics of creating a template in Dreamweaver aren't difficult to master. A single command creates the template file. Dreamweaver takes care of the details of giving that file a special extension (.dwt) and creating the Templates subfolder in the root folder of your local site to store your template files. Another single command enables you to define editable areas of the template. All the page elements that appear in the template are the same as in any other web document—you create and work with them in exactly the same way you do on any other web page.

You have two choices in creating a template. You can start from scratch and build a template from a blank web document, or you can convert an existing web document (and all its contents) into a template.

Dreamweaver expects you to work with templates in Design view. Some template-related commands are unavailable when you work in Code view. To access the template-related commands, simply switch to Design view.

Save an Existing Page as a Template

Perhaps the most common technique for creating a template is to start with an existing web document and save a copy of that document as a template. This technique makes it easy to visualize how the template-based documents will look, because the template itself starts out as a completed web document. The existing web document serves as a prototype for the documents based on the template created from that original document.

If you're building a new web site, you may want to create a sample web document with the intent to use it as the basis for a template. You can work out the details of the page layout and the placement of various page elements in the sample document. Then, when the sample document meets your approval, you create a template based on the document.

If, however, you're continuing development of an existing site, you can select one of the existing pages to serve as the basis for your template. Any new pages you create based on the template will match the existing page. You can also apply the template to existing web documents in the site so you can take advantage of Dreamweaver's ability to automatically update template-based pages.

To create a template based on an existing web document, follow these steps:

1. Select or create a web document to serve as the prototype for the template. Open that web page in Dreamweaver's Design view window.

2. Choose File | Save as Template. Dreamweaver opens the Save As Template dialog box.

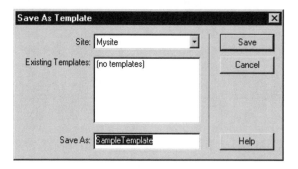

3. Select the site in the Site box and enter a name for the template in the Save As box. Click Save to close the Save As Template dialog box and create the template file. Dreamweaver saves a copy of the web document with the .dwt extension. The file is saved in the Templates folder of your local root folder for the site you selected. If the Templates folder does not exist, Dreamweaver creates it.

The newly created template file is open in the Design view window, ready for editing. To make the template functional, you'll need to delete text and other page elements that you don't want duplicated on to every template-based document, and you need to define editable areas of the template (see the later section in this chapter, "Define Editable Areas of a Template").

Create a Template from Scratch

Templates don't have to be based on an existing web page. You can create a template from scratch. You typically use this technique when you're building a new web site from scratch and you have a well-defined page layout worked out in advance. Here's how you do it:

1. Click the Templates button in the Assets panel. (Choose Window | Assets to open the Assets panel if it isn't already open.)

2. Click the New Template button at the bottom of the Assets panel. Dreamweaver adds a new "Untitled" template to the list of templates in the Assets panel.

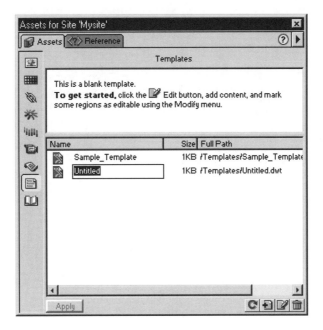

3. Enter a name for the template and press ENTER.

4. Click the Edit Template button at the bottom of the Assets panel to open the template in Design view and begin developing the page settings, layout, and content that will be passed on to the template-based pages.

CAUTION *Dreamweaver expects to find template files in a specific location in your site. Do not move the Templates folder. Do not move template files to another folder. And do not place nontemplate files in the Templates folder. If you move the template, the paths to files referenced in the template may not work properly.*

10

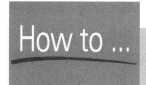 **Rename and Remove Templates**

It always happens. You create a template, give it a name, and use it as the basis for some pages in your site. Then you (or your boss/client) decide that the template needs another name or it should be removed from the site completely. You can handle both these maintenance chores in the Assets panel.

To rename a template, follow these steps:

1. Click the Templates button in the Assets panel to display the list of templates in the site.

2. Right-click the template name in the list and choose Rename from the context menu that appears. Dreamweaver highlights the template name.

3. Type a new template name and press ENTER. Dreamweaver changes the template name in the Assets panel and offers to update all the files based on the template.

To delete a template from your site, follow these steps:

1. Click the Templates button in the Assets panel to display the list of templates in the site.

2. Click the template you want to delete in the Assets panel list to select it.

3. Click the Delete button at the bottom of the Assets panel. Dreamweaver displays a confirmation message box.

4. Click Yes to confirm the deletion. Dreamweaver removes the template from the Assets panel and deletes the corresponding file from the Templates folder in your site.

Deleting the template from your site doesn't automatically unlock all the content in all the pages based on that template. To edit the locked text in any of the template-based pages, you must first disconnect the page from the template. For instructions, see the later section in this chapter, "Disconnect a Page From a Template."

Define Editable Areas of a Template

Templates exist to impose a degree of conformity on all the template-based pages. But that doesn't mean that every page is an exact duplicate of the template. Some areas of the page must vary from one page to the next. The variable areas might be small (just enough room for an image and some text), or the situation might be reversed and only a small area of the page is tied to the template, leaving the bulk of the page freely editable.

What portion of a template-based page is editable and what portion of the page is locked to the template is not something that is left to whim. The editable regions are carefully delineated and defined in the template. Then, when you create a page based on the template, you can edit the editable regions of the page, but you can't change the locked regions of the template-based page. To edit locked regions of a template-based page, you must edit the template and then update the page, or you can disconnect the page from the template.

When you create a new template, it starts out with the entire page locked. You must define one or more editable areas in the template in order to make the template useful. Here's how to mark existing page content as editable:

1. Select the text or other content that you want to be able to change in the template-based pages.

   ■ You can select an individual paragraph of text, an image, or other individual page element, or you can select a large area of the page containing several page elements. Just be sure your selection doesn't include page elements that you want to remain consistent throughout the site.

   ■ You can select an individual table cell or an entire table as an editable region, but you can't select multiple table cells and mark them as one editable region. If you must make multiple cells editable, create a separate editable region for each cell.

   ■ To mark the contents of a table cell as editable without making the cell itself editable, create a text paragraph in the cell and carefully select the paragraph and not the cell (check the Tag Selector to confirm that the <p> tag is selected but not the <td> tag).

   ■ If you mark a layer as editable, both the layer position and contents are editable. If you mark the layer contents as editable, only the content is editable, not the layer itself.

TIP *You don't need to select all the editable portions of a template at once. You can define multiple small editable areas one at a time.*

2. Choose Modify | Templates | New Editable Region, or right-click the selection and choose New Editable Region from the context menu. Dreamweaver displays the New Editable Region dialog box.

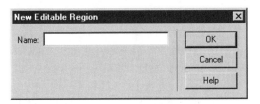

3. Enter a name for the editable region in the Name box. The editable region name must be unique within the current template and the name can't include angle brackets (<>), quotation marks (" '), or the ampersand (&) character.

4. Click OK to close the New Editable Region dialog box. Dreamweaver marks the editable region of the template with a light blue (cyan) outline and labels it with a small tab at the upper-left corner, as shown in Figure 10-1.

10

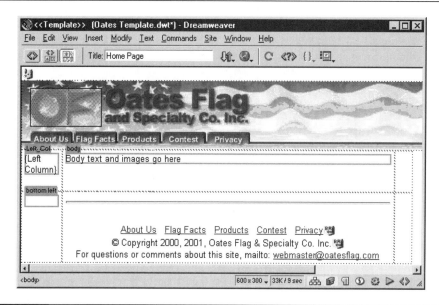

FIGURE 10-1 A newly defined editable region in a template

NOTE

The editable and locked regions of a template control what you can and cannot edit in a template-based page. All areas of the template are accessible for editing when the template itself is open in the Design view window. Dreamweaver automatically updates template-based pages with any changes you make to locked regions of the template. Changes to editable regions of the template don't trigger automatic updates.

You can also create a new, empty editable region on a template. Here's how:

1. Position the insertion point cursor at the location in the template where you want to create a new editable region.

2. Choose Modify | Templates | New Editable Region, or right-click and choose New Editable Region from the context menu that appears. Dreamweaver opens the New Editable Region dialog box.

3. Enter a name for the editable region in the Name box. The editable region name must be unique within the current template, and the name can't include angle brackets (<>), quotation marks (" '), or the ampersand (&) character (shown previously).

4. Click OK to close the New Editable Region dialog box. Dreamweaver creates the new editable region and marks it with a light blue (cyan) outline and a label tab at the

upper-left corner. The name of the editable region also appears as text in curly brackets inside the outline. This text serves as a placeholder to keep the editable region outline from collapsing to nothing.

5. Edit the placeholder text in the editable region as needed. You can replace the editable region name with a prompt or instructions.

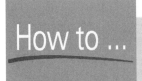 **Lock an Editable Region**

Occasionally, you may change your mind about the status of an editable region of a template and decide that it shouldn't be editable after all. To lock an editable region of a template, follow these steps:

1. Open the template file in the Design view window (if it isn't already open).

2. Choose Modify | Templates | Remove Editable Region, or right-click anywhere on the template and choose Remove Editable Region. Dreamweaver displays the Remove Editable Region dialog box.

3. Select the region you want to lock from the list in the dialog box and click OK. Dreamweaver closes the Remove Editable Region dialog box and removes the blue outline and name from the selected region.

Since all content in a template is locked unless it is specifically defined as an editable region, removing the editable region status of the selected content locks it so that it can't be changed in the template-based pages.

TIP *Dreamweaver generally does a good job of keeping track of paths to links, image files, and other content in templates and adjusting those paths for the new locations of the pages based on the template. However, you can reduce the chances of broken links if you use root-relative paths instead of document-relative paths for all links and file references in a template.*

10

Work with a Template

Creating a template is just the beginning. To use templates effectively, you need to be able to apply the template to the pages in your web site. Then you need to be able to work with those template-based pages, which means knowing how to select and edit content in the editable areas, as well as knowing how to identify the locked areas so you don't waste time trying to edit them.

How to Apply a Template

The most common way to apply a template to a web document is to create a new document based on the template. When you use this technique, Dreamweaver creates a new web document, copies the template settings and content to the new document, and opens that document in a Design view window for editing. Depending on the completeness of your template, the result is often a nearly complete web page that lacks only some custom content that you need to enter into the editable areas of the page.

You can also apply a template to an existing web page. When you do, Dreamweaver scoops up the content on the existing page and pours it into the editable areas of the template. You can use this technique when you need to go ahead and create the body content for some or most of the pages on your site before the page design and graphics are finalized. Then, when the graphics are approved, you can incorporate them into a template and apply the template to the pages containing the body content to quickly create the finished pages.

Applying a template to an existing web page works best when there is just one large editable area in the template. If there are several editable areas, you may need to go through an additional step to tell Dreamweaver where to place the existing page content.

Create a Page Based on a Template

Creating a new web document based on a template actually combines two operations into one. First of all, you create a new web document and open it for editing in the Design view window. Secondly, you instruct Dreamweaver to apply the selected template to that new, blank web document.

To create a new template-based document, follow these steps:

1. Choose File | New from Template. Dreamweaver opens the Select Template dialog box.

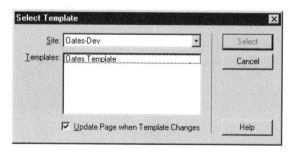

2. Select the site from the Site list box. Dreamweaver lists the templates available in the selected site.

3. Select a template from the Templates list and make sure the Update Page When Template Changes option is checked.

NOTE   *If you uncheck the Update Page When Template Changes option in the Select Template dialog box, Dreamweaver creates a new web document and copies the template content into that document, then disconnects the document from the template. As a result, everything in the new document is editable—there are no locked or protected areas—and Dreamweaver can't update the document to reflect changes in the template.*

4. Click Select to close the Select Template dialog box and create the new template-based page. Dreamweaver opens a Design view window containing the newly created web document with the template applied.

Apply a Template to an Individual Page

You can also apply a template to the page you are editing in Design view. Here's how:

1. Click the Templates button in the Assets panel to display the list of available templates on the site.

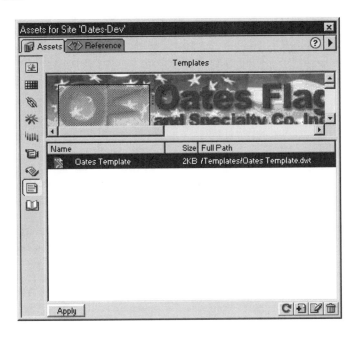

2. Select a template from the list and click the Apply button, or simply drag the selected template from the Assets panel and drop it on the page in the Design view window. Dreamweaver applies the selected template to the document.

> **TIP** *You can also apply a template to a page using a menu command. Choose Modify | Templates | Apply Templates to Page to open the Select Template dialog box. Select a site and a template; then click Select to close the dialog box and apply the template.*

Here are a few things you should know about what happens when you apply a template to an existing document.

- If no template had been previously applied to the document, Dreamweaver copies the template settings and content to the document and places the existing document content into the editable area of the template.

- If there are multiple editable areas in the template and multiple blocks of content on the page, Dreamweaver displays a dialog box where you can select the editable area into which the content is placed.

- If the document was based on another template, Dreamweaver replaces the old template content with the new template settings and content and tries to match the content of editable areas based on their names. For example, the content of the "Middle Column" editable area in the old template will be transferred to the "Middle Column" editable area of the new template, assuming that such an area exists.

- Behaviors and scripts located in the document header that belong with content in the document body are retained but other header items (such as meta tags) are discarded and replaced by the header content from the template.

Edit a Template-Based Page

The very nature of the connection between a page and the template on which it is based places some constraints on editing a template-based page. The portions of the page that are copied from the template and controlled by the template connection are locked—rendered uneditable—on the page in Design view. Only the portions of the page that are designated as editable in the template are accessible for editing. The editable regions may constitute most of the page or be limited to a few small areas.

Dreamweaver identifies the locked and editable portions of the page with color coded outlines in the Design view window, as shown in Figure 10-2. The locked area is marked with a yellow outline and labeled with a tab in the upper-right corner that bears the name of the template. Since the template is all locked except for the designated editable areas, the locked outline normally extends around the entire perimeter of the work area in the Design view window. The editable areas are marked with light blue outlines and labeled with the name of the editable region in a tab in the upper-left corner.

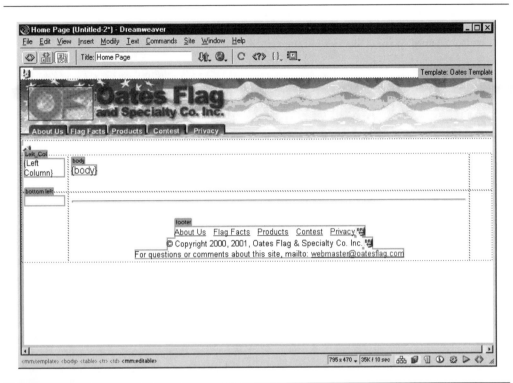

FIGURE 10-2   Colored outlines mark the locked and editable areas of a template-based page.

TIP *You can customize the colors Dreamweaver uses for the outlines marking locked and editable areas. The relevant settings are in the Highlighting category of the Preferences dialog box. See Chapter 20 for details.*

■ To edit a template-based document, you can simply click inside an editable area and then use any of the normal editing techniques to select, insert, delete, and modify the page content.

TIP   *If the locked and editable region outlines don't appear in Design view, choose View | Visual Aids | Invisible Elements to display Dreamweaver's clues to the existence of elements that don't show up in the browser window.*

 ■ As you move the mouse pointer over locked areas of the page, the pointer takes on the shape of the universal "do not" symbol to indicate that you can't select or edit content in that area.

■ To go directly to a specific editable region, choose Modify | Templates | *editable region name*. Dreamweaver selects the region and all its contents. To replace the contents with text, just start typing. Click within the selected area to edit the contents.

 *You can't convert tables to layers or layers to tables in a template-based page. You can still work with both tables and layers; you just can't convert one to the other.*

Update Template-Based Pages

One of the most powerful aspects of Dreamweaver's Templates feature is the program's ability to automatically update template-based pages throughout the site to reflect changes in the template. This means that you can make a change in one place—in the template file—and Dreamweaver automatically makes that change in all the web documents based on the template. You avoid the mind-numbing tedium of opening file after file and repeating the same edit on each one—Dreamweaver does the job for you and does it faster and more accurately.

Open a Template to Make Changes

Dreamweaver gives you two options for accessing a template file. You can open the template file directly, or you can open the template from any of the pages based on the template. Either way, you end up with the template file open in a Dreamweaver Design view window.

To take the direct approach to accessing a template file, follow these steps:

 1. Click the Templates button in the Assets panel to display the list of templates in your site.

2. Select the template you want to edit from the list in the Assets panel.

 3. Click the Edit Template button. Dreamweaver opens a Design view window to display the template for editing.

 You can also open a template by double-clicking the template's file icon in the Site files list in the Dreamweaver Site window.

If, as is often the case, you're working with a template-based page and you discover that you need to edit the template, you can just choose Modify | Templates | Open Attached Template to open the template. When you use this technique, there's no question about which template to select for editing, since Dreamweaver opens the template to which the page is connected.

Edit a Template

Editing a template is a straightforward process. You can edit all the text, images, tables, and other page elements using any normal editing technique.

The editable regions of the template are clearly marked, but, unlike when you are editing template-based pages, there are no restrictions imposed by the editable and locked regions of the template. Everything is fully editable on the template itself. You can edit the content of locked regions just as you can the content in editable regions. You can even change the editable regions themselves.

Even though you can edit anything on the template page, you need to pay attention to whether or not your edits fall within an editable region because that determines how Dreamweaver updates template-based pages in your site. Here's what happens when you save your changes to a template file:

■ If you edit a locked region (anything outside the editable regions), Dreamweaver opens the Update Template Files dialog box and offers to update all the web documents based on the template with the changes. If you click Update, the edited page content from the template replaces the old content in all the template-based pages listed in the dialog box.

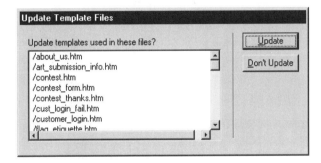

■ If you edit the content of an editable region, Dreamweaver does NOT automatically copy the changes to any existing documents based on the template. The newly edited content will be copied to any new documents that you create based on the template.

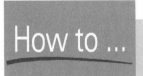
To make sure the current document is updated with the latest edits from the template, choose Modify | Templates | Update Current Page.

How to ... Update a Complete Site After Changing a Template

Although Dreamweaver offers to update all the template-based pages automatically when you save the template file after making changes in the template, there may be times that you want to trigger an update manually. Perhaps you deferred an earlier update after editing the template, or perhaps you edited the template outside Dreamweaver and now need to update the pages to reflect those changes. Here's how to initiate an update manually:

1. Choose Modify | Templates | Update Pages in any Design view window. Dreamweaver opens the Update Pages dialog box.

10

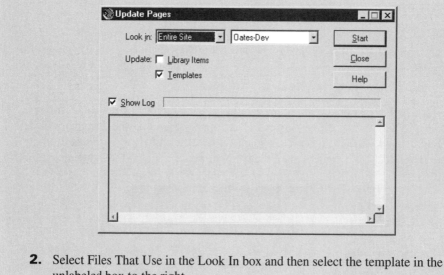

2. Select Files That Use in the Look In box and then select the template in the unlabeled box to the right.

3. Make sure the Templates check box is checked.

4. Click Start to begin the update. Dreamweaver displays a log of its progress in the large box in the lower half of the dialog box.

5. After the update process is complete, click Close to close the Update Pages dialog box.

Disconnect a Page from a Template

When you're editing a template-based page, Dreamweaver won't let you make any changes to a locked region of the page. To edit a locked region, you must make the changes on the template and then update the template-based pages. This ensures that the locked regions of all the template-based pages remain consistent.

Usually, that consistency is exactly what you're trying to accomplish with a template. However, there may be times when you need to change something in a locked region of one page without affecting all the other template-based pages in the site. To deal with these situations, you can break the connection between the page and the template and thereby remove the lock on the previously locked regions. Of course, the trade-off is that the link between the page and the template is broken, so Dreamweaver can no longer update the page to reflect any changes in the template.

If you need to disconnect a document from its template, simply choose Modify | Templates | Detach from Template. Dreamweaver removes from the page's source code all the HTML comments containing the links between the document and the template and designating editable and locked regions. The editable and locked region outlines disappear from Design view, and all areas of the page become editable.

Part IV

Add Graphics and Media

Chapter 11

Create and Optimize Images with Fireworks

How to...

- Create an image in Fireworks
- Draw objects in Fireworks
- Work with text
- Optimize images

One of the most popular ways to buy Dreamweaver is as part of the Dreamweaver 4/Fireworks 4 Studio package. The Studio package combines Dreamweaver with Fireworks, Macromedia's image editing program. Together, they give you a complete solution for designing web pages and the graphics that are so prominent on those web pages. Dreamweaver and Fireworks exhibit a truly symbiotic relationship. And by using the two programs together, you can shave hours off the time it takes to build your sites.

Get to Know Fireworks

So what, exactly, is Fireworks? And why did it come bundled with Dreamweaver?

To put it succinctly, Fireworks gives you the ability to create complex images using vector graphics, bitmapped images, or a combination of both, to visually enhance your web site. You can build animations or rollover buttons, and Fireworks will generate the HTML code to make sure your work turns out as you envisioned it when people view it on the Web. But perhaps the most-used feature of Fireworks is its ability to convert images to web-standard formats such as GIF and JPEG and to optimize the images so they load quickly on a web page while retaining the highest quality possible. It is, to say the least, an invaluable tool in your web design arsenal.

Create and Edit Bitmaps with Vector Tools

Fireworks is an unusual program. It's a cross between a pixel-based image editor for bitmap images and a vector drawing program. Although it's a capable image editor that excels at manipulating and optimizing bitmap or pixel-based images, it also contains a full set of vector drawing tools and maintains its native documents as vector drawings.

Fireworks can open and edit most common bitmap image files such as GIF, JPEG, TIFF, and BMP. When you paint and edit bitmap images with tools such as the paint brush and the bucket, you're manipulating pixels. No surprises there. The concept is familiar to anyone who has used simple paint programs such as Windows Paint. Fireworks' implementation is much more powerful, but the concept is the same.

However, when you create text, polygons, and other vector shapes in a native Fireworks document, you're working with vector objects. For its native documents, Fireworks uses the PNG file format, which supports both bitmap and vector elements. As a result, a Fireworks document can contain imported bitmap images, but the objects you draw with the Fireworks drawing tools are vector objects unless and until you deliberately convert them to a bitmap.

Did you know?

Bitmap Images vs. Vector Drawings

Bitmap images (sometimes called *raster* images) are composed of tiny, individual colored dots, called *pixels* (short for *picture elements*). Bitmap images work on the same principle as a television screen or the halftone printing in newspapers and magazines At the intended viewing size, individual pixels are too small for the human eye to distinguish; instead you see the shapes and shading of the overall image. However, if you magnify a bitmap image, the individual pixels become readily apparent.

The file size of a bitmap image is dependent on the size of the image and its resolution. Size refers to the physical dimensions of the image, such as 3 by 4 inches. Resolution refers to the size of the pixels that make up the image. The smaller the pixel, the sharper and more detailed the image appears, and so the more pixels that are required to produce the image. Resolution is measured by the number of pixels that will fit in one inch (or centimeter, or whatever). For example, a 2-inch square image with a resolution of 100 pixels per inch is composed of a grid of pixels measuring 200 by 200 for a total of 40,000 pixels. Obviously, the more pixels there are in a bitmap image file, the larger the file. File size is also affected by the number of colors in the image.

Vector drawings, in contrast, record a graphic as instructions for drawing a series of lines, shapes, text characters, and other objects. The objects in a vector drawing are defined with mathematical precision that remains unaffected by changes in magnification or display size. Furthermore, each object retains its individual identity, which means that you can select, edit, and move each object independently of the others. As a result, vector drawings are generally much easier to edit than bitmap images.

The file size of a vector drawing is directly related to the number of objects in the drawing and the complexity of the individual objects (how many characters are in a text object or how many sides are in a polygon). However, since output devices such as computer monitors display images as a series of dots, vector drawings must be translated into a dot pattern (just like bitmap images) for display. That extra step means that extra software and more processing time are required to translate the vector image into a viewable image.

11

Actually, it's not unusual to have drawing tools for creating text and hard-edged shapes in an image editor. Furthermore, it's common for the shapes you create with those tools to behave like vector objects up to a point, but the shapes typically merge with the underlying bitmap image as soon as you click on the next tool. The same thing happens in Fireworks when you're editing a bitmap image, but not so in a Fireworks document. Text and other shapes retain the characteristics and editability of vector objects even after you save the Fireworks document. Even some of the traditional painting tools, such as the paintbrush and the pencil, exhibit the characteristics of vector drawing tools when you use them in a native Fireworks document.

Fireworks gives you the option to convert your document to a bitmap at any time. And the program automatically merges the raster and vector components of the document into a single pixel-based image when you export the image for use as a web graphic.

Because of the number and variety of tools for creating and editing images and shapes in Fireworks, and because the program blurs the lines between vector and bitmap images, Fireworks can seem a little daunting. But most of the tools are remarkably intuitive, and you can probably discern their function quickly if you just get in there and try them out. This chapter gives you a good start with descriptions of the more common tools and features and instructions for performing some common tasks.

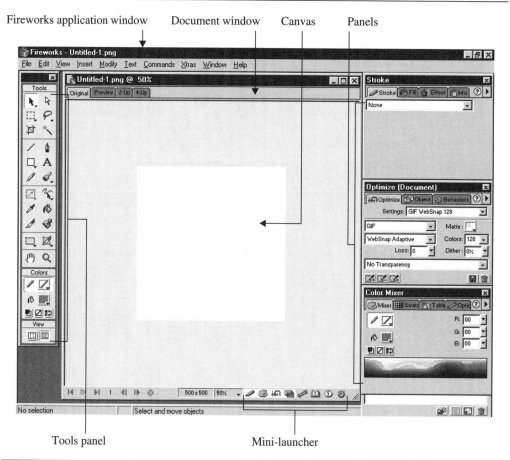

FIGURE 11-1   The Fireworks 4 user interface closely resembles the interfaces of other Macromedia programs.

The Fireworks Interface

The main Fireworks program window (see Figure 11-1) contains several smaller windows. The largest of these is the Document window (see Figure 11-2), sometimes called the *workspace*. The white box in the Document window is the *canvas*, the actual image work area. In Fireworks it's common to work on images that are smaller than the Document window. If the image is larger than the Document window, Fireworks displays scroll bars on the right and bottom edges of the Document window to enable you to scroll the image so you can view the area you're working on.

TIP *You can use the gray area surrounding the canvas as a scratch pad or temporary storage place for objects as you work on your image.*

One unusual feature of the Fireworks Document window is the tabs in the upper-left corner. These tabs enable you to preview your document as it will appear with different optimization settings applied. (See the section "Optimize Images" later in this chapter.)

At the bottom left of the Document window is the animation playback control. You use these to play back animations you have built inside Fireworks. These controls are set up like a VCR's, allowing you to play, fast forward, rewind, and move forward or back one frame at a time. These animations can be simple rollover animations or more complicated, Flash-style animations where various objects move from one spot on the canvas to another.

Along with the Document window, the window you will probably use the most is the Tools panel. This is where all the drawing and editing tools are housed. As with all Macromedia products, pointing to a tool for a second reveals a pop-up Tool Tip box that displays the name of that particular tool.

Some of these tools, such as the Pointer tool and the Lasso tool, have a small arrow in the lower-right corner of the tool button. The arrow signifies that you can click and hold the mouse button on the tool to reveal a subset of tools.

11

FIGURE 11-2   The Document window

> TIP *When you select a tool, Fireworks displays a message in the status bar at the bottom of the Fireworks window describing what the tool does.*

Here's a rundown on the tools in the Fireworks Tools panel:

Button	Tool	Description
	Pointer tool	Lets you select and move objects in an image. The additional pop-up tools are the Select Behind tool, which will select an element that is positioned behind another, and the Export Area tool, which allows you to select a portion of the image you are working on and export it as its own, stand-alone image.
	Subselection tool	Lets you select a point along a path that has been created, which then allows you to change the shape of the path by moving the selected point.

Button	Tool	Description
	Marquee tool	Lets you select a rectangular area of an image. Then you can modify anything within that selected area. Areas outside the selected area will not be affected. The pop-up gives you access to the Oval Marquee tool.
	Lasso tool	Gives you the ability to select an irregularly shaped area of an image by drawing around it. This is the perfect tool to use to trace around an element in your image. The pop-up gives you access to the Polygon Lasso tool, which you can use to draw a selection area with straight sides.
	Crop tool	Used to delete any unwanted areas around an image. Click and drag over the image to define the specific area you want to retain. Double-click inside the selected area (or press ENTER) to remove the rest of the image.
	Magic Wand tool	Use this tool to select specific areas of an image based on color or grayscale information. You click the magic wand on the image, and Fireworks automatically selects adjacent areas of the same or similar color.
	Line tool	Lets you draw a line in your document.
	Pen tool	Use this to draw paths for masks or vector graphics.
	Rectangle tool	Lets you draw a rectangular box in your document. The pop-up gives you access to the Rounded Rectangle tool, the Ellipse tool, and the Polygon tool.
	Text tool	Use this to add text to your document.
	Pencil tool	As its name implies, use this to draw on the canvas as if you were using a pencil to draw on a sheet of paper.
	Brush tool	Paint areas of an image as if you were using a paintbrush. The pop-up gives you access to the Redraw Path tool, which lets you redraw a path without erasing any fill color associated with it.
	Scale tool	Use to enlarge or reduce the image. The pop-up gives you access to the Reshape Area and Path Scrubber tools.
	Freeform tool	Gives you the ability to reshape paths you have created.

11

Button	Tool	Description
	Eyedropper tool	Use this to select a color from the image you're working on. Click the dropper on a sample of the desired color to add that color to the color well, where it can be used by other drawing and painting tools.
	Paint Bucket tool	Fills an enclosed area with the selected color, much like pouring paint into a receptacle.
	Knife/Eraser tool	In vector drawing mode, the Knife tool cuts paths into separate objects. In bitmap editing mode, the Knife becomes the Eraser to erase areas of an image.
	Rubber Stamp tool	Lets you select an area of a picture and then "clone" that selection onto other areas of the image.
	Rectangle Hotspot tool	Lets you assign an area of the image that will act as a hyperlink. Use this tool to create image maps. The pop-up gives you access to the Circle Hotspot tool and the Polygon Hotspot tool.
	Slice tool	Gives you the ability to cut an image into smaller sections so the image doesn't take as long to load on a web page. The pop-up gives you access to the Polygon Slice tool.
	Hand tool	Use this to move the entire image or layer around in the Document window.
	Zoom tool	Use this to zoom in on or out from a specific area of the image.
	Line Color	Lets you choose a color that will be applied to borders and lines.
	Fill Color	Lets you choose the fill color of a vector graphic.
	Set Default Brush/ Fill Colors	Lets you choose the default colors that are assigned to the Line and Fill color wells.
	No Stroke or Fill	Removes assigned color from the selected border or object.
	Swap Brush/ Fill Colors	Switches the assigned brush and fill colors.

A number of other floating panels house the rest of the controls at your disposal (see Figure 11-3). It isn't practical to have each panel open in its own window because the panels would take up too much screen real estate. So, as in Dreamweaver, Fireworks lets you open, close, resize, and move these panels to give yourself more working room. You can even dock multiple panels into a single window as you can with Dreamweaver panels (see Chapter 1).

Stroke panel with docked
Fill, Effect, and Info panels

Styles panel with docked
Library and URL panels

History panel with docked
Layers and Frames panels

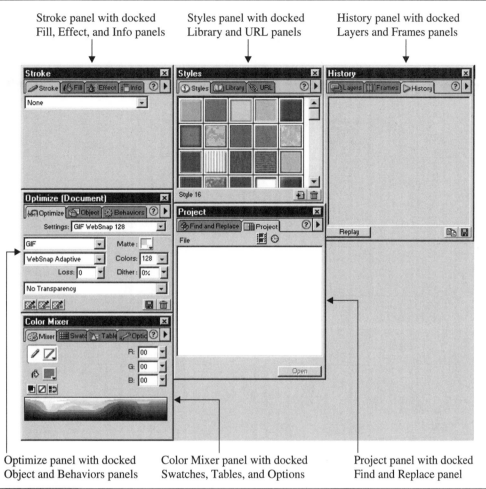

Optimize panel with docked
Object and Behaviors panels

Color Mixer panel with docked
Swatches, Tables, and Options

Project panel with docked
Find and Replace panel

FIGURE 11-3   An assortment of floating panels

Create a Fireworks Image

When you first start Fireworks, the program window appears without any documents open. Unlike many other programs, Fireworks doesn't automatically assume that you want to create a new document. After all, much of the work you do with Fireworks is editing existing images. The simplest way to learn about the Fireworks tools is to begin experimenting in a blank document.

Create a New Document

To create a new, blank Fireworks document, follow these steps:

1. Choose File | New, or press CTRL+N. Fireworks displays the New Document dialog box, where you can define the size and resolution of the canvas (image area) in the document and its canvas color (background).

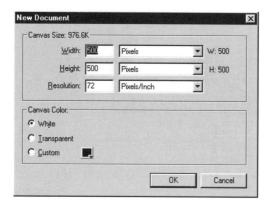

2. Enter a value in the Width and Height boxes and select a measurement. You can specify the size in inches, centimeters, or pixels.

3. Enter a value in the Resolution box and select a measurement. You can specify Pixels/Inch or Pixels/cm.

The default resolution of 72 pixels/inch is perfect for images intended for use on the Web. A typical computer monitor's resolution is about 72 pixels/inch, so a higher resolution would be overkill.

4. Specify a background color in the Canvas Color area. You can choose the default White, Transparent, or select Custom and then pick a color with the color picker box.

5. Click OK to close the New Document dialog box and create the document. Fireworks creates a new, untitled document and displays it in a Document window (see Figure 11-2).

Set Rulers, Grids, and Guides

Fireworks sports some useful tools to help you measure and position objects on the canvas in the Document window. The Rulers and Grid features are similar to their counterparts in the Dreamweaver Design view Document window (see Chapter 1).

- To show or hide the rulers on the top and left sides of the Document window (see Figure 11-4), choose View | Rulers, or press CTRL+ALT+R.

- To reposition the zero mark on the rulers, click the off-centered cross hair in the upper-left corner where the rulers meet and drag to the new zero position.

- To show or hide grid lines in the Document window, choose View | Grid | Show Grid, or press CTRL+ALT+G.

- To toggle the Snap to Grid feature on or off, choose View | Grid | Snap to Grid, or press CTRL+ALT+SHIFT+G.

- To adjust grid spacing and color, choose View | Grid | Edit Grid to open the Edit Grid dialog box. Edit the settings and click OK to apply them.

In addition to rulers and grids, Fireworks has another very useful positioning tool called *Guides*. Guides are a little like the lines that make up the grid, except that, instead of being positioned at fixed intervals, individual guide lines can be placed wherever you want on the

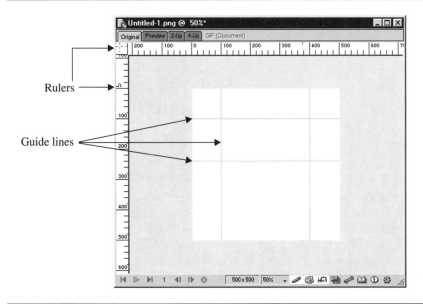

FIGURE 11-4   A Document window with rulers and guides

canvas. This makes guides much more flexible than the grid. You can set Fireworks to snap objects into place on guide lines, just as you can on the grid.

- To show or hide guide lines, choose View | Guides | Show Guides, or press CTRL+; (the CTRL key plus the semicolon key). Guides appear as green horizontal and vertical lines on the canvas.

- To create a guide line, click on a ruler and drag onto the canvas, then drop the guide line in the desired location.

- To move a guide line, simply click and drag to the new location.

- To delete a guide line, click and drag it off the canvas.

- To lock the guides into position to prevent accidental repositioning, choose View | Guides | Lock Guides, or press CTRL+ALT+;. Repeat the command to unlock the guides.

- To toggle the Snap to Guides feature on or off, choose View | Guides | Snap to Guides, or press CTRL+ALT+SHIFT+;.

- To adjust guide colors, choose View | Guides | Edit Guides to open the Guides dialog box. Edit the settings and click OK to apply them.

 **Save a Fireworks Document**

The procedure for saving a Fireworks document is similar to the corresponding procedure in most any other program. You choose File | Save As to open the Save As dialog box, navigate to the folder where you want to save the file, type a filename in the File Name box, then click the Save button to close the dialog box and save the file. The surprising thing about Fireworks is that there is only one selection—Fireworks (*.png)—in the Save As Type box.

That's right, despite the fact that Fireworks can open and edit files stored in more than a dozen different file formats, you can save files in only Fireworks native PNG format. If you need to create a file in another format, you must use the Export command.

Draw Objects in Fireworks

Just as a long journey begins with a single step, your exploration of Fireworks as a tool for creating web graphics begins with some simple drawing exercises. Mastering all the intricacies of Fireworks' many features is beyond the scope of this book, but you can do quite a lot with a few basic tools. For example, a typical button graphic is nothing more than a rectangle with some text superimposed on it. Then you can apply some styles and effects to transform a functional but plain graphic into something striking. And it all starts with Fireworks' simplest tools.

Draw Simple Shapes

The simplest shapes to draw in Fireworks are the graphic primitives, such as straight lines, rectangles, and ellipses. You can draw any of them by simply selecting the tool from the Tools palette and then dragging on the canvas to indicate the size and position of the object.

- To draw a line, click the Line Tool in the Tools palette. Position the pointer on the canvas where the line should start; then click and drag to the end point of the line. The line appears.

- To draw a rectangle, click the Rectangle Tool in the Tools palette. Position the pointer on the canvas where one corner of the rectangle should be, then click and drag diagonally to the opposite corner position. The rectangle appears.

Press and hold the SHIFT *key as you draw a rectangle to constrain the rectangle so that you get a perfect square. Press* SHIFT *as you draw with the Ellipse Tool to create a circle.*

- To draw an ellipse, click the Ellipse Tool in the Tools palette. Position the pointer on the canvas and drag diagonally as if drawing a rectangle. Fireworks creates an ellipse that fits within the imaginary rectangle you defined with the drag operation.

- To draw a regular polygon (such as a pentagon or a hexagon) or a star, double-click the Polygon Tool in the Tools panel to open the Options panel. Select Polygon or Star in the Shape box and the number of sides (or points) in the Sides box. Position the pointer on the canvas at the center of the object and drag to one point. A polygon (or star) appears.

Select, Move, and Color Objects

When you draw objects in a Fireworks document, you're drawing vector objects; and the great thing about vector objects is that they are easy to edit. You can select an object and move it, change its size, change its color, or do any number of other things to it without affecting other objects in the document.

■ To select an object, click the Pointer Tool in the Tools panel; then move the pointer over the object you want to select. Fireworks outlines the object in red when the pointer tool hovers over it. Click the object to select it. Fireworks displays a blue outline with small square handles at the corners to indicate the selected object.

■ To move a selected object, just drag it to a new location.

■ To resize the selected object, click the Scale Tool in the Tools panel. Larger sizing handles appear around and on the outline of the selected object. Drag a handle to resize the object. Drag a corner handle to scale the object proportionally. Drag a handle in the middle of a side to scale the object nonproportionally.

■ To change the color of the interior of the selected object, click the Paint Bucket Tool; then click the color picker and select the new color. Fireworks changes the color immediately.

■ To change the color of the outline of the selected object, click the Line Color Tool; then click the color picker and select a new color.

■ To delete an object from the document, select the object and then choose Edit | Clear.

Draw Complex Shapes

You can draw more complicated shapes in Fireworks using the Pen Tool and then modify them with the Freeform Tool and/or the Subselection Tool. The Pen Tool is a versatile tool that enables you to draw both lines and closed shapes composed of both straight and curved segments.

To draw an irregular polygon with the Pen Tool, follow these steps:

1. Click the Pen Tool in the Tools panel.

2. Click on the canvas with the Pen Tool to place the first corner point.

3. Move the pointer and click again. Fireworks connects the points with a straight line.

4. Continue to click the Pen Tool to add corner points to define the perimeter of the shape. As you lay down more points on the canvas, they are joined by lines. These lines act as the border that defines the shape.

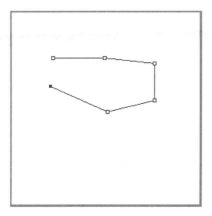

5. Click back on the starting point to close the shape. Fireworks closes the shape.

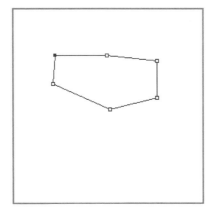

11

> **TIP** *To draw a line instead of a closed shape, just don't click back on the starting point to close the shape. Instead, click the Pointer Tool and then click the canvas to deselect the line without closing it.*

To draw a curved-sided shape, use the same Pen Tool; however, the drawing technique is a little different. Here's how you do it:

1. Click the Pen Tool in the Tools panel.

2. Click on the canvas with the Pen Tool to place the first point, but, instead of using just a simple click, click and drag toward the next point. Fireworks places a curve point (or vertices) where you first click and a control point under the moving Pen Tool with a line extending from the control point under the Pen Tool, through the curve point, and projecting an equal distance on the other side of the curve point. This line is called the *control handle*, and it represents the vector to the control point, not the actual line or curve you are drawing. Release the mouse button to drop the control point.

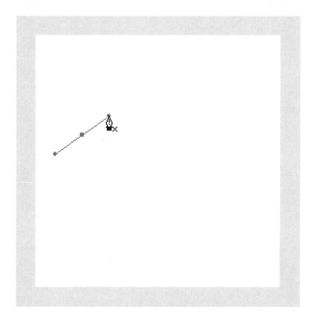

3. Click and drag again to place the next curve point and drag out the control handle. Fireworks draws the curve between the first curve point and the new curve point.

Note how it curves toward the control handle instead of being a straight line between the two curve points.

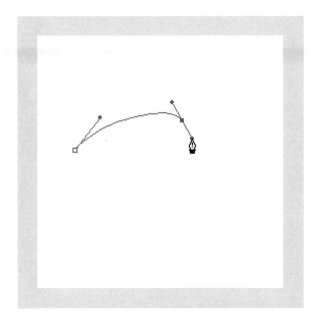

4. Continue to click and drag the Pen Tool. Add curved line segments to define the outline of a shape.

11

5. Click the Pen Tool back on the first point to close the shape. Fireworks fills the shape with color.

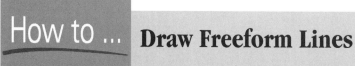

You can mix straight and curved-line segments in the same line or shape just by varying your drawing technique with the Pen Tool. Use simple clicks for corner points to define straight segments and the click-and-drag technique for curve points to define curve segments.

How to ... Draw Freeform Lines

Drawing lines with the Pen Tool is deliberate and precise. But sometimes you may want to draw fluid, free-flowing lines, which is something the Pen Tool doesn't do very well. So use the Pencil Tool or Brush Tool instead. Just select the Pencil Tool or the Brush Tool from the Tools panel; then click and drag across the canvas with the tool. Fireworks creates a line tracing the path of the pointer. The Pencil Tool produces thin, hard-edged lines, and the Brush Tool can be configured with various stroke effects such as soft-edged brushes, airbrush, or calligraphy pen. Both tools produce a line defined by a series of corner points, curve points, and control handles, just like the lines you create with the Pen Tool; however, Fireworks places all the points for you automatically.

Manipulate Points and Lines

You can revise the shapes you create at any time with the Subselection Tool. The Subselection Tool gives you the ability to work with both the corner points and curve points on a line as well as the control points at either end of the control handles.

- Click the Subselection Tool in the Tools panel to select it.

- You can click an object with the Subselection tool to select it, just as you can select an object with the Pointer Tool.

- Click and drag a corner point or a curve point to move the point.

- Click a curve point to select it and make the control handle appear. Then you can click and drag the control points to change the curve.

Work with Text in Fireworks

One of the things you will probably do the most in Fireworks is add text to your images. As with everything you do within Fireworks, you can modify text to meet your specific design needs. You can add basic effects such as drop shadows, glow effects, and much more.

Enter and Edit Text

Placing text into a Fireworks document is fairly straightforward.

1. Click the Text Tool in the Tools panel.

2. Click with the Text Tool on the canvas. The position you click on the canvas will be the point at which your text will be placed. Fireworks opens the Text Editor dialog box.

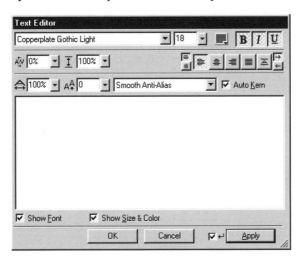

3. Type your text into the large text box in the Text Editor.

11

4. Adjust the text formatting controls as needed. These controls are as follows:

- **Font**   Select any font that you have installed in your computer.
- **Font Size**   Choose the point size of the font you are using.
- **Font Color**   Select the color for the font by clicking on this button and choosing a color from the pop-up screen.
- **Font Styles**   Select Bold, Italic, and/or Underline to be assigned to your text.
- **A/V**   Controls the spacing between the letters of your text, which is known as *kerning*.
- **Leading**   Precisely controls the vertical space between lines of text.
- **Alignment Controls**   Select whether the text flows vertically or horizontally, and whether it's aligned left, center, right, or justified.
- **Text Width**   Expands or contracts the width of individual letters or text blocks.
- **Baseline Shift**   Gives you the ability to move the bottom alignment of the selected text. It causes the text to be reduced to half size.
- **Anti-Aliasing Level**   Controls the smoothness of the text to reduce the "jaggies."
- **Auto Kern**   Use this to have Fireworks automatically select the proper kerning between letters.
- **Show Font**   Shows the font and style you are using as you type in the Text Box.
- **Show Size & Color**   Shows the point size and the color you selected as you type in the Text Box.

NOTE   *It's usually a good idea to enable the Show Font and Show Size & Color options so you can preview your text formatting in the Text Editor dialog box. However, if you have an older computer or are running low on RAM, you may want to deselect these two options to improve performance.*

5. Click OK to close the Text Editor dialog box and add the text to your Fireworks document.

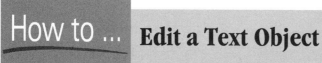

How to ... Edit a Text Object

Fireworks doesn't let you edit text directly on the canvas, but you can easily reopen the Text Editor dialog box with the text displayed for editing. You can either select and then double-click the text object with the Pointer Tool, or click once on the text with the Text Tool. When the Text Editor dialog box opens, you can edit the text itself and also take advantage of the full assortment of formatting controls.

Apply Styles and Effects

Of course, you can change the line color and fill color of any Fireworks object, including text. But that's just the beginning of the formatting and effects you can apply in Fireworks. Three Fireworks panels—Stroke, Fill, and Effect—provide a powerful set of tools that enable you to transform simple text and objects into striking images with rich textures and sophisticated effects.

The Stroke panel lets you control the thickness and the color of the outline or border of an object. But thickness and color are just the beginning. You can also control various characteristics of the stroke to give the outline softened edges, texture, and transparency. You can simulate the lines drawn with various media, such as a felt tip marker, watercolor brush, crayon, and airbrush.

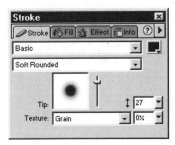

The Fill panel provides options for controlling the appearance of the interior of the shape. In addition to being able to pick a color to fill the shape, you can choose from more than a dozen different gradations, and that's before you add edge effects, textures, and transparency settings.

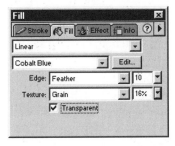

11

The Effect panel is a treasure trove of special effects that you can add to any Fireworks object. You can choose effects such as bevels, glows, drop shadows, blurs, and more. You can mix and match effects and fine-tune the settings for each one to achieve just the look you want.

Using the Effect panel is a little different from using some of the other panels. You start by selecting a basic effect from the pop-up menu at the top of the panel. Then you adjust the settings for that effect in the pop-up box that appears. When you click outside the pop-up, Fireworks adds the selected effect to the list that makes up the body of the panel and applies the effect to the selected object in your document. If you need to go back and adjust the settings for the effect, click the information button (the italic letter *i* on a blue circle) next to the effect name.

The Styles panel contains a series of buttons, each of which represents a preset combination of stroke, fill, effect, and text formatting settings. To apply a style, you need only select an object in your Fireworks document, open the Styles panel (choose Window | Styles), and click a button in the Styles panel. Fireworks adds the settings from the style to the selected object. It's quick. It's easy. And it's very effective.

Import and Edit Images in Fireworks

One of Fireworks most-used features undoubtedly is its ability to open bitmap images in a variety of different file formats. After you get the image into Fireworks, you can edit and manipulate it in a variety of different ways. Then, you can export the image in a web-friendly file format, optimized for fast downloads over the Internet.

You can bring a bitmap image into Fireworks in one of two ways:

- **Import the image and place it into a Fireworks document** To do this, start with a blank Fireworks document; then choose File | Import to open the Import dialog box. Locate and select the file you want to import and then click the Open button. Fireworks closes the Import dialog box and returns to the Document window. Click and drag as if you were drawing a rectangle to define the size and position of the imported image. When you complete the drag operation, Fireworks displays the image in your document.

- **Open the image directly in its own Document window** To do this, choose File | Open to open the Open dialog box. Locate and select the file you want to open and then click the Open button. Fireworks displays the bitmap image in its own Document window. A striped border surrounding the canvas indicates that Fireworks is in bitmap editing mode, which means that any additions and alterations to the image are immediately merged with the bitmap image—you can't go back and edit text and objects independently.

Optimize Images

When working with images for display on the Internet, it's critical to optimize your files. You could spend hour upon hour tweaking your images so they are perfect, but if you don't optimize them correctly, no one will spend the time to wait for an overly large file to download or pay any attention to the results if they don't display properly.

Optimizing a file means saving it using the combination of file format and option settings that achieve the optimum balance between image quality on a computer monitor and the time it takes for that file to load onto a web page.

This is where the tabs at the top of the Fireworks Document window come into play, as we discuss shortly. Understanding what file format to save an image in is extremely important. If you save a file in an inappropriate manner, you could be adding unnecessary load time to the image. The main image file formats for the Web are as follows:

- **GIF** (pronounced like the popular peanut butter brand)   This is the perfect file format for hard-edged graphics or images that contain no smooth color shadings. GIF has a limited color palette—a maximum of 256 colors. As a result, GIF images don't reproduce smooth color variations well. A photographic image or an image that has a lot of graduated colors and smooth transitions will exhibit *banding* (sharply defined color jumps). However, the GIF format has good compression features that usually result in smaller file sizes than do other formats. Also, you can create transparent backgrounds in GIF images to allow other page elements to show through.

- **JPEG** (pronounced "jay-peg")   This is today's standard for photographic images and other images with smooth color transitions because the JPEG format supports millions of colors. The JPEG format also supports variable compression settings to reduce file size. However, the JPEG format uses *lossy* compression, which means that some picture information is lost in the compression process. Using high-compression settings can produce small files but at the expense of a fuzzy, low-quality image. You may need to experiment with JPEG compression settings to find the best compromise between quality and file size for a given image.

- **PNG** (pronounced "ping")   This format attempts to be the best of all worlds, with color support that equals the JPEG format, transparency features like the GIF format, efficient compression for small file sizes, plus other features such as the ability to record vector drawing data as well as bitmap image data. This versatility is the reason Fireworks uses PNG as its native file format. The problem is that PNG is a newer format, and it doesn't enjoy the same universal browser support as do JPEG and GIF images. Although the current versions of the major browsers display PNG images, there are still some web surfers out there who cannot view PNG files without the aid of external helper applications that aren't always installed. This problem is gradually disappearing as web surfers migrate to newer browsers, but it is still something to consider when you optimize your files. Also, although PNG files containing only bitmap image data with limited color depth are relatively small, the file size can mushroom dramatically as you increase the color depth and add vector objects, layers, and other advanced features. As a result, GIF and moderately compressed JPEG files are often smaller than the same image saved as a PNG file.

Optimizing an image is usually a matter of experimenting with a variety of different file formats and settings to see which combination produces the best results. One of Fireworks' strengths is its ability to preview the effects of different export settings without actually exporting the image file. Furthermore, the 2-Up and 4-Up preview tabs enable you to view side-by-side preview panes showing the same portion of the image with different export settings applied so you can see and evaluate the effect of different settings.

11

Here's how you use this feature to optimize the export settings for an image:

1. Open any Fireworks document or bitmap image. The image appears in the Original tab of the Document window.

2. Click the 4-Up tab to display the four-pane preview shown in Figure 11-5. Fireworks shows the same portion of the image in all four panes. Normally, the original image is in the upper-left corner. The other three preview images start out with the default export settings.

3. Click one of the preview images to select it. The selected preview has a bold border around the image and the info box below the image.

4. Adjust the settings in the Optimize panel. You can select a preset combination of settings from the Settings box or adjust the individual settings yourself. To adjust individual settings, always start by selecting the file format from the list box in the upper-left portion of the Optimize panel. The other options available in the Optimize panel change

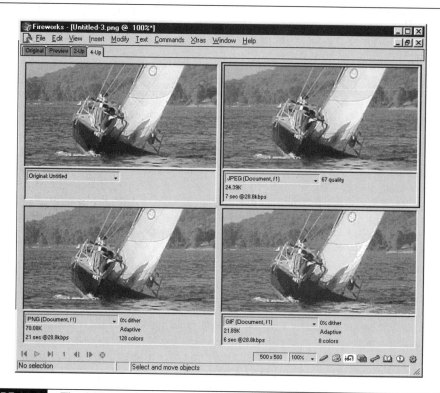

FIGURE 11-5   The 4-Up preview tab in the Fireworks Document window

depending on the file format selected. For example, GIF has a Transparency setting and an option to select the number of Colors, whereas the options for a JPEG include Smoothing and Quality (compression).

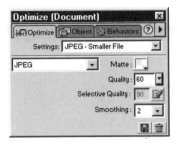

As you adjust settings in the Optimize panel, Fireworks previews the results in the selected preview pane. The status area below the preview image shows the file size and the estimated download time.

5. Repeat steps 3 and 4 on the other preview panes. Try different optimization settings in each pane so you can compare the result with the other panes, both visually and according to file size/download time estimates.

6. Click on the preview pane with the preferred settings. Fireworks uses the settings from the selected preview pane when you export the image.

7. Choose File | Export to open the Export dialog box.

11

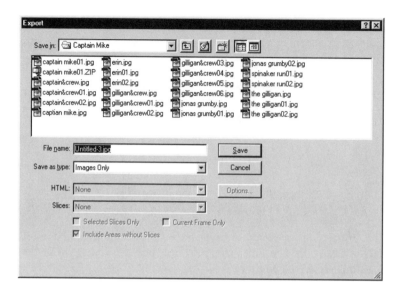

8. Select the location where you want to save the exported file and enter or edit the filename. Select Images Only in the Save As Type box to save a bitmap image file—you don't need to export HTML code or other options when you're just optimizing an image. Click the Save button to close the Export dialog box and save the optimized image.

Chapter 12

Use Fireworks and Other External Programs with Dreamweaver

How to...

- Use external editors in Dreamweaver
- Use Fireworks' ability to optimize, crop, and resize images from within Dreamweaver
- Create Fireworks rollover buttons for use in Dreamweaver
- Insert Fireworks HTML into a Dreamweaver document

Minimizing the amount of time it takes to complete projects is of utmost importance in this day and age. Designing and developing a web site is a multifaceted project that typically requires a web author to work with a variety of different programs. Even a program as powerful and versatile as Dreamweaver can't create and edit all the different image and media file formats that you deal with. However, switching from program to program can be a time-consuming drag.

Fortunately, Dreamweaver includes a feature that streamlines the process of switching to external programs when you need to edit an image or other media file. Dreamweaver allows you to define external programs for editing specific file types. Then, when you need to make modifications to an image, media file, or other element on your page, you can quickly open the appropriate program and do so without having to close Dreamweaver and manually open the external editor. Finally, when you return to Dreamweaver after editing the file in the external editor, the changes are reflected in Dreamweaver's Document window. Dreamweaver's ability to coordinate work with external editors makes your workflow smoother and simpler.

This chapter shows you how to use Fireworks, Macromedia's premier image-editing program, as an external program for editing images placed in Dreamweaver. Fireworks is uniquely suited to this purpose and even includes features designed specifically to complement Dreamweaver. However, the basic techniques for defining an external editor and accessing that editor to edit images and other elements from a page in the Dreamweaver Document window apply equally to any other external editor you may choose.

Use Fireworks and Other External Editors from Within Dreamweaver

What exactly is an external editor? In Dreamweaver parlance, an external editor is not just any external program that you use as an editor for images and other elements on your web page—it's one of a list of such programs that you associate with specific file types so Dreamweaver can launch the program when you need to edit a file of the related type.

Suppose you need to modify an image after placing it in your Dreamweaver document. Without having an external editor defined in Dreamweaver, you would need to note the filename of the image and then get out of Dreamweaver (either minimize or exit the program), open your image editing program, locate and open the file you want to modify, make the changes and resave the image, quit the image editing program, reopen Dreamweaver, and reopen or refresh the document to view the updated image. That's a lot of steps to go through.

Now suppose Dreamweaver knows what program you want to use to edit a given file type, such as the image we just mentioned. In that case, the workflow goes like this: You merely double-click the image in the Dreamweaver document. Dreamweaver automatically sends the necessary commands to launch the external editor and load the image file. You use the external editor to make the necessary changes and resave the file. When you switch back to Dreamweaver, the updated image appears in the Document window.

Launching the external editor from within Dreamweaver doesn't enable you to do anything you couldn't do manually before. What it does is automate some of the steps, thus making this oft-repeated process go faster and smoother. And that saves you time and hassle.

You can assign any program you might have in your graphic design arsenal as an external editor for a given file type. However, defining Fireworks 4 as the external editor for images is an obvious choice because of the strong symbiotic relationship between Dreamweaver and Fireworks. So, naturally that's the example that appears throughout this chapter. Here's how you define an external editor in Dreamweaver:

NOTE *If you install Fireworks 4 along with Dreamweaver 4 as part of the Dreamweaver/Fireworks Studio package, Fireworks is automatically configured as the primary external editor for images in Dreamweaver.*

1. Choose Edit | Edit With External Editor to open the Preferences dialog box with the File Types/Editors category selected (see Figure 12-1).

2. In the Extensions list, select the file extension that identifies the file type for which you want to define an external editor. The file types for web images are: GIF, JPEG, and PNG. You need to assign an image editor for each of these file types. Note that some of the file extension entries show alternate extensions (such as .jpg, .jpe, and .jpeg for JPEG files). When you select a file extension, the defined editors appear in the Editors list.

NOTE *To add a file type to the Extensions list, click the plus (+) button to add a blank entry to the bottom of the list. Type the file extension (don't forget to start each extension with a period) and press* ENTER *to add it to the list.*

3. If the desired editor doesn't appear in the Editors list, click the plus (+) button over the Editors list to open the Select External Editor dialog box. Locate and select the executable program file for the program and click the Open button to close the dialog box, as shown next, and add the editor to the Editors list.

12

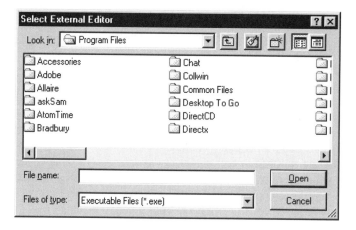

4. To change the primary editor for the selected file type, select the editor in the Editors list and click the Make Primary button.

5. Repeat steps 2–4 to define external editors for other file types.

6. Click the OK button to close the Preferences dialog box and record your external editor settings.

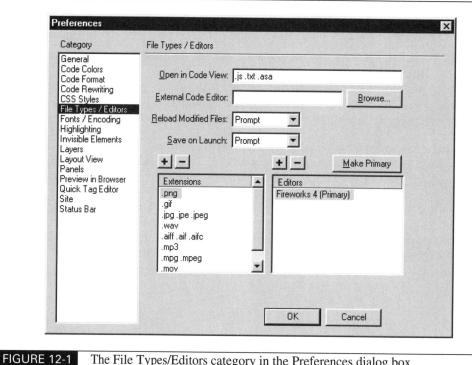

FIGURE 12-1   The File Types/Editors category in the Preferences dialog box

Insert Fireworks Images in Dreamweaver

When you insert images and media files into a web page you're editing in Dreamweaver, you don't need to do anything special to connect files to an external editor. Simply insert the image or other file using any of the standard techniques. (See Chapter 4 for information on adding images and Chapter 13 for information on other media files.)

Dreamweaver uses the three-letter extension that is part of the filename to identify the file type and to launch the appropriate external editor when you elect to edit the file. It's all automatic; all you need to do is make sure the images and media files you insert into your web pages have the proper extensions.

Launch Fireworks from Within Dreamweaver

After you define an external editor, using it to edit files from within Dreamweaver is a simple process. Here are the basic steps, as they apply to most external editors:

1. In the Dreamweaver Document window, select the image or other element that you want to edit with an external editor.

2. Use any of the following techniques to launch the external editor and instruct the editor to open the image or media file associated with the selected page element:

    ■ Click the Edit button in the Property Inspector panel. (If the Edit button isn't visible in the Property Inspector panel, click the arrow button in the lower-right corner to show the expanded options.)

    ■ Right-click the image and choose Edit With *Editorname*.

    ■ Right-click the image and choose Edit With | *Editorname* to launch one of the secondary external editors instead of the designated primary editor.

    ■ Press and hold the CTRL key as you double-click the image (this technique works only in Design view).

3. Edit the file in the external editor and save the changes.

4. Switch back to Dreamweaver. The revised image appears in Design view.

When you use Fireworks as your external editor for image files, the process is basically the same. But Fireworks introduces a couple of wrinkles. Because you normally save a Fireworks document in one file and export to another file format to create a web graphic, Fireworks prompts you to identify the original Fireworks document for editing and reexport instead of simply opening the image file from the web document. Also, the Document window in Fireworks shows evidence of the tight integration with Dreamweaver with a prominent reminder that you are editing an image from Dreamweaver. Here's how it works when you use Fireworks as your external image editor:

1. In the Dreamweaver Document window, select the image you want to edit with Fireworks.

12

2. Click the Edit button in the Property Inspector panel, or use any of the other techniques described earlier for launching an external editor. As Fireworks opens, the Find Source dialog box appears.

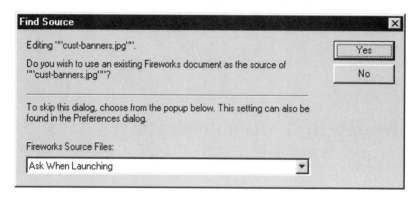

3. Click the Yes button if you want to open the existing Fireworks document (PNG file) that is the basis for the image you want to edit. Fireworks displays the Open dialog box. If there is no existing Fireworks document associated with the image, click the No button and skip the next step.

TIP

If you don't want to see the Find Source dialog box each time you launch Fireworks, you can change the setting in the Fireworks Source Files list box at the bottom of the dialog box. Select Always Use Source PNG to go straight to the Open dialog box. Select Never Use Source PNG to skip both dialog boxes and open the web image in Fireworks.

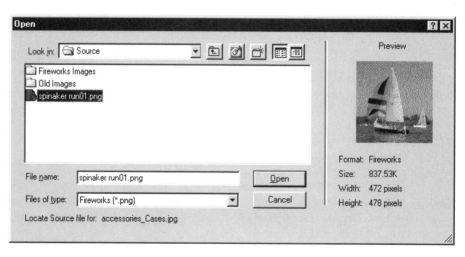

4. Locate and select the Fireworks PNG file in the Open dialog box; then click the Open button to close the dialog box and open the document. The document to be edited appears in a Fireworks Document window.

Note that the Fireworks Document window looks a little different. There is a Done button and a reminder immediately above the image that says Editing from Dreamweaver.

5. Edit the image in Fireworks.

6. After you complete your edits, click the Done button. Dreamweaver reappears immediately with the edited image updated in the Dreamweaver Document window.

12

Optimize and Edit Images from Within Dreamweaver

Nowhere is the symbiotic relationship between Dreamweaver and Fireworks more apparent than in the ability to access Fireworks' image-optimizing features from within Dreamweaver. With a single command, you can go directly to the Fireworks Optimize/Export Preview dialog box without even opening the full Fireworks program. There, you can optimize, crop, and resize the image quickly and efficiently and then get right back to Dreamweaver. It's almost as though the Optimize dialog box from Fireworks has been grafted onto the Dreamweaver program.

Optimize Your Image

Web surfers are an impatient lot. They seem to enjoy the visual richness of sites with a lot of graphics, but they're not willing to wait very long for those images to load in a web browser window. So, if you want the visitors to your site to have a good browsing experience, every image on your page must load as quickly as possible and deliver maximum impact.

Toward that end, it's essential that you *optimize* your image files. Optimizing an image means to create an image file that is as small as it can possibly be and still deliver the necessary information to the browser to display the image with adequate quality. Smaller files require less download time and therefore reduce the time the visitors have to wait for your page to appear in their browser windows. You optimize a file by experimenting with different file formats and settings in order to find a combination that produces the best compromise between file size and image quality.

To optimize an image that you have placed on a web page in Dreamweaver, follow these steps:

1. Select the image in the Dreamweaver Design view window.

2. Choose Commands | Optimize Image In Fireworks, or right-click the image and choose Optimize in Fireworks. The Find Source dialog box appears.

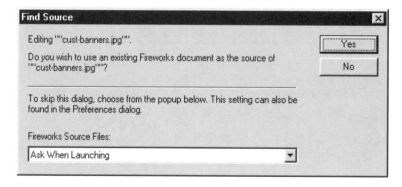

3. Click the Yes button if you want to open the existing Fireworks document (PNG file) that is the basis for the image you want to edit. The Open dialog box appears. If there is

no existing Fireworks document associated with the image, click the No button and skip the next step.

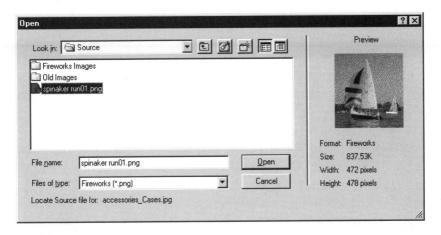

4. Locate and select the Fireworks PNG file in the Open dialog box, then click the Open button to close the dialog box and open the document. Dreamweaver opens the Optimize dialog box (the same dialog box you see when you choose File | Export Preview in Fireworks), as shown in Figure 12-2.

5. Select a preset combination of file format and settings in the Saved Settings box located above the preview image. Here's a list of the default settings and what they mean:

- **GIF Web 216**   GIF format that forces all the colors in the image to change to the 216 web-safe colors.

- **GIF WebSnap 256**   GIF format that uses a 256-color palette and automatically converts all non-web-safe colors to the closest web-safe color.

- **GIF WebSnap 128**   Same as WebSnap 256, only this selection uses a color palette of 128 colors.

- **GIF Adaptive 256**   GIF format that uses the actual colors present in the image for the color palette—up to 256 colors.

- **JPEG—Better Quality**   JPEG format with a Quality setting of 80 and no smoothing to produce a high-quality image with only mild file compression. The result is usually a larger file size than other JPEG settings.

- **JPEG—Smaller File**   JPEG format with a Quality setting of 60 and Smoothing 2 to create a significantly smaller file than the JPEG Better Quality setting. The image quality is impaired, however.

12

Note the status display above the preview image and to the left of the Saved Settings box. This area shows the key settings and also the resulting file size and an estimate of the download time for the image. Also note the visual effect of your setting selection on the preview image.

6. Further adjust the Format and other settings near the top of the Options tab. (When you select a file format in the Format box, the options below that box change to show the appropriate settings for the selected format.)

7. Repeat steps 5 and 6 as needed to produce the best-looking preview image with the smallest file size.

8. Click the Update button to close the Optimize dialog box. Dreamweaver/Fireworks automatically saves the file with your selected settings. The updated image appears in the Dreamweaver Design view window.

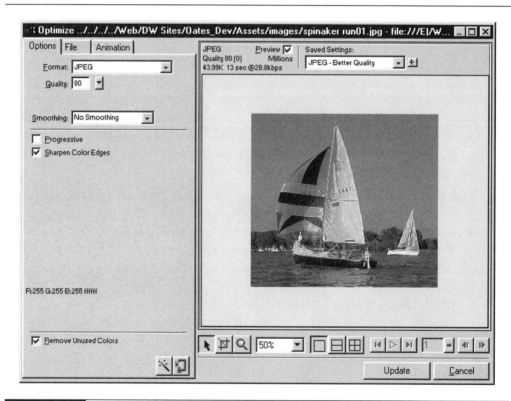

FIGURE 12-2   The Optimize dialog box

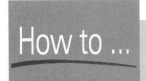

Create Your Own Saved Optimize Settings

You aren't locked into always using the same default settings in the Optimize window to start the optimization process. You can save your own favorite settings in the following manner.

1. Adjust the settings on the Options tab of the Optimize dialog box to the ones you want to save.

2. Click the plus (+) button beside the Saved Settings box. The Preset Name dialog box appears.

3. Type a name for the settings in the Name box and click OK to close the dialog box and record your settings.

The settings will now be available from the Saved Settings list the next time you use them

NOTE *You can remove saved presets from the Saved Settings pop-up by selecting it from the list and then clicking the Delete button (the one that looks like a trash can) in the lower-right part of the Optimize panel.*

12

Crop an Image

When you crop an image you remove superfluous material by trimming unwanted image area from the outer edges. The idea is to get rid of portions of an image that detract from the main subject matter by drawing attention away from the subject—for example, too much open space above a person's head.

The same dialog box you use to optimize images with Fireworks also includes a Cropping tool (called "Export Area") that you can use to crop an image from within Dreamweaver. Here's how:

1. Follow steps 1–4 in the instructions for optimizing an image. (Right-click the image and choose Optimize With Fireworks. Locate and select the Fireworks PNG file if appropriate.) The Optimize dialog box (refer to Figure 12-2) appears with the selected image displayed in the preview pane.

2. Click the Export Area button below the preview image. A dashed rectangle with cropping handles (small boxes) at the corners and in the middle of each side appears surrounding the preview image.

3. Drag the cropping handles toward the center of the image to reduce the image area. Adjust the various cropping handles to achieve the desired effect.

4. Click the Update button to close the Optimize dialog box. Dreamweaver/Fireworks automatically saves the file, without the superfluous area you cropped away. The updated image appears in the Dreamweaver Design view window.

As you edit and optimize an image for the Web, make sure that you export a copy of the image and record all edits in the exported copy, not the original image file. Cropping, resizing, and optimizing the image all discard image data that you may need if you ever reuse the image at a different size.

Resize an Image

Very often an image that you have scanned, shot with a digital camera, or acquired from another source is too large to fit into the designated space on your web page. Then you need to resize the image so that it fits on your page and doesn't take an inordinate amount of time to download to a browser.

CAUTION *Resizing an image means that you change the dimensions of the picture—and you can use the resize tools to make an image larger as well as smaller. However, for bitmap images, you can only reduce the dimensions safely. You can't make a bitmap image larger without adversely affecting the quality.*

As with cropping an image, you can resize an image using the Optimize dialog box. Here's how you do it:

1. Select the image on your page in Dreamweaver's Design view window.

2. Resize the image to fit your layout using the sizing handles on the bottom and right edges of the selection box around the image (or type dimensions into the H and W boxes in the Property Inspector panel). (See Chapter 4 for more information on sizing an image.) This instructs the browser to enlarge or reduce the image display to fit certain dimensions; it doesn't affect the actual size of the image recorded in the image file. Note the height and width measurements shown in the Property Inspector panel.

3. Follow steps 2– 4 in the instructions for optimizing an image presented earlier in this chapter. (Right-click the image and choose Optimize With Fireworks. Locate and select the Fireworks PNG file if appropriate.) The Optimize dialog box (refer to Figure 12-2) appears with the selected image displayed in the preview pane.

4. Click the File tab, as shown next, and check the image dimensions shown in the Scale area. Confirm that they match the desired image dimensions you noted in step 2. If the dimensions don't match, enter the desired dimensions in the W and H boxes.

12

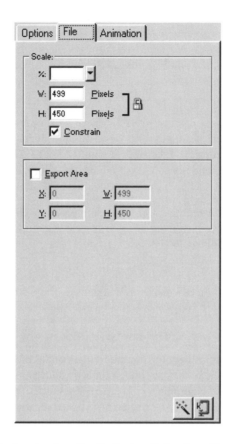

5. Click the Update button to close the Optimize dialog box. Dreamweaver/Fireworks automatically saves the file, reduced to the new dimensions. The updated image appears in the Dreamweaver Design view window.

For best results when performing multiple operations on an image, first crop, then resize, and finally optimize. Working in this sequence ensures the best quality by maintaining maximum image information in preliminary steps.

Create Graphics Effects with Fireworks

In addition to the tight integration with Dreamweaver for optimizing images, Fireworks offers some special features and tools designed specifically for creating web graphics. In contrast to the image-optimization process in which you start with an image in Dreamweaver and turn to

Fireworks to alter that image, you create these web graphics in Fireworks, save them, and then place the resulting graphics onto your web page in Dreamweaver.

The special integration between Dreamweaver and Fireworks comes into play with the programs' ability to manage the multiple image files and the HTML code required to implement effects such as buttons with rollover effects. Fireworks can produce the HTML code as well as the collection of image files needed for such an effect. Dreamweaver features special provisions for importing the images and HTML code generated by Fireworks and incorporating everything into the source code for your web page.

The following section gives brief instructions for creating buttons in Fireworks. But this is just one example of the many kinds of web graphics you can produce with Fireworks. See the section of this chapter called "Work with Fireworks HTML in Dreamweaver" to learn how to add Fireworks graphics to your page in Dreamweaver.

Create Buttons with Rollovers

Buttons are among the most common graphic navigation elements on most modern web pages. Of course, for simple buttons, you can use Fireworks to create an image that you can insert into your web page; then you add a link to that image in Dreamweaver and you've got a functional button.

Simple buttons work, but buttons with rollover effects provide the visitor with more feedback, thus making for a richer browsing experience. Besides, rollover effects are cool.

Fireworks includes a special wizard-like dialog box that greatly simplifies the process of creating buttons with rollover effects. Here's how it works:

1. Create a new Fireworks document. Make sure it is large enough to give you room to work with; you can always crop the image when you have completed your button.

2. Choose Insert | New Button to open the Button.png dialog box (see Figure 12-3). The dialog box contains five tabs, four of which correspond to the four button states plus one used to define the size of the button:

   ■ **Up**   The base look for the button

   ■ **Over**   The button appearance when the pointer moves over it

   ■ **Down** (optional)   The way the button appears when clicked

   ■ **Over While Down** (optional)   The way the button looks when the mouse button is held down while the pointer is over the button

   ■ **Active Area** (optional)   The location within the button that will trigger the rollover effect

   Down, Over While Down, and Active Area are all designated as optional because it is not necessary to assign effects in these sections unless you want to. To create a basic rollover button, all you need to use is the Up and Over states.

12

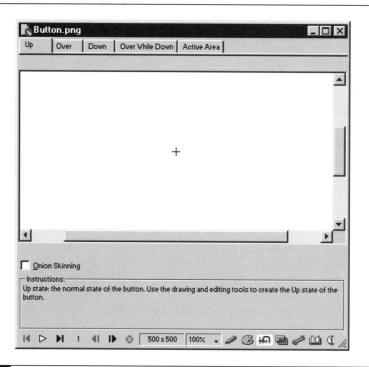

FIGURE 12-3   The Fireworks Button dialog box

3. Click the Up tab to select the Up button state.

4. Draw a shape to serve as the body of the button. Adjust the stroke, fill, and effects for the shape as needed. (See Chapter 11 for information on drawing in Fireworks.) As a starter, you might want to try drawing a rounded-corner rectangle with no stroke, a solid color fill in a rich color, and the Inner Bevel effect.

5. Use the Text tool to add some text over the image you created in the previous step. Select the font, size, color, and other text attributes as appropriate and position the text on the face of the button.

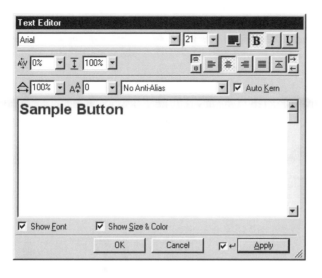

(Again, see Chapter 11 for details on using the Text tool.) This completes the basic button graphic for the Up state. You can add all sorts of embellishments if you want, but a simple button serves to illustrate this example.

6. Click the Over tab. The work area in the middle of the dialog box goes blank because there is no image defined for the Over button state—yet.

7. Click the Copy Up Graphic button. Fireworks places a copy of the button from the Up tab into the Over tab workspace.

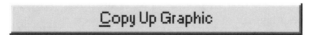

8. Adjust the button image as needed to produce the effect you want when the pointer hovers over the button. Suggestion: Select the text and add a Glow effect. Select the rectangle and edit the bevel effect to change it from Raised to Highlighted.

12

NOTE

You can repeat steps 6–8 on the Down and Over While Down tabs to create button graphics for those button states as well. However, for a simple rollover, you can leave those tabs blank—in which case the corresponding button states are ignored.

9. Click the Active Area tab to display the slice/hotspot applied to the button image. You can adjust it if necessary, but you'll normally just accept the default.

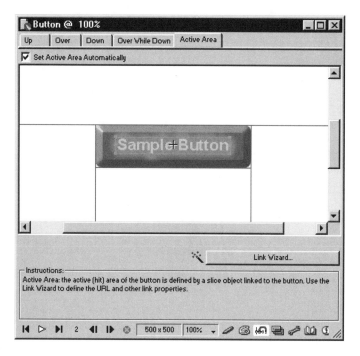

10. Click the Link Wizard button to open the Link Wizard dialog box. The dialog box opens with the Export Settings tab displayed.

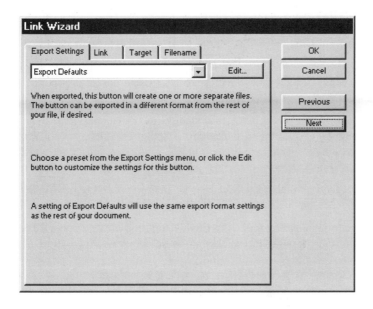

11. Select your preferred export settings from the drop-down list box and then click Next. The Link tab appears.

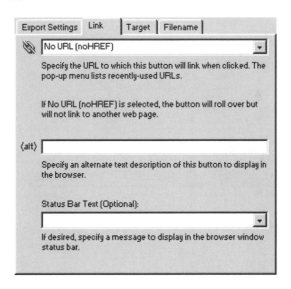

12

12. Select or enter the URL the button should link to. Also, in the respective text boxes, enter alt text for the image and the text of a message that appears in the browser's status bar when the visitor's pointer is over the button. Click Next to display the Target tab.

13. If you're working with a frameset, select or enter the target frame where the linked URL should appear. Usually, you leave this blank. Press Next. The Filename tab appears.

14. Check the Auto-Name check box if you want Fireworks to automatically name the button graphic files based on the current document name. Otherwise, clear the check box and enter a base filename in the text box. Fireworks gives the individual button files names such as *basename_r1-c1.gif* or *basename_f2.gif*.

15. Click the OK button to close the Link Wizard dialog box and return to the Button dialog box.

16. Close the Button dialog box (click the Close (×) button in the title bar). The button appears on the canvas in the Fireworks Document window.

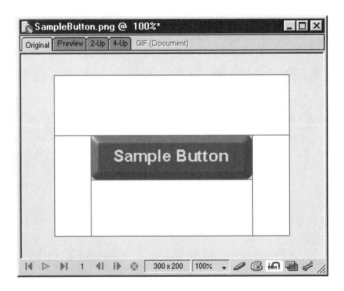

17. Choose Modify | Trim Canvas to eliminate the excess canvas area around the button image.

18. Choose File | Export. The Export dialog box appears.

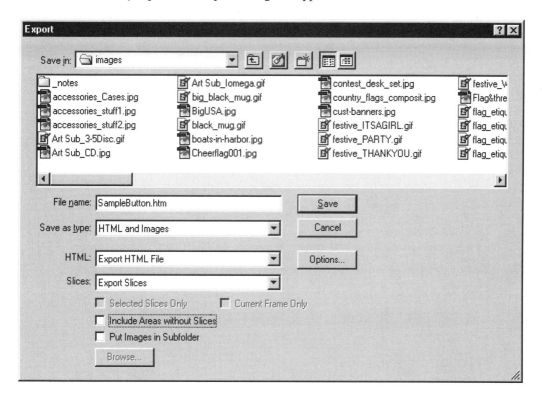

19. Navigate to the location where you want to save the button graphics (usually a subfolder of your site's local folder). Select HTML and Images in the Save As Type box to have Fireworks create HTML code as well as button images. Select Export HTML File in the HTML box and Export Slices in the Slices box. Click the Save button to close the Export dialog box and generate the image files and an HTML file containing the HTML and JavaScript code for the rollover effect.

12

Work with Fireworks HTML in Dreamweaver

When you use Fireworks to create sliced images, rollover buttons, navigation bars, or pop-up menus, the program not only exports the image files needed for those objects but also generates a file that contains the HTML code to make the effects work. The HTML code contains references to all the image files related to the effect, tables to assemble multipart images, JavaScript script code for rollover effects, and so on.

Dreamweaver uses this code to make the images do what you intend them to do when viewed in a browser. Without this Fireworks HTML code, you would have to recreate the effect by writing the code using a text editor or rebuild the effect using Dreamweaver behaviors. Since the code usually contains scripts, integrating it into the source code for your Dreamweaver documents isn't as simple as cutting and pasting a few HTML tags into Code view. The code for the tables containing sliced images can be quite complex, and blocks of JavaScript code often need to be inserted into the document header.

Fortunately, Dreamweaver includes an intelligent import feature for Fireworks HTML code that takes care of all the details for you. Here's how it works:

1. Open your Dreamweaver document and position the insertion point at the location where you want to insert the Fireworks button, pop-up menu, sliced image, or whatever.

2. Choose Insert | Interactive Images | Fireworks HTML. The Insert Fireworks HTML dialog box appears.

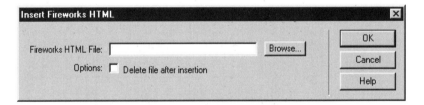

3. Enter the path and filename of the Fireworks HTML file, or click the Browse button to open the Select Fireworks HTML File dialog box (a standard File Open dialog box) where you can locate and select the file.

NOTE   *Check the Delete File After Insertion option to have Dreamweaver automatically delete the Fireworks HTML file after inserting its contents into your document's source code.*

4. Click the OK button to close the dialog box. Dreamweaver reads the Fireworks HTML file and automatically inserts the code into the appropriate locations in your document's source code. The Fireworks-created button (or other graphic) appears in the Design view window.

Chapter 13

Add Sound, Movies, and Media Objects

How to...

- Insert media files into Dreamweaver
- Utilize audio files
- Work with Flash movies and text and button objects
- Utilize Shockwave movies
- Manage Netscape Navigator plug-ins
- Utilize ActiveX controls
- Set parameters for media objects

If you're like most people, you want to add Flash, sound clips, movies, and/or streaming video to your web site. With the recent advent of digital home video and MP3 audio, more people than ever are incorporating some kind of sound or video on their sites. Media enhancements like these can greatly enhance your web pages, and you can use Dreamweaver to incorporate a multitude of sound, video, and other media objects and formats.

Remember, however, that sound, video, and other multimedia files aren't *created* using Dreamweaver. Instead they are created with "external media editors" and later *imported* into Dreamweaver. So, using such multimedia files involves either creating them in another application or using files created by someone else. The Web is full of multimedia files that you can download or share with others through your web site. Maybe you're not a Flash whiz who can create snazzy Flash animations, but you've probably come across sound or video files on the Web that you'd like to add to your site. Or maybe you want to show off some homemade video, or a cool little Java applet you came across.

Besides showing you how to incorporate such enhancements into your site, this chapter will describe how you can set many of the parameters and properties of different media source files directly from within Dreamweaver. Also, you'll learn how to configure Dreamweaver so that it will automatically launch the appropriate external media editor when you double-click on a media file.

 *Most of the sounds, movies, and other multimedia files on the Web are copyrighted. Be sure any files you download from the Web for reuse on your site are not copyrighted and are intended for public use before you display them on your site; otherwise, apply for reuse permission from the copyright holder.*

Insert Media Objects

Almost every day a new media format emerges along with new standards on how to deploy it on the Web. Because there are so many different media formats and standards for displaying these in a browser, it can get very complicated trying to track down all the necessary code required to embed them into an HTML page. Dreamweaver, however, makes it easy to add these media components without doing any hand-coding. Adding sound, video, or other media objects is simply a matter of clicking a few buttons. Dreamweaver even allows you to edit many of the source file's playback parameters without ever leaving the program.

In Dreamweaver, you can work with five main kinds of external media objects: Flash, Shockwave, ActiveX, Java, and Netscape Navigator plug-ins. Each of these different file types has its own special button in the Objects panel that lets you add a component with just a mouse click. In addition, if you've ever wanted to add Flash files to your pages but don't know how to use Flash, Dreamweaver 4 even lets you create Flash text and buttons without ever using the Flash application. As you read on, you'll find detailed instructions on how to deploy and use each of these different media files.

Work with External Media Editors

External media editors are programs used to create sound, video, and other media objects. Dreamweaver allows you to work with the following kinds of media, all of which are created using external media editors:

- **Sound**   Sound files are created in a sound application or captured from an audio device and saved into an appropriate audio format. External sound editors include SoundEdit16, SoundForge, Beatnik, RealAudio Encoder, QuickTime Pro, and Windows Media. Some of the more common file formats for web-enabled sound include .midi, .wav, .aif, .mp3, .ra, .ram, and .rpm.

- **Movies**   Video files are created in video-editing applications or captured from a video device and saved into an appropriate video format. External video editors include Adobe Premiere, Final Cut Pro, QuickTime Pro, RealProducer, and the like. Some of the more popular file formats for web-enabled video include .mov, .avi, .mpg, and .mpeg. Many of these files use Netscape Navigator plug-ins to display in a browser, since browsers don't natively understand how to handle video.

- **Flash**   Flash files are vector-based animations created with Macromedia's Flash application. Other applications such as Adobe's Live Motion can also create Flash formatted files. Dreamweaver 4 also allows you to create simple Flash text and buttons directly within Dreamweaver.

- **Shockwave**   Shockwave files are bit-mapped animations created with Macromedia's Director application. These typically are used for more complicated games and animations which require a greater amount of interactivity than Flash.

- **Netscape Navigator plug-ins**   Navigator plug-ins refer to a type of media object that uses a browser plug-in to display in the browser. Most of the sound and video formats deployed on the Web use plug-ins. Because Navigator plug-ins have a standard architecture, they are also used by Microsoft Internet Explorer, despite their name. Usually the user viewing the content will need to download a plug-in to display the media object, although some of the more popular plug-ins are included with the major browsers. External editors for encoding plug-in media files are usually available from the manufacturers of the plug-ins.

13

■ **ActiveX Controls**   ActiveX controls are miniprograms that run on your web page. They are usually written by programmers and are fairly complicated to create. ActiveX controls run only on Windows machines.

■ **Java applets**   Java applets are also miniprograms that run on your web page. Java is a programming language that allows you to view programs or applets on a web page. Java applets can run on any computer platform that has Java Virtual machine software installed.

Configure an External Editor for Media Objects

Just as you can double-click a graphic in the Site window to launch Fireworks or another external graphics editor (see Chapter 12, "Using Fireworks and Other External Programs with Dreamweaver"), you can also double-click on various media objects to launch their corresponding external editors. This is important because Dreamweaver doesn't let you edit these files directly; you need to use the program they were created in.

Normally, when you double-click on a file in the Site window, the file is launched by the associated application. This application is the same application that would launch if you double-clicked the file's icon on the desktop. However, you can have Dreamweaver associate a different external editor for each file type, or even multiple editors for a single file type, if you want to be able to pick from a list of editors for different tasks on different occasions. This is a great timesaving feature because, rather than having to switch applications and locate the file you want to edit within another application, you can just launch the file into the external editor right from within Dreamweaver.

To associate a given file extension (for example, .swf, .mov, .wav) with a particular application (for instance, Flash, QuickTime, or a sound-editing app), you edit an extension's preferences or add a new extension using the File Types/Editors category in the Preferences dialog box (see Chapter 20 for details). Whenever you double-click a media object with that particular extension from within Dreamweaver, it will automatically launch into the external application, where you can edit the file and resave it.

Launch an External Editor

Launching an external editor from within Dreamweaver is easy: double-click any media file in the Site window, and it will launch into the primary editor associated with it. You can also right-click media files in the Site window to display a pop-up list of editors associated with that particular file extension, as shown in Figure 13-1. In this figure, you'll notice that the Open With menu option displays a list of editors for .wav files that I have assigned to the .wav sound extension. My primary .wav editor, CoolEdit 2000 (a popular sound-editing application), has its own listing in the menu above the submenu because I defined this as the primary editor for the .wav extension. Below that are the other editors associated with the .wav extension; I can choose from any of these alternate editors by using the Context menu.

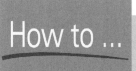

FIGURE 13-1   Right-clicking media files in the Site window displays a list of associated
editors you can use to launch and edit the file with.

How to ... Add Design Notes to a Media Object

13

Design Notes are a great way to attach information to files that you can share with others.
You attach Design Notes to media objects in the same way that you attach them to HTML
or graphics files (see Chapter 18).

1. Right-click on a media object in Design view or its file icon in the Site window to
    bring up the context menu. Select Design Notes… from the bottom of this menu.
    This brings up the Design Notes dialog box.

2. Enter the status of the file, if any, in the Status pull-down menu.

3. Enter any notes or comments in the Notes field and click OK. Your design note is
    now attached to the media object and saved along with it. When you are viewing the
    Site window you can tell that a media object has an attached design note because a
    notes icon appears in the Notes column of the Site window.

Add Sound to Your Web Page

Adding sound is one of the most common ways to enhance or personalize a web page. Just as Dreamweaver makes it easy to add images to a page, adding sound isn't a whole lot different. The main difference is that there are a lot more sound file formats to deal with and several different methods for incorporating them into a page. Which format you decide to use and how you go about adding the sound depends on how you want the sound to be presented, who your audience is, the size and quality of the sound file, and, of course, the age-old caveat—browser compatibility differences.

> **TIP** *If you are just looking to add a short sound bite to your page, either as a clickable file or as a background sound, .wav and .aif files are the best-supported formats for web sounds. Most browsers will be capable of playing these formats without the need for an additional plug-in. Any good sound-editing application will allow you to save a sound file into .wav or .aif formats. Make sure, however, that you don't add any compression options when saving the files, even though you can compress .wav and .aif files in many editing applications; they won't be suitable for playing on the Web.*

Besides coming in many different formats, sound can also take up a lot of space, and anything more than a few seconds of sound can take a very long time to download off the Web. Because of this, longer sound samples, like radio broadcasts, whole songs, and so on often use a technology called *streaming*, which allows them to play while they download. Streaming formats also incorporate very heavy compression, which lowers the sound quality in order to decrease file size. Streaming sounds usually require special encoding software and dedicated servers and players such as Real Player to play from the Web. Shorter sound files of a few seconds or less, such as .wav or .midi files, can play natively within a browser, without the need for extra plug-ins or dedicated servers. Many stand-alone sound files like .wav or .midi can be downloaded from the Web or created in a sound-editing application. A good sound-editing application is a must if you want to take raw sound files and save them into a variety of different formats for delivery on the Web.

> **CAUTION** *Remember that whenever you import or link to an external media file in Dreamweaver, the file should be kept inside the current site's root folder (the folder containing all your site's files and assets). If the media file is located outside the site's root folder, Dreamweaver will ask you if you want to copy the file to your root folder when you try to import it. If you get this prompt, select Yes; otherwise, your link may not work when you upload your site to a server.*

Link to an Audio File

Linking to an audio file with a hyperlink from text or an image is the easiest way to add sound to a web page. It's also the least obtrusive method because it allows your viewers to decide whether or not they want to listen to the file rather then being forced to listen to it. Many times a site that plays a sound over and over when you visit the page without the option to turn it off can be downright annoying. When you think about the extra time that it takes to download audio and the fact that some people don't even have sound cards or speakers, it's not a bad idea to give your visitors an option. You can link to any of the sound formats listed earlier by linking directly to the source file.

Linking to an audio file in Dreamweaver is just like linking to an image file.

1. First select the text or image you want to use as a link.

2. In the Property Inspector, click the folder icon to the right of the link field to open a browse dialog box.

3. Browse your drive for the audio file. Once you have located the file, click Select to close the browse box and create the link.

This creates a hyperlink between the text or graphic on your web page and the audio file. When viewers click on this link in their web browsers, the file will download and play using the associated plug-in or helper application.

NOTE *What's a helper application? A helper application is a program that plays specific media types when they are downloaded from the Web, since they can't usually be played by the browser. For Windows computers, most media types use Windows Media Player as the standard helper app. On a Mac, QuickTime handles this task. You can customize which helper apps handle which media types by editing the preferences within your web browser.*

Embed an Audio File

Embedding an audio file is useful when you want a sound to play automatically as background music, or you want to include a sound player (with play, stop, pause, and volume controls) directly on the page. To embed an audio file, you start by inserting a plug-in object, as shown in Figure 13-2 (see the "Work with Netscape Navigator Plug-In Content" section later in this chapter).

1. In Design view, place your cursor anywhere on the page where you want the player to appear.

2. Choose Insert | Media | Plugin or click the Insert Plug-in button in the Objects panel to open the Select File dialog box. Use the Select File dialog box to browse your drive for the audio file you want to place. It's best if you have already placed the audio file in your site folder; otherwise, Dreamweaver will ask you if you want to copy it there since all your site assets should reside in the same folder. After clicking Select, a blank plug-in placeholder graphic appears on the page in Design View (see Figure 13-2).

Plug-in placeholder   Insert Plug-in icon

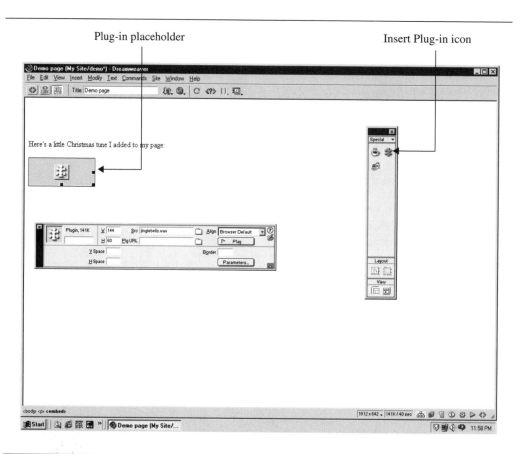

FIGURE 13-2   Sound file embedded in a web page

3. Resize the placeholder graphic by entering a height and width in the Property Inspector (or by dragging the resize handles) to determine the size of the audio player as it appears in the browser. A width of 144 pixels and height of 60 pixels is a good size to try. Be sure to view the page in both Netscape and Internet Explorer as each browser's audio player will look slightly different.

Embed a Sound Without Displaying the Player Controls

You can also embed a sound file into your web page without including visible player controls. Here's how:

1. Follow steps 1–3 above.

2. For step 4, type in a height and width of 2 pixels. Even though you want the controller to be invisible, some browsers require you to still set a visible height and width.

3. In the Property Inspector, click the Parameters button to open the Parameters dialog box.

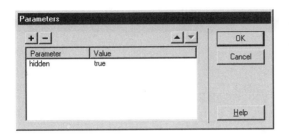

4. In the Parameters dialog box, click the add (+) button and enter **hidden** in the Parameter column. You have now created a new parameter and will define its status in the next step.

5. Press the TAB key and enter **true** in the Value column. Values refer to different states of a parameter. Hidden=True means the player will remain hidden; similarly, if you entered **false**, then the player would be visible.

6. Click OK to close the Parameters dialog box.

When the page is viewed in a browser, the sound will now play without a visible audio controller—a perfect situation for including automatic background sound on your web page.

 Use this technique with discretion! If you embed a sound in your page without any visible controls, the visitor will not have any convenient way to prevent or stop the sound playback. Make sure your audience wants the sound, or else you might drive visitors away from your site.

Work with Flash Content

Macromedia Flash is a popular program for creating vector-based animations for display on the Web. Flash files (.swf) display within a browser with the help of the Flash plug-in, which is included with many browsers (though you'll still need to visit the Macromedia web site periodically to update the plug-in). The big benefit of using Flash on the Web is that Flash uses vector graphics. With vector graphics, file sizes can be significantly reduced. Often vector files are a lot smaller than similar bit-map graphics created in programs such as Photoshop or Fireworks. Flash also allows for animated effects and interactivity. Moreover, Flash files can be scaled up or down in size without affecting the image quality.

Since Flash is also a Macromedia product, Dreamweaver makes it especially easy to incorporate Flash movies, which are usually embedded directly into the page, where they can be sized and positioned exactly as needed. Dreamweaver also allows you to control many attributes of how a Flash movie displays within a page.

13

Most of the Flash movies you see on the Web are created using Flash, a separate program. However, Dreamweaver has some Flash creation capabilities too. With Dreamweaver you can create simple buttons and animated text to include in your web sites. Inserting these kinds of movies involves a slightly different procedure, which I'll cover a bit later in this chapter.

Insert Flash Movies

Inserting Flash movies created in the Flash application is similar to inserting other media objects (see Figure 13-3).

1. In Design view, place your cursor anywhere on the page where you want the Flash movie to appear.

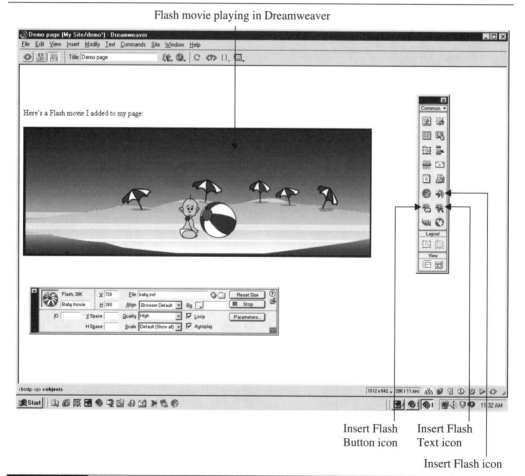

FIGURE 13-3   Inserting a Flash movie

2. Choose Insert | Media | Flash, or click the Insert Flash icon in the Objects panel to open the Select File dialog box.

3. Browse your drive for the file you want to place. Click Select. A Flash placeholder icon appears on the page in Design view. This icon will automatically size to the native dimensions of the Flash movie. (You can resize the Flash movie by typing in a new size in the height and width fields in the Property Inspector panel.)

4. Press F12 or choose File | Preview in Browser | *browser name* to view the Flash movie in action.

Insert Flash Button Objects

Flash is a great application for creating animated movies, but if you don't have access to Flash, or your needs are too simple to justify the cost and steep learning curve of another program, you might get by with some of Dreamweaver's built-in Flash capabilities. Dreamweaver 4 now includes more than 40 professionally designed, customizable Flash buttons, allowing you to add Flash content to your pages without ever leaving Dreamweaver. You can even import new buttons created in Flash to increase your button library. Just like regular image buttons, Flash buttons can be linked to other pages or media elements when a user clicks on them. And Flash buttons share the advantages of other Flash objects in that the file sizes are very small, and you can resize the button without any loss in quality or increase in file size.

1. In Design view, place your cursor anywhere on the page where you want the Flash button to appear.

2. Choose Insert | Interactive Images | Flash Button, or click the Insert Flash Button icon in the Objects panel. The Insert Flash Button dialog box appears.

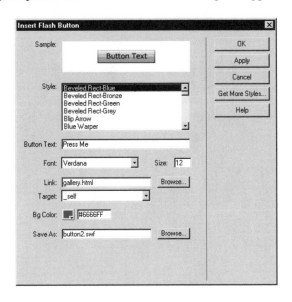

13

3. Scroll through the different button styles in the Style category by using the up or down arrow keys to select a style that you like. Each style appears in the sample window allowing you to preview it.

TIP *You can add more button styles by clicking the Get More Styles button in the Insert Flash Button dialog box. Clicking this button will launch your browser and take you to a section of the Macromedia site where you can download additional button styles.*

4. To customize the button text, type in new text in the Button Text field. You can also customize the display font and font size in the corresponding fields.

5. Enter the file you want the button to link to by typing it into the Link field or by using the Browse button to locate it on your drive. If you are working with a frameset page, include the target using the Target pull-down menu.

6. Apply a background color using the pop-up color picker in the Bg Color field. You usually want to select the same background color for your button that you have specified on your web page so that the button blends in correctly.

7. Type a filename in the Save As box, or click the Browse button to open a browse box where you can select a folder location and enter a filename for the file. Remember to save it in the same site folder as your current site.

TIP *If you use a consistent naming scheme for all your Flash buttons, they'll be easier to find and work with in your site. I like to preface all button filenames with btn_ as in btn_buttonname.swf.*

8. Click OK to close the Insert Flash Button dialog box. The button appears on the page in Design view (see Figure 13-4). Note that the button doesn't get fuzzy when enlarged.

9. Press F12 or choose File | Preview in Browser | *browser name* to view the button in action.

After you create a Flash button, you can resize it by simply selecting the button and dragging the sizing handle. Unlike GIF and JPEG images, the quality of the Flash button doesn't suffer by being resized, so there's no need to reoptimize the button after changing its size. If you need to make other changes to the button, just double-click it to reopen the Insert Flash Button dialog box and edit any of the settings there.

Insert Flash Text Objects

Dreamweaver's Flash text objects allow you to create text-only Flash movies. A Flash text object looks pretty much like a text graphic, except that you can easily incorporate rollover effects so

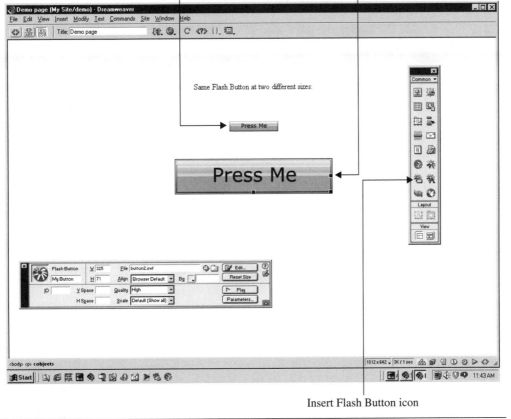

Original Flash button   Enlarged Flash button

Insert Flash Button icon

FIGURE 13-4   Flash buttons can be scaled up or down without affecting image quality.

13

that the text changes color when the pointer passes over the text. Again, the benefits of Flash vector graphics also apply to text: you get smaller file sizes than with bitmapped images, and you have the ability to scale up or down without degrading image quality.

1. In Design view, place your cursor anywhere on the page where you want the Flash text object to appear.

2. Choose Insert | Interactive Images | Flash Text, or click the Insert Flash Text icon in the Objects panel. The Insert Flash Text dialog box appears.

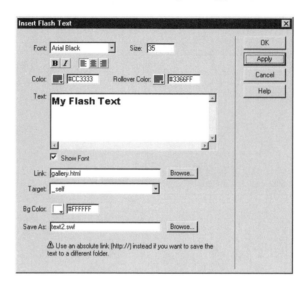

3. Select the display font, type sizes, and attributes in the appropriate fields. Check the Show Font option box to preview what the font will look like.

4. If you want the text to change color when a user rolls their mouse over it, select a different color as the Rollover Color.

5. Enter the file you want the text to link to by typing it into the Link field or using the Browse button to locate it on your drive. If you are working with a frameset page, include the target using the Target pull-down menu.

6. Apply a background color using the pop-up color picker in the Bg Color field. You usually want to select the same background color for your text that you have specified on your web page so that the text blends in correctly.

7. Type a filename in the Save As box or click the Browse button to open a browse box where you can select a folder location, and enter a filename for the file. Once again, remember to save it in the same site folder as your current site. The text movie will appear on the page in Design view

8. Press F12 or choose File | Preview in Browser | *browser name* to view the text movie in action.

Set Flash Movie Properties

Flash movies have a number of properties that you can modify using the Property Inspector. When you first insert a Flash object in Dreamweaver, the Property Inspector displays the most commonly used properties. To see additional properties, click the expander arrow in the lower-right corner of the Inspector. This allows you to further customize the appearance of the movie within your page. The Inspector also contains a Play button, which allows you to preview the Flash movie within Dreamweaver.

Properties of Flash Movies

The following is a complete listing and description of Flash button and text properties that you can modify using the settings in the Property Inspector.

- **Name**   An optional name to identify the Flash object for use with scripting.

- **W** and **H**   Enter the width and height of the Flash movie. You can use picas (pc), points (pt), inches (in), millimeters (mm), centimeters (cm), or percentages of the object's original size (%). Do not include a space between the number and the measurement when entering a value.

- **File**   The path to the Flash movie. You can also click the Browse… button to locate the file.

- **Align**   Specifies the alignment of the movie within the page.

- **Bg**   Specifies the background color of the Flash movie.

- **Edit**   Opens up the Flash Text or the Button object dialog box.

- **Reset Size**   Resets the Flash object to its original size.

- **Play/Stop**   Allows you to preview the Flash animation.

- **ID**   Defines the parameter used for passing information to ActiveX controls.

- **V Space/H Space**   Specifies the amount of white space around the object as measured in pixels.

- **Quality**   Specifies the appearance quality of the Flash file. A higher setting looks better but requires a faster computer processor to render. There are four possible settings. Low sacrifices appearance to accommodate slower computers, whereas High favors appearance at a penalty for slower computers. Auto Low accommodates slower computers but will improve appearance when possible. Auto High accommodates any computer if possible but when necessary sacrifices appearance when running on a slower computer.

- **Scale**   Defines how the movie displays within the parameters set for Width and Height.

- **Parameters**   Opens a dialog box for entering additional custom parameters.

13

Additional Properties Used by Imported Movies but Not by Text and Button Objects

The following properties pertain only to files created in Flash and imported into Dreamweaver.

- ■ **Loop**   Replays the movie indefinitely.
- ■ **Autoplay**   Plays the movie automatically when the page loads.

Work with Shockwave Movies

Shockwave is a compressed file format that allows you to deploy interactive multimedia files created with Macromedia Director on the Web. Shockwave uses bitmap graphics, so the file sizes are generally larger than Flash files, but Director allows much more complicated programming and interactive features. Shockwave files require a separate plug-in to display in a browser. The Shockwave plug-in is included as part of the default installation of recent versions of the popular browsers, and it's also available for free from the Macromedia web site.

Insert Shockwave Movies

Shockwave movies are normally a bit complicated to insert into raw HTML because Netscape Navigator and Internet Explorer browsers require different code. To code for both browsers, you need to include two different kinds of HTML tags and accompanying code. Fortunately, Dreamweaver takes care of all this behind the scenes, so inserting and editing Shockwave movies involves only a few clicks of the mouse.

1. In Design view, place your cursor anywhere on the page where you want the Shockwave movie to appear.

2. Choose Insert | Media | Shockwave, or click the Insert Shockwave icon in the Objects panel to call up the Select File dialog box.

3. Use the Select File dialog box to browse your drive for the Shockwave file you want to place. Click Select. A Shockwave placeholder icon appears on the page in Design view.

4. Resize the Shockwave icon on your page if necessary. The icon will automatically size to the native dimensions of the Shockwave movie (see Figure 13-5). You can resize the movie by typing in a new size in the height and width fields in the Property Inspector or by dragging the sizing handles on the icon.

5. Press F12 or choose File | Preview in Browser | *browser name* to view the Shockwave movie in action.

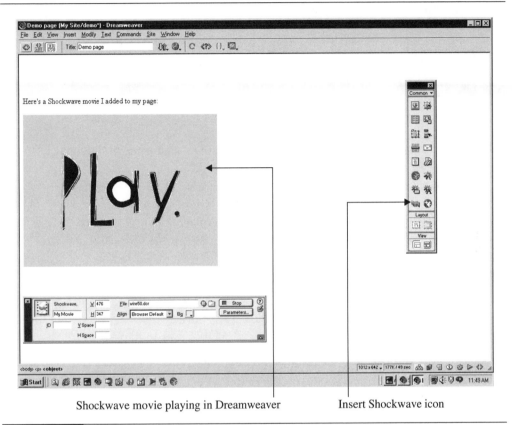

Shockwave movie playing in Dreamweaver   Insert Shockwave icon

FIGURE 13-5   Inserting a Shockwave movie

13

Set Shockwave Movie Properties

Shockwave movies have a number of properties that you can modify using the Property Inspector. When you first insert a Shockwave movie in Dreamweaver, the Property Inspector displays the most commonly used properties. To see additional properties, click the expander arrow in the lower right corner of the Inspector. This allows you to further customize the appearance of the movie within your page. The Inspector also contains a Play button, which allows you to preview the Shockwave movie within Dreamweaver. The following is a complete listing and description of Shockwave movie properties that you can modify using the settings in the Property Inspector.

- ■ **Name** An optional name to identify the Shockwave movie for use with scripting.

- ■ **W and H** Enter the width and height of the Shockwave movie. You can use picas (pc), points (pt), inches (in), millimeters (mm), centimeters (cm), or percentages of the object's original size (%). Do not include a space between the number and the measurement when entering a value.

- ■ **File** The path to the Shockwave movie. You can also click the Browse… button to locate the file.

- ■ **Align** Specifies the alignment of the movie within the page.

- ■ **Bg** Specifies the background color of the Shockwave movie.

- ■ **Play/Stop** Allows you to preview the Shockwave movie.

- ■ **Parameters** Opens a dialog box for entering additional custom parameters.

- ■ **ID** Defines the optional parameter used for passing information to ActiveX controls.

- ■ **V Space/H Space** Specifies the amount of white space around the object as measured in pixels.

Work with Netscape Navigator Plug-In Content

A long time ago, when Netscape Navigator was the dominant browser on the Web, Netscape invented a method of extending a browser's display capabilities by developing a new kind of plug-in architecture. Using this new standard plug-in architecture, third-party companies could extend the capabilities of Netscape's browser by developing new plug-ins that conformed to the standard. Users then had only to download the new plug-in and install it to enjoy all sorts of new viewing possibilities with their browser. Today the generic plug-in standard developed by Netscape still exists and is also used by other browser makers. In fact, Navigator plug-ins are used by the majority of web media formats, including audio, video, 3D, and many others. Any format that uses the <embed> tag employs a plug-in for browser display.

NOTE *See the table later in this chapter, "Common Audio and Video File Formats and the Browser Plug-Ins Needed to Play Them," for a quick description of which media types require Netscape Navigator plug-ins for viewing.*

Insert Netscape Navigator Plug-In Content

The process for inserting Navigator plug-ins is basically the same as the procedure for embedding sound file. Here are the steps:

1. In Design view, place your cursor anywhere on the page where you want the plug-in object to appear.

2. Choose Insert | Media | Plugin, or click the Insert Plug-in icon in the Special pane of the Objects panel to open the Select File dialog box.

3. Use the Select File dialog box to browse your drive for the file you want to place. Click Select. A plug-in placeholder icon appears on the page in Design view, as shown in Figure 13-6.

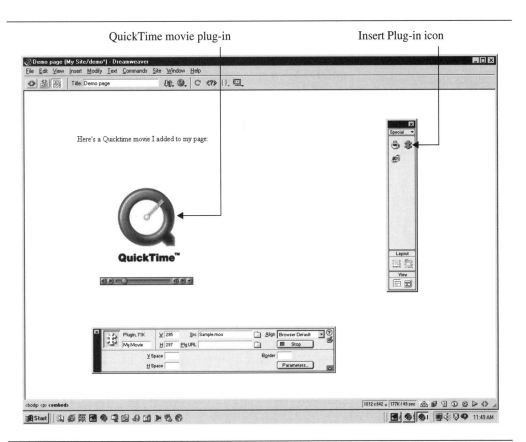

FIGURE 13-6   Inserting a QuickTime movie as a Netscape Navigator plug-in object

The kind of media file you embed into your page determines which plug-in Dreamweaver and the visitor's browser will call upon to play or display the media file. Table 13-1 lists some of the more common media file formats and their corresponding plug-ins.

Format	Plug-In	Description
.midi or .mid (Musical Instrument Digital Interface)	Windows Media Player (IE), Live Audio (NN), both built into the browser.	Instrumental-music-only format. It provides good sound quality (though varies depending on the computer's sound card) and very small file sizes compared to other formats.
.wav (Waveform Extension)	Windows Media Player (IE), LiveAudio (NN), both built into the browser.	One of the most common file formats for sound. It provides good sound quality but also a very large file size as the sound length increases.
.aiff, .aif (Audio Interchange File Format)	Media Player (IE), Live Audio (NN), both built into the browser.	Similar to .wav, good sound quality and same issue with file size.
.rmf (Rich Media Format)	Beatnik (plug-in may not be present on most browsers).	A hybrid audio/music format used by Beatnik.
.mp3 (Motion Picture Experts Group Audio or MPEG-Audio Layer-3)	Windows Media Player (IE), QuickTime, Winamp, RealAudio (older computers may need to download a compatible plug-in).	MP3 files offer very high sound quality while keeping file sizes relatively small.
.ra, .ram, .rpm (RealAudio)	RealAudio (plug-in must be downloaded).	Real Audio offers a very high degree of compression resulting in considerably smaller file sizes. Uses streaming technology, which allows listeners to begin listening to a selection before it has completely downloaded. Sound quality is lower than the other formats listed above but is still acceptable for most purposes.
.mov	QuickTime (standard on Macs, optional on Windows).	Popular format for video and audio content. Can be made to stream.

TABLE 13-1   Common Audio and Video File Formats and the Browser Plug-Ins Needed to Play Them

Format	Plug-In	Description
.mpg, .mpeg, .mpe	Windows Media Player (older computers may need to download a compatible plug-in).	Motion Picture Experts Group video format. MPEG files offer much greater compression than noncompressed Quicktime and .avi movies while still offering very good quality.
.avi	QuickTime or Windows Media Player (older computers may need to download a compatible plug-in).	Popular but older video format.

TABLE 13-1   Common Audio and Video File Formats and the Browser Plug-Ins Needed to Play Them *(continued)*

Set Netscape Navigator Plug-In Properties

Just like you can set the properties of other media types using the Property Inspector, Navigator plug-ins also allow you to set their properties. Below is a listing of all the Navigator plug-in properties that you can edit in the Property Inspector.

- ■ **Name**   An optional name to identify the plug-in object for use with scripting.

- ■ **W** and **H**   Enter the width and the height of the plug-in object. You can use picas (pc), points (pt), inches (in), millimeters (mm), centimeters (cm), or percentages of the object's original size (%). Do not include a space between the number and the measurement when entering a value.

- ■ **Src**   The path to the media file. You can also click the folder icon to locate the file using the file browser.

- ■ **Plg URL**   This field provides a place to include a URL where the plug-in can be downloaded in case a user doesn't have the correct plug-in. Entering a URL redirects visitors to the download page if they don't have the plug-in. Consult the manufacturer of the specific plug-in for the correct URL.

- ■ **Align**   Specifies the alignment of the plug-in object within the page.

- ■ **Play/Stop**   Allows you to preview the plug-in content.

13

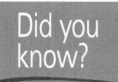

Did you know?

Dreamweaver Uses Plug-Ins, Too

Dreamweaver uses the same plug-ins to display files in the Document window that your browser uses for display. In fact, when Dreamweaver first starts up, it searches your computer for all the installed plug-ins so that it can display the plug-in content when you click the Play button in the Property Inspector.

- **V Space/H Space**   Specifies the amount of white space around the object as measured in pixels.
- **Border**   Specifies the width of the border around the plug-in object.
- **Parameters**   Opens a dialog box for entering additional custom parameters.

Work with ActiveX Controls

An ActiveX control is a kind of miniprogram that can function like a browser plug-in. However, ActiveX controls run only in Internet Explorer on Windows computers. Dreamweaver allows you to add ActiveX controls as well as access some of the properties of ActiveX objects through the Property Inspector.

Insert ActiveX Controls

Inserting ActiveX controls works the same way as inserting other media objects.

1. In Design view, place your cursor anywhere on the page where you want the ActiveX object to appear.

2. Choose Insert | Media | ActiveX, or click the Insert ActiveX icon in the Special pane of the Objects panel to call up the Select File dialog box.

3. Use the Select File dialog box to browse your drive for the file you want to place. Click Select. An ActiveX placeholder icon appears on the page in Design view, as shown in Figure 13-7.

4. Press F12 or choose File | Preview in Browser | *browser name* to view the ActiveX control in action.

Set ActiveX Properties

Just as you can set the properties of other media types using the Property Inspector, ActiveX controls also allow you to set their properties. Below is a listing of all the ActiveX properties that you can edit in the Property Inspector.

- **Name** An optional name to identify the ActiveX control for use with scripting

- **W** and **H** Enter the width and the height of the object. You can use picas (pc), points (pt), inches (in), millimeters (mm), centimeters (cm), or percentages of the object's original size (%). Do not include a space between the number and the measurement when entering a value.

- **Class ID** Used to identify the ActiveX control. Enter a value or choose one from the pop-up menu.

- **Embed** Click this box to make the ActiveX component compatible with Netscape Navigator if it has an equivalent plug-in for Netscape.

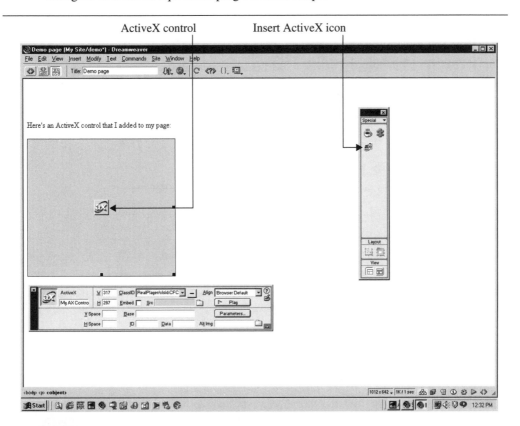

FIGURE 13-7 Inserting an ActiveX control

- **Align**   Specifies the alignment of the object within the page.
- **Parameters**   Opens a dialog box for entering additional custom parameters.
- **Src**   The path to the media file. You can also click the folder icon to locate the file using the file browser.
- **V Space/H Space**   Specifies the amount of white space around the object as measured in pixels.
- **Base**   Provides a place to include a URL where the ActiveX control can be downloaded in case a user doesn't have it installed. Entering a URL will allow Internet Explorer to download the control. Consult the manufacturer of the control for the correct URL.
- **Bg**   Specifies the background color of the object.
- **Alt Img**   Allows you to specify an alternate image to display in place of the control if a browser doesn't support ActiveX. Not available if the Embed option is checked.
- **ID**   Defines the parameter used for passing information to other ActiveX controls.
- **Data**   Specifies a data file for the ActiveX control to use.
- **Borders**   Specifies the width of the border around the object.

Add Java Applets

Java applets are miniprograms created in the Java programming language that you can run on your web page. Java applets can run on any computer platform with Java Virtual machine software installed.

Insert Java Applets

Inserting Java applets works the same way as inserting other media objects:

1. In Design view, place your cursor anywhere on the page where you want the Java applet to appear.
2. Choose Insert | Media | Applet, or click the Insert Applet icon in the Special pane of the Objects panel to open the Select File dialog box.
3. Use the Select File dialog box to browse your drive for the file you want to place. Click Select. A Java applet placeholder icon appears on the page in Design view (pictured in Figure 13-8).
4. Press F12 or choose File | Preview in Browser | *browser name* to view the applet in action.

Set Java Applet Properties

Just like you can set the properties of other media types using the Property Inspector, Java applets also allow you to set their properties. Below is a listing of all the Java applet properties that you can edit in the Property Inspector.

- ■ **Name**   An optional name to identify the Java applet for use with scripting.

- ■ **W** and **H**   Enter the width and the height of the applet. You can use picas (pc), points (pt), inches (in), millimeters (mm), centimeters (cm), or percentages of the object's original size (%). Do not include a space between the number and measurement when entering a value.

- ■ **Code**   The path to the file containing the Java code. You can also click the folder icon to locate the file using the file browser.

Java applet   Insert Applet icon

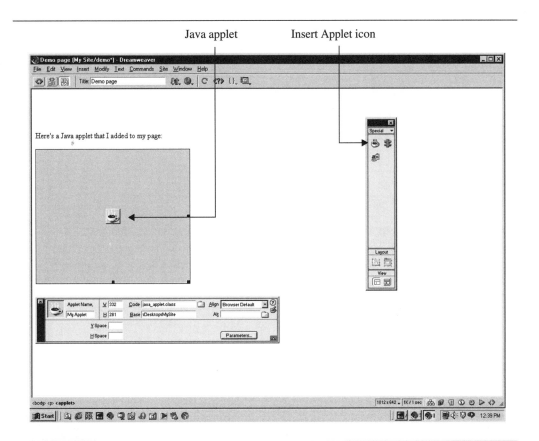

FIGURE 13-8   Inserting a Java applet

- **Base**   The folder containing the selected applet. This field is automatically filled in when you fill in the Code field.

- **Align**   Specifies the alignment of the applet within the page.

- **Alt**   Specifies alternative content to display in the event the user's browser doesn't support Java or Java is disabled.

- **V Space/H Space**   Specifies the amount of white space around the object as measured in pixels.

- **Parameters**   Opens a dialog box for entering additional custom parameters.

Set Parameters for Media Objects

Many media objects allow additional, proprietary parameters to be set in order to control various different aspects specific to each individual media format. Because each plug-in type and media object uses different sets of parameters, Dreamweaver allows you to create and edit custom parameters for each object. Access the Parameters dialog box by clicking the Parameters button in the Property Inspector. You can also right-click an object in Design view or Site view and select the Parameters option from the Context menu to call up the Parameter dialog box.

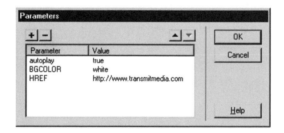

In the example illustrated, I set some additional parameters for a QuickTime movie. As can many plug-in objects, QuickTime can utilize many additional, optional parameters to further customize the display of the movie within the browser. To find out more about parameters specific to a particular media type, consult the manufacturer of the plug-in or media object.

1. In the Parameters dialog box, click the plus (+) button to enter a new parameter or the minus (−) button to delete a parameter.

2. Enter the name of the parameter and press TAB.

3. Enter a value for the parameter and press OK.

4. Repeat steps 1–3 as needed to add more parameters, then click OK to close the Parameters dialog box.

Part V

Expand Your Horizons

Chapter 14

Create and Use Style Sheets

How to...

- Create Cascading Style Sheets
- Link to an external style sheet
- Reformat an entire site using Cascading Style Sheets
- Convert Cascading Style Sheets to HTML tags

If you've spent any time trying to control the look and layout of text in a web document, you've no doubt been frustrated by the lack of accurate layout capabilities available using HTML tags. To address the shortcomings of HTML design, the committee that devises many of the new web standards and technologies introduced Cascading Style Sheets (CSS) as a way to give web designers much greater control over the look of their pages.

With standard HTML, the only way to control the font and formatting characteristics of text was through a few, very limited `<font>` tag attributes. Basically, you can affect only font faces and a few style attributes such as bold, underline, italic, and so on. Sizing options are limited to seven relative text sizes that aren't particularly accurate, since text appears at different sizes in different browsers and on different platforms.

Cascading Style Sheets, or CSS, are a kind of "extended HTML" that provides a way to control text much more precisely. CSS also enables you to apply formatting changes to multiple pages, or even to an entire site, quickly and easily by changing the style definitions in a style sheet. Besides providing text formatting and layout control, CSS also provides a way to specify and control some unique web page features such as layer positioning, special effects, and mouse rollovers. CSS can apply to other elements besides text, but this chapter concentrates on CSS as it applies to providing advanced formatting and design options for text.

Even though CSS has been around for a few years now, many web designers have yet to embrace it, despite its obvious advantages. The biggest roadblock has been the fact that CSS requires version 4 web browsers or higher. Furthermore, even version 4 browsers offer incomplete and inconsistent support for CSS. Until solid browser support for CSS reaches widespread use, designers have no incentive to use the technology. However, as time moves on, this becomes less and less of an issue. Today major browsers are well beyond version 4, and improved CSS support is a major goal of new browser versions. As the user base migrates to these newer browsers, CSS will enjoy much wider use.

Another obstacle to acceptance of CSS is the need for designers to learn the syntax and rules involved in coding CSS. Although CSS syntax is actually fairly simple, most web designers aren't eager to learn it. Fortunately, as a Dreamweaver user, you can access the tremendous power of CSS without actually having to learn any extra coding. Dreamweaver provides a simple and intuitive interface for accessing and implementing virtually all the powerful text-formatting features of CSS.

What Are Cascading Style Sheets?

Designed to propel web design to a much higher standard than previously possible, CSS allows you to specify many font attributes with far greater precision than you can with traditional HTML tags alone. For example, you can specify font sizes based on absolute measurements such as pixels, points, picas, inches, millimeters, and more. You can also set line heights, font weights, and upper- or lowercase letters, to name a few customizable options.

CSS also allows you to define new rules that affect how a browser renders HTML tags. These rules define how the browser displays text or how it interprets HTML tags, even to the point of overriding the normal rules of HTML. Each time you create a style sheet using CSS, you can define a new set of rules, and the document that uses the style sheet knows which rules to follow because you've instructed it to do so. You can embed these instructions within individual HTML tags, add them to the page as part of the `<header>` tag, or save the style sheet instructions in an external file (called an *external style sheet*) that can be linked to one or more web documents.

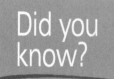

The Difference Between HTML Styles and CSS Styles

Dreamweaver includes another kind of styles—HTML styles, which are covered in Chapter 3. Like CSS styles, HTML styles provide a way to implement control over text attributes in Dreamweaver. However, HTML styles are very different from CSS styles.

- HTML styles are a unique feature of Dreamweaver that provides a shortcut for applying a group of normal HTML text attributes all at once. CSS styles, in contrast, are a much more powerful industry-wide standard.

- HTML styles work only in Dreamweaver. The effects of applying an HTML style are viewable in any web browser, but the styles themselves are available only when you are working on a site in Dreamweaver. CSS styles are independent of Dreamweaver. CSS style sheets that you create in Dreamweaver can be used and edited by other applications or HTML editors.

- Modifying an HTML style affects only subsequent applications of that style. Modifying a CSS style affects all instances where that style is used throughout the document or site. When you change CSS attributes, they automatically update any text or pages that utilize the CSS rules. This means you can change a single CSS rule, and it can update an entire site, or even multiple sites, if they all use the same style sheet.

14

- HTML styles are limited to the standard HTML text attributes such as typeface, color, bold, italic, and so on. CSS styles give you far greater control over the formatting and layout of type, plus control over layers and other new web document features.

- HTML styles are compatible with all commonly used browser versions. The use of CSS styles requires newer browser versions.

The CSS Styles Panel

The CSS Styles panel is your main access point for creating and editing style sheets in Dreamweaver. To open the CSS Styles panel, simply choose Window | CSS Styles, or click the Show CSS Styles button in the Launcher. The CSS Styles panel (see Figure 14-1) has several elements.

As you can see in Figure 14-1, the CSS Styles panel lists any styles currently associated with the document. There are also four commands that you can execute from this panel, displayed as buttons along the lower-right corner of the panel. All the commands are also accessible in the pop-up menu that appears when you click the triangle in the upper-right corner of the panel. You can create new style sheets, attach external style sheets, and edit or delete existing style sheets using these commands. Anytime you work with style sheets, you'll want to have the CSS Styles panel window available.

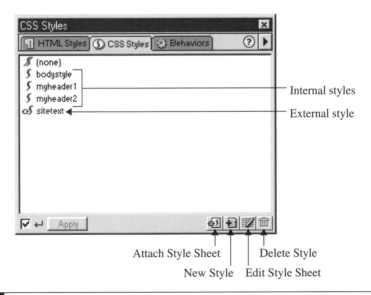

FIGURE 14-1   The CSS Styles panel

You can also use the shortcut SHIFT+F11 *to toggle the CSS Styles panel on and off.*

Create a CSS Style Sheet

You can create two different kinds of CSS style sheets: internal style sheets and external style sheets. Internal style sheets are embedded in the code of the existing web document. External style sheets reside in an external file that can be referenced much as you reference another HTML page using a hypertext link. For each type of style sheet you can also create three different and distinct kinds of styles:

- Custom styles
- Redefined HTML tag styles
- CSS selector styles

Create a Style Sheet in Dreamweaver

To work with CSS styles, you first need to open the CSS Styles panel (shown in Figure 14-1). In the CSS Styles panel, you can define styles for your document (or site). A collection of CSS styles is called a *style sheet*.

Initially, you'll probably want to store those styles in an internal style sheet, which is code located in the header section of the current document to describe the styles. Later, after you define a selection of styles, you can export those styles to a separate external style sheet that you can use to format multiple documents and even multiple sites.

NOTE   *Actually, Dreamweaver enables you to create styles directly in an external sheet, but most web designers tend to start with an internal style sheet in a document that can serve as a test page for the styles.*

Create a Custom Style

Custom CSS styles are what people usually think of when they imagine a style sheet. If you've worked with Dreamweaver's HTML styles, the concept is similar, but the capabilities of custom CSS styles are far greater than HTML styles. With a custom style, you can create and modify a diverse set of attributes and apply them to any selection of type on your page.

For example, you can create a custom style to use for level-one headings in a document. You might define your level-one headings to display in 14pt Verdana, bold and colored blue. Then, whenever you want to apply that style, you can just highlight some text and apply the level-one heading style. If later you decide to change the color to red, you just change the style sheet and all the level-one headings in your whole document automatically change to reflect the updated style specification.

In the parlance of CSS, a custom style is referred to as a *class*. This term refers to a collection of CSS *rule declarations* (list of formatting specifications) that you create and save either in your existing document or in an external file. When you name a custom style, you can

14

pretty much use any name you want, but the name must begin with a period. To create a custom style, follow these steps:

1. Click the New Style button in the CSS Styles panel. This opens the New Style dialog box.

2. Select the Make Custom Style (Class) radio button.

3. Enter a name for your style in the Name box. Any name is appropriate providing it starts with a period. If you forget to enter a period, Dreamweaver will enter one for you.

 When naming custom style classes, try to avoid using names that are used by HTML tags, such as head, body, title, and so forth.

4. Select the This Document Only radio button. This saves your style information in an internal style sheet in the current web document. (For information on saving styles in an external style sheet, see the section later in this chapter on external style sheets.)

5. Click the OK button to open the Style Definition dialog box. This is where you define the actual attributes for your new style.

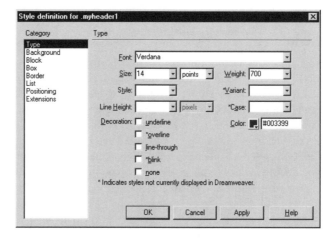

6. Click Type in the Category list. Adjust the Type settings in the Style Definition dialog box to define the text formatting attributes for your style.

■ Enter a font name for your style, or select one from the Font pop-up menu.

■ Enter a size for the font in the Size box and select a measurement in the pop-up menu to the right of the Size box.

TIP *Many designers like to use points to specify text size with CSS because points provide the most consistent size appearance across computer platforms. This is one of the most compelling reasons to use CSS.*

■ Select other options and attributes using the different fields in the Style Definition dialog box. Refer to Table 14-1 for further descriptions of each field and the available attributes.

7. Click OK to close the Style Definition dialog box and finish creating your style. Dreamweaver adds the style definition to the internal style sheet for your document and also adds the style name to the list of styles shown in the CSS Styles panel.

CAUTION *Cascading Style Sheets are a still-evolving specification. Many of the attributes in the Style Definition dialog box are not supported by current browser versions but are expected to be supported by future versions. Even though the attributes aren't currently supported, Dreamweaver includes the ability to set many of these attributes for future compatibility. The attributes listed in the Style Definition dialog box with an asterisk next to their names do not preview in Dreamweaver and are less likely to be supported by current browsers. Always preview your styles in different browsers to confirm which attributes will display properly.*

Attribute	Description
Font	Specify a font face or font family.
Size	Select a font size and measurement system. Relative sizes such as small, medium, large, and so on are set relative to the normally displayed font size.
Weight	Specify the boldness of the type. A normal setting (nonbold) is equal to about 400. You can set the weight bolder than normal or lighter than normal by entering a value or selecting one from the pop-up menu. Relative values such as normal, bolder, lighter, and so forth are set relative to the normally displayed weight.
Style	Specify the style attributes such as normal, oblique, or italic. Oblique is similar to italic but is usually created by electronically slanting a normal (roman) font.
Variant	Select either normal or small caps. Small caps displays the text in all uppercase letters, set at the height of lowercase letters. Shifted characters appear slightly larger.
Line Height	Specify the vertical spacing, also known as *leading,* between lines of text. You can also select a measurement system. The normal setting is equivalent to one or two points more than the selected type size.

TABLE 14-1   CSS Type Attributes

14

Attribute	Description
Case	Select type case. Options include capitalize (initial caps), uppercase (all caps), lowercase, and none (normal).
Decoration	Specify the text decoration effects by selecting one or more options.
Color	Use the color selector to specify a color for the font.

TABLE 14-1 CSS Type Attributes *(continued)*

These steps describe how to create a style that controls text attributes. However, you can also create custom styles for any other category listed in the Style Definition dialog box (see Table 14-2).

Apply Your Style

After you create a style, applying it to text in your document is easy. Here's how:

1. Make sure the CSS Styles panel (shown in Figure 14-1) is visible by choosing Window | CSS Styles or clicking the Show CSS Styles button in the Launcher.

2. Select the text to which you want to apply the style. You can highlight a block of text in the Document window by dragging the pointer across the text, or you can simply click anywhere within a paragraph or table cell to apply the style to the whole paragraph or cell.

Category	Description
Type	Allows you to specify text formatting attributes such as font, size, and weight.
Background	Allows you to specify background images or colors within a style.
Block	Allows you to alter options such as word or letter spacing and alignment and justification of paragraphs.
Box	Allows you to use CSS to alter spacing around elements (such as images) in much the same way that tables do.
Border	Allows you to control the characteristics of border elements around objects including text, images, and other media objects.
List	Gives you control over bulleted points for lists, allowing you to customize the bullet or even substitute your own graphic in place of a bullet.
Positioning	Gives you exact control over positioning of elements on the page using a variety of measurement systems.
Extensions	Includes advanced-level CSS options such as defining page breaks, specifying a custom cursor, and enabling special effects with filters.

TABLE 14-2 Style Categories Available with CSS

3. Click the style you want to apply in the CSS Styles panel. The new style is applied to the current selection or to the entire paragraph if no text is selected (see Figure 14-2).

TIP

You can remove a CSS style from a selection by simply repeating this same procedure.

CAUTION

Manual paragraph formatting with HTML tags (which includes HTML styles) will override any formatting you do with CSS. For example, if you change the color of some text using the Property Inspector panel, that text will not accept a different color applied with a CSS style. Be sure to remove any manual formatting if you want to control your text using CSS.

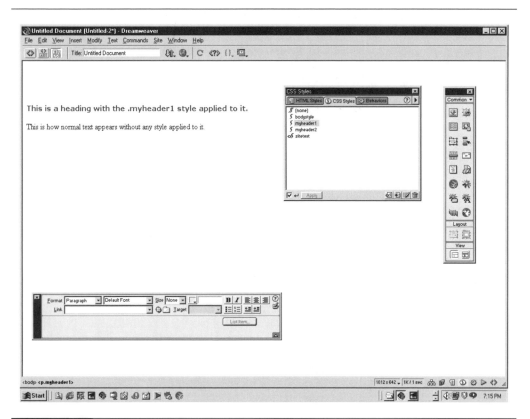

FIGURE 14-2   Applying a CSS style

14

How Cascading Style Sheets Got Their Name

Cascading Style Sheets are referred to as *cascading* because of the way in which styles closest to a styled element override styles farther from the element. Any style applied to an element on a page may have other styles above it, which may or may not apply to the same element. Because of the way that HTML works, successive nested style rules override previous style rules in defining how the browser renders an element. So the formatting of a paragraph overrides the general body text formatting and character formatting on a word overrides the paragraph formatting. In other words, the formatting priority flows from style to style in much the same way that water cascades over ledges in a waterfall.

 *If you apply two or more styles to the same text, try to avoid applying conflicting styles since they can produce unexpected results. Conflicting styles specify different values for the same attribute. So, two styles that both specify different colors do conflict, but one style that specifies font and size and another style that specifies color and weight do not conflict.*

Redefine HTML Tags

In addition to defining custom styles from scratch, CSS enables you to redefine the attributes of the standard HTML tags. Redefined HTML tag styles allow you to change the way that existing HTML tags are rendered by the viewer's browser. This feature can be very useful for making quick, global changes to a page or a web site. For example, when you apply the bold attribute to text by clicking the Bold button in the Property Inspector panel, Dreamweaver marks the text with the <b> tag, which instructs the browser to render text in bold face. However, using redefined HTML tag styles, you could specify additional attributes for the <b> tag, and all text marked with the <b> tag would take on the new attributes. For example, you could redefine the <b> tag such that any text marked with that tag displays in red as well as being bold.

To create a redefined HTML tag style, follow these steps:

1. Click the New Style button in the CSS Styles panel. This opens the New Style dialog box.

2. Select the Redefine HTML Tag radio button.

3. Select an HTML tag to redefine from the Tag list box. The list shows all the available HTML tags without the angle brackets that normally surround the tags in HTML code.

4. Select the This Document Only radio button. This saves your style information in the internal style sheet for the current HTML document.

5. Click the OK button to open the Style Definition dialog box, allowing you to define the attributes for your new style.

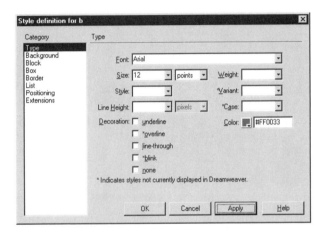

6. Click Type in the Category list. Adjust the Type settings in the Style Definition dialog box to define the text formatting attributes for your style.

■ Enter a font name for your style, or select one from the Font pop-up menu.

■ Enter a size for the font in the Size box, and select a measurement in the pop-up menu to the right of the Size box.

■ Select other options and attributes using the different fields in the Style Definition dialog box. Refer to Table 14-1 for further descriptions of each field and the available attributes.

7. Click OK to close the Style Definition dialog box and finish creating your style. Dreamweaver adds the style definition to the internal style sheet for your document.

No further steps are necessary to apply the style since it will automatically apply anywhere in your page where you have used the redefined HTML tag to format your text (see Figure 14-3).

14

TIP

By modifying the <a> tag and selecting the None option in the Decoration attribute, you can turn off underlining for hypertext links. This is a commonly used CSS technique to change the appearance of links in a web browser.

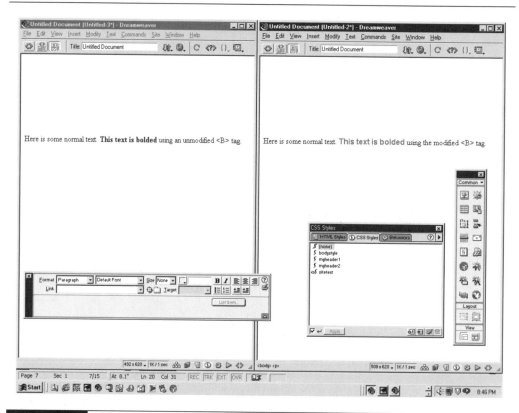

FIGURE 14-3   Altering the `<b>` (bold) tag using the redefine HTML tag style

Modify a CSS Selector

In a way, CSS selector styles combine both custom styles and redefined HTML tag styles. With CSS selector styles you can change the attributes of the `<a>`, or anchor tag, used to create a hypertext link. This feature allows you to change how links appear in a browser and interact when the mouse hovers over them or the user has already visited the link. With CSS selector styles you can also redefine the formatting of a particular combination of tags—that is, tags nested within other tags. For example, a `<blockquote>` tag nested within another `<blockquote>` tag will format differently than the first.

Apply Styles to Hypertext Links Using the `<a>` (Anchor) Tag   You can create CSS selector styles (also called *pseudoclasses*) to control the way hypertext links appear in a browser. This technique allows you to control link colors and rollover colors by using CSS.

Click the New Style button in the CSS Styles panel. This opens the New Style dialog box.

CAUTION   *Converting CSS styles to HTML tags causes irreversible changes to the current document. Always perform this operation on a copy of your document, not the original.*

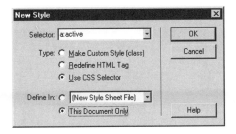

1. Select the Use CSS Selector radio button.

2. Select a click state from the Selector list box. For example, select a:active to set the appearance attributes for active links. Here's a list of the available states:

    ■ **a:active**   The way the link appears when the user clicks it

    ■ **a:hover**   The way the link appears when the pointer is hovering over it

    ■ **a:link**   The way the link appears normally

    ■ **a:visited**   The way the link appears after the user has already visited it

3. Select the This Document Only radio button to save the style in the document's internal style sheet.

4. Click the OK button to open the Style Definition dialog box, where you can define the formatting attributes for your link.

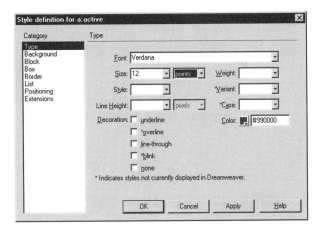

5. Click the Type category and enter the text attributes for the link text. Remember that you're setting the way a link should appear in a particular state—active, hover, normal link, or visited. Usually you'll want to select different colors for each state.

6. Click OK to close the New Style dialog box and apply the style.

14

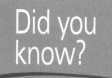

Selector Styles Are the Most Common CSS Styles

CSS selector styles for the <a> tag are one of the most commonly used CSS implementations on the Web, since they allow you to create rollover effects without using JavaScript or creating extra images. Large web sites such as Microsoft.com and others make common use of this CSS feature.

This procedure defines the attributes for one state of the <a> tag, which marks hypertext links. You can repeat the steps to create style definitions for the remaining link states to complete the effect.

 *The CSS selector styles applied to the <a> tag do not display in Netscape Navigator 4 or earlier versions of Netscape. Internet Explorer 4 and above, or Netscape Navigator 6 and above, is required to view them properly.*

Redefine the Formatting for a Combination of Tags (Nested Tags)   Another design task you can achieve by using CSS selector styles is defining how a certain tag renders when it is nested inside another tag.

For example, when using indented text, suppose you want to format that text differently from nonindented text to set it apart. In this case, you could use the Indent button in the Property Inspector panel to indent the text, which marks that text with the <blockquote> tag. You could use CSS to redefine the HTML tag <blockquote> to add other text formatting in addition to indenting the text. Now suppose you want to insert a quote within the indented text; this item needs additional indentation, as well as a different style setting to set it off from the nonquoted text. Again you use the Indent button in the Property Inspector panel, which creates a new <blockquote> tag nested within the first <blockquote> tag. By creating a CSS selector style for this combination of tags, you can define how the nested <blockquote> tag will display differently than the nonnested version (see Figure 14-4).

1. Click the New Style button in the CSS Styles panel. This brings up the New Style dialog box.

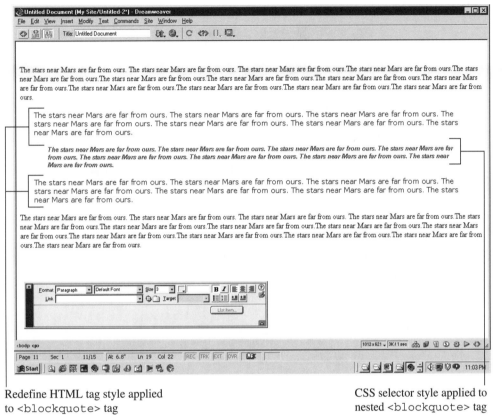

Redefine HTML tag style applied
to <blockquote> tag

CSS selector style applied to
nested <blockquote> tag

FIGURE 14-4   Nested <blockquote> text renders differently than nonnested
<blockquote> text.

14

2. Select the Use CSS Selector radio button.

3. Enter the combination of tags you want to define in the Selector box. Type in the tag
   names without angle brackets. For example, to define attributes for the <blockquote>

tag only when it is nested within in another `<blockquote>` tag, enter **blockquote blockquote**.

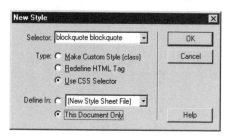

4. Select the This Document Only radio button. This saves your style information in the internal style sheet in the current HTML document.

5. Click the OK button to open the Style Definition dialog box, where you can define the actual attributes for the style.

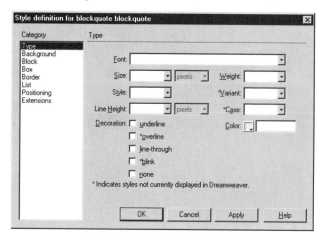

6. Click Type in the Category list and enter or select the text attributes you wish to apply to the nested tag.

7. Click OK to close the New Style dialog box and apply the style.

Create an External Style Sheet

The CSS style definition procedures covered elsewhere in this chapter describe how to create an internal style sheet that is saved in the current web document. But you can also save styles in an external style sheet. An external style sheet differs from an internal one only in that the code used to define the styles is saved as a separate text file instead of within the current document.

The advantage of saving style information in an external file provides one of the most powerful and compelling reasons to use style sheets—you can link to the external file from multiple pages within a site, rather than having to include the style information on each page in the site. This feature allows you to apply consistent styles to an entire site and update the entire site simply by making a few changes to the external style sheet. Many large web sites, such as Yahoo, CNN, and Microsoft, utilize external style sheets to provide consistent styling and formatting throughout their sites.

One of the easiest ways to create an external style sheet is to simply select the external style sheet option when you create a new style. Here's how:

1. Click the New Style button in the CSS Styles panel. This brings up the New Style dialog box.

2. Select the appropriate type of style—custom style, redefine HTML tag, or CSS selector—in the New Style dialog box.

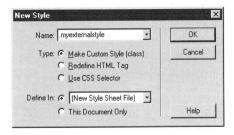

3. Instead of selecting the This Document Only radio button, click the other radio button in the Define In area, and choose New Style Sheet File in the list box. Then click OK to open the Save Style Sheet File As dialog box.

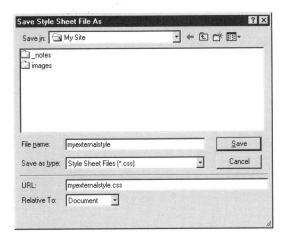

14

4. Locate the folder where you want to save your new style sheet file, and enter a name for your file. Dreamweaver automatically adds the extension .css to the end of the name when you enter it. Click Save to close the Save Style Sheet File As dialog box and open the Style Definition dialog box.

 A .css file is a text file containing all the style sheet information.

5. Set the attributes for your new style in the Style Definition dialog box. Click OK to close the dialog box and create the style.

 *You must save the external CSS style sheet in a location that is accessible via the Web if you expect visitors' web browsers to use it to display pages.*

Link to an External Style Sheet

Since an external style sheet is a separate file, you need to create a link between your web document and the external style sheet so that you can apply the formatting specified in the external .css file to the current document. When a browser accesses a web document that references an external style sheet, the browser retrieves the information from that style sheet in order to correctly render the page. The style sheet information can reside on the same server as the web document or anywhere else on the Web.

To link the current web document to an external style sheet, follow these steps:

1. In the CSS Styles panel, click the Attach Style Sheet button in the lower-right corner of the panel (refer to Figure 14-1). This opens the Select Style Sheet File dialog box.

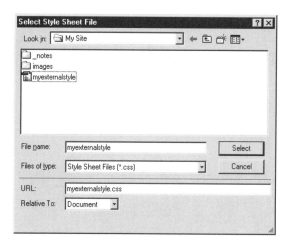

2. Locate an existing style sheet (.css), or enter an external URL if the style sheet resides somewhere on the internet.

3. Click Select to close the dialog box and finish attaching the style sheet.

NOTE   *If you've created an external style sheet and want to link to it using an external URL (for example, when the HTML page and style sheet reside on different servers), you need to make sure to upload your .css file to the appropriate server so that it can be accessed by the public through the external URL.*

Export an External Style Sheet from Existing Internal Styles

If you've created CSS styles in an internal style sheet in the current document, you can easily export those styles to an external style sheet. Here's how:

1. Choose File | Export | Export CSS styles (this option is grayed out if the current document does not contain any style sheet information). The Export Styles As CSS File dialog box appears.

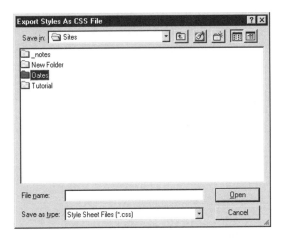

2. Enter a filename for the style sheet and locate a folder in which to save it. Click Save to exit the dialog box and save the style sheet.

3. Follow the instructions in the previous section for linking the current document to the external style sheet.

14

 *You can also export an external style sheet from internal styles by pressing the* CTRL *key (*COMMAND *key on the Mac) while clicking the Done button in the Edit Style Sheet dialog box.*

Edit an External Style Sheet

Editing an external style sheet is similar to editing an internal style sheet; the only difference is that you need to have access to the external style sheet in order to make the edits. You can edit only those style sheets that reside locally on your computer. To edit a style sheet on a remote site, you must first transfer the style sheet file to your computer, where you can make the edits; then you upload the revised style sheet back to the remote server. Once you edit an external style sheet, any changes you make will automatically be reflected in all pages that are linked to it. This is a great way to update an entire site: Simply edit a single style sheet that it is linked to. Here's the procedure for editing an external style sheet.

1. In the CSS Styles panel, click the Edit Style Sheet button in the lower-right corner of the panel (refer to Figure 14-1). This brings up the Edit Style Sheet dialog box.

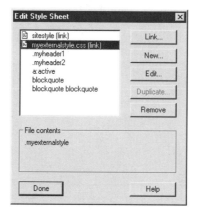

2. Select a style sheet from the list. Both local and remote external style sheets linked to the current page appear in the style sheet list. However, you can edit only local style sheets in Dreamweaver. When you select a style sheet, its contents appear in the File Contents area. Click Edit to continue editing the selected style sheet. A new window appears listing each defined style in the selected style sheet.

3. Select the individual style to edit, and click the Edit button to open the Style Definition dialog box. This dialog box allows you to edit any of the attributes of the style. After making any changes to the attributes, click OK to exit the dialog box. Dreamweaver returns you to the window that lists the styles available within the currently selected style sheet.

4. Repeat step 3 as needed to edit other styles. Click Save to close the dialog box and return to the Edit Style Sheet dialog box. Click Done to close this dialog box and complete the editing process.

Convert CSS Styles to HTML Tags

CSS styles are powerful formatting tools, but your site visitors must use an up-to-date browser to properly view web pages that include CSS styles. So, Dreamweaver gives you the option to create a copy of your web page with the same formatting but without relying on CSS. You can use this option to convert your CSS styles to HTML tags compatible with a wider range of browsers. This process attempts to convert all the CSS style attributes into existing HTML tags. Naturally, not all CSS style attributes will convert, because HTML has much more limited type display capabilities. Still, if you need to make a 3.0 browser–compatible version of your page, the convert command makes this possible without having to redo all the page formatting. Note that any CSS styles that do not have HTML equivalents are ignored when you use this command. To convert CSS styles to HTML, follow these steps:

1. Open an existing web file that contains CSS style sheet specifications.

2. Choose File | Convert | 3.0 Browser Compatible to open the Convert to 3.0 Browser Compatible dialog box

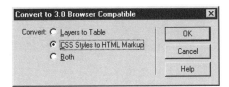

3. Select CSS Styles to HTML Markup. Click OK. Dreamweaver closes the dialog box and creates a copy of the current page with CSS styles converted to HTML markup. The converted document appears in a new Untitled Document window.

14

Chapter 15 Work with Layers

How to...

- Create layers
- Use layers for precise page layout
- Manage multiple layers
- Convert layers to tables
- Use the timeline to create animated layers

Chapter 14 covers using Cascading Style Sheets to control text formatting on a web page. But CSS can do more than format text. A newer implementation of the CSS specification offers the same level of control for additional page elements, including images, tables, forms, media objects, and almost anything else you can include on a web page. This new specification is called *CSS-P,* or *Cascading Style Sheets-Positioning.* CSS-P is the foundation of a web design feature more commonly known as *layers,* which allows pixel-level control of almost any element on a page.

Like CSS, CSS-P has had some difficulty gaining wide usage (at least among the nongeek web design folks). Programming layers takes a pretty high degree of coding skill. Nonetheless, thanks to Dreamweaver's easy and intuitive layers implementation, all the benefits of layers are readily accessible to Dreamweaver users. Layers offer a whole new level of design and interactive capability never before possible with just HTML.

What Are Layers?

Although the raw code needed to create and manipulate layers is quite complicated, the basic concept behind layers is extremely simple. Think of a layer as a kind of container within a web page. This container can be sized much smaller than a web page and can contain pretty much anything a web page can contain—images, text, tables, media files, etc. The difference between a layer and the HTML page containing it is that you can move the layer around wherever you want on the page using precise pixel-accurate measurements. For example, you could create a layer, insert an image, and then position the layer exactly 100 pixels from the top of the page and 100 pixels from the left of the page. Web designers have been clamoring for this capability since day one. Layers provide the exact kind of page layout control that has been sorely missing from HTML since its inception.

In addition to providing exact positioning capabilities, layers also enable you to overlap items, animate them, and control their appearance and behavior using scripting languages such as JavaScript and Dynamic HTML (DHTML). You can use layers together with DHTML (known as behaviors in Dreamweaver) to add many advanced special effects and interactive capabilities to your web pages that might otherwise require external plug-ins or media applications.

Manage Layers with the Layers Panel

The Layers panel, shown in Figure 15-1, is the main access point for creating, editing, and managing layers in Dreamweaver. To bring the Layers panel into view, simply choose Window | Layers, or press the F2 key.

Did you know?

Compatibility Problems with Layers

Like all great new features on the Web, there's always at least one drawback. The biggest problem with layers is that they don't work with browsers earlier than version 4.0. Pre-4.0 browsers simply don't understand layers and so ignore them.

When you think about it though, having something not show up on a page is not as bad as having something totally wreck your page. Anything in a layer just disappears on a 3.0 version browser.

However, there are ways to work around this. One solution is to create alternate versions of your site. Dreamweaver even includes a special command that enables you to convert layers to tables. Think about who your audience is and what kind of browsers you need to support when you plan on using layers.

Another compatibility problem with layers involves a different layer specification introduced by Netscape when it first released version 4 of Navigator. Most layer examples you see on the Web today use the original layer specification proposed by the W3C, which is based on the `<div>` and `<span>` tags. Early on, Netscape introduced a system of creating layers that relied on different tags: `<layer>` and `<ilayer>`. The Netscape tags offer similar functionality, but other browsers such as Internet Explorer don't support them.

When layers first appeared, nobody knew which standard would gain the widest acceptance. Over time, the original W3C spec has gained wide usage, while the Netscape spec has slipped into oblivion. While Dreamweaver still allows you to create layers using the Netscape tags, even Netscape itself has abandoned them in the latest version of their browser, Netscape 6.

The Layers Panel

The Layers panel has several elements that facilitate creating and working with layers.

The Layers panel lists all the existing layers in the document and enables you to control their appearance and behavior. You can include as many layers as you want in your document; the Layers panel provides the interface for managing them. The Property Inspector panel displays various layer properties whenever a layer is selected and enables you to modify them by changing the values and the settings.

Set Layer Preferences

Layer preferences define the default characteristics of any layers you create in Dreamweaver. You can keep the default layer settings that Dreamweaver uses, or you can set your own using the Layers category in the Preferences dialog box. Either way you can still change all the characteristics after you create a layer. See Chapter 20 for information on changing preference settings.

15

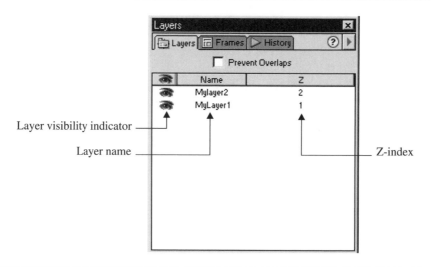

Layer visibility indicator

Layer name

Z-index

The Layers panel

Create Layers

Dreamweaver provides a fabulously simple interface for accessing the power of layers. It may be difficult to appreciate this if you've never coded layers by hand, but this feature is good. After you create your first layers, take a look at the HTML source code to see what I mean.

Using Dreamweaver's visual tools, you can create and position layers precisely by simply dragging them around on the page or by entering exact measurements into the Property Inspector panel. Dreamweaver even includes rulers and a grid to further facilitate layout (see Chapter 1 for information on the rulers and grid).

Insert a Layer

There are two ways to insert a layer into a page in Dreamweaver. This first involves manually drawing a layer using the draw layer tool. The second involves using the Insert Layer command. If you've ever worked with page design programs such as QuarkXPress or PageMaker, you're probably familiar with the concept of creating a text box on a page and later filling it with content.

To manually draw a layer:

1. Click the Draw Layer button in the Objects panel. Your pointer becomes a crosshair cursor.

2. Click anywhere in the document and drag the cursor diagonally to create a rectangular shape approximating the size and positioning of your desired layer. When you release the mouse button, Dreamweaver creates the layer.

To insert a layer into your web document using the Insert Layer command:

1. Choose Insert | Layer. Dreamweaver automatically places a new empty layer in the upper left corner of the document, as shown in Figure 15-2. The layer's default size is 200 pixels wide by 115 pixels high unless you change the setting in the preferences (see Chapter 20 for information on changing layer preferences).

2. Move or resize the newly created layer as needed.

> **CAUTION**   *After you insert a layer, a blinking cursor appears inside the new layer to indicate that you can insert content. If you immediately insert another layer using the Insert | Layer command, the second layer will become nested within the first. To create a nonnested layer, either click the cursor outside the first layer before inserting the second, or use the Draw Layer button to draw a new layer. (See the section on creating nested layers later in this chapter for more information about nested layers.)*

When you insert a new layer with Dreamweaver, two new objects appear on the screen. In the upper left-hand corner of the page you'll notice the layer icon, a small yellow square with the letter C inside. This is an invisible element that anchors the layer onto the page. Like other invisible elements, you can cut, copy, paste, and reposition the element anywhere else on the page, but the layer itself does not move when the icon moves. Moving the icon simply moves

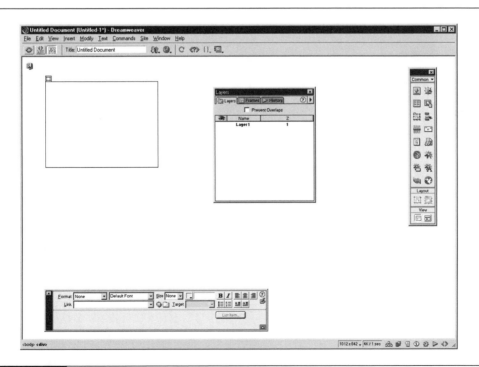

15

FIGURE 15-2   Inserting a layer

the source code for the layer to another location in the HTML without affecting the functionality of the layer (though generally it's a good idea to keep layer icons together in one location on the page). Deleting the icon deletes the layer and all its associated code from the page.

The second object that appears when you insert a layer is the layer bounding box. This box indicates the size and the position of the layer, and you can use it to move and resize the layer.

Move and Resize Layers

After you create a layer, you can move it by clicking and dragging the selection handle, which appears any time you click inside the layer. To select the layer for resizing and other manipulations, click the selection handle or the layer border to make the sizing handles appear. You can resize the layer by clicking and dragging any of the resizing handles (see Figure 15-3).

You can also move or resize layers by selecting the layer and typing new coordinates into the Property Inspector panel. When you select a layer on the page, the Property Inspector panel displays its size and location on the page in the corresponding Property Inspector fields. (See the following "Set Layer Properties" section for an illustration of the panel and descriptions of the layer properties.)

The L field in the Property Inspector panel represents the number of pixels the layer is positioned from the left edge of the page; the T field represents the number of pixels from the top edge of the page. You can type in new values in either of these fields to move the layer to

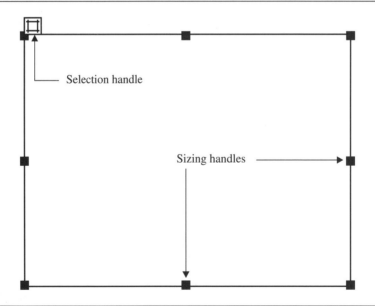

FIGURE 15-3   Selecting a layer

a new coordinate. Likewise, the size of the layer is represented by the W (width) and H (height) fields; you can enter new values into either of these fields to resize the layer.

Icons representing invisible elements in Dreamweaver can push layers out of position in Design view. Always preview your page in a browser to judge its true position and size.

It's possible to enter negative values into the L and T fields in the Property Inspector panel to position the layer off the page. This can be useful for creating layers that will move into view from somewhere offscreen after the page has loaded. Later on in this chapter you'll learn how to animate layers to achieve this effect.

Insert Content into Layers

Layers are basically containers—containers that can hold almost any kind of content including text, images, tables, forms, media objects, and even other layers. By placing your content into a layer you can control its exact placement on the page when you reposition the layer. Another great advantage to working with layers is that you can overlap them on a page. Thus, even though you can't place an image on top of another image using ordinary HTML, you can place images into separate layers and position one layer on top of the other to achieve the same effect.

Inserting content into a layer is exactly like inserting content into a regular web document. You can drag and drop, use the Insert command, type text with the keyboard, or click object buttons in the Objects panel to insert them into a layer. However, before you insert anything into a layer, make sure that the layer is selected and that the cursor is blinking inside it.

To insert items into a layer you can:

- Insert text by simply typing with the keyboard or copying and pasting.
- Insert images and other media by dragging and dropping them into the layer or by clicking any of the insert object buttons in the Objects panel.

Set Layer Properties

Layers have many different customizable properties that you can access through the Property Inspector panel. The following table lists the layer properties available in the Property Inspector panel along with a description of each.

15

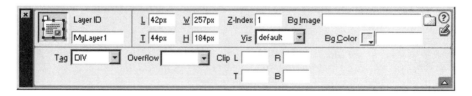

Property	Description
Layer ID	A required field used to uniquely identify a layer as a document object and for use with scripting. Dreamweaver names layers incrementally beginning with Layer1, Layer2, and so on. You can replace the name with your own descriptive name to help you manage multiple layers.
L (Left)	Specifies the distance of the layer as measured from the left edge of the page.
T (Top)	Specifies the distance of the layer as measured from the top edge of the page.
W	Specifies the layer's width.
H	Specifies the layer's height.
Z-Index	Specifies the stacking order of the layer in relation to other layers. Layers with higher numbers will appear in front of layers with lower numbers.
Vis (Visibility)	Specifies whether the layer is visible or not. The inherit option takes on the visibility of the parent layer when a layer is nested.
BgImage	Specifies the background image for the layer.
BgColor	Specifies the background color for the layer.
Tag	Specifies the HTML tag used to define the layer. Unless you have reasons not to, use the default <div> tag.
Overflow	Specifies how the contents of a layer should be displayed when they are larger than the dimensions of the layer. The scroll option adds horizontal and vertical scroll bars enabling the user to scroll the hidden content. The auto option adds scroll bars only if needed.
Clip	Specifies the region of a layer (left, top, right, bottom) that you want cropped from view by entering numerical values as measured from each edge of the layer. If no values are specified, the layer displays in its entirety. Clipping is a useful feature for creating interactive and animated effects that change over time.

Create Nested Layers

Nesting layers is a technique in which you insert new layers inside of existing layers, sometimes several levels deep. These kinds of layers are often described as having a parent-child relationship because the outer layer is like a parent and the inner layer is like a child (see Figure 15-4). One of the main benefits of nesting layers is that child layers usually move in unison with the parent as you move the parent layer around the page. Using nested layers, you can move complicated multilayer structures around as a unit, just by moving the parent layer.

 *Nested layers use the upper-left corner of the parent layer as their origin point for ruler measurements instead of the upper-left corner of the document.*

To nest a new layer into an existing layer:

1. Place the cursor inside the existing layer so that you see a blinking cursor in the upper left-hand corner of the layer.

2. Choose Insert | Layer to create a new child layer inside the parent layer. After creating the child layer you can reposition it by clicking and dragging the selection handle to move it anywhere else on the page.

To nest an existing layer into another existing layer:

1. Make the Layers panel visible by choosing Window | Layers or pressing the F2 key.

2. Press and hold the CTRL key as you click the name of the layer in the Layers panel that you want to make the child and drag it over the name of the parent layer. As you move the pointer over the parent layer's name, a selection rectangle appears around it. Drop the child layer onto the parent layer. Note that the Layers panel now shows the name of the child layer indented beneath the parent layer (see Figure 15-4).

NOTE   *Child layers don't have to be located inside their parent layer; they can be located anywhere on the page but nonetheless will always use the upper-left corner of their parent layer as their origin point instead of the upper-left corner of the document.*

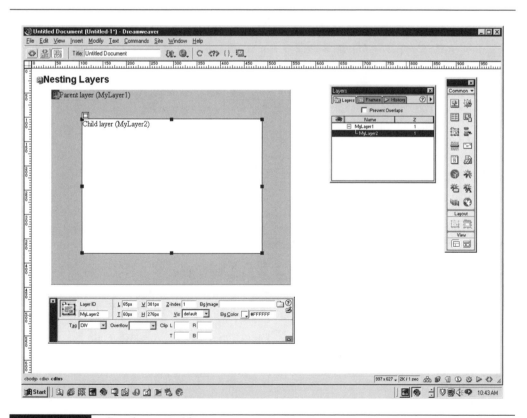

FIGURE 15-4   Creating nested layers

15

Work with Layers

In order to work with layers you need to be able to modify and manipulate them in numerous ways. Many of the layer features and functionality are accessed through various interface tools unique to Dreamweaver such as the Layers panel and the Timelines panel.

Select Layers

To manipulate and modify layers you need to be able to select them. You can tell when a layer is selected because the selection and sizing handles appear around it, and the Property Inspector panel displays the layer properties for the selected layer. Basically, there are two ways to select layers in Dreamweaver:

- Click anywhere on the layer in the Document window and then click the selection handle or layer border so that the sizing handles are displayed. To select multiple layers, hold down the SHIFT key as you click other layers.

- Click the layer name in the Layers panel to highlight it. To select multiple layers, SHIFT+click on other layer names.

 *Using the Layers panel to select layers is usually easier and more efficient when several layers are stacked on top of one another in the document. Otherwise, it can be difficult to manually click on the layer in the Document window.*

 *When you are selecting layers containing images or other content, it's easy to accidentally select the content inside the layer instead of the layer around it. If the layer selection handle and resizing handles are visible after you click the layer, the layer itself is selected; if they are not visible, you may have selected only the layer's contents.*

Change Layer Visibility

Layers include a visibility attribute that enables you to make them either visible or invisible on the page. There are at least two reasons for making a layer invisible. The first is to allow special interactive effects such as turning a layer on or off when the user interacts with it. The second reason is to facilitate design and layout; sometimes you need to hide a layer temporarily to make it easier to work with other layers on the page.

You control layer visibility through the Layers panel (see Figure 15-5). The first column in the Layers panel shows an eye icon. An open eye icon indicates that the layer is visible. To make the layer invisible click the eye icon next to a layer so that the eye appears closed. When the eye is closed, the associated layer is invisible.

If you click the eye icon one more time, you'll notice that it disappears. When no eye icon is visible it means that the layer inherits the visibility status of its parent layer. In the event that the layer is not a child layer, this means that the layer is visible since the parent is the document itself, which is always visible. By clicking the eye icon at the top of the column, you can control the visibility for all the layers in the document.

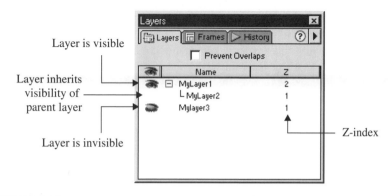

Layer is visible

Layer inherits visibility of parent layer

Layer is invisible

Z-index

FIGURE 15-5   Icons are used to control the visibility of layers.

Change Layer Stacking Order

One of the greatest benefits of using layers is the ability to overlap content on a page. Dreamweaver uses a stacking order to determine whether a given layer is in front of or behind other layers. This stacking order is also referred to as the Z-index (shown in Figure 15-5). The Z-index simply uses a numerical value to determine the position of a layer along the Z-axis, which runs from the front of the page to the back. Layers with a lower-numbered Z-index are stacked closer to the back, while layers with a higher Z-index are stacked closer to the front. If a layer with a Z-index of 2 is placed in the same page position as a layer with a Z-index of 1, the layer with Z-index 2 obscures the other layer (assuming its contents are not transparent). If you assign two layers the same Z-index, they stack in the order in which they were created. As you begin working with layers you will find that controlling their stacking order is an important function.

The Z-index is displayed for each layer in two different locations: the Z-index field in the Property Inspector panel and the Z-index column in the Layers panel. You can change the Z-index value in one of three ways:

■ Enter a new value in the Z-index field in the Property Inspector panel.

■ Enter a new value in the Z-index column in the Layers panel.

■ Click and drag a layer's name in the Layers panel into a new position relative to the other layers. Layers listed at the top of the panel have the highest index, and layers at the bottom of the panel have the lowest. When you move a layer into a new position by dragging its name in the Layers panel, Dreamweaver automatically gives it a new Z-index to correspond with its new position in the Layers panel.

15

Use Layers for Page Layout

Layers are one of the greatest page layout innovations to have made their way into web designers' toolkits. Using layers, designers can exactly mimic any design created in traditional design programs that existed long before the Web. Unfortunately, a significant drawback to using layers is that there are still browsers out there on the Net that can't view layer content—any browser earlier than version 4 of Netscape or Internet Explorer. The number of potential visitors out there still surfing with pre-4.0 browsers is steadily diminishing, but they still exist in significant numbers. Fortunately, there's a way to design pages using layers and then convert the layers tables for compatibility with pre-4.0 browsers.

Convert Layers to Tables

Dreamweaver includes a handy Convert Layers to Tables feature that enables you to take a layout created with layers and automatically convert all the layers in the document to tables. A page created with this feature will look similar to the layers version but will still be viewable in pre-4.0 browsers.

To convert a page that has been designed using layers to a page that uses tables instead, choose Modify | Convert | Layers to Tables. This opens the Convert Layers to Table dialog box, which presents you with several options for outputting your tables (see Figure 15-6).

 *Since the Convert Layers to Tables command modifies and replaces the existing document, apply the command to a copy of your layers page if you want to preserve a version of the page that uses layers as well.*

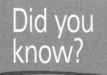

The Difference Between Layers and Tables, and When to Use Each

Layers permit precise, pixel-level page layout using CSS-P, a recent implementation of Cascading Style sheets that works only in version 4.0 and later browsers. Tables, in contrast, use cells laid out in rows and columns. Tables use empty cells to separate elements on a page in order to approximate the desired positioning. But it's still not the same kind of precise layout that you can achieve with layers. The benefit of using tables, however, is that they display in the majority of browsers—probably close to 100% of web browsers. If you need to cater to an audience that is likely to be using older browsers, you might want to at least have a nonlayers version of your web site available as an alternative to the layers version.

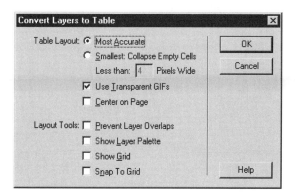

Options for converting layers to tables

Options available when converting tables to layers:

■ **Table Layout**   These options affect the construction of the new table.

■ **Most Accurate**   Select this option to most closely mimic the layout of the layers-based page. This option creates the most complex table and is the default setting. Use this option when you want to match the layers-based layout as closely as possible, regardless of the complexity of the resulting table.

■ **Smallest**   This option simplifies the table structure by joining adjacent empty cells that are smaller than the number specified into single cells. The higher the number you enter, the simpler the table structure (fewer cells) but, conversely, the less accurate the layout compared to the layers version. Use this option when you want to avoid creating an overly complex table and you're willing to sacrifice a degree of accuracy in matching the layers-based layout.

■ **Use Transparent GIFs**   This option uses transparent GIF images to fill the empty cells in the layout as spacer cells. This guarantees a greater degree of uniformity across browsers. The default setting is to use transparent GIFs.

■ **Center on Page**   Select this option to center the table in the browser window instead of the usual position at the upper-left corner.

■ **Layout Tools**   These options affect the attributes of the document after the conversion to tables takes place. Any of these options can still be turned on or off after the layers have been converted.

■ **Prevent Layer Overlaps**   Select to enable this option for the document (refer to next section for more information about overlapping layers).

15

- ■ **Show Layer Palette**   Select to keep the Layers panel in view.
- ■ **Show Grid**   Select to turn the grid on.
- ■ **Snap to Grid**   Select to enable this option for the document.

Prevent Layers from Overlapping

Whenever you use the Convert Layers to Tables command, you'll want to make sure that you haven't used any overlapping layers in your document. Because tables do not support overlapping content, if you attempt to convert a document with overlapping layers to tables, Dreamweaver will give you a warning message and prevent you from doing so. Since it's easy to get carried away with layers and overlook this situation, Dreamweaver includes a special option to prevent you from creating any overlapping layers in the first place. Dreamweaver does this by not allowing you to place one layer on top of another in the same way that snap-to-grid forces layers to snap-to-grid intersection points. To enable this option, choose Modify | Arrange | Prevent Layer Overlaps. When this option is enabled, you will not be able to create overlapping layers in your document. Note, however, that any existing overlapping layers created before this option was enabled still need to be moved before you use the Convert Layers to Tables command.

Animate Layers

Using layers to achieve accurate page design is a compelling enough reason to use layers. But there's another great reason to use layers: the ability to animate layers.

Layers are actually page objects that can be manipulated and moved around the page interactively, even after the page has already been loaded into the browser. This is made possible via an extension to HTML called *Dynamic HTML*, or *DHTML*. DHTML, another web technology introduced by the W3C organization, displays only in 4.0 and later browsers. DHTML works in conjunction with JavaScript—a scripting language—to enable designers and programmers to create dynamic, interactive content on web pages. Normally programming in DHTML and JavaScript requires a high degree of scripting knowledge and experience. However, once again, Dreamweaver enables mortal web designers to access much of the power of DHTML and layers using easy-to-understand visual tools.

Use the Timelines Panel

The heart of Dreamweaver's layer animation capabilities is based on a timeline metaphor. If you've ever used a program like Flash or Director, you may be familiar with how a timeline works. It's basically a way to control frame-by-frame animation over time. Traditional cartoon animators use a similar process to create frame-by-frame animations with drawings. New frames appear several times per second, each with a slightly different drawing. Over time, the illusion of motion is created. The Dreamweaver timeline allows you to move layers, frame by frame over time, thus creating the same illusion.

To access the timeline, open the Timelines panel by choosing Window | Timelines (see Figure 15-7).

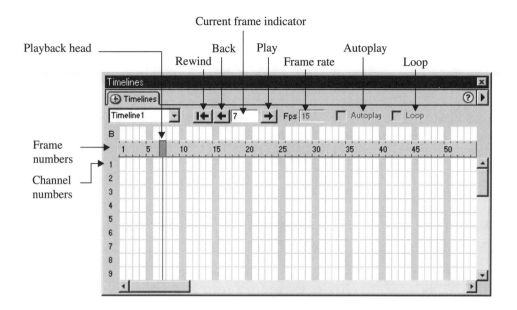

Playback head

Current frame indicator

Rewind   Back   Play   Frame rate   Autoplay   Loop

Frame numbers

Channel numbers

FIGURE 15-7   The Timelines panel

Create a Timeline Animation

Timeline animations allow you to change the size, position, visibility, and stacking order of layers over a specified period of time. You can also change the source file of images in a layer or add behaviors to create rollovers and other interactive effects.

1. Choose Window | Timelines to make the Timelines panel visible.

2. Select a layer on the page to animate. You may want to insert text, images, or other content into the layer first.

3. Choose Modify | Timeline | Add Object to Timeline, or simply click and drag the layer from the page onto the first cell of the Timelines panel. When you release the mouse button, you'll notice that a bar appears in the first channel of the timeline. The bar displays the name of the layer you just added (see Figure 15-8).

4. Click the small circle in the last frame occupied by the bar. This circle represents a keyframe. Keyframes represent starting, ending, or intermediary points in an animation.

15

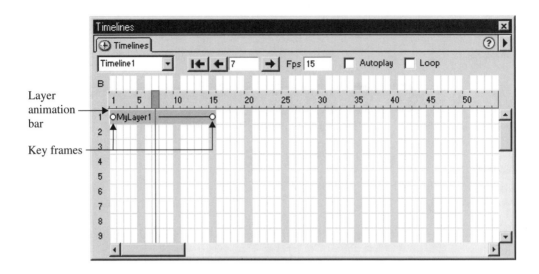

Layer animation bar

Key frames

FIGURE 15-8 Inserting a layer into a timeline

5. In Dreamweaver's Document window, drag the layer somewhere else on the page. After you move the layer, a line appears representing the motion path of the layer between frame 1 and the ending keyframe of the animation (see Figure 15-9).

6. Click and hold the play button to see the layer move across the page.

7. Repeat steps 1–6 if you want to add additional layers to the timeline. When you add additional layers, each new layer occupies a different channel in the timeline, identified by its layer name. Channels are displayed as the horizontal numbered rows across the Timelines panel.

NOTE

You can also add images to a timeline by dragging them from the Document window into the Timelines panel. Though you can't animate images on a page unless they are placed in a layer first, you can add behaviors to them to create rollovers and other interactive effects (see Chapter 16).

Modify a Motion Path

You're not limited to just straight motion paths between animation keyframes. To create more interesting animated movements, you can customize the motion path of your layer either by adding new keyframes or by having Dreamweaver automatically record the onscreen path of the layer as you move it around the page.

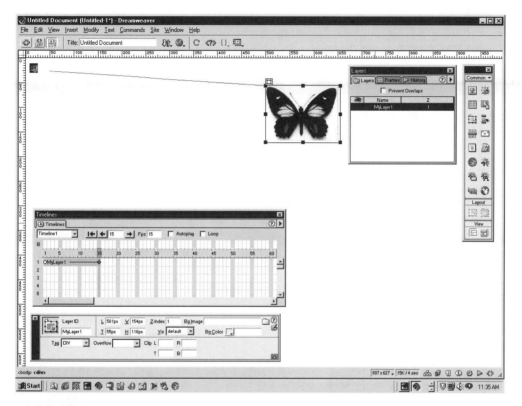

FIGURE 15-9   Moving the layer at the last keyframe in the animation to create a motion path

Define a Path by Adding a Keyframe

The previous example shows how to create a timeline animation with two keyframes and a straight path. This example shows how to modify such a path by adding additional keyframes.

1. Click anywhere near the middle of the layer bar in the Timelines panel to select a frame somewhere between the first and the last frames. When you select the frame, the playback head moves to the frame indicating that it is the current selected frame. The layer also changes its position in the Document window to reflect where it is at that point in the timeline.

TIP   *You can also* CTRL+click *the layer bar where you want to add a keyframe.*

2. Choose Modify | Timeline | Add Keyframe, or press the F6 key. This places a new keyframe into the timeline at the current frame.

15

3. Reposition the layer to alter its motion path (see Figure 15-10).

4. Repeat steps 1–3 as needed to further modify the path. You can continue to add keyframes and alter the motion path until the desired path is achieved.

Define a Path by Recording Mouse Movement

When you need to create a complicated motion path, it's sometimes easier to draw the path with your mouse pointer and let Dreamweaver record the motion automatically. This works really well when it's too difficult or involved to create the path by inserting new keyframes and moving

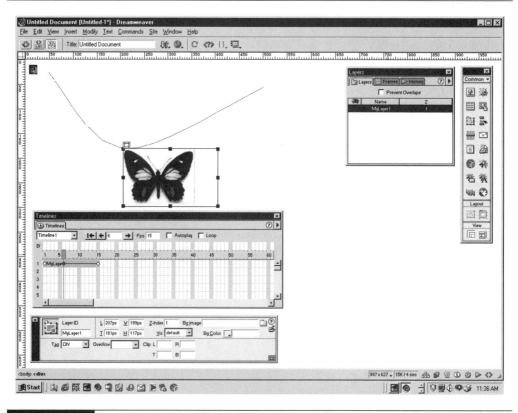

FIGURE 15-10   Modify the animation page by creating a new keyframe and repositioning the layer.

layers around. An example might be an animated image of a butterfly circling the page for a few times before landing.

1. Select the layer in the Document window whose path you want to record and drag it to its starting position on the page.

2. Choose Modify | Record Path of Layer. This opens up the Timelines panel if it is not already visible.

3. Click the layer again and drag it around on the page to define the movement path (see Figure 15-11). As you draw, Dreamweaver creates keyframes to capture the movement. The more slowly you move the mouse, the closer the keyframes are spaced together. The faster you move the mouse the farther apart they are spaced.

4. Release the mouse button to stop the recording and complete the motion path.

5. Press and hold the Play button in the Timelines panel to preview the animation effect.

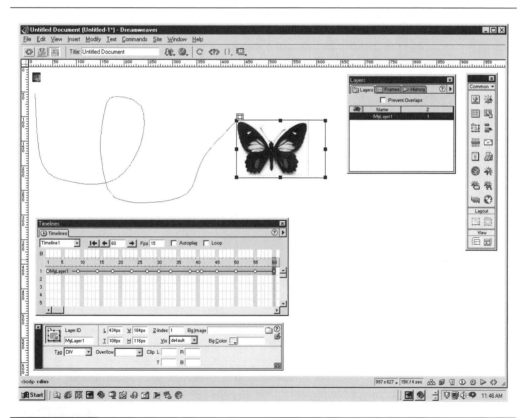

FIGURE 15-11   Use the Record Path of Layer command to manually create a motion path using your mouse.

Refine the Timeline

The timeline uses total number of frames, total number of keyframes, and the positioning of the layer in each keyframe to define the way the animation appears over time. You can make further refinements to the animation by modifying any of these components.

Change the Animation Speed

Frame-based animation works by tricking the eye with a rapid succession of changing images. To achieve a smooth animation, a certain number of frames per second must be displayed (frame rate). In Dreamweaver you can modify the frame rate to control how smoothly the animation appears. To do this, enter a different frame rate value in the timeline's Fps (frames per second) field, found just to the right of the Play button in the Timelines panel. In motion picture animation, the smoothest playback usually occurs at around 24–30 frames per second. Unfortunately, web-based layer animation frame rates depend on the speed of the computer running the browser. While fast computers may be able to display 30 frames in 1 second, slower computers just can't keep up. As a result, it's better not to go too much higher than the default frame rate of 15 frames per second, which is usually fast enough to produce smooth animation without degrading too significantly on slower computers. In fact, you might get by with 8–12 frames per second, which approximates the speed of animated cartoons.

Another way to alter the speed of an animation is to increase or decrease the number of frames used. By clicking the last keyframe in an animation and dragging the bar out to the right on the timeline, you can increase the number of frames used. The number of frames displayed each second remains constant, so the more frames it takes to move the layer from the first keyframe to the last, the slower the animation. Moving the last keyframe to the left has the opposite effect of speeding up the animation by reducing the number of frames.

Modify the Position of Layers in the Time Sequence

Keyframes define the position of a layer at a given point in the timeline sequence. To change the position of a layer, simply select a keyframe and reposition the layer in the Document window. Whenever you reposition a layer in a keyframe, Dreamweaver looks at the position of the layer in that keyframe and the one preceding it to automatically calculate the layer positions for intermediate frames. For example, to move the beginning position of the layer in an animation, change its position in the first keyframe. To move to the ending position, change the position in the last keyframe. Move the position in any middle keyframes to change the middle positions.

Use Multiple Timelines

For creating more complicated layer animations you can use additional timelines. However, only one timeline can be displayed in the Timelines panel at any one time. To add a new timeline, choose Modify | Timeline | Add Timeline. A new blank timeline appears that Dreamweaver automatically names Timeline2. You can continue to add timelines in this manner and modify each one to create multiple timeline animations. Use the pop-up window to select which timeline to view in the Timelines panel (see Figure 15-12). To delete a timeline, select it using the pop-up window and choose Modify | Timeline | Remove Timeline. You can rename timelines by either typing in a new name in the name field or choosing Modify | Timeline | Rename Timeline.

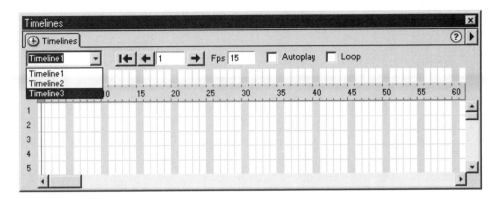

FIGURE 15-12   You can create multiple timelines in the Timelines panel.

Apply a Timeline

When you create a timeline and preview it in a browser, nothing will happen unless you instruct the timeline to begin playing after the page loads—it won't play on its own. The normal way to tell a timeline to begin playing is to select the Autoplay option by clicking the Autoplay field in the Timelines panel. Autoplay instructs the browser to begin playing the animation as soon as the page has loaded. With Autoplay selected, the animation plays once and stops at the last frame in the animation every time the page is loaded. If you want the animation to continue playing over and over, select the Loop option.

TIP   *To make looping animations appear continuous, make the position of the layer in the last frame of the animation very close to the position in the first frame so that it appears as if there is no disruption and it is all one continuous movie.*

Another way to control when a timeline begins playing is to call (start playback of) the timeline using a behavior. When you use a behavior to control when a timeline plays, do not check the Autoplay option. Using behaviors is covered in Chapter 16.

15

Chapter 16

Work with Rollovers and Other Interactive Elements

How to…

- ■ Understand the technology and process behind Behaviors
- ■ Add interactive elements to your page
- ■ Plan for browser compatibility
- ■ Create interactive buttons, navigational elements, and menus

Behaviors are one of the many ways that Dreamweaver helps implement real interactivity in a web site. Behaviors enable you to take your site from the realm of "digital magazine" to full-blown multimedia showcase. Behaviors unlock the power of JavaScript and add visual effects, navigational tools, and rich media control to your web site.

Understand and Work with Behaviors

For many people, technical computer terms are confusing, especially when they involve programming or scripting in a computer language. It can be both intimidating and frustrating for beginners to "cross the line" between simply using computers and writing instructions for computers. The good news is that Dreamweaver makes it relatively easy for designers, writers, and editors (read: nonprogrammers) to make a transition to the technical side of web development in a user-friendly, visual environment.

You're probably aware that Dreamweaver automates the process of creating web documents; you don't have to spend hours hand-coding the HTML tags that tell a browser how to interpret your design. What you may not know is that Dreamweaver can also produce scripts that respond to the way users interact with your web site. These scripts are called *Behaviors,* and you access them through the Behaviors panel.

Behaviors allow you to enhance the interactivity of your web site by offering visual feedback for buttons and navigational elements. You can also use Behaviors to build menus, alter the appearance of web pages, control media objects, and so on. Dreamweaver allows you to expand the interactive possibilities of a site while keeping the technical aspects to a bare minimum. However, you do need to understand the anatomy of Behaviors before you can use them both creatively and effectively.

What Are Behaviors?

Behaviors is an appropriate and self-explanatory name. In the most basic sense, Behaviors tell elements of a web page how to "act" or "behave." Think of Behaviors as a set of instructions that you can apply to text, graphics, buttons, links, timelines, and other web page elements. After you select an object on your page (let's say a button graphic), you use menus in the Behaviors panel to define the way this button acts when a site visitor clicks on or points to it. Meanwhile, Dreamweaver automatically inserts these instructions into your web document.

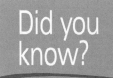

JavaScript Is Everywhere

JavaScript is a key component of the World Wide Web today. This language, developed by Netscape, can add interactive functionality to HTML-based web pages. *Java*, the programming language, and *JavaScript* are not the same thing, although they do have some similarities. For resources and detailed documentation on JavaScript, visit Netscape DevEdge Online at: **http://developer.netscape.com/**.

Behavior "instructions" are added to your document as lines of JavaScript code. As does HTML, JavaScript talks to the web browser and tells it how to display a web page. As you probably guessed, Dreamweaver handles all the JavaScripting automatically. So, if you are daunted by hand-coding but impressed by the functionality JavaScript can provide, Behaviors are definitely for you.

Now that you know what Behaviors are, let's talk about what they can do. If you are new to web development, you may not be aware of the flexibility and sophistication that JavaScript can add to your site. This powerful language has an enormous variety of applications, many of which go beyond the scope of this book. However, Dreamweaver Behaviors serve as an excellent introduction to JavaScript; they expand the interactivity and user-friendliness of a web site. You can use Behaviors to do the following:

- Create rollover button effects
- Create navigational elements
- Open a new browser window
- Toggle images on and off
- Play a sound
- Control animations
- Manage frames and hyperlinks

This list is not exhaustive by any means. Dreamweaver ships with a large assortment of Behaviors, and you can add more (see Appendix B).

16

Fancy Effects Aren't Always Good

Behaviors, and the effects they offer, are some of the "bells and whistles" of web development. While they can add a level of sophistication and "wow" to your site, they do not ensure that your message will get through to your audience. As the web designer you have responsibility to communicate the message and information offered by your site as clearly as possible. Just because you *can* add fancy effects with Behaviors doesn't mean you *should* add them. Before using a Behavior, ask yourself if the Behavior reinforces your message or distracts from it.

Let's take, for example, a button. On a web page, buttons allow users to make choices. From a design standpoint, buttons can be visually appealing, and they offer a clear means of accessing information. Buttons are a metaphor from our physical world; we use buttons every day to summon an elevator or make a telephone call. Buttons are interactive. We push them and something happens; this is why the concept of a button translates so well into the realm of digital media. What does not translate, however, is the sensory experience of pressing the button. In the real world, a combination of sound, light, and/or resistance offers feedback and tells you that the button has performed its duty. Behaviors provide this feedback in the digital world. Behaviors allow buttons to:

- Change appearance when the mouse is positioned over the button
- Change appearance when it is being "pressed"
- Play a sound to acknowledge the mouse click

Understanding Events and Actions

A Behavior is nothing more than a sequence that causes an element of your web site to change in response to the requests of a user. This sequence has two major components: an *event* and an *action*. An event is the catalyst, the trigger that sets a sequence into motion. Clicking or pointing the mouse, key presses, and loading an HTML document into memory are events. An action is a response to the event, and it is handled by JavaScript.

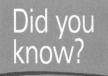

Events Must Be Initiated

In the case of a button, the browser sends a message that says, "The mouse has just pointed to an element of this web page; is there anything that is supposed to happen?" The Behavior responds to this request by saying, "Yes, you need to perform an action defined by JavaScript. Please replace the previous graphic file the mouse crossed over with a new one named *buttonOver.gif.*"

Clearly there is no polite, conversational exchange that takes place within your computer. But in a basic sense, a Behavior manages this communication.

Behaviors monitor events and provide appropriate responses. For a visual representation, see Figure 16-1.

In the button example, a behavior is attached to a graphic to create the illusion that the button changes appearance when the mouse rolls over it. In reality, the original button graphic is switched and replaced with a slightly different image.

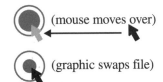 *It is common practice for designers to use multiple images for a single button—one for each state or condition of the button. For example, a button could have three states: a normal, or up, state; an over, or standby, state; and a down, or active, state.*

Additional changes can be created. By attaching another Behavior to the button you can once again create the illusion that the button changes appearance. This additional Behavior waits for a browser message saying that the user has clicked on the image. When the Behavior receives that message, it switches another image into place that represents the button in a depressed state (Figure 16-2).

(mouse moves over)

(graphic swaps file)

FIGURE 16-1   An event followed by an action: The mouse rolls over a button to trigger a "swap," or a change of graphic, that represents the button.

16

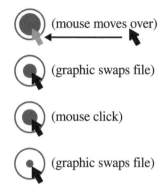

FIGURE 16-2   Behavior sequence: An event triggers an action, followed by a new event that triggers a new action.

The detailed description of events and actions of a simple button may seem tedious, but it provides a good example of the conceptual framework on which all Behaviors are based. After you grasp this idea you can create and apply a variety of other Behaviors on your own.

Use the Behaviors Panel

The first step in creating a Behavior is to access the Behaviors panel (Figure 16-3). If the Behaviors panel is not already available, choose Window | Behaviors, or press SHIFT+F3. (For further discussion on accessing and managing panels please refer to Chapter 1.) The Behaviors panel allows you to add and change Behaviors by attaching them to elements of your web page. Once a Behavior is attached to an element, Dreamweaver displays the element's HTML tag in the title bar of the Behaviors panel.

> **NOTE**   *Behaviors are not attached to an object in the manner of a graphic or a link. Rather, they are placed within the tag for the element, similar to an attribute.*

In addition, the Behaviors panel displays the event and action that make up the Behavior. If there is more than one set of events and actions, the Behaviors panel lists them from top to bottom either alphabetically or in the order in which they occur. If a tag has no Behavior attached to it then the Behaviors panel appears empty.

The Behaviors panel contains several buttons that allow you to edit the Behavior parameters. Most predominant is the Actions button, represented by a large plus (+) sign. This button opens a menu of JavaScript actions that are available to you in Dreamweaver. Although actions are really the second component in a Behavior sequence, you attach Behaviors by first defining the action. Adjacent to the Actions button is the Delete Actions button, represented by a minus (–) sign. Clicking this button removes any selected (highlighted) Behaviors in the panel.

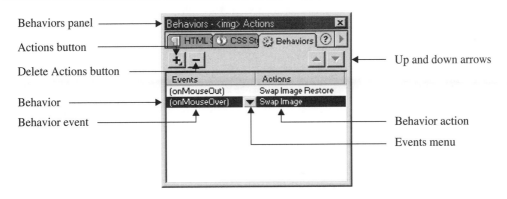

Behaviors panel

Actions button

Delete Actions button

Behavior

Behavior event

Up and down arrows

Behavior action

Events menu

FIGURE 16-3   The Behaviors panel: Note that the selected Behavior comprises an
onMouseOver event and a SwapImage action.

If a Behavior is selected in the panel, a small button appears beside it. This is the Events
menu. Click it to display a list of events that will set the adjacent action into motion.

TIP   *The Events menu displays some events in parentheses, such as (onClick). These
events are to be used for links only. For more details, see "Use Behaviors with Text
and Links" later in this chapter.*

The final two components of the Behaviors panel are the up and down arrows. These do not
apply to all Behaviors, but they are extremely useful for reordering the actions that make up
some Behavior sequences. To reorder a Behavior simply select it from the list and use the up or
down arrows to change its position in the list. For Behaviors where order is not important, the up
and down arrows are disabled.

Attach a Behavior

Using the Behaviors panel to attach Behaviors to objects on your web page is a simple process
involving a few quick clicks of the mouse. Before you begin, be sure that both the item that
requires a Behavior and the Behaviors panel are visible on your computer screen. Then follow
these steps:

1. Select the element of your web page where you wish to attach the Behavior. Both the
Tag Inspector and Behaviors panel (Figure 16-3) indicate the element's HTML tag.

NOTE   *If you want to attach a Behavior to a link, you can either select the entire link, or just
click anywhere within the link text.*

16

2. Click the Actions button in the Behaviors panel. The drop-down list of possible actions appears.

Some actions in the menu are dimmed. This simply means that they do not apply to the document you are currently editing. For example, the "Drag Layer" action will be unavailable if your document contains no layers.

3. Select the desired action from the menu. A dialog box appears where you can select the various options for the specified action. The contents of the dialog box vary depending on the action you select.

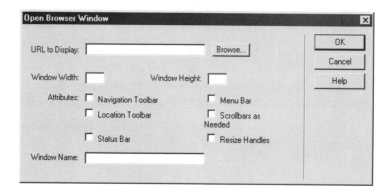

4. Define the action by entering and selecting options in the dialog box. Click OK to close the dialog box and return to the Behaviors panel. The Behaviors panel displays the action alongside the default event that triggers it.

5. Choose the event that sets the Behavior into motion. To do this, simply click on the Events menu in the Behaviors panel and select the desired event. Again, some of the menu choices may be dimmed either because the events are not applicable to the object to which you are attaching the Behavior or because the events are not recognized by some browsers (see the section on browser compatibility later in this chapter).

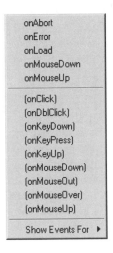

You can't preview Behaviors in Dreamweaver. To test your new Behavior you must preview the document in a web browser. Choose File | Preview In Browser, and choose a browser from the list. (For additional information on previewing Dreamweaver documents, see Chapter 1.) When the document appears in the browser window you can test your Behavior and see that it performs properly.

Once you attach a Behavior to an object on your web page it remains intact until you delete or modify the Behavior.

Modify a Behavior

After a Behavior is attached you may wish to edit its attributes. Within the Behavior panel you can make changes to actions and the events that trigger them. You can also add or delete Behavior events and actions.

1. Select the object that has an attached Behavior you would like to modify.

2. Open the Behaviors panel if it is not already available.

16

3. Do any of the following:

■ To edit action parameters, double-click on the action to display its dialog box. Make any necessary changes and click OK.

■ To change an event, select the event in the Behaviors panel. Click on the events menu and choose a new event from the list.

■ To remove a Behavior, select it and press the minus (–) button, or press the DELETE key.

■ To add to a Behavior, select a new action, assign its parameters, and choose an event to serve as the trigger. Behaviors appear on the list in alphabetical order by event name. In the case that a single event has two or more actions associated with it, use the up and down arrows to sort the list from top to bottom in the order you want the actions to occur.

Use Behaviors with Text and Links

We know that Behaviors consist of two parts: a trigger event and a JavaScript action; however, some portions of a web page cannot pass event messages to the web browser. Text is one example of this. Within an HTML document, text is usually bound by tags such as <p> and <font>. These tags are for display and formatting purposes only. To apply a Behavior to a text element you have to make that element a link. As a link it can communicate with the browser and access the JavaScript necessary to perform a Behavior.

To attach a Behavior to a word or section of text, follow these steps:

1. Select the text. The Property Inspector panel changes to reflect any formatting that may be applied to the text already.

2. In the Link field of the Property Inspector panel type **javascript:;**. This creates a *null link*—a link that goes nowhere. The purpose of a null link is to tell the browser that the link will be handled by the JavaScript of the attached Behavior.

 Notice the colon (:) and semicolon (;) following javascript *in the null link. You must type the link exactly as shown.*

3. In the Behaviors panel, choose the action you wish the Behavior to perform, and select an event to trigger it. For more details, see "Attach a Behavior" earlier.

Here are some Behaviors that apply to text links:

■ **Go to URL**   This Behavior opens a new page in the active window or specified frame.

- **Open Browser Window**   This Behavior opens a URL in a fresh, new browser window of your own design. The Behavior allows you to specify window attributes including dimensions, title, presence of scroll and toolbars, and so on.

- **Pop-up Message**   When this Behavior is attached to a link, it can open a JavaScript alert when the link is clicked.

Use Behaviors with Images

Dreamweaver Behaviors allow you to access several JavaScript actions that can be helpful for managing images and the graphic interactivity on your web site. Image-related Behaviors are used to create interactive diagrams, navigational menus, and interactive buttons. Once your graphics are designed and prepared for the Web, Dreamweaver allows you to incorporate them in a variety of applications.

NOTE   *The actions contained in Dreamweaver are only a sample of the possibilities that JavaScript can offer for an interactive web site. For suggestions to expand Dreamweaver's library of actions, see Appendix B.*

The most common use of JavaScript in relation to images is the rollover button. In its most basic form, a rollover button changes appearance when a user moves the mouse pointer over the button; it reverts to its original appearance when the pointer moves away. To complete this effect a button must have two different Behaviors attached to it: Swap Image and Swap Image Restore. These action names clearly define what each Behavior does to the image.

- **Swap Image**   Changes the `src=` portion of the `<img>` tag to display a new graphic file within the same tag.

- **Swap Image Restore**   Resets images to their original state before an `onMouseOver` event initiated the action. This action is not limited to the `onMouseOver` event, but it is one of the most common uses.

TIP   *For detailed instructions on creating rollovers please refer to the section "Create Rollover Effects," which appears later in this chapter.*

A rollover button is only one example of what this Behavior can do. The Swap Image action can be applied to any image on the web page. The action also allows you to switch multiple images, meaning that one button can alter several graphics on the basis of a single trigger event.

Other image-related Behaviors use the Preload Images action, which loads images into a browser's cache. This action is useful for loading images that will not be displayed immediately, such as images in invisible layers and images referenced in a timeline.

16

NOTE *Preload Images is also a key component of the Swap Image action because it prevents the action from lagging or delaying the swap process. A check box in the Swap Image dialog box allows you to automatically attach a Preload Images action in an additional Behavior.*

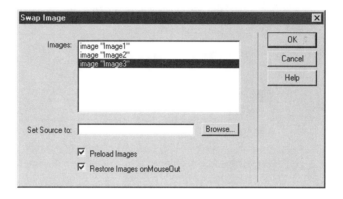

Use Behaviors with Frames

Frames provide a useful means of dividing a web page into sections that can be controlled independently. Frames allow web designers to load new information into one area of the browser window while leaving static page elements (such as navigation menus or site maps) untouched. Generally, you set your links to target one specific frame, and the new link is loaded within that frame. However, it is possible that your design scheme demands that multiple frames change simultaneously. To do this, you must use a Behavior.

The Go to URL action is most helpful when it comes to managing frames. You can create a Behavior that, when triggered by the correct event, loads as many frames as the web page holds. To create and attach the Behavior:

1. Select the link or button you wish to use to target several frames. (For more information on attaching Behaviors to links or buttons, see the previous sections of this chapter.)

2. From the Actions menu, select the Go to URL action. The Go To URL dialog box appears showing where the link can be opened. You can choose the main window or any frame on the page.

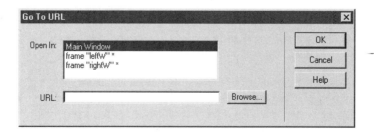

3. Select the frame you would like to target, and then either type the URL for the linked document or click the Browse button to locate the file you want.

4. Click OK, and the Go to URL action appears in the Behavior panel beside an event. Since you will be using this action in conjunction with a link or a button, the default event is either `onClick` or `onMouseDown`.

5. Repeat steps 1–4 to add other target frames to the link.

Don't forget to preview the page in a browser to test the Behavior.

Use Behaviors with Layers

Like frames, layers are a tool that can help with the layout and design of your page. But rather than holding entire HTML documents, layers serve as containers for text, images, and other elements. Layers offer a great deal of flexibility by allowing designers to position layer elements at exact pixel coordinates. Combining Behaviors with layers can add exciting interactive flair to your web page.

> NOTE   *For complete information on layers and how to create and manage them, please refer to Chapter 15.*

The Show-Hide Layers action controls the visibility of a layer. You can use it to create complex rollover responses, dynamic maps with hidden overlays, digital dress-up dolls, and so on. Once you attach this kind of Behavior to an element of your page, that element becomes a kind of light switch that turns a layer on or off. The kind of switch depends on the event you assign to the Behavior.

Another interactive JavaScript command that you can use in Dreamweaver Behaviors is the Drag-Layer action. The Drag-Layer action allows users to physically move the graphic and text elements that reside in the layers of an HTML document. This makes the action ideal for creating digital jigsaw puzzles and board games, moveable interface controls, customizable cartoons and comics, and so on. In addition to the interactivity afforded by moveable graphics, the Drag-Layer action allows you to define parameters such as the following ones that enhance the drag:

- **Movement**   Unconstrained or bounded by pixel coordinates.
- **Drop Target**   Defined by pixel coordinates; sets layers to "snap" to coordinates when they are within a particular range.
- **Drag Handle**   Defines the area that serves as a layer's "handle."
- **Stacking**   A layer can change stacking order when it is dragged.
- **JavaScript**   Calls additional JavaScript code while the drag is in progress or when a layer is dropped.

16

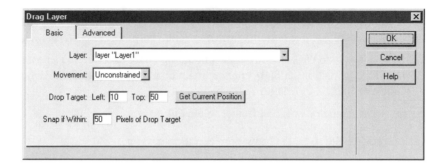

Use Behaviors with Timelines

In Dreamweaver, Timelines allow you to animate the contents of a layer. You can use layers to create quick intro animations, "slide show" picture sequences, and other kinds of visual changes over time. By incorporating Behaviors into a Timeline you can create controls to run an animation and to use animation sequences as events that trigger other Behaviors.

Use the Play/Stop Timeline actions for Behaviors that control Timeline animations. This Behavior is often attached to a link, a button, or the <body> tag of the web page. When the element receives an event message, such as a mouse click, the event triggers the Timeline animation to either begin or stop playing.

You can also create Behaviors that allow you to jump to any point in an animation. To do this, use the Go to Timeline Frame action. When cued by an event, this action causes the Timeline to automatically advance to the frame number specified in the Behavior. Think of this as a means of creating fast-forward and rewind buttons for your animation.

Many Behaviors are attached to elements outside the Timeline, such as buttons and links; however, it is also possible to attach Behaviors to frames of the Timeline itself (Figure 16-4). The Behavior Channel in the Timelines panel is used to attach Behaviors to a Timeline. Events are defined by frame numbers. When the playback head reaches the event frame, the action is executed. In this case, the event is onFrame15.

Placing a Behavior (or more accurately an action) in the Timeline creates a timed event. When the playback head arrives at the designated frame, the JavaScript action executes. In Figure 16-4 there is an animation on Layer 1 that lasts 15 frames and a Go to URL action in frame 15 of the Behavior Channel. When frame 15 is played, the action executes, and a new URL is launched. This technique is useful for triggering introductory animations to immediately link to a home page when the animation is complete.

Behaviors and Browser Compatibility

Dreamweaver Behaviors provide a wide range of effects, but unfortunately there are limits to Behaviors. Not all web browsers are able to interpret the events and actions associated with Behaviors. As a result, browser compatibility is an issue that must be considered by web designers who wish to use Behaviors. Not only do different browsers interpret JavaScript in different ways; some browsers do not support it at all. In most cases it is best to test your site on

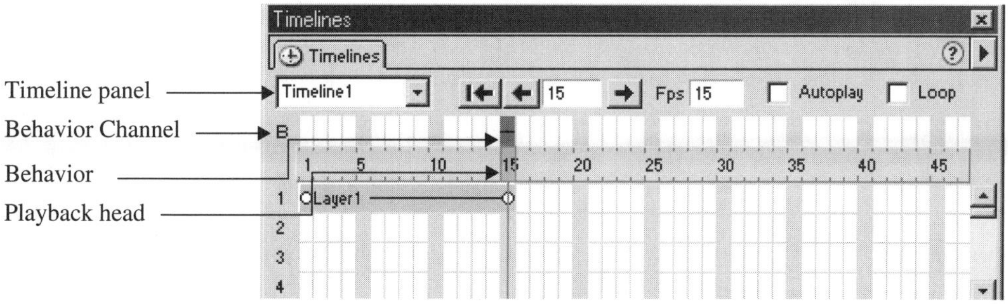

FIGURE 16-4   Attach Behaviors to a Timeline using the Behavior Channel in the
Timelines panel.

a variety of machines and browsers to insure both design and functional consistency. For a
complete list of JavaScript actions available in Dreamweaver, see Table 16-1.

According to Macromedia, Dreamweaver 4 shipped with Behavior actions designed to work
with all versions of Netscape Navigator 4.x, and Internet Explorer 4.x and 5.x. Macromedia has
taken steps to ensure that the JavaScript generated by Dreamweaver Behaviors is as cross-platform
and cross-browser compatible as possible.

NOTE   *Netscape 6 and Dreamweaver 4 were released at nearly the same time. Because of the
time pinch, Macromedia was unable to address all compatibility issues found in the newest
version of Netscape. Consult the Macromedia web site, **http://www.macromedia.com**,
for details on Netscape 6.*

Action	Description
Call JavaScript	Allows a Behavior to perform a custom JavaScript function
Change Property	Action that changes the property of a web page element, such as the stacking order of a layer
Check Browser	Detects the type of browser a visitor is using and redirects them to different pages depending on its capabilities
Check Plugin	Searches for installed plug-ins and redirects visitors accordingly
Control Shockwave or Flash	Action that can play, stop, rewind, and skip frames in a Macromedia Shockwave or Flash movie
Drag Layer	Allows users to drag and move layers in an HTML document
Go to Timeline Frame	Action that moves the Timeline playback head to a specific frame
Go to URL	Opens a link in the main browser window or specified frame(s)

TABLE 16-1   All JavaScript Actions Make Up Part of a Behavior and Must Be Triggered
by an Event

16

Action	Description
Jump Menu	Action that allows a menu object to perform as a Jump menu
Open Browser Window	Opens a new browser window with the properties (size, menu bar, and so on) that you specify
Play Sound	Action that plays a sound when cued by a Behavior event
Play Timeline Stop Timeline	Actions that start or stop the playback of a Timeline
Popup Message	Displays a JavaScript alert message with the text you specify
Preload Images	Action that loads images that are not immediately displayed on a web page
Set Nav Bar Image	Converts an image to a nav bar image or changes the properties of nav bar images
Set Text of Frame	Action that dynamically changes the content and design of a frame with HTML that you specify
Set Text of Layer	Action that dynamically changes the content and design of a layer with HTML that you specify
Set Text of Text Field	Replaces the information in a form text field with information that you specify
Show-Hide Layers	Sets the visibility property of a layer
Swap Image	Action that switches one graphic with another
Swap Image Restore	Resets a swapped image to its original source
Validate Form	Action that confirms that all text field data has been entered correctly and is in the right format

TABLE 16-1   All JavaScript Actions Make Up Part of a Behavior and Must Be Triggered by an Event *(continued)*

Select Browser Compatibility Level for Events

Macromedia has done the drudgework of figuring out which browsers support what Behavior functionality. To help you select appropriate events for compatibility with target browsers, Dreamweaver provides a menu option that limits your choices based on the browser(s) for which you design.

With a Behavior selected, click the inverted triangle button to display the events menu. Near the bottom you will see a choice that reads Show Events For (Figure 16-5). Point to this option, and a submenu appears. Dreamweaver displays the events for:

- 3.0 and Later Browsers
- 4.0 and Later Browsers
- Internet Explorer 3, 4, and 5
- Netscape 3 and 4

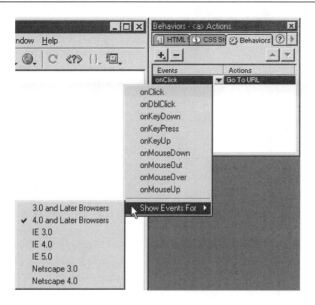

FIGURE 16-5	Show Events For reveals a subsection of the Events menu. The browser version selected here shows which events are recognized by the selected browser(s).

Select the browser your audience is most likely to use when viewing your web site. If you are designing an intranet site and you know that all employees browse the Web with Netscape 4.7, you can comfortably select the Netscape 4.0 option. However, if you are planning a site for the general public and you want to reach the widest possible audience, it is probably best to go with a more restricted set of browser events. Refer to Table 16-2 for complete event descriptions and their browser compatibility.

Event	Supported Browsers	Description
onAbort	NN3, NN4, IE4, IE5	Initiated when a user stops the browser from loading an image completely.
onAfterUpdate	IE4, IE5	Initiated when a bound data element has updated its source.
onBeforeUpdate	IE4, IE5	Initiated when a bound data element has been changed (lost its focus) and is prepared for an update.
onBlur	NN3, NN4, IE3, IE4, IE5	The opposite of onFocus—initiated when the element is no longer the main object of user interaction.

TABLE 16-2	All Behavior Events Are Not in All Browsers. NN = Netscape Navigator, IE = Internet Explorer; Followed by a Version Number

16

Event	Supported Browsers	Description
onBounce	IE4, IE5	Initiated when the contents of a marquee have reached the marquee boundary.
onChange	NN3, NN4, IE3, IE4, IE5	Initiated when a user changes the value of an element.
onClick	NN3, NN4, IE3, IE4, IE5	Initiated when the user clicks an element such as a button or a link.
onDblClick	NN4, IE4, IE5	Initiated when the user quickly clicks the mouse twice on an element.
onError	NN3, NN4, IE4, IE5	Initiated by an error encountered while loading an image or HTML document.
onFinish	IE4, IE5	Initiated when marquee contents have finished a loop cycle.
onFocus	NN3, NN4, IE4, IE5	Initiated when an element becomes the main object of user interaction (see also onBlur).
onHelp	IE4, IE5	Initiated when the user selects the Help option from a browser button or a menu.
onKeyDown	NN4, IE4, IE5	Initiated when the user presses any key and it is in the down position. The browser cannot detect which key has been pressed.
onKeyPress	NN4, IE4, IE5	Initiated when the user presses any key. The browser cannot detect which key has been pressed.
onKeyUp	NN4, IE4, IE5	Initiated when the user presses any key and it returns to the up position. The browser cannot detect which key has been pressed.
onLoad	NN3, NN4, IE3, IE4, IE5	Initiated when an image or HTML document finishes loading.
onMouseDown	NN4, IE4, IE5	Initiated when a user presses the mouse button.
onMouseMove	IE3, IE4, IE5	Initiated when a user moves the mouse within the bounds of the specified element.
onMouseOut	NN3, NN4, IE4, IE5	Initiated when the user points the mouse away from (off of) the specified element.

TABLE 16-2 All Behavior Events Are Not in All Browsers. NN = Netscape Navigator, IE = Internet Explorer; Followed by a Version Number *(continued)*

Event	Supported Browsers	Description
onMouseOver	NN3, NN4, IE4, IE5	Initiated when the user points the mouse over (on to) the specified element.
onMouseUp	NN4, IE4, IE5	Initiated when a depressed mouse button is released.
onMove	NN4	Initiated when a user moves a window or a frame.
onReadyStateChange	IE4, IE5	Initiated when the state of an element changes.
onReset	NN3, NN4, IE3, IE4, IE5	Initiated when a form is restored to its default values.
onResize	NN4, IE4, IE5	Initiated when a user resizes a browser or a frame window.
onRowEnter	IE4, IE5	Initiated when the current record pointer of a bound data source changes.
onRowExit	IE4, IE5	Initiated when the current record pointer of a bound data source prepares to change.
onScroll	IE4, IE5	Initiated when a user scrolls the window contents up or down.
onSelect	NN3, NN4, IE3, IE4, IE5	Initiated when text is selected in a text field.
onStart	IE4, IE5	Initiated when marquee contents begin to loop.
onSubmit	NN3, NN4, IE3, IE4, IE5	Initiated when a user submits a form.
onUnload	NN3, NN4, IE3, IE4, IE5	Initiated when a user exits a page.

TABLE 16-2   All Behavior Events Are Not in All Browsers. NN = Netscape Navigator, IE = Internet Explorer; Followed by a Version Number *(continued)*

Create Rollover Effects

One of the most common uses for Behaviors is to create rollovers. The effect of a rollover can be impressive, although it is really quite simple to create and implement in your web page design. Dreamweaver will, of course, handle all the JavaScript. But what it can't do is produce the necessary graphics. At a bare minimum, you need two: one for the idle state and one for the rollover state. To create these you must use a separate graphics program such as Macromedia Fireworks or Adobe Photoshop.

16

Once your graphics have been created you should be ready to add them to your web page and create the rollover. This is how you do it:

> *Before bringing rollover graphics into the Dreamweaver environment place them in your local site folder or one of its subfolders.*

1. Position the insertion point in your document at the location where you want to insert the rollover button.

2. To insert the rollover image, do any of the following:

   ■ Click the Insert Rollover Images icon on the Objects panel.

   ■ Drag the Insert Rollover Images icon from the Objects panel onto your document.

   ■ Choose Insert | Interactive Images | Rollover Image.

   The Insert Rollover Image dialog box appears.

3. Select the options for your rollover image:

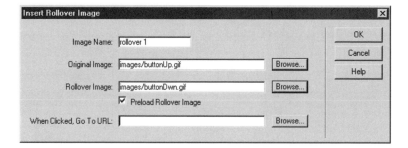

   ■ **Image Name**   Type a name for the rollover here. It is not necessary but can be helpful if you plan to use several rollovers in a single document.

   ■ **Original Image**   Type a path or click Browse to select the "idle state" image.

   ■ **Rollover Image**   Type a path or click Browse to select the "active state" image.

   ■ **Preload Rollover Image**   Check this option to preload your rollover image (recommended).

   ■ **When Clicked, Go To URL**   If your rollover is a hyperlink button you can enter the link's URL in this field.

4. Click OK to close the Insert Rollover Image dialog box. The rollover image you defined appears in the Document window. To test the rollover, preview your page in a browser.

This procedure streamlines the process of attaching Behaviors for a rollover effect. Dreamweaver automatically inserts the image and attaches the necessary Behaviors to create a rollover image with the link you specify. You can also insert the image into your page manually and attach three or four separate Behaviors, but this procedure requires more work.

Create a Navigation Bar

Navigation bars offer an immediately recognizable, clear means of exploring a web site. Navigation bars (or nav bars) serve both as a bookmark and a table of contents (Figure 16-6). They are stacked horizontally or vertically on the web page and offer two kinds of information: (1) a visitor's current location and (2) other locations that can be visited within the site.

Similar to using rollover images, you must create nav bar graphics in an external imaging program. Nav bar components can have up to four states:

- **Up**   "Idle" or inactive state
- **Over**   "Ready" state when the cursor points to the nav bar selection
- **Down**   "Active" state that marks a selection
- **Over While Down**   "Ready" state for a selection in the down position

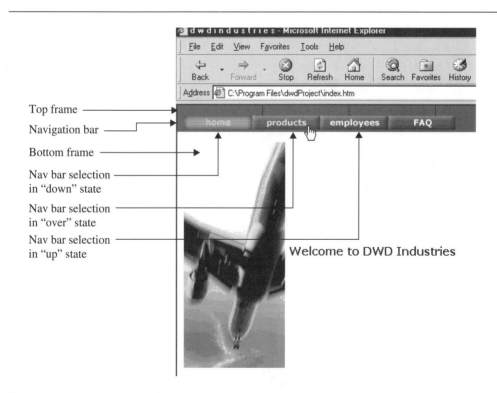

FIGURE 16-6   This navigation bar sits in the top frame. Visitors click on the different selections (employees, FAQ, and so on) to load links into the bottom frame.

16

Basically, a nav bar is a set of rollover buttons. As you can with single rollovers, you could manually insert the base images for each button and then attach behaviors to each one, but it's a lot easier to use Dreamweaver's Insert Navigation Bar feature to automate much of the process. Here is how to create a navigation bar:

1. Position the insertion point cursor in your document at the location where you want to insert the navigation bar.

2. To insert the navigation bar you can either:

   ■ Select the Insert Navigation Bar icon from the Objects panel.

   ■ Choose Insert | Interactive Images | Navigation Bar.

   The Insert Navigation Bar dialog box appears.

3. Dreamweaver lists the first Nav Bar Element as "unnamed1." Click on Browse beside the Up Image field and select the graphic you wish to use for the inactive state of the first nav bar element.

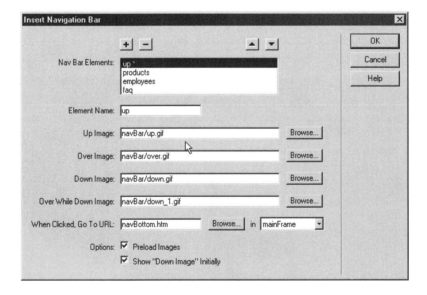

4. Click on Browse to select graphics for the remaining states: Over Image, Down Image, and Over While Down Image.

5. Beside the When Clicked, Go To URL field click Browse to select the linked document and choose a location for the new link from the In pop-up menu.

6. If you want an element to be in the "down" state when the nav bar is first loaded, check the box next to Show "Down Image" Initially. Dreamweaver tracks this by inserting an asterisk next to the element.

7. To add more elements to the nav bar click the plus (+) button and repeat steps 4–7. Click the minus (–) button to remove elements, and use the up/down arrows to reorder them.

Other options:

■ Preload Images attaches the necessary Behaviors to load nav bar graphics into cache before they are used. This option prevents lag when the graphics change from one state to the next.

■ Choose Horizontal or Vertical orientation for your nav bar from the Insert pop-up menu.

■ To insert the nav bar as a table, check the Use Tables box.

8. Click OK to close the Insert Navigation Bar dialog box. Dreamweaver inserts the images into your page, attaches Behaviors to the images, and adds the necessary code to your web document.

NOTE   *There can be only one navigation bar per page. If you are working with a frameset be sure to select the correct frame before inserting or editing a nav bar. To make changes to an existing navigation bar choose Modify | Navigation Bar and edit as needed.*

Create a Jump Menu

Jump menus offer an economic approach to web site navigation because they provide many link options without taking up much space on the web page. A Jump menu is a drop-down list in which each item on the list coincides with a link. When a visitor selects a menu item, the Jump menu loads its link into a frame or a browser window (Figure 16-7).

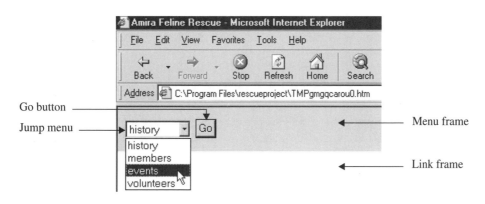

FIGURE 16-7   This Jump menu, located in the top frame, loads any of the four links into the frame below it. The Go button is optional. Clicking it will load the selected Jump menu link.

16

To add a Jump menu to your project:

1. Position the insertion point cursor in your document at the location where you want to insert the navigation bar.

2. Choose Insert | Form Objects | Jump Menu. The Insert Jump Menu dialog box appears; you must specify:
   - Menu Items
   - Text
   - Linked URL

3. The dialog box opens with a default "unnamed" menu item. Click Browse and select the file you want to link to this first choice on the menu. Click OK.

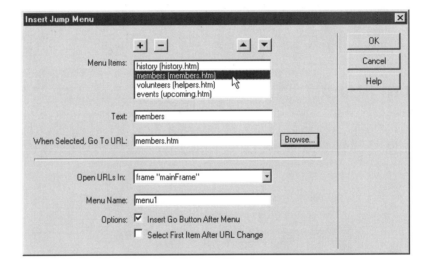

4. When you return to the dialog box, the previously "unnamed" menu item has been replaced with your choice of link. To specify the way the link will appear on the Jump menu, type the name into the Text field.

5. Next, select where you want the link to open using the Open URLs In pop-up menu. Links can be opened either in the main browser window or in frames, if they are available.

6. To add additional menu items, click on the plus (+) button and repeat steps 3–5.

7. Click OK to close the Insert Jump Menu dialog box. Dreamweaver inserts the menu into your page, attaches Behaviors, and adds the necessary code to your web document.

Part VI

Manage Your Site with Dreamweaver

Chapter 17

Publish Your Site

How to...

- Prepare your site for publication
- Publish your site to a web server
- Keep your site up-to-date

You have your site built. All the pages are done, and the links are in place. You're ready to show your creation to the world—or are you?

First, you need to examine your site and all its pages to check for browser compatibility issues and common code errors so you can detect and correct those problems before you publish the site for all to see. Second, you need to get all the files that make up your web site transferred to a web server where they will be available to the Internet population (or to a server on your corporate intranet).

You are now moving into the realm of webmaster. The webmaster is the person (or persons) responsible for online content—making sure that the site is up and running properly as well as keeping the site content fresh by updating it on a fairly regular basis. This chapter describes how to do all that—make the final preparations before uploading, upload the site, and do incremental updates after the site is online.

Prepare Your Site for Publication

Before transferring your site to your web server, you need to make sure that everything is working correctly. It is one thing to create pages in Dreamweaver, but to see the site as your visitor will see it, you need to check the pages for browser compatibility. Check how various browsers render the HTML codes and the scripts in your pages and confirm that all the links work as expected.

 The techniques described in this section all identify and report potential problems with your web pages, but they don't automatically make any changes in the HTML source code. It's up to you to decide what, if any, action to take to correct the reported problems.

Check Pages Against Target Browsers

Each browser, be it Internet Explorer, Netscape Navigator, AOL, or any of several other, less-well-known browsers, has its own way of displaying content. Default font sizes might be different. Certain HTML tags and attributes might be rendered differently. Certain scripts might or might not be recognized, which means that the really nifty layered animation you built might not work in a particular browser. Browsers vary from brand to brand, from version to version; even the computer platform can make a difference. In addition, a linked site's URL might have changed, making that link on your page useless. All these factors can negate the hard work you put into designing your site. So you need to test your site carefully before posting it in order to find and eliminate the many small—and not so small—glitches that invariably turn up.

Dreamweaver's Preview in Browser feature is your first line of defense, enabling you to quickly preview your page in a browser window as you work. When you install Dreamweaver, it automatically configures itself to use your default browser for previews. And if you have other browsers installed on your system, you can add them to the Preview in Browser list (see Chapter 20). This feature enables you to visually check each page in a couple of different browsers as you create and edit it.

As useful (and essential) as the Preview in Browser feature is, it can't test a page for all the various browsers and versions of browsers that site visitors might use. You can't keep that many browsers installed on your system; even if you did, it wouldn't be practical to preview every page in every version of each browser.

Dreamweaver's Check Target Browsers feature addresses this problem by providing a way to check your pages against a series of *browser profiles*. A browser profile lists browser characteristics for a specific browser, such as what HTML tags and attributes the browser supports. Dreamweaver can scan the source code for your pages, compare it to the browser profile for a given browser, and generate a report listing any known problems such as unsupported HTML tags.

> **NOTE** *For those who care, the Check Target Browser feature is a code parsing and validation process, and the browser profile is a DTD (Document Type Declaration).*

The Check Target Browsers feature is quite versatile. Dreamweaver has browser profiles for several versions of both major browsers, and other profiles are available as extensions that you can download and install. (See Appendix B for instructions on locating and installing extensions.) You can use Check Target Browsers to check a single document, selected files, all the files in a selected folder, or all the files in an entire site.

Here's how to run a target browser report:

1. Select the file or files that you want to check against one or more browser profiles. You can use any of the following techniques to select the web documents to check:

   ■ Open the document you want to check in the Dreamweaver Document window.

   ■ Select one or more files in the file list in the Site window.

   ■ Select a folder in the file list in the Site window.

   ■ Select the root folder of the file list in the Site window to check the entire site.

2. Choose File | Check Target Browsers. Dreamweaver opens the Check Target Browsers dialog box.

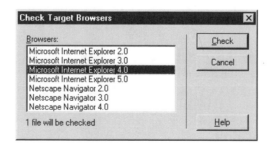

17

3. Select one or more browsers in the Browsers list. You can select from the following choices plus any additional browser profiles you've installed:

- Microsoft Internet Explorer 2.0

- Microsoft Internet Explorer 3.0

- Microsoft Internet Explorer 4.0

- Microsoft Internet Explorer 5.0

- Netscape Navigator 2.0

- Netscape Navigator 3.0

- Netscape Navigator 4.0

4. Click the Check button to close the Check Target Browsers dialog box and begin the check. Dreamweaver displays a message box showing the status of the process. When the checking process is complete, Dreamweaver launches your default browser to display a report listing the results (see Figure 17-1).

Checking a single file against one browser profile takes only a few seconds, but checking multiple files against multiple browser profiles can take several minutes. The progress bars showing the status of the browser check aren't very informative. Be patient. Give Dreamweaver time to do its thing.

The Check Target Browsers report lists the filenames of files with potential problems and displays the line numbers where the offending tags and/or attributes can be found in the source code.

The Check Target Browsers report requires some interpretation. The report points out potential problems, but it's up to you to determine whether a particular problem is serious enough to require action or if it's something you can safely ignore. In other words, just because the report lists a potential problem, such as an unsupported tag or attribute, that doesn't necessarily mean your page will crash or fail to display correctly. It just indicates something you need to check on.

For example, Internet Explorer and Netscape Navigator support different attribute names for page margins. It's common practice to insert duplicate margin settings into the <body> tag, one set for IE and one for Navigator. Each browser sets its margins according to the attribute it recognizes and ignores the unsupported attributes. The Check Target Browsers report correctly points out the unsupported attributes, even though they are intentional.

Run a Site Report

In addition to the Check Target Browsers report, Dreamweaver includes a report you can run to check your web documents for potential problems before publication. The Site Report feature includes seven different reports that cover everything from the Design Notes attached to web documents to a number of common HTML code errors and omissions. You can select which

Dreamweaver Target Browser Check

29-April-2001 at 07:56:55 PM Eastern Daylight Time.

This report covered 1 file.

Target Browser	Errors	Warnings
Microsoft Internet Explorer 4.0	2	1
Total	2	1

Files containing errors:

D:\Sites\Oates\

about_us.htm

File	D:\Sites\Oates\about_us.htm (Back to Index)
Error	The marginheight attribute of the Body tag is not supported. Microsoft Internet Explorer 4.0
line 179	`<body bgcolor="#FFFFFF" text="#000000" link="#0000CC" vlink="#990099" alink="#CC0033" leftmargin="0" topmargin="0" marginwidth="0" marginheight="0" onLoad="MM_preloadImages('Assets/Tob%20banner%20&%20nav/Nav_About_Us_btn_f2.jpg','Assets/Tob%20banner%20&%20nav/Nav_Privacy_btn_f2.jpg')">`
Error	The marginwidth attribute of the Body tag is not supported. Microsoft Internet Explorer 4.0
line 179	`<body bgcolor="#FFFFFF" text="#000000" link="#0000CC" vlink="#990099" alink="#CC0033" leftmargin="0" topmargin="0" marginwidth="0" marginheight="0" onLoad="MM_preloadImages('Assets/Tob%20banner%20&%20nav/Nav_About_Us_btn_f2.jpg','Assets/Tob%20banner%20&%20nav/Nav_Privacy_btn_f2.jpg')">`
Warning	Warning: Attributes and values for the <EMBED> tag vary by plug-in. Please check that all attributes and values are valid. Microsoft Internet Explorer 4.0
line 233	`<embed src="Assets/Buttons/btn_contact.swf" base="." quality=high pluginspage="http://www.macromedia.com/shockwave/download/index.cgi? P1_Prod_Version=ShockwaveFlash" type="application/x-shockwave-flash" width="93" height="33" bgcolor="" name="Contact Us Button">`

End of report.

FIGURE 17-1   The results of a Check Target Browser scan

reports to run, and you can elect to run the reports on the current document, selected files, all the files in a selected folder, or your entire site. Here's how to do it:

1. Select the file or files on which you want to run site reports. You can use any of the following techniques to select the web documents for checking:

- Open a document in the Dreamweaver Document window.
- Select one or more files in the file list in the Site window.

■ If you want to run reports on the contents of a folder or the entire site, you don't need to preselect the folder. You can do that in the Reports dialog box.

2. Choose Site | Reports to open the Reports dialog box.

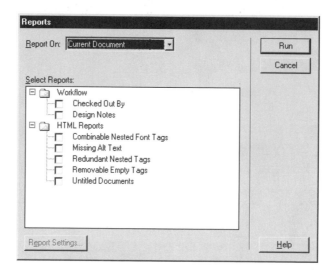

3. Select the subject of the report from the Report On list box. You can select Current Document, Entire Local Site, Selected Files in Site, or Folder. If you select Folder, another text box appears below the Report On list box where you can type in the folder name or click the folder icon beside the text box to open the Choose Local Folder dialog box, where you can locate and select the folder.

4. Select one or more reports in the Select Reports box by clicking the check box beside the report name. You can select any of the following reports:

   ■ **Checked Out By**   Lists files that are locked by Dreamweaver's Check Out feature and shows who checked out the file.

   ■ **Design Notes**   Lists which files have Design Notes attached and shows the contents of those notes.

   ■ **Combinable Nested Font Tags**   Lists nested font tags that could be combined to clean up the source code.

   ■ **Missing Alt Text**   Lists images that lack Alt text attributes.

   ■ **Redundant Nested Tags**   Lists instances of a tag nested within another tag of the same kind to no effect.

   ■ **Removable Empty Tags**   Lists empty tags that could be removed to clean up the source code.

   ■ **Untitled Documents**   Lists documents that still have the default "Untitled Document" title.

5. Click Run to run the selected reports. Dreamweaver opens the Results dialog box to display the results as it scans the selected documents and shows what it found.

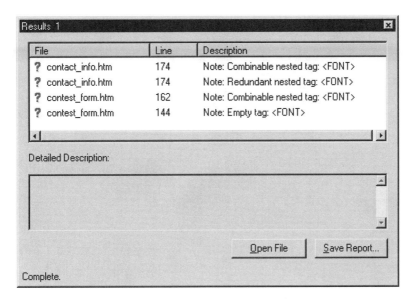

6. Click an item in the list box at the top of the Results dialog box to see more information in the Detailed Description area below.

7. Select a file in the Reports dialog box and click the Open File button to open that document for editing. Dreamweaver opens the file in a Document window and highlights the error so you can deal with it quickly and easily.

Publish Your Dreamweaver Site to a Web Server

After you have made sure all the elements of your site are working correctly, it's time to publish your site by placing it on a web server. To publish your site, you need to duplicate the local site that you worked so hard to develop onto the remote site. The remote site is usually a directory on a web server at your Internet Service Provider or a web hosting service, although it can also be a web server on your local area network. Typically, you access the web server via the Internet using FTP (File Transfer Protocol). Dreamweaver includes built-in FTP capabilities that handle all file transfer duties necessary to publish and maintain most web sites, so there's no need to use an external FTP utility program.

17

Define the Remote Site

To publish your site to the remote server with Dreamweaver, you must supply Dreamweaver with some information about the server location and the settings you use to access it. This is all part of the Dreamweaver Site definition; you may have completed it when you originally defined your site in Dreamweaver (see Chapter 2). However, if you didn't define the Remote Site earlier, you must do so now. Here's how:

1. Choose Site | Define Sites, or select Define Sites from the Site list box in the Sites window toolbar. Dreamweaver opens the Define Sites dialog box.

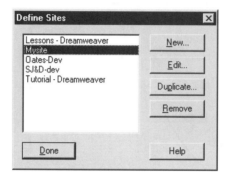

2. Select the site you want to publish from the list box in the Define Sites dialog box; then click Edit. Dreamweaver displays the Site Definition for *sitename* dialog box.

3. Click Remote Info in the Category list to display the settings for the remote site.

4. Select the appropriate access mode in the Access box. Normally, that's FTP, but you can also select Local/Network, SourceSafe Database, or WebDAV. Dreamweaver displays options for the selected access mode in the dialog box. The FTP options are shown below.

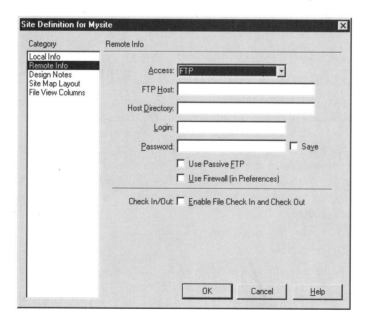

5. Enter or select the information as needed. Here is what you will need to supply for an FTP connection:

   ■ **FTP Host** The address for the host FTP site. This address is usually in the form of ftp.hostname.com.

   ■ **Host Directory** The directory on the host system where web documents are stored—the root directory of the web site. You may not need to enter anything here if the FTP host address points directly to the web root directory. Otherwise, you need to enter a directory path from the FTP host root to the web root—for example, ~username/webroot/.

   ■ **Login** This is your User Name for access to the FTP/web server. It's usually the same as your account user ID for this service provider.

   ■ **Password** Input the password for FTP access—usually the same as your master account password for this service provider.

   ■ **Save** Check this option to have Dreamweaver save the password so you don't have to enter it manually each time you connect.

   ■ **Use Passive FTP** and **Use Firewall (in Preferences)** If your Internet access goes through a firewall that requires special passive-mode FTP operation, check one or both options. If you're not sure, leave these options unchecked unless you have a problem establishing an FTP connection; then consult with your network system administrator for the proper settings.

   ■ **Check In/Out** Check this option to enable the file Check Out feature (see Chapter 18). This feature is for workgroups collaborating on web site development. If you work alone, ignore it.

6. Click the OK button to close the Site Definition dialog box and record the remote site access settings.

Transfer Site Files to the Remote Site

Once you have the access information for the remote site configured, you're ready to transfer your files to the host server. Dreamweaver uses the remote site definition to take care of all the mechanics of establishing a connection to the remote site and transferring files. All you need to do is tell Dreamweaver what files to transfer. Here's how to do that:

NOTE *You must have an established connection to the Internet in order to connect and transfer files to the remote site. Depending on your system configuration, if you don't have a full-time Internet connection, you may need to initiate a dial-up connection outside Dreamweaver.*

1. If the Site window isn't already displaying the site you want to publish, choose Site | Open Site | *sitename,* or select the site from the Site menu in the Site window toolbar.

2. Choose Window | Site Files, or click the Site Files toolbar button to display the Remote Site and Local Site files lists, not the Site Map, in the Site window.

3. Choose Site | Connect or click the Connect button in the toolbar. Dreamweaver establishes a connection to the remote site (usually via an FTP connection over the Internet) and updates the Remote Site files list. The Connect button changes to show the two plugs connected. (This step is unnecessary if the remote site is located on your local area network.)

4. Select the files in the Local Folder file list that you want to transfer to the server. To upload the entire site, select the root folder of the local site.

NOTE *Make sure all your files are saved before you transfer them; Dreamweaver will prompt you to save any unsaved files before the transfer begins.*

5. Choose Site | Put or click the Put button in the toolbar to begin the transfer. If you selected the entire site for upload, Dreamweaver prompts you for confirmation before proceeding. Dreamweaver begins copying files and folders from your local site to the remote server. Dreamweaver automatically creates folders on the remote site as needed to duplicate the folder structure of your local site and copies files into the correct folders. The Site window status bar shows the filename of each file as it is transferred to the remote site.

NOTE *If you select individual folders or files for upload instead of the entire site, Dreamweaver displays a message box asking whether to include dependent files. Click Yes to have Dreamweaver automatically transfer those files along with your web pages.*

6. When the transfer is complete, click the Connect button again, or choose Site | Disconnect to break the connection to the remote site. (If you accessed the Internet via a dial-up connection, you may also want to end the modem connection outside Dreamweaver.)

NOTE *Check with the system administrator or webmaster for your web host to find out if it's necessary to change or set file access permissions for the files you upload to your remote site in order to make them available to anonymous web surfers. If you do need to adjust permission settings, you'll need to get instructions on how to do so.*

Dependent Files

In Dreamweaver parlance, *dependent files* are the images, buttons, media objects, and other page elements that are stored in separate files and referenced by your web documents. Dependent files are often stored in folders on your web site separately from the main web documents. Dreamweaver automatically scans your web pages before uploading or downloading them and offers to copy dependent files along with the web pages.

Keep Your Site Up-to-Date

After you initially publish your site by copying all the files and folders from the local site folder to the remote server, you'll rarely need to go through a full-site transfer again. But that doesn't mean you just load your site onto a web server and forget it. Web sites, like pets, need constant care and feeding in the form of frequent updates to freshen content, repair broken links, and add new pages and features.

Upload and Download Files

The same Dreamweaver tools you use to publish your site in the first place also help you maintain it. You can establish a connection and transfer files back and forth between the local and remote sites at any time. The procedure is essentially the same as outlined previously for publishing the site. The only differences are in the files you select to transfer and the choice of the Put or Get command.

- To transfer (upload) selected files from the local site to the remote site, select the files you want to transfer in the Local Folder file list and choose Site | Put, or click the Put button on the toolbar.

- To transfer (download) selected files from the remote site to the local site, select the files you want to transfer in the Remote Site file list and choose Site | Get, or click the Get button on the toolbar.

- To delete files or folders from the remote site, select the files or folders you want to delete in the Remote Site file list; then right-click one of the selected files and choose Delete from the context menu that appears. (You can do the same in the Local Folder file list to delete files from the local site.)

> **TIP**   *When you transfer to or from a remote site, Dreamweaver creates a transfer log that you can refer to if a problem occurs. You can even show your client this record after you have uploaded or changed files on the site. To view the log, choose Window | Site FTP Log from the Site window. Dreamweaver displays the FTP Log window shown in Figure 17-2.*

Synchronize Files

Web sites can quickly become quite large. It is not uncommon to have hundreds of files to keep track of. In addition to the web pages themselves, you have all the image files, slices of image files, buttons, animations, and other dependent files to worry about. Identifying what files have been changed and need to be updated can make the process of maintaining a site rather tedious.

Dreamweaver includes a special feature to automate the process of synchronizing the files in your Local Folder and Remote Site. When you use the Synchronize command, Dreamweaver compares the file dates for the selected files in the Local Folder and the Remote Site and transfers only the files that have changed, not files with the same modification date. The Synchronize command works for transferring files in either direction between the local and remote sites. You can synchronize an entire site or only selected files.

17

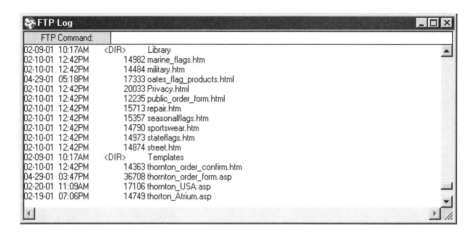

FIGURE 17-2   The FTP Log window shows a record of the Dreamweaver file transfers.

Here's how to synchronize your files:

1. Choose Site | Connect, or click the Connect button in the toolbar to establish a connection to the remote server. (This step isn't necessary if the remote site is located on your local area network.)

2. Select the files you want to synchronize in the Dreamweaver Site window. (If you want to synchronize the entire site, you can skip this step.)

3. Choose Site | Synchronize. Dreamweaver opens the Synchronize Files dialog box.

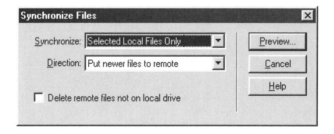

4. In the Synchronize box, select either Entire *sitename* Site to synchronize the entire site or Selected Local Files Only to synchronize only the files you selected in step 2. (If you selected files in the Remote Site file list, the option reads Selected Remote Files Only.)

5. Select the appropriate option in the Direction box. Your choices are as follows:

- **Put newer files to remote** Replaces outdated files on the remote site by uploading newer versions from the local site but ignores any newer files that may be located on the remote site

- **Get newer files from remote** Replaces outdated files on the local site by downloading newer versions from the remote site but ignores any newer files that may be located on the local site

- **Get and Put newer files** Uploads and downloads as necessary to replace outdated files with newer versions

6. Check Delete Remote Files Not On Local Drive if you want Dreamweaver to automatically delete files from the remote site if there isn't a matching file on the local site. This option is useful if you've deleted some old files from the local site and need to make corresponding deletions on the remote site. (This option changes depending on the selection in the Direction box. If you choose Get Newer Files From Remote, this option is Delete Local Files Not On Remote Server. If you select Get and Put Newer Files, this option is unavailable.)

7. Click the Preview button. Dreamweaver closes the Synchronize Files dialog box, scans and compares the files in the local and remote sites, and then displays the Synchronize dialog box.

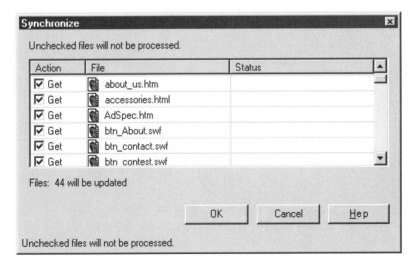

8. Review the proposed synchronization actions in the dialog box. The dialog box lists each file transfer and/or deletion Dreamweaver deemed necessary to implement your instructions. You can cancel an individual action by unchecking the check box in the first column.

9. Click OK to start processing the files. Dreamweaver updates the list to show the status of each file as it is transferred or deleted.

10. When synchronization is complete, click the Close button to close the Synchronize dialog box.

17

Chapter 18

Site Testing, Maintenance, and Workgroup Collaboration

How to...

- ■ Manage links in your site
- ■ Use file Check Out and Check In
- ■ Use Design Notes

Dreamweaver excels in link maintenance and workgroup collaboration. Dreamweaver automatically assists you in updating changed links and makes it easy to alter links in the Site window. When it comes to collaboration, Dreamweaver's Design Notes remind you of a task's status and keep other members of your workgroup informed.

Manage Links in Your Site

Chapter 4 described how to set up links in your site. But links often don't always remain static; they need to be updated and changed periodically. Fortunately, Dreamweaver makes it easy to do just that.

Change Links in the Site Map

One of the fastest and simplest ways to change links in your site is to make your changes in the Site Map view. The Site Map, shown in Figure 18-1, is a graphical representation of the links between pages in your site, so it's a logical place to go when you need to update those links. To change an existing link in the Site Map, follow these steps:

> TIP
>
> *Remember that the Site Map shows links between pages as lines connecting page icons. The page containing links is at the top of the map, and the linked pages are in the row below. You can click the + beside a page icon in the row to show the links in that page, but it's usually easier to right-click the page and choose View As Root to elevate that page to the top position and work with the linked pages in the wide row beneath it.*

1. Navigate through the Site Map so that the page containing the links you want to change is displayed in the Root position at the top of the map. (Right-click a page icon in the Site Map and choose View As Root.)

2. Locate the icon for the link you want to change in the wide row beneath the root. Right-click the page icon and choose Change Link from the pop-up menu that appears. Dreamweaver displays the Select HTML File dialog box.

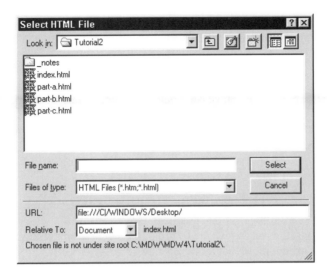

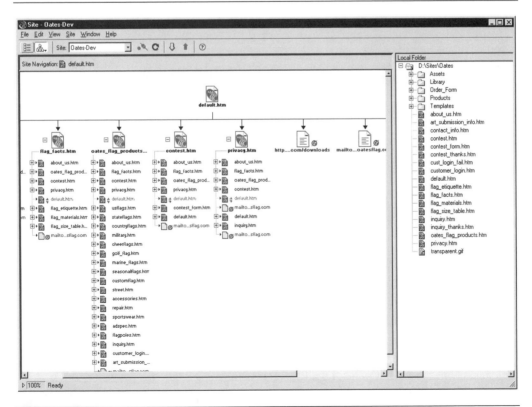

FIGURE 18-1   The Site Map is a natural place to update links.

3. Locate and select the new file you want the link to point to. Select the appropriate option in the Relative To box to finish defining the link.

4. Click the Select button to close the Select HTML File dialog box. Dreamweaver presents the Update Files dialog box shown in Figure 18-2.

5. Click the Update button. Dreamweaver changes the link in the page that appears in the root position in the Site Map and also in all other pages listed in the Update Files dialog box. (Depending on your preference settings, Dreamweaver may skip this confirmation step and update all the links automatically.)

Change Links Sitewide

Another way to change a link throughout your site is to use the Site | Change Link Sitewide menu command. When you use this command, Dreamweaver performs a search-and-replace operation on all the HTML files in your site. The program searches for any link to a given filename and changes it to another filename. Here's how it works:

1. Select the old linked file in the Local Folder file list. This is the file that the existing links point to.

2. Choose Site | Change Link Sitewide. Dreamweaver opens the Change Link Sitewide dialog box. The selected file appears in the Change All Links To box.

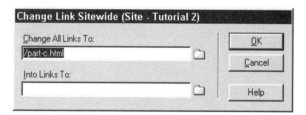

3. Enter the path and the filename for the replacement linked file in the Into Links To box. You can either type the path and the filename or click the folder icon to the right of the text box to open a dialog box where you can locate and select the file.

4. Click OK to close the Change Link Sitewide dialog box. Again, Dreamweaver displays the Update Files dialog box shown in Figure 18-2.

5. Click the Update button. Dreamweaver changes the link in all the other pages listed in the Update Files dialog box. (Depending on your preference settings, Dreamweaver may skip this confirmation step and update all the links automatically.)

Test Your Pages for Broken Links

Broken links—links that point to invalid URLs—are an ongoing challenge for webmasters. Links can be broken in any number of ways. The most common cause is files that are moved or

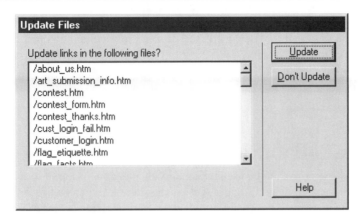

FIGURE 18-2   The Update Files dialog box

renamed. If you move or rename a file within Dreamweaver's Site window, the program tracks the effect the move will have on links to and from that file and offers to update those links automatically. However, if you (or someone else) move, delete, or rename a site file outside Dreamweaver, the links to that file are broken.

Test your site for broken links. Dreamweaver provides a link checker for this task. Here's how to check the entire site for broken links:

1. Choose Site | Check Links Sitewide from the menu. Dreamweaver scans the source code for all the pages in the site, checking all the links in each page. When it is done, Dreamweaver displays the results in the Link Checker dialog box.

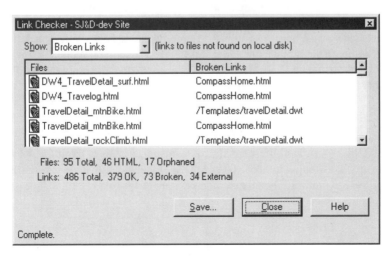

2. To fix a broken link, click on the filename under Broken Links, type in the correct URL, and press the ENTER key to make the correction. (You can also click the folder icon that appears when you click the filename in the Broken Links column to open a dialog box where you can locate and select the file.) If the URL is referenced from more than one file, Dreamweaver displays the Update Files dialog box shown in Figure 18-2.

3. Click the Update button. Dreamweaver changes the link in all the other pages listed in the Update Files dialog box.

Dreamweaver's Collaboration Features

Dreamweaver is versatile enough to be used by an individual or a megacorporation's web design team. After all, the basic web page design process is the same whether you're working solo or as part of a team. The difference between the two work environments is that a solo web author does everything alone, whereas the design team typically assigns different tasks to different team members. The collaborative nature of the team-working environment requires communication to keep everyone informed of the project's status. To facilitate communication Dreamweaver includes two key features—file Check Out/Check In and Design Notes.

Use File Check Out and Check In

One of the problems that a development team runs into when collaborating on a web site is the possibility that two (or more) team members are editing the same file on their local systems at the same time. Then, when the team members upload the edited files to the common remote site, the changes made by one team member overwrite the changes made by another team member.

The accepted solution to this problem is to institute a *check out* system on the remote site. That's what Dreamweaver does with its Check Out/Check In feature. When the feature is enabled, you check out a file from the remote site before editing it. Dreamweaver locks the file on the remote site so no one else can change it and marks the file so other team members know who has the file checked out. While the file is checked out, other team members can view the file, but they can't make changes. When you complete your edits, you check the file back in, which uploads the changed file to the remote site and releases the lock so the file becomes available for edits by other team members. This system effectively eliminates the problem of conflicting updates being posted by different team members.

Check Out Files for Editing

Although file Check Out sounds like it could be complicated, the process is actually quite simple. When file Check Out/Check In is enabled, Dreamweaver adds two buttons—Check Out and Check In—to the Site window toolbar. To use the file Check Out feature, use those buttons instead of the Get and Put buttons. Dreamweaver takes care of the rest.

■ To check out a file for editing, select the file in the Site Files list and click the Check Out button. Dreamweaver downloads the latest version of the file from the remote site (like a Get operation) and marks it as checked out to you. A green check mark appears next to the filename on your screen, and a red one appears on your partners' screens (see Figure 18-3).

TIP *If you activate the Check Out Files When Opening option (see the following section, "Set Up Check Out and Check In"), Deamweaver automatically checks out the file from the remote site when you open it for editing. You can skip the manual check out step and simply open the file.*

■ To check in a file after editing it, select the file in the Site Files list and click the Check In button. Dreamweaver uploads the file to the remote site (like a Put operation) and clears the lock created by the check-out status. The check mark beside the filename in the Local Folder file list changes to a padlock to indicate that you can't edit the file unless you check it out again.

CAUTION *Don't forget to check in each file when you finish working with it. Remember that other team members can't update the file if you've got it checked out.*

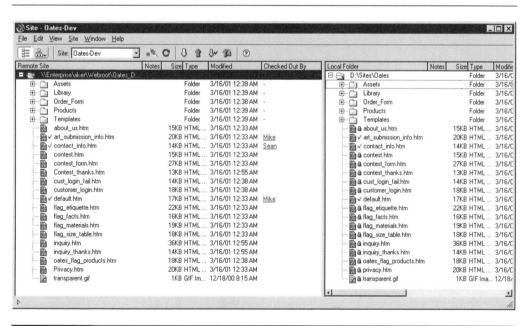

FIGURE 18-3   A Site window showing checked-out files

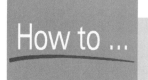

Inquire About a Checked-Out File

Sooner or later, you'll need to edit a file only to find it locked because someone else has it checked out. You need to contact that person to find out when the file will be available for editing. Dreamweaver can help. The program not only marks checked-out files in the file lists in the Site window, it also lists who has the file checked out in the Checked Out By column. (You may need to scroll the file list horizontally to see the Checked Out By column.) The name in the Checked Out By column works like a mailto link; click the name to open a preaddressed e-mail message. Type your message, and click Send to send the message to the person who checked out the file.

Set Up Check Out and Check In

The file Check Out/Check In feature is usually enabled at the time the site is first created. However, if you have a site that you want to change from a solo project to a group project, you can follow these steps:

1. Choose Site | Define Sites from the menu in the Site window. Dreamweaver opens the Define Sites dialog box.

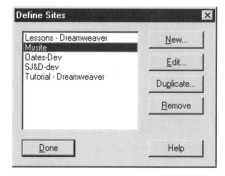

2. Select the site you want to alter from the list; then click the Edit button. Dreamweaver opens the Site Definition dialog box.

3. Select Remote Info in the Category list to display the options shown in Figure 18-4.

The Remote Info options vary depending on what type of remote connection you are using. Figure 18-4 shows the commonly used FTP connection version. Also, all the Check In/Out options don't appear until you enable that option.

4. Click the Enable File Check In and Check Out option and select/fill in the other Check In/Out options.

■ **Check Out Files When Opening**   Enable this option to have Dreamweaver automatically perform a file Check Out when you open a file for editing. This eliminates the need to manually check out a file before you edit it. The drawback is that Dreamweaver doesn't know whether you are opening a file to make significant editing changes or just opening the file to view its contents. It checks out the file in either case, thus making it unavailable to other team members.

■ **Check Out Name**   Enter the name you want to appear on the remote site labeling the files you check out.

■ **Email Address**   Enter your e-mail address, so team members can contact you to inquire about a checked-out file.

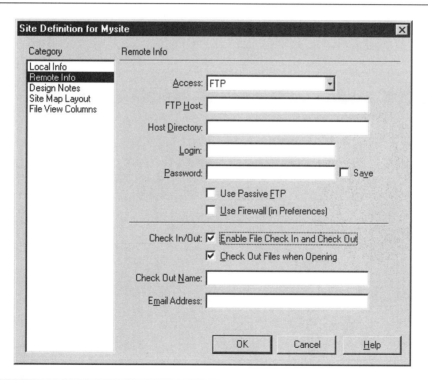

5. Click the OK button to close the Site Definition dialog box and return to the Define Sites dialog box.

6. In the Define Sites dialog box, click the Done button.

From here on in, all you have to do to check a file out or in is click on the Check Out or Check In button in the Site window.

Use Design Notes

Design Notes are Dreamweaver's equivalent of stick-on notes. They allow you to attach notes to various files so that you and others can know about any special requirements relating to those files. To add a Design Note to a file, follow these steps:

1. Right-click on the file in the Site window file list; then choose Design Notes from the pop-up menu that appears, or select a file and choose File | Design Notes. Dreamweaver opens the Design Notes dialog box, as shown in Figure 18-5.

2. Select an entry from the Status drop-down list.

3. Expand the note with comments, a date, or detailed information:

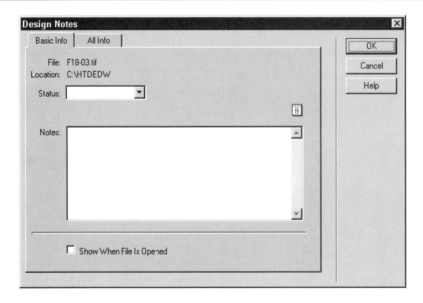

FIGURE 18-5 The Design Notes dialog box

- Type comments in the Notes text area.

- Click on the calendar icon to enter the current date.

- Check the Show When File Is Opened option to have Dreamweaver automatically display the Design Note when you open the file to which it is attached.

- To enter more detailed customized information, click on the All Info tab (see Figure 18-6). You can add a new field by clicking on the plus button, then entering the field's name in the Name text box. Follow this up by entering the corresponding value in the Value text area, then pressing the TAB key. You can add any number of new name/value pairs to your Design Note via this approach.

4. Click the OK button to close the Design Notes dialog box.

After you add a Design Note to a file, the Site window indicates its presence with a balloon symbol in the Notes column, as shown in Figure 18-7. You can open and edit the Design Note by simply double-clicking that symbol in the Site window.

NOTE   *Make sure to double-click the Design Note symbol, not the name of the file it is attached to.*

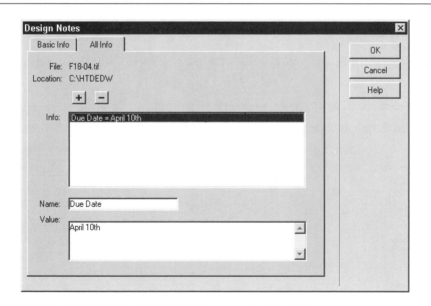

FIGURE 18-6   The All Info tab

18

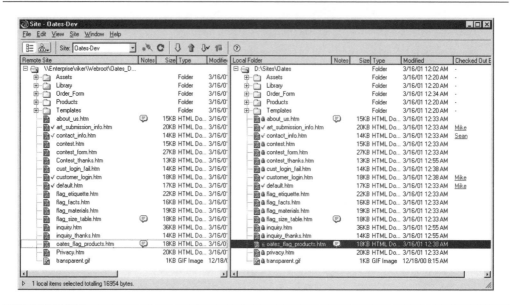

The Site window showing a Design Note attached to a file

To delete a Design Note, follow these steps:

1. Double-click the Design Note symbol in the Site window to open the note for editing.

2. Click the All Info tab.

3. Select each entry one at a time (unfortunately, you can't select all the entries as a group).

4. Click on the minus button in the Design Notes dialog box to remove the selected entry.

5. After you delete all the entries, click the OK button. Dreamweaver deletes the entire Design Note, and it no longer appears in the Site window.

Customize Dreamweaver

Chapter 19

Use Objects, Commands, and Other Time-Saving Features

How to...

- Use objects to insert page elements
- Use commands to automate tasks
- Use the Assets panel
- Use the History panel

Dreamweaver is carefully designed to make web page creation as speedy and easy as possible. Wherever possible, it provides quick and easy-to-use shortcuts through a series of panels that group related items and tasks for fast access and use. This chapter summarizes the Objects panel, the Command menu, the Assets panel, and the History panel, each of which makes its own unique contribution to Dreamweaver.

Use Objects to Insert Page Elements

The Objects panel is a series of seven "categories" of objects that you can click or drag and drop onto a Design view window to quickly add elements to your web pages. The categories are Character, Common, Forms, Frames, Head, Invisibles, and Special. The following sections describe which objects are available in each category.

Character

The Character category contains an assortment of special text characters, most of which are difficult to enter directly from the keyboard. (See Chapter 3 for more information on working with text.)

Button	Object	Description
	Line Break	Inserts a line break, the same as pressing SHIFT+ENTER
	Nonbreaking Space	Inserts a nonbreaking space, which looks like a normal space in text, but prevents the browser from breaking the line at the nonbreaking space
	Copyright	Inserts the copyright mark: ©

Button	Object	Description
®	Registered Trademark	Inserts the registered trademark, or circle R: ®
™	Trademark	Inserts the superscript "TM" trademark symbol: ™
£	Pound	Inserts the British pound symbol: £
¥	Yen	Inserts the Japanese yen symbol: ¥
€	Euro	Inserts the Eurodollar symbol: €
"	Left Quote	Inserts the double opening "curly" quote: "
"	Right Quote	Inserts the double closing "curly" quote: "
—	Em Dash	Inserts the long dash: —
國	Other Character	Opens the Other Character dialog box, where you can select other special characters to insert into your text

Common

The Common page of the Objects panel includes the most commonly used web page elements. When you click or drag most of these icons onto your page, Dreamweaver opens a dialog box prompting you for more information about the object.

Button	Object	Description
🖼	Image	Opens the Select Image Source dialog box. Locate and select the image file and click OK to insert the image into your page (see Chapter 4 for more information).
🖼	Rollover Image	Opens the Insert Rollover Image dialog box, where you can specify two images and a link for a simple rollover.
▦	Table	Opens the Insert Table dialog box. Specify the number of rows and columns to create an empty table (see Chapter 7 for more information).
📊	Tabular Data	Opens the Insert Tabular Data dialog box, where you can specify a data file and table settings to import tabular data into your document (see Chapter 7).

19

Button	Object	Description
	Layer	Drop on your document to insert a new layer.
	Navigation Bar	Opens the Insert Navigation Bar dialog box, where you can specify images and links for a multibutton navigation bar, complete with rollover effects.
	Horizontal Rule	Inserts a horizontal rule into your document (see Chapter 3).
	Email Link	Opens the Insert Email Link dialog box to insert a mailto: link (see Chapter 4).
	Date	Opens the Insert Date dialog box. Select the day, date, and time formats, and insert the results into your document (see Chapter 3).
	Server-Side Include	Opens the Select File dialog box, where you can select or specify server content files to include in your document.
	Fireworks HTML	Opens the Insert Fireworks HTML dialog box, where you can specify a Fireworks HTML file to insert into your document (see Chapter 12).
	Flash	Opens the Select File dialog box, where you can select a Flash file to insert into your document (see Chapter 13).
	Flash Button	Opens the Insert Flash Button dialog box, where you can define a flash button object and insert it into your document (see Chapter 13).
	Flash Text	Opens the Insert Flash Text dialog box, where you can define a Flash text object and insert it into your document (see Chapter 13).
	Shockwave	Opens the Select File dialog box, where you can select a Shockwave file to insert into your document (see Chapter 13).
	Generator	Opens the Insert Generator dialog box, where you can specify Flash files and set parameters to insert Generator content into your document.

Forms

The Forms category of the Objects panel includes icons for everything you need to make and populate an HTML form. Clicking one of these objects inserts the corresponding form or form element into your document immediately, without going through any dialog boxes or other prompts. But don't forget to adjust the settings for the form element in the Property Inspector panel. At the very least, you need to edit the default name for each form element. (See Chapter 9 for information on how to use these tools.)

Button	Object	Description
	Form	Inserts an empty form box into your document.
	Text Field	Inserts a generic text box into the form. Use the Property Inspector panel to modify the default settings to create a password box or a multiline text area.
	Button	Inserts a Submit button into the form. Use the Property Inspector panel to modify the Submit button or change it to a Reset button.
	Checkbox	Inserts a check box into the form.
	Radio Button	Inserts a single radio button into the form. Use the name setting in the Property Inspector panel to group multiple radio buttons into a selection group.
	List/Menu	Inserts a generic pop-up menu (selection list) into your document. You can use the Property Inspector panel to modify the settings to produce a scrolling list instead. Also define the list item in the Property Inspector panel.
	File Field	Inserts a file field into your document for file uploads.
	Image Field	Inserts an image into your form—primarily for creating graphical Submit buttons.
	Hidden Field	Inserts a hidden field into your form. Use hidden fields to pass information to the forms processor script.
	Jump Menu	Opens the Insert Jump Menu dialog box, where you can define a list of menu items and links for a pop-up menu of hyperlinks. When you click OK, Dreamweaver creates the Jump menu and even puts it into its own form.

Frames

The Frames page of the Objects panel contains icons for eight preconfigured framesets that enable you to quickly and easily create and modify frames and framesets. (See Chapter 8 for more information.)

Button	Object	Description
	Left Frame	Creates a frameset with an empty frame on the left and existing content on the right.
	Right Frame	Creates a frameset with an empty frame on the right and existing content on the left.

19

Button	Object	Description
	Top Frame	Creates a frameset with an empty frame on the top and existing content on the bottom.
	Bottom Frame	Creates a frameset with an empty frame on the bottom and existing content on the top.
	Left, Top-Left Corner, and Top Frames	Creates a frameset with empty frames on the left, top-left corner, and top and with existing content in the lower-right quadrant.
	Left and Nested Top Frame	Creates a frameset with an empty frame on the left and another empty frame nested above the existing content in the lower-right corner.
	Top and Nested Left Frame	Creates a frameset with an empty frame across the top and another empty frame nested to the left of the existing content in the lower-right corner.
	Split Frame Center	Creates a frameset arranged in a four-way split—existing content is in the lower-right frame.

Head

The Head category of the Objects panel includes icons for the elements that do not belong in the body of the web page.

Button	Object	Description
	Meta	Opens the Insert Meta dialog box, where you can define a meta tag and its content.
	Keywords	Opens the Insert Keywords dialog box, where you can type keywords for search engine indexing.
	Description	Opens the Insert Description dialog box, where you can type a page description (also for search engine indexing).
	Refresh	Opens the Insert Refresh dialog box, where you can set automatic refresh parameters for the page.
	Base	Opens the Insert Base dialog box, where you can set a base address for document-relative links in the page.
	Link	Opens the Insert Link dialog box, where you can define a link to another web document, such as a link to an external style sheet.

Invisibles

The Invisibles page in the Objects panel includes items that are not visible on a web page.

Button	Object	Description
	Named Anchor	Opens the Insert Named Anchor dialog box. Enter a name for the anchor, and click OK to insert an anchor (bookmark) into your page.
	Script	Opens the Insert Script dialog box. Select a script language from the Language box and then type (or paste) your script into the Content box. Then click OK to insert the script into your page.
	Comment	Opens the Insert Comment dialog box. Type a comment into the Comment box and click OK to insert that text into the source code for your page as an HTML comment.

Special

The icons on the Special page of the Objects panel are for adding Java applets, browser plug-ins, and ActiveX controls.

Button	Object	Description
	Applet	Opens the Select File dialog box, where you can select a Java applet file for insertion into your page.
	Plugin	Opens the Select File dialog box, where you can select a Netscape plug-in file for insertion into your page.
	ActiveX	Inserts a placeholder icon for an ActiveX control into your page. Use the Property Inspector panel to adjust settings for the control.

Use Commands to Automate Tasks

The Command menu is home to an assortment of special-purpose commands to automate various tasks in Dreamweaver. The default installation includes the following choices:

- **Start Recording**   Select this command to start recording a series of steps and commands for reuse. Choose Commands | Stop Recording to end the recorded sequence. The effect is similar to creating a custom command from a series of History steps (see the section later in this chapter, "Use the History Panel"), but it creates a single, temporary command without going through the History panel.

19

- **Play Recorded Command**   Executes the temporary command created by Start Recording.

- **Edit Command List**   Opens the Edit Command List dialog box, which lists the custom commands added to the Command menu (such as those you create by converting History steps to a command). Select a command and click Delete to remove it from the list. Click Close to close the dialog box.

- **Get More Commands**   Opens your default browser and links to the Macromedia Exchange web site, where you can download Dreamweaver extensions (see Appendix B).

- **Manage Extensions**   Opens the Macromedia Extension Manager utility program, which enables you to install and remove Dreamweaver Extensions (see Appendix B).

- **Apply Source Formatting**   Applies source code formatting (line lengths, indenting, color coding, and so on) to the code in Code view or Code Inspector per your preference settings. (See Chapter 5 for information on working with code and Chapter 20 for information on setting preferences.)

- **Clean Up HTML**   Opens the Clean Up HTML dialog box. Select the cleanup operations you want Dreamweaver to perform; then click OK. Dreamweaver scans the current document's source code and removes empty tags, combines nested `<font>` tags, and so on per your selections. (See Chapter 5 for more details.)

- **Clean Up Word HTML**   Opens the Clean Up Word HTML dialog box, which is the beginning of a special cleanup procedure designed to remove proprietary codes generated by Microsoft Word. (See Chapter 5 for more details.)

- **Add/Remove Netscape Resize Fix**   Adds (or removes) JavaScript code in the document header that fixes a problem with layer sizing in Netscape 4 browsers.

- **Optimize Image In Fireworks**   If you have Fireworks installed, select an image and then issue this command to launch Fireworks and load the image in the Fireworks' Export Preview for quick size and optimization adjustments and then reexport the image.

- **Create Web Photo Album**   Another command that requires Fireworks. This command creates a web photo album consisting of a page containing thumbnail images with links to larger versions of each image. Start with all the source photo files (they can be any bitmap file format Fireworks recognizes) in a separate folder; then choose the command. Dreamweaver opens the Create Web Photo Album dialog box. Enter the information in the dialog box and click OK. Dreamweaver launches Fireworks to create the thumbnail images and large images and plugs those into pages created by the command.

- **Set Color Scheme**   Opens the Set Color Scheme Command dialog box, where you can select one of several preset color schemes for the background, text, and link colors. (See Chapter 3 for details.)

■ **Format Table** Select a table; then choose this command to open the Format Table dialog box, where you can select one of several preset combinations of table and cell border, color, and alignment settings. (See Chapter 6 for details.)

■ **Sort Table** Select a table; then choose this command to open the Sort Table dialog box, where you can select sort criteria. Then click OK to sort the contents of the table. (See Chapter 6 for details.)

In addition to the default commands, you can create and install custom commands that you create from the History panel. (See the section, "Use the History Panel," later in this chapter.) You can also download and install custom commands as Dreamweaver extensions. See Appendix B for information on locating and installing extensions.

Use the Assets Panel

The Assets panel is a convenient central access point for the various page elements you use to build your web site. Dreamweaver keeps track of just about everything you place on your pages throughout your entire site and arranges it all into categories. The asset categories are as follows:

■ Images	■ Flash	■ Scripts
■ Colors	■ Shockwave	■ Templates
■ URLs	■ Movies	■ Library

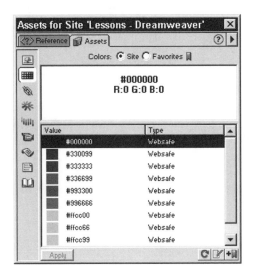

19

A column of icons located on the left side of the Assets panel gives you easy access to the various categories. To choose any category, simply click the icon that represents it. Dreamweaver displays the inventory of items in that category in the main list. A thumbnail preview of the selected item appears above the list.

To add a particular asset from any category to your page, either drag it from the Assets panel into your web page or select the item and then click the button on the bottom left of that panel. The button changes from "Insert" to "Apply" depending upon the type of asset. Images, for instance, are inserted, while colors are applied.

The asset list can become incorrect because of deletions. To refresh it, click the Refresh button (the first of the buttons on the lower-right side of the Assets panel).

To edit an asset, click the Edit button (the second of the buttons on the lower-right side of the Assets panel). Dreamweaver opens items such as templates and library items in a Dreamweaver Document window. For images and other external files, Dreamweaver launches the external editor associated with the file type to edit the item.

Use Favorite Assets

The problem with the Assets panel is that it lists every single asset in the entire site. This can be a huge amount of material to wade through. You may, for instance, use a color only once, yet it will show up in the Assets panel just as do colors you use a hundred times. The solution to this is to use Favorites to cull the list.

Favorites is a special subcategory containing only those assets you want to include. To make any asset into a favorite, simply select it; then click the Add to Favorites button (the third of the buttons on the lower-right side of the Assets panel). To view the Favorites for a selected category, click the Favorites radio button at the top of the Assets panel.

Group Assets in the Favorites

You can also create special groupings of Favorites. To do so, click the New Favorites Folder button (the first button at the bottom right of the Favorites listing in the Assets panel). Dreamweaver adds an "untitled" folder to the folder list. Type a new name for the folder. Once the folder is created, simply drag any favorites into it. Dreamweaver adds a + box next to the folder icon in the Assets panel. You can click the + to display the contents of the folder, or click again to hide the folder contents—just as you do when working with folders in the Site files list.

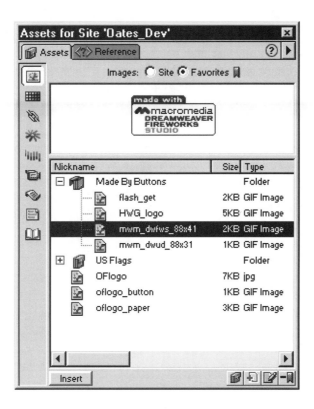

The Repeating Elements Library

The Library category, like the templates discussed in Chapter 10, is a special type of asset. Instead of being a simple listing of existing assets, such as the colors used in a site, library items are something that you must define before you can use. You create and control library items via the Assets panel, just as you do templates. Library items, in fact, have a great deal in common with templates. The main difference is in how they are used.

You create a template to lay out those portions of a web page that should remain the same from page to page, throughout the site. If you need to change the layout, you can change it in one place, the template file, and let Dreamweaver update all the template-based pages throughout the site.

A library item serves a similar purpose. You create a library item and save it in a separate file. Then you add the library item to several different web pages. You can update every instance of the library item on pages throughout your site by changing the main library item and letting Dreamweaver update the individual pages. In this sense, a library item is the same as a template. The difference is that library items are used for small entities, such as a corporate logo and address text, a copyright notice (the information that normally appears at the bottom of each page), a set of buttons that you use together, or anything else that could change from time to time and need to be updated across the site.

Create a Library Item

A library item can be most anything you place on a web page—a paragraph of text, a table and its contents, an image and some accompanying text. The only limitation is that you must be able to select the library item as a solid block without including any unwanted elements. So, for example, you could select the contents of a table cell and save it as a library item, and you could select an entire table and all its contents, but you couldn't select a table and exclude its contents from the library item.

To create a library item, start with existing elements on a web page that you want to reuse on other pages. You can start with elements of an existing page, or create a new page from scratch.

To transform anything on a web page into a library item, simply choose the Library category in the Assets panel; then select the page elements that you want to include in the library item and drag the selection into the bottom of the Assets panel. Dreamweaver creates a new library item called "Untitled" and highlights it. Type your own descriptive name and press ENTER. From here on in, any time you want to add that library item to a web page, all you have to do is to drag it from the Assets panel onto that page.

Edit and Update a Library Item

To edit a library item, select it and then click the Edit button at the bottom of the Assets panel. Dreamweaver opens the library item in its own Document window, and you can work with it just as any web page. Then, when you save your changes (choose File | Save), Dreamweaver automatically applies the changes to every instance of the library item throughout your site.

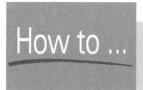

How to ...   Break the Connection to a Library Item

Dreamweaver prevents you from editing the contents of a library item on the individual web pages where it is used. As are the locked regions of a template, the library item is protected from local change in order to preserve the ability to make changes to the master library item in the Assets panel and have them automatically reflected in pages throughout the site. However, if you find it necessary to change the content of a library item on an individual page, you can do so by selecting the library item and then clicking the Detach From Original button in the Property Inspector panel. This action breaks the connection to the library item file and transforms the former library item content into plain, editable HTML code. However, Dreamweaver won't be able to perform automatic updates on the detached library items when it updates other pages.

Use the History Panel

The History panel provides a supercharged way to undo and redo steps you have taken. Instead of relying on the old-fashioned method of using the Edit menu (or its shortcut key equivalents), you are able to have in front of you at all times the complete listing of all your recent steps. More important, you are able to work with them in unique ways.

Suppose, for example, that you need to undo several steps. Instead of choosing Edit | Undo repeatedly, you can simply push the slider button on the left side of the History panel as far up the list as you want to go. Everything in your path will be undone. You can redo steps by reversing direction with the slider. Just slide up for undo, down for redo.

Perhaps the best feature of the History panel, however, is its ability to redo only selected steps. By choosing certain steps and leaving out others, you can create a customized set of steps. Simply press CTRL+click on the steps you want to redo; then click the Replay button (found in the lower-left corner of the History panel).

CAUTION   *Replaying selected steps from the History panel works only with redo, not with undo.*

Create Commands from History Steps

You can add a series of steps from the History panel to the Command menu for later replay as well. To do so, select the desired steps; then right-click one of them. Choose Save As Command from the pop-up menu that appears. Dreamweaver prompts you to give the new command a name. After you have done so, Dreamweaver adds the command to the Command menu. Then, to repeat the action, you can choose the new command just as you can any other command.

Copy History Steps from One Document to Another

If you simply want to replay a series of steps in another document on a one-shot basis and don't need to create a command for it, then the easiest solution is to simply copy and paste the steps. Select the desired steps just as if you were going to make a command out of them. However, when you right-click the steps, choose Copy Steps from the pop-up menu that appears. Next, open the document you want to play the steps in and choose Edit | Paste from the menu. The steps will be played in order.

Chapter 20

Customize Dreamweaver Settings

How to...

- Set Dreamweaver preferences
- Define site settings
- Add extensions

Macromedia engineered Dreamweaver to be a remarkably adaptive program. You can customize an impressive array of settings to adjust and tailor the software to your own working style and preferences. In most cases, the default settings provide a highly workable configuration. But as you become comfortable with the program, you can then begin to tinker with various settings, changing them to better conform to your individual needs.

Set Preferences

The master control center for Dreamweaver customization is the Preferences dialog box, shown in Figure 20-1. From this one dialog box, you can make changes to almost every aspect of the program. Dreamweaver packs a lot of settings into this dialog box. The secret to its versatility is the long list of categories on the left side. For each category, Dreamweaver displays a different set of preference settings in the body of the dialog box.

The basic process for changing any of the Dreamweaver preference settings is the same. The following steps summarize the procedure, and the subsequent sections describe the options in each category.

1. Choose Edit | Preferences to open the Preferences dialog box (see Figure 20-1).

2. Select a category from the Category list. Dreamweaver displays the settings for that category.

3. Adjust the settings as needed. Most of the settings are check boxes that you click to enable or disable an option. But there are also text boxes, pop-up menus, color pickers, and so on, depending on the settings available in each category.

4. Repeat steps 2 and 3 as needed to change settings in other categories.

5. Click OK to close the Preferences dialog box and record your settings. Most settings take effect immediately. A few settings will become effective the next time you start Dreamweaver. All settings apply to the Dreamweaver program as a whole, not just to individual sites or documents.

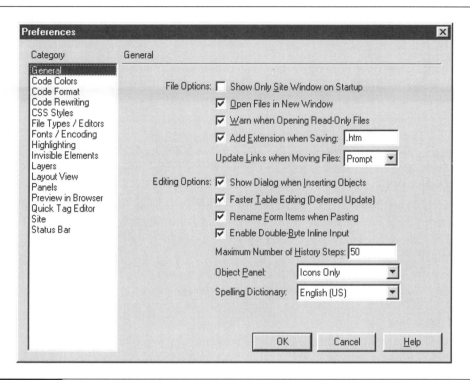

FIGURE 20-1   The Preferences dialog box

General

The General settings (refer to Figure 20-1) set some file-handling rules and editing preferences as well as telling Dreamweaver what to do every time you open the program.

■ **Show Only Site Window on Startup**   Shows the selected tool panels and the Site window when you open Dreamweaver but does not open a new document for you to work on.

■ **Open Files in New Window**   This is a PC-only option that gives you the ability to open multiple documents in separate windows. If this option is turned off, when you open a document, it replaces the one in the open Document window.

■ **Warn When Opening Read-Only Files**   Causes Dreamweaver to issue a warning when you open a file that is locked by the file Check Out option and gives you the ability to unlock the file before opening it.

- **Add Extension When Saving**   Tells Dreamweaver to automatically add an extension to the document name when you save the file. Specify the extension (usually .htm or .html) in the adjacent text box.

- **Update Links When Moving Files**   Tells Dreamweaver how to handle links that need to change to reflect new file locations when you move a file in your site. You can have Dreamweaver automatically update links, ignore the changes and not update the links, or ask you if you want to update the links.

- **Show Dialog When Inserting Objects**   Enabling this option causes Dreamweaver to open a dialog box to prompt you for information when you place an image, a table, or a Shockwave object onto the page. If you disable the option, you can go to the Property Inspector panel to make the changes.

- **Faster Table Editing (Deferred Update)**   When this feature is active, column width and row height are automatically adjusted only *after* you finish typing in a table cell. This eliminates the delay that often occurs as Dreamweaver tries to redraw the table as you type each character.

- **Rename Form Items When Pasting**   When this feature is enabled, Dreamweaver automatically updates a form element's name when you cut and paste it into your document. If deselected, the form element retains its original name (which could result in duplicate names).

- **Enable Double-Byte Inline Input**   Enable this setting to activate support for double-byte text (such as Japanese characters). You'll probably want to disable this option unless you plan on creating a multilingual site.

- **Maximum Number of History Steps**   Lets you assign how many actions Dreamweaver remembers. This controls the maximum capacity of the History panel and the number of steps you can undo with the Edit | Undo command. The more steps you assign, the more memory Dreamweaver has to use when running.

- **Object Panel**   Controls the appearance of the object icons in the Objects panel. You can choose icons, text, or both.

- **Spelling Dictionary**   Lets you choose which dictionary Dreamweaver uses for spell checking.

Code Colors

The Code Colors preferences (see Figure 20-2) enable you to control the appearance of the HTML source code in Code view and the Code Inspector panel. You can select background and text colors, and also pick distinctive colors for specific HTML tags using standard Dreamweaver color picker boxes. The color coding is just for your reference in Dreamweaver windows and doesn't affect the web document or the way it displays in a browser.

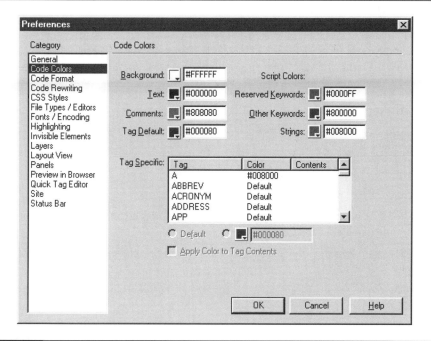

FIGURE 20-2   Code Colors category

You can set colors to control the way the following items appear in the Code view window and the Code Inspector panel.

- **Background**   Assigns a background color to the Code view window and the Code Inspector panel.
- **Text**   Sets the default text color.
- **Comments**   Sets a color for HTML Comment tags.
- **Tag Default**   Sets the color for all tags except the Comment tags.
- **Reserved Keywords**   Sets the color for reserved keywords in scripts.
- **Other Keywords**   Sets the color of other script keywords.
- **Strings**   Sets the color for any strings in scripts.
- **Tag Specific**   This scrolling list lets you select individual HTML tags and specify colors that override the default tag color. Just click a tag in the list and then use the color picker below the list to pick the color.

20

Code Format

The Code Format preferences (see Figure 20-3) control formatting such as indenting and capitalization in the Code view window and the Code Inspector panel. These preferences apply to code generated in Dreamweaver. You can also apply the same preferences to imported code by choosing the Commands | Apply Source Formatting command.

- **Indent**   Turns automatic code indenting on or off. Select spaces or tabs for indenting.
- **Table Rows and Columns**   Indents code for table rows and columns.
- **Frames and Framesets**   Indents code for frames and framesets.
- **Indent Size**   Sets the number of spaces for indents.
- **Tab Size**   Sets the size of tabs for tab indents.
- **Automatic Wrapping**   Activates automatic line wrapping and sets the maximum number of characters in a line.
- **Line Breaks**   Sets the line break character in code. Select a carriage return, line feed, or both.
- **Case for Tags**   Sets the capitalization for HTML tags—all lowercase or all uppercase.

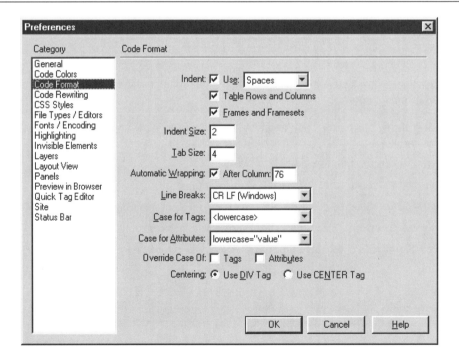

Code Format category

NOTE   *Many people like to use uppercase for HTML tags and attributes to make those elements stand out in the HTML source code, and web browsers are generally tolerant of such capitalization schemes in HTML code. However, the XML standard is stricter and requires lowercase text for tags and attributes. With XML becoming increasingly important to web sites, it's a good idea to stick with lowercase tags and attributes for compatibility with this emerging standard.*

- **Case for Attributes**   Sets the capitalization for attribute names in HTML tags— all lowercase or all uppercase.
- **Override Case Of**   Tells Dreamweaver whether to override the case of existing HTML tags and attributes in the source code.
- **Centering**   Select the tag to use for centering objects on the page.

Code Rewriting

The Code Rewriting preferences (see Figure 20-4) let you set how Dreamweaver reformats HTML documents when you open them in the program. Depending on the settings you select here, you can instruct Dreamweaver to automatically fix a variety of common code problems or take a hands-off approach and respect the code that was generated in other programs and by programmers working in text-based HTML editors.

Here's a rundown of the options in the Code Rewriting category.

- **Fix Invalidly Nested and Unclosed Tags**   Rewrites overlapping tags to achieve proper nesting and supplies missing closing quotation marks and angle brackets.
- **Remove Extra Closing Tags**   Deletes closing tags that have no matching opening tags.
- **Warn When Fixing or Removing Tags**   Causes Dreamweaver to display a warning before altering tags.
- **Never Rewrite Code**   Check this option to disable all code rewriting for any files with the extensions listed in the adjacent text box.
- **Encode Special Characters in URLs Using %**   Use the percent character to mark special characters in URLs so that they are not misinterpreted as HTML code.
- **Encode <, >, &, and " in Attribute Values Using %**   Use the percent character to mark special characters in attribute values so that they are not misinterpreted as HTML code.

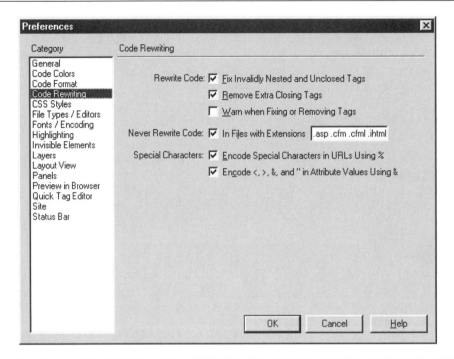

FIGURE 20-4   The Code Rewriting preferences

CSS Styles

The CSS Styles preferences set (see Figure 20-5) gives you control over how Dreamweaver writes the code for CSS styles. If you are working with Cascading Style Sheets, you must determine whether you want to have Dreamweaver write the code using alternative "shorthand" attributes or write out the full code. Many programmers find shorthand easier to work with, but it's not as widely supported by web browsers as is full code.

You can instruct Dreamweaver to use shorthand for Font, Background, Margin and Padding, Border and Border Width, and List Style attributes when creating new CSS styles. Then, when you are editing existing CSS styles, you can instruct Dreamweaver to use the same shorthand settings or use shorthand only if the existing styles use shorthand. If you're not familiar with shorthand attributes and don't have a reason for using them, just leave the default settings alone.

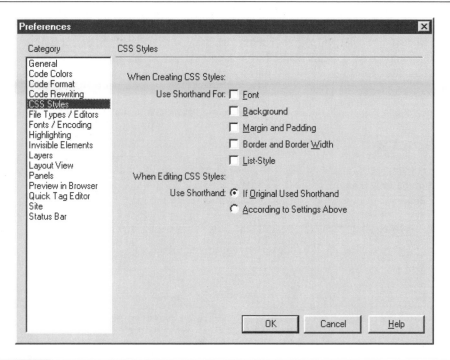

FIGURE 20-5   The CSS Styles category

File Types/Editors

The File Types/Editors preferences window (see Figure 20-6) gives you the ability to tell Dreamweaver what program to launch when you need to edit a specific file type. You can set the program used to edit code and text (.js, .txt, .asa), as well as your favorite image editor (Fireworks, of course) and editors for the various multimedia file types. You do this by linking a file extension to the viewer/editor you want to use for that file type. Here's how:

1. Open the Preferences dialog box (choose Edit | Preferences) and select File Types/Editors from the Category list.

2. Select a file extension in the Extensions list box. If the file extension you want isn't in the Extensions list, click the plus (+) button above the Extensions list to add a blank line to the list; then type in the new file extension. The default editor for the selected file type appears in the Editors list. In some cases, more than one program may be listed.

20

3. Select the program you want to use as the main editor and click the Make Primary button to make it the primary editor for the file type. If the desired editor doesn't appear in the Editors list, click the plus sign (+) above the Editors list to open the Select External Editor dialog box. Use this dialog box to locate and select the application to associate with the file extension; then click the Open button to close the dialog box and add the program to the Editors list.

4. Repeat steps 2 and 3 as necessary to define your preferred editors for other file types.

Fonts/Encoding

The Fonts/Encoding preferences (see Figure 20-7) determine the default encoding for the pages you create and the fonts Dreamweaver uses to display your documents in Design view. You can adjust the following settings:

- **Default Encoding**   Sets the default encoding for new pages you create
- **Font Settings**   Specify the font set Dreamweaver uses for the encoding selected in the Default Encoding list

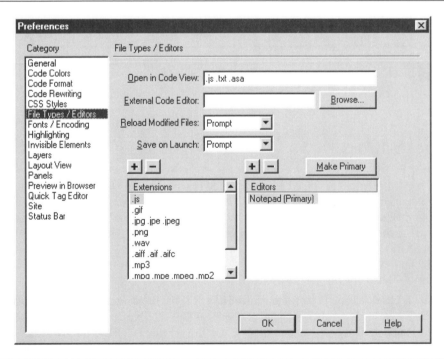

FIGURE 20-6   The File Types/Editors category

■ **Proportional Font/Size**   Sets the font face and size Dreamweaver uses
to display normal text in Design view

■ **Fixed Font/Size**   Sets the font face and size Dreamweaver uses to display
fixed-width (monospaced) text in Design view

■ **Code Inspector/Size**   Sets the font face and size Dreamweaver uses in Code
view and the Code Inspector panel

Highlighting

The Highlighting preferences (see Figure 20-8) tell Dreamweaver how to display highlighted
elements such as template regions when you're working in Design view. You can specify
colors for Editable Regions and Locked Regions of templates, Library Items, and Third-Party
Tags. You can select a color using the color picker for each option or type a hexadecimal value
in the text box. Check or clear the Show check box to control whether Dreamweaver displays
the associated highlight.

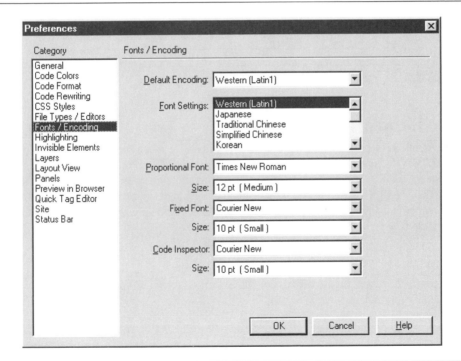

FIGURE 20-7   The Fonts/Encoding category

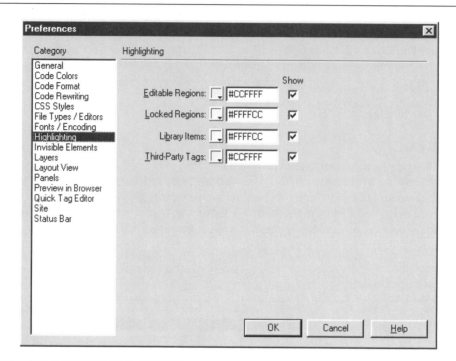

FIGURE 20-8   The Highlighting preferences

Invisible Elements

Invisible elements are page elements that are normally invisible when the page is viewed in a web browser, but Dreamweaver can display icons in Design view to represent those elements so you can select and manipulate them. You toggle the Invisible Elements display on and off by choosing the View | Visual Aids | Invisible Elements command. The options in the Invisible Elements category (see Figure 20-9) determine which elements appear when the Invisible Elements display is enabled.

Layers

The Layers preferences (see Figure 20-10) enable you to set the default parameters for new layers you add to your document.

- **Tag**   Specify the type of HTML tag to use when creating layers. The default tag is `<div>`, but you can select `<span>`, `<layer>`, or `<ilayer>`. The last two tags function only in Netscape (see sidebar on Layer compatibility in Chapter 15).

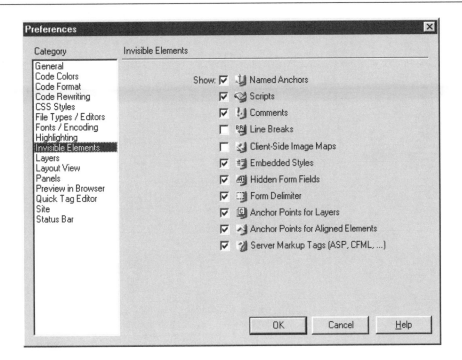

FIGURE 20-9   The Invisible Elements preferences

- ■ **Visibility**   Specify the initial visibility state of a layer. The options are default, inherit, visible, and hidden.

- ■ **Width**   Specify the layer width. The default size is 200 pixels.

- ■ **Height**   Specify the layer height. The default size is 115 pixels.

- ■ **Background Color**   Specify a background color for the layer by selecting from the pop-up menu of colors. The default is no color (transparent).

- ■ **Background Image**   Specify a background image for the layer by clicking the Browser button and locating an image.

- ■ **Nesting**   When checked, automatically nests one layer into another when that layer is inserted over another layer. Default is unchecked.

- ■ **Netscape 4 Compatibility**   When checked, provides a fix for a known bug in Netscape 4 that causes problems when the user resizes the browser window. Default is checked.

20

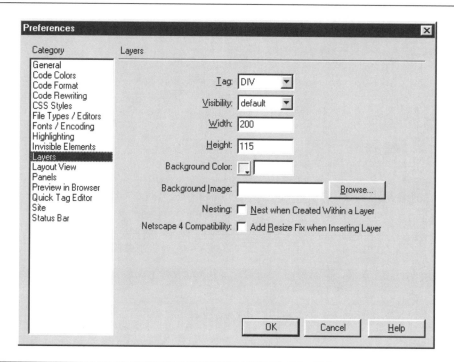

FIGURE 20-10 Layers preferences

Layout View

The Layout View preferences (see Figure 20-11) allow you to assign parameters for spacer images and other settings relating to Layout Tables and Layout Cells. Here is what each of these selections does:

- **Autoinsert Spacers**   Tell Dreamweaver to automatically add a spacer image to each column if a column in the table is set to Autostretch. This ensures that columns maintain their minimum width, even when they are empty.

- **Spacer Image**   Defines a specific image file to use as a spacer for the selected site. You can either have Dreamweaver create its own spacer image or you can specify another spacer image by typing the pathname for the image in the Image File box or by clicking the Browse button and using the dialog box that appears to locate and select the image file.

- **Cell Outline**   Sets the color for the border of a layout cell.

- **Cell Highlight** Sets the color for the border of a layout cell when the pointer is pointing to that cell.
- **Table Outline** Sets the color for the border around a layout table.
- **Table Background** Sets the background color for the empty placeholder cells in a layout table.

Panels

The Panels category (see Figure 20-12) is where you control which panels always remain in front of the Document window when they overlap and which panels are represented in the Launcher in the Design view status bar. Some users prefer panels to stay on top of the Dreamweaver Document window when the windows overlap so that the panel contents are accessible.

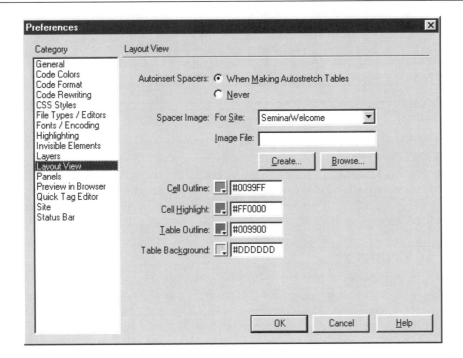

FIGURE 20-11   Layout View preferences

20

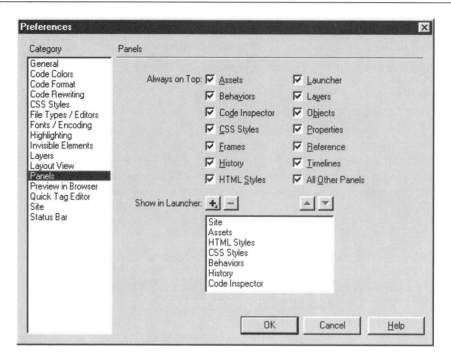

FIGURE 20-12 The Panels preferences

Click the check box beside a panel name to ensure that it stays on top of the Document window. The Show in Launcher list shows all the panels that appear in the Launcher. To add a panel to the Launcher, click the plus (+) button and choose the panel from the menu that appears. To remove a panel from the Launcher, select the panel in the Show in Launcher list and then click the minus (–) button.

Preview in Browser

The Preview in Browser category (see Figure 20-13) enables you to build a list of web browsers that are available to preview your Dreamweaver documents. Since browsers display information differently, it's important to preview your web documents in several different browsers. When you installed Dreamweaver, the installation program automatically configured Dreamweaver to

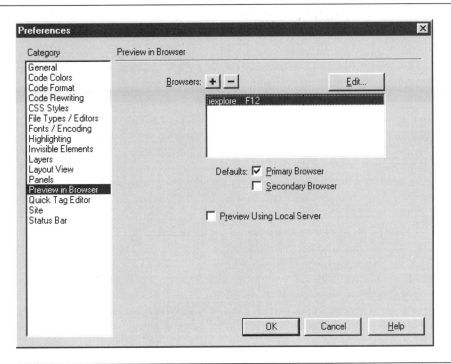

FIGURE 20-13   The Preview in Browser preferences

use your default browser for preview. You need to tell Dreamweaver where to find any other browsers you have installed. Here's how:

1. Select Preview in Browser from the Category list in the Preferences dialog box.

2. Click the plus (+) button to open the Add Browser dialog box.

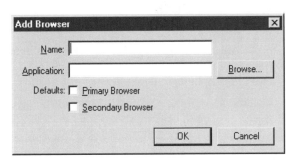

20

3. Type a name for the browser in the Name box. This is the name that appears on the Dreamweaver menus.

4. Click the Browser button to open the Select Browser dialog box. Locate and select the browser's executable file in the dialog box; then click the Open button to close the Select Browser dialog box and enter the path and filename in the Application box in the Add Browser dialog box.

5. Click OK to close the Add Browser dialog box and add the new browser to the Browsers list back in the Preview in Browser category of the Preferences dialog box.

6. Repeat steps 2–5 to add other browsers to the list.

7. Select a browser from the Browsers list and click the Primary Browser check box to make that browser the one Dreamweaver launches when you press F12 to preview your web document.

8. Select a different browser from the Browsers list and click the Secondary Browser check box to make that browser the one Dreamweaver launches when you press CTRL+F12 to preview your web document.

NOTE   *You can specify only two browsers to be linked to keyboard shortcuts for previewing your web documents. But you can access any of the other browsers in the list by choosing File | Preview in Browser |* browser name.

Quick Tag Editor

The Quick Tag Editor preferences (see Figure 20-14) let you determine whether changes you make while working in the Quick Tag Editor are immediately applied to the document or are applied when you close the Quick Tag Editor. You can also enable hints (a pop-up menu of tags or attributes) to appear as you are typing and specify a delay before they appear.

Site

The Site category (see Figure 20-15) is where you control the configuration of the Site window as well as some important FTP connection settings that control access to the remote server. Here's a rundown of the Site category options:

■ **Always Show**   Lets you select whether the Local Folder or the Remote Site is the primary file list and on which side of the Site window it appears. By default, the Local Folder file list is shown in the right pane.

■ **Dependent Files**   Determines whether a prompt appears when you transfer files that have dependent files such as images, external style sheets, and animations.

■ **FTP Connection**   Tells Dreamweaver to disconnect from an FTP site after the set number of minutes has elapsed without any activity.

■ **FTP Time Out**   Lets you set the amount of time that Dreamweaver will continue to try to connect to an FTP site. If no response is received from that site in the set amount of time, Dreamweaver stops trying to connect.

■ **Firewall Host**   Specifies the address of the proxy server if you have a firewall installed.

■ **Firewall Port**   Specifies the port on the firewall to use for the FTP connection to a remote server.

■ **Put Options**   Tells Dreamweaver to automatically save unsaved files before transferring them.

■ **Define Sites**   Opens the Define Sites dialog box, where you can edit an existing site or create a new site.

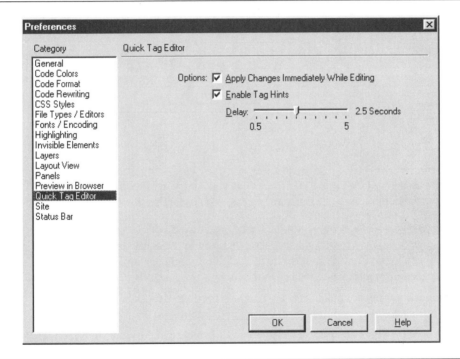

FIGURE 20-14   The Quick Tag Editor preferences

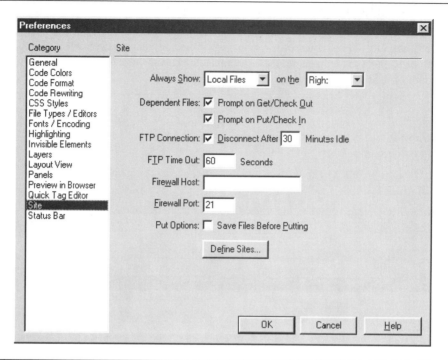

FIGURE 20-15 The Site preferences

Status Bar

The Status Bar category (see Figure 20-16) enables you configure options for the status bar that appears at the bottom of the Document window. You can adjust the following settings:

- **Window Sizes** Create and edit the list of preset window sizes that appear in the Window Size Selector in the status bar. Click any of the entries in the Window Sizes list to edit them. Click a blank space at the bottom of the list and enter a width, height, and description to add a new entry to the list.

- **Connection Speed** Selects the connection speed Dreamweaver uses to calculate the estimated download time that appears in the status bar.

- **Launcher** When enabled, displays the mini-launcher in the status bar.

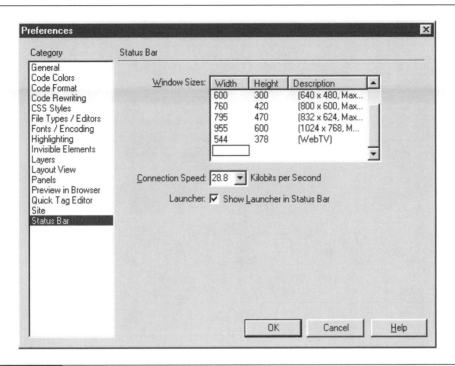

FIGURE 20-16   Status Bar preferences

Define Site Settings

Another area of Dreamweaver where you can customize the program significantly is in the site definition. Choose Site | Define Sites to open the Define Sites dialog box; then select a site and click the Edit button to open the Site Definition dialog box (see Figure 20-17). As does the Preferences dialog box, the Site Definition dialog box has a Category list on the left side. Select a category to display the options for that category in the rest of the dialog box. You can customize the site settings on a site-by-site basis.

Chapter 2 covers the critical Local Info and Remote Info categories, where you actually set up the locations of the local and remote sites. Chapter 18 covers the Design Notes category.

20

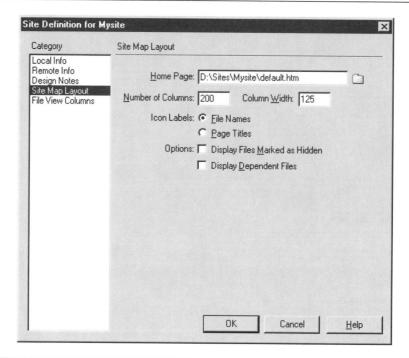

FIGURE 20-17   The Site Definition dialog box showing the Site Map Layout options

The Site Map Layout category offers the following options for controlling the display of the Site Map in the Site window:

- **Home Page**   Shows the page specified as the site's home page, which is the root of the Site Map. You can set the home page here if you want, but you'll usually select the home page in the Site window.

- **Number of Columns**   Sets the number of page icons per row in the Site Map and the width of each column (page icon width) in pixels.

- **Icon Labels**   Select filenames or page titles to label page icons in the Site Map.

- **Options**   Select what files to display in the Site Map. You can display hidden files and/or dependent files in addition to regular web pages.

The File View Columns category (see Figure 20-18) enables you to customize the file list display by adding or editing column headings in the file list. The list box at the top of the dialog

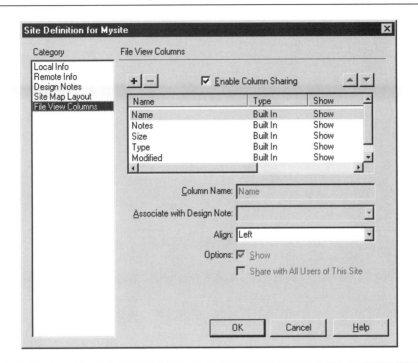

FIGURE 20-18 File View Columns options

box displays the column headings. Select a heading and adjust the settings in the option boxes below the list to change the way Dreamweaver displays that heading in the Site window file lists. You can rearrange the column order by selecting a column and clicking the up and down arrow buttons above the list to change the list order.

Add Extensions

Dreamweaver is an open-architecture program, which means that users can create extensions that expand the program's capabilities with new objects, behaviors, and commands that add features or automate common tasks. Macromedia has created numerous extensions for Dreamweaver, and so have many Dreamweaver users and developers. See Appendix B for information on how to find and install Dreamweaver extensions.

Part VIII

Appendixes

Appendix A

Dreamweaver, Fireworks, and Companion Programs

How to...

■ Install Dreamweaver 4, Fireworks 4, and the Dreamweaver/Fireworks Studio

■ Locate and install HomeSite

■ Locate the other Macromedia products on the CD

■ Locate other programs on the CD and elsewhere

From the user's perspective, the procedure for installing Dreamweaver 4, Fireworks 4, and the Dreamweaver 4/Fireworks 4 Studio is simple and straightforward. However, for the sake of completeness, this appendix includes brief instructions to get you started. But there's a lot more on the Dreamweaver 4 and the Dreamweaver 4/Fireworks 4 Studio CDs than just the core program. Macromedia packs each CD with sample versions of several other Macromedia programs, plus an assortment of companion programs and other resources from other vendors. This appendix serves as an overview of those resources (and a few others) to help you identify the ones you might want to try.

Install the Main Software

Installing modern computer programs is a complicated procedure. Fortunately, you don't have to do it manually; an installer program handles all the details for you. All you need to do is to launch the correct installer to install the program of your choice.

■ To install the Dreamweaver 4/Fireworks 4 Studio, run the installer program located at \Studio 4 Installer.exe on the Studio CD.

■ To install Dreamweaver 4, run the installer program located at \Dreamweaver 4\ Dreamweaver 4 Installer.exe on the Studio CD or \Dreamweaver 4 Installer.exe on the Dreamweaver CD.

■ To install Fireworks 4, run the installer program located at \Fireworks 4\Fireworks 4 Installer.exe on the Studio CD.

It's always a good idea to shut down any other programs that are running on your system before starting to install Dreamweaver or any other software. After you start the installer program, simply follow the instructions onscreen to complete the installation.

 The installer program locations specified above are for the Dreamweaver 4/Fireworks 4 Studio CD. If you have a stand-alone Dreamweaver 4 program, the Studio 4 installer won't be available, and you get a trial version of Fireworks instead of the full version.

Install HomeSite or BBEdit

For Windows users, Macromedia supplies a full commercial version of HomeSite 4.5, the text-based HTML editor from Allaire. HomeSite provides programmers with the kind of complete control over their code possible only in a text-based HTML editor. Dreamweaver and HomeSite complement each other nicely, enabling you to work on pages visually in the/Dreamweaver, launch HomeSite to work on the source code, and then return to Dreamweaver, all with a minimum of fuss and bother. You can find HomeSite in the \Dreamweaver 4\HomeSite 4.5 folder on the Studio CD or the \HomeSite 4.5 folder on the Dreamweaver CD. For updates and information about HomeSite and other Allaire products, such as ColdFusion, check out **http://www.allaire.com**.

Macintosh users get a trial version of BBEdit instead of HomeSite. The Macintosh version of Dreamweaver features special integration with BBEdit that allows you to switch back and forth between the two programs to take advantage of the visual editing in Dreamweaver and the HTML/text editing in BBEdit. You can install the trial version of BBEdit from the Dreamweaver Macintosh CD, or download it from **http://www.bbedit.com**.

Other Macromedia Programs

Macromedia includes trial versions of many of the other Macromedia consumer products on the Dreamweaver CD.

- ■ **Fireworks**   An image editing and creation tool optimized for creating web graphics. If you didn't get the Dreamweaver 4/Fireworks 4 Studio, a trial version of Fireworks is on the Dreamweaver CD.

- ■ **Authorware**   An authoring tool for creating online learning applications that include multimedia elements as well as student tracking features. Authorware is located in the \Other Macromedia Software\Authorware 5.2 folder on the CD.

- ■ **Director**   An authoring tool for creating Shockwave multimedia content for Web and CD applications. Director enables you to integrate text, graphics, sound, animation, and video to create interactive multimedia content. The Director trial is located in the \Other Macromedia Software\Director 8 folder on the CD.

- ■ **Dreamweaver UltraDev**   The big brother to Dreamweaver. UltraDev includes the full Dreamweaver feature set plus added features that enable you to develop database-driven web sites and ASP, JSP, and ColdFusion web applications. The UltraDev trial is located in the \Other Macromedia Software\Dreamweaver UltraDev 4 folder on the CD.

- ■ **Flash 5**   Creates vector-based animations for high-speed, interactive web sites. You can find the trial version of Flash 5 in the \Other Macromedia Software\Flash 5 folder on the CD.

- **Freehand 9**   A graphic artist's drawing tool for creating vector illustrations for use in desktop publishing and web use via Flash 5. The trial version of Freehand is located in the \Other Macromedia Software\Freehand 9 folder on the CD.

- **Generator 2 Developer Edition**   A tool for building automatically updating web sites in which data-driven graphics automatically change to reflect changes in content. The trial version of Generator is located in the \Other Macromedia Software\Generator 2 Developer Edition folder on the CD.

Freebies

In addition to the trial versions of some of Macromedia's commercial software, the CD also includes convenience copies of some player plug-ins and graphics that Macromedia makes available for free.

- **Shockwave Player**   The browser plug-in required to play Shockwave movies is located in the \Other Macromedia Software\Shockwave Player folder on the CD.

- **Flash Player**   The browser plug-in required to play Flash content is located in the \Other Macromedia Software\Flash Player folder on the CD.

- **Made with Macromedia**   Images of buttons promoting Macromedia software are available in the \Other Macromedia Software\Made with Macromedia\Images folder on the CD.

Other Programs You Might Need

Macromedia didn't hog the entire Dreamweaver CD for shameless self-promotion. In addition to the external text editor, they include a few third-party programs.

Browsers

No doubt, you have your favorite web browser already installed. But if you plan to develop web sites for others to visit, you need to have other browsers available for preview and testing. So, Macromedia included copies of the two major browsers on Dreamweaver CD.

- **Internet Explorer 5.5**   Located in the \Browsers\Internet Explorer 5.5 folder on the CD.

- **Netscape Communicator 4.75**   Located in the \Browsers\Communicator 4.75 folder on the CD.

- **Opera 5.5**   Not supplied on the Dreamweaver CD but a very useful alternative to the "big two" browsers. You can download a copy from **http://www.opera.com**.

NOTE   *You may also want to download copies of the newer versions of Internet Explorer and Netscape Navigator.*

A

MGI PhotoVista

MGI Software provides some interesting imaging technology that enables you to create 360-degree panoramas that require no plug-ins to view in a web browser. Other MGI software creates high-resolution images that the site visitor can zoom to see more detail. Trial versions of the software, as well as Dreamweaver extensions to facilitate implementation of the enhanced image-viewing features, are supplied on the Dreamweaver CD.

- **PhotoVista 2.0**   Creates 360-degree panoramas. It's located in the \Dreamweaver 4\ More Extensions\MGI Software\PhotoVista 2.0 folder on the Studio CD or the \More Extensions\MGI Software\PhotoVista 2.0 folder on the Dreamweaver CD.

- **Zoom Objects**   Provides a collection of Dreamweaver extensions for use with PhotoVista panoramas and MGI zoom images. They are located in the \Dreamweaver 4\ More Extensions\MGI Software\Zoom Objects folder on the Studio CD or the \More Extensions\MGI Software\Zoom Objects folder on the Dreamweaver CD.

- **Zoom Server 3.5**   Delivers zoomable high-resolution images to web visitors. The trial software is located in the \Dreamweaver 4\More Extensions\MGI Software\Zoom Server 3.5 Trial folder on the Studio CD or the \More Extensions\MGI Software\Zoom Server 3.5 Trial folder on the Dreamweaver CD.

Appendix B

Install and Use Dreamweaver Extensions

How to…

- Locate extensions
- Install extensions
- Identify some popular extensions

Extensions are objects, commands, behaviors, and so on that have been created by Macromedia and by other Dreamweaver users to automate certain tasks. There is a lively exchange of these extensions on the Macromedia site and elsewhere. This appendix lists examples of some of the most popular extensions and gives instructions on how to install and use extensions to enhance Dreamweaver.

Where to Find Extensions

Macromedia set aside a special section of its web site, called *Macromedia Exchange*, as a clearinghouse where Dreamweaver users can go to find and download extensions. At the Macromedia Exchange, you can view lists of extensions for Dreamweaver and other Macromedia programs, check out descriptions of the extensions, and download extensions that you want to try.

The Dreamweaver section of the Macromedia Exchange is located at **http://www.macromedia .com/exchange/dreamweaver/** (see Figure B-1). You can also go to the Macromedia Exchange from within Dreamweaver by choosing Commands | Get More Commands or Help | Dreamweaver Exchange. If you're working in the Behaviors panel, clicking the plus (+) button and choosing Get More Behaviors from the menu that appears has the same effect.

At the Macromedia Exchange web site, you can browse through the ever-expanding list of available extensions for Dreamweaver, sorted into various categories. Click an extension name to drill down to the detail page with a description of the extension and its function. Then, with a click of your mouse, you can download the extension file and save it in a convenient location on your system. (If you haven't already registered at the Macromedia web site, you'll need to do so before downloading extensions.)

Install Extensions with the Extension Manager

Installing extensions in previous versions of Dreamweaver could be a chore, but Dreamweaver 4 includes a new utility—*Extension Manager*—that automates the process of installing extensions. Macromedia Extension Manager works with extension package files (.mxp) that contain all the files you need to install and use the extension. All the extensions on the Macromedia Exchange web site are in MXP format for use with the Extension Manager utility.

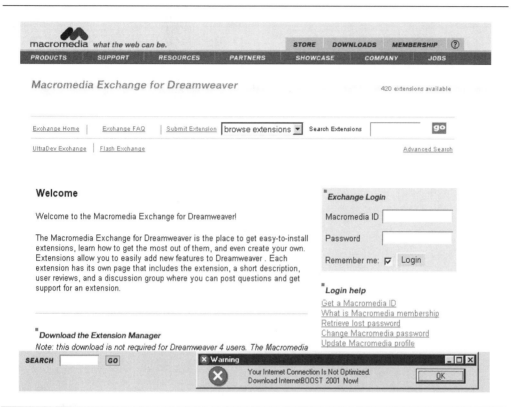

FIGURE B-1   Macromedia Exchange for Dreamweaver on the Web

NOTE   *Depending on your browser, you may have the option of opening the extension package file from its web location without downloading it first. If you choose to go this route, the Extension Manager application opens automatically to install the extension. Although this direct-install method works, I can't recommend it unless you enjoy an exceptionally fast and reliable Internet connection. Even then, you sacrifice the security of having the .mxp file available to reinstall.*

After you download an extension, follow these steps to install it with Extension Manager:

1. Launch the Extension Manager utility. (Choose Start | Programs | Macromedia Extension Manager | Macromedia Extension Manager.) The Macromedia Extension Manager window opens.

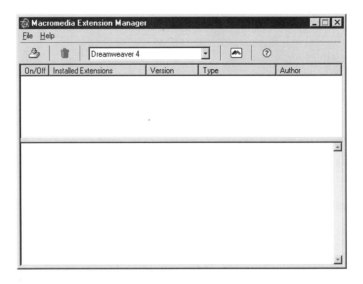

2. Select Dreamweaver 4 from the list box in the Extension Manager toolbar.

3. Choose File | Install Extension, or click the Install New Extension button in the toolbar. The Select Extension to Install dialog box appears.

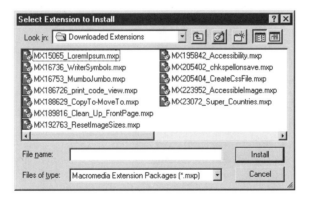

4. Locate and select the MXP extension file you want to install.

5. Click Install to close the Select Extension to Install dialog box and start the installation process. The Extension Manager may display one or more message boxes asking you to accept license terms and/or confirm file replacements. Macromedia Extension Manager displays a message after it successfully installs the extension and adds the extension to the list in the Extension Manager window.

NOTE *Depending on the extension, you may need to shut down and then restart Dreamweaver to make the extension functional.*

B

When you select an extension in the Installed Extensions list in the Extension Manager window a description of the extension appears in the bottom half of the window. The description text for some extensions is pretty skimpy, but you will almost always see a short description of the extension and information on where to find it in Dreamweaver (on the Command menu, in the Objects panel, or whatever). Some extension authors display some helpful instructions on how to use the extension in this space.

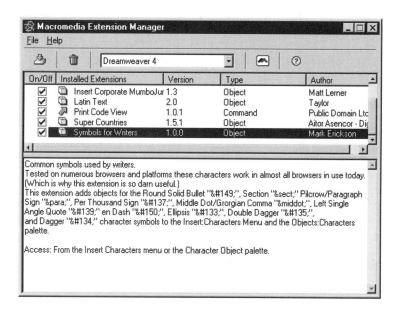

 If you decide that you want to remove an extension from Dreamweaver, simply select the extension name in the Macromedia Extension Manager window and click the Remove Extension button in the toolbar. Click Yes to confirm the action. Extension Manager reports its success in another message box.

 You can disable an extension without removing it by simply clicking the On/Off check box beside the extension name in the Macromedia Extension Manager window. Click the check box again to reenable the extension.

List of Popular Extensions

There are a lot of extensions available on the Macromedia Exchange web site (more than 400 at the time of this writing). I can't begin to list them all on these pages. The following list is a rather capricious and random sampling of what's available. It's not intended as an endorsement or recommendation of specific extensions (although I have used many of the extensions on the list). Instead, this list is intended to give you an idea of the variety of extensions that are available and to encourage you to check the Macromedia Exchange for extensions that might make your work with Dreamweaver a little faster and/or easier.

Accessible Image Object Extension   This extension replaces the standard Insert Image object on the Objects panel. Using the Accessible Image opens a dialog box that prompts for Alt text and a longdesc URL, which are both used by assistive devices such as screen readers.

Add To Favorites Extension   A behavior that enables visitors to automatically add your page to their Internet Explorer Favorites list.

Additional Flash Button Styles Extension   Adds new button styles to the Insert Flash Button dialog box.

Alternate Table Rows Extension   Formats a table with rows of alternating colors.

Auto Backup Extension   Creates an automatic backup copy of your current document when you open or save the document.

Banner Image Builder Extension   Creates a series of images that change automatically at a preset interval.

Button Rollover Extension   Creates and applies CSS styles to convert normal text links into buttons, complete with rollover effects.

Calculate Form Extension   A behavior that enables you to perform calculations using the contents of form fields and display the results.

Check Page for Accessibility Extension   Evaluates web pages for conditions that would cause problems for site visitors using assistive devices such as screen readers. The extension generates a report that specifies the location of any problems found and includes reminders of the W3C Accessibility guidelines for web page design.

Check Spelling on Save Extension   Automatically runs the spell checker before saving your document.

Clean Up FrontPage HTML Extension   Works like the Clean Up Word HTML command to remove proprietary tags from an HTML file generated by FrontPage.

Close Child Window Extension   Creates a link, button, or image that the visitor can click to close a pop-up child browser window.

Context Builder Extension   Facilitates adding syndicated media content from Context Media to your web sites.

Copy To, Move To Folder Extension   A command that appears on the right-click context menu in the Site window to facilitate copying or moving multiple selected files within the local folder.

Create CSS Files from Style Tags Extension   Builds an external CSS style sheet from the internal style tags in the document, removes the internal tags, and creates a link to the external style sheet.

dHTML Outlines Extension   Creates an expandable/collapsible outline using Dynamic HTML.

Documents Used During Session Extension   Creates a list of the documents used during the current Dreamweaver session.

DW4 Save All Extension   Adds a Save All command to Dreamweaver's File menu, thus enabling you to save all open documents with a single command.

Form Builder Extension   An assortment of prebuilt pop-up menus for use in forms. Menus include marital status, age group, date of birth, education, occupation, and so on.

Insert Corporate MumboJumbo Extension   Inserts dummy text into your document for use on mockup pages. Works like the Latin Text Extension mentioned below, but this text reads like notes from a corporate board meeting full of the latest buzzwords. Very funny!

Insert ImageReady HTML Extension   Works like the Insert Fireworks HTML command. Facilitates importing HTML generated by the Adobe ImageReady program.

JustSo Picture Window Extension   Creates a pop-up image window for displaying a higher resolution version of an image. The pop-up browser window is automatically sized to the image.

Latin Text Extension   Inserts a specified amount of "Latin" dummy text into your document.

Layer Transitions Extension   A collection of preconstructed transition effects for moving layers on or off the page.

Macromedia CourseBuilder Extension   A set of tools for creating web-based instructional content. Includes a gallery of prebuilt interactions for creating questions and a visual Action Manager for creating interactivity.

Meta Generator Extension   A dialog box that helps you create various meta tags for the header portion of your document.

New Document from Selection Extension   Creates a new document from the current selection in the current document.

News Ticker Extension   Creates a news ticker or marquee to display scrolling text from an external text file.

Nokia WML Studio for Dreamweaver   A set of tools for creating content for delivery to Nokia cell phones and other WAP-enabled wireless devices.

Nowhere Link Extension   Creates null links to which you can attach behaviors.

Page Transitions Extension   Facilitates adding Internet Explorer page transitions to your document.

Previous Page Link Extension   Inserts a "Previous Page" link into your document.

Print Code View Extension   Prints the contents of the Code view window or Code Inspector panel.

Reset Image Sizes Extension   Automatically resets all images to their original default size.

Set HTML Comment Extension   Changes the selected text into an HTML comment.

Site Import Export Extension   Saves your site definition data in a file. You can use the resulting file as a backup of your site definition or to share site definition data with workgroup members. Also includes an import command to load save site data into Dreamweaver.

Super Countries Extension   Inserts pop-up menus into forms preloaded with values such as a list of world countries or U.S. states.

Super Email Extension   Creates e-mail links with added features not found in the plain Dreamweaver Insert E-Mail object.

Superscripts and Subscripts Extension   Adds superscripts and subscripts to your web pages.

Symbols for Writers Extension   Adds buttons for a bunch of extra symbols, such as the en-dash, ellipsis, or paragraph sign (pilcrow), to the Characters pane of the Objects panel.

Table of Contents Extension   Automatically creates a table of contents linked to either anchors or heading paragraphs in the page.

TableLines Extension   Formats tables to display lines between rows and/or columns.

UltraDeviant - Meta Keywords Report Extension   Generates a list of pages that are missing meta keywords.

Word Count Extension   Finds out how many words are on the current web page, excluding the HTML code.

Zero Page Borders Extension   Sets page margins to zero, which is something you can do easily in the Page Properties dialog box, but this extension automates the process.

Index

INTERNATIONAL CONTACT INFORMATION

AUSTRALIA
McGraw-Hill Book Company Australia Pty. Ltd.
TEL +61-2-9417-9899
FAX +61-2-9417-5687
http://www.mcgraw-hill.com.au
books-it_sydney@mcgraw-hill.com

CANADA
McGraw-Hill Ryerson Ltd.
TEL +905-430-5000
FAX +905-430-5020
http://www.mcgrawhill.ca

GREECE, MIDDLE EAST,
NORTHERN AFRICA
McGraw-Hill Hellas
TEL +30-1-656-0990-3-4
FAX +30-1-654-5525

MEXICO (Also serving Latin America)
McGraw-Hill Interamericana Editores S.A. de C.V.
TEL +525-117-1583
FAX +525-117-1589
http://www.mcgraw-hill.com.mx
fernando_castellanos@mcgraw-hill.com

SINGAPORE (Serving Asia)
McGraw-Hill Book Company
TEL +65-863-1580
FAX +65-862-3354
http://www.mcgraw-hill.com.sg
mghasia@mcgraw-hill.com

SOUTH AFRICA
McGraw-Hill South Africa
TEL +27-11-622-7512
FAX +27-11-622-9045
robyn_swanepoel@mcgraw-hill.com

UNITED KINGDOM & EUROPE
(Excluding Southern Europe)
McGraw-Hill Education Europe
TEL +44-1-628-502500
FAX +44-1-628-770224
http://www.mcgraw-hill.co.uk
computing_neurope@mcgraw-hill.com

ALL OTHER INQUIRIES Contact:
Osborne/McGraw-Hill
TEL +1-510-549-6600
FAX +1-510-883-7600
http://www.osborne.com
omg_international@mcgraw-hill.com

And Don't Forget These...

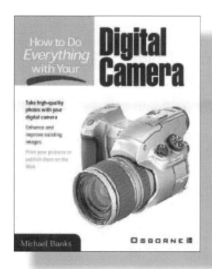

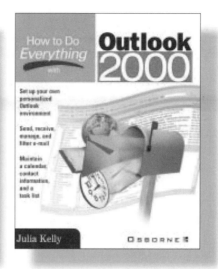

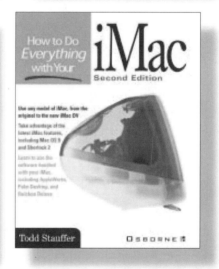

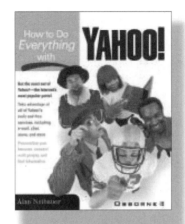
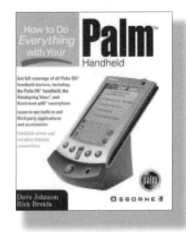